Traversing THE Divide

Honouring Deborah Cass's
Contributions to Public and
International Law

Traversing THE Divide

Honouring Deborah Cass's
Contributions to Public and
International Law

**Edited by
Kim Rubenstein**

Australian
National
University

PRESS

ANU PRESS

Published by ANU Press
The Australian National University
Acton ACT 2601, Australia
Email: anupress@anu.edu.au

Available to download for free at press.anu.edu.au

ISBN (print): 9781760464226
ISBN (online): 9781760464233

WorldCat (print): 1240187379
WorldCat (online): 1240188659

DOI: 10.22459/TD.2021

Cover design and layout by ANU Press. Cover photograph: Deborah Cass, estimated date of the photo is 1993, Deborah's first year at ANU.

Contents

Preface vii

Traversing the Divides: Remembering Deborah Cass 1
Hilary Charlesworth

Part 1: Constitutional Work

Introduction to 'Constitutional Work' 11
Jenny Morgan

Returning to 'Representation/s of Women': Feminist analysis
and job-sharing as core constitutional concerns 13
Kim Rubenstein

Part 2: Natural Resources and Self-Determination

Introduction to Professor Anghie 35
Catherine Hawkins

Self-Determination and Beyond: Reflections on the Aftermath
of the Nauru Case 39
Antony Anghie

A Quiet Revolution: The Exclusivity of Exclusive Economic Zones 59
Margaret A Young

Part 3: International Law and the World Trade Organization

Introduction to International Law and the World Trade Organization . .89
Rosanne Kennedy

Deborah Cass, *The Constitutionalization of the World Trade
Organization*: A Reading in Time 91
Kerry Rittich

Part 4: Personal Reflection and Conclusions

Traversing Divides: My 'Integrated' Sister 115
Dan Cass

Concluding Remarks 129
Gerry Simpson

Part 5: Reproductions of Articles Discussed

The Quiet Revolution: The Development of the Exclusive Economic
Zone and Implications for Foreign Fishing Access in the Pacific 135
Deborah Cass

Rethinking Self-Determination: A Critical Analysis of Current
International Law Theories 157
Deborah Z Cass

Representation/s of Women in the Australian Constitutional
System. 179
Deborah Cass and Kim Rubenstein

Navigating the Newstream: Recent Critical Scholarship
in International Law. 227
Deborah Z Cass

Commonwealth Regulation of Campaign Finance – Public Funding,
Disclosure and Expenditure Limits 273
Deborah Z Cass and Sonia Burrows

Contributors 325

Preface

This book started its journey on Friday 14 August 2015, in the Springbank Room of the Crawford Building at The Australian National University (ANU). Much earlier, Hilary Charlesworth had been the Director of the Centre for International and Public Law (CIPL) at ANU when Deborah was one of its academic members. By 2015 I was the Director of CIPL, and Hilary and I decided to organise a day-long symposium, under CIPL's auspices, to honour the work of our friend and colleague Deborah Cass, 15 February 1960 – 4 June 2013.

Deborah's parents Moss and Shirley Cass, her husband Gerry Simpson and their daughters Hannah and Rosa, her brother Dan, as well as extended family from Sydney, were moved by the presentations that all included a personal and professional dimension.

Deborah was a brilliant Australian constitutional and international lawyer who had studied at the University of Melbourne and Harvard Law School, and taught at Melbourne Law School, ANU and the London School of Economics. As a member of CIPL from 1993 to 2000, her work offered illuminating new perspectives in a range of fields, from the right to self-determination, critical international legal theory and feminist legal theory to the international trade law system.

The symposium drew together academics from around the globe to reflect on Deborah's scholarship and contributions to public law and international law, and how they might influence current controversies. Beyond the contributors to this collection, both Jennifer Clarke and Kristen Walker also presented illuminating papers on the day.

It is six years since that event, but the material in this collection, including some of Deborah's original law review pieces, are testament to the foresight of Deborah's work and thinking, which continue to inform current pressing debates.

Thank you to all the people who have been involved in ensuring the outcomes of that workshop have resulted in this book being available for more people to benefit from Deborah's work. I would also like to thank the journals in which Deborah's articles first appeared for permission to reproduce them in this book, so readers can go straight to the source that inspired each contribution. I also thank the ANU Publication Subsidy Committee for the financial contribution supporting the editing. Finally, I would like to thank ANU Law student Ella Beniamini, who undertook a CIPL internship, for her role in ensuring this book has seen the light of day, and Beth Battrick for her excellent editing!

Kim Rubenstein
February 2021

Traversing the Divides: Remembering Deborah Cass

Hilary Charlesworth

This collection celebrates the life and work of Deborah Cass (1960–2013).[1] Both an international and public lawyer, Deborah[2] studied and/or taught at the University of Melbourne, Harvard Law School, The Australian National University (ANU) and the London School of Economics. Deborah was a significant presence in all the institutions with which she was connected, as well as being a wonderful spirit in the lives of her family and friends.

I encountered Deborah when she was an undergraduate law student at Melbourne University. I recall our first meeting vividly. I turned up for work on my first day as a junior lecturer in 1987, rather nervous and uncertain about where I should report for duty. Deborah greeted me on the steep Law Faculty staircase, saying, 'You must be the new lecturer, let me show you your room'. She marched me to my rather dingy office and counselled that I might think of asking for something better. Deborah then introduced me to the Law Faculty office staff and left me with them, saying she would call in again to see how I was settling in. I assumed that she was a very friendly colleague and looked forward to her continuing advice on navigating the Law Faculty. Deborah dropped in a few days

---

1   There is strong feminist philosophical reasoning for referring to femme-identifying academics by their full names, and this collection uses Deborah Cass's full name in referring to her academic work. This enforces an acknowledgement of the unique standpoint from which femme-identifying academics are thinking and writing from, and complements the sort of work Deborah was trying to achieve in her work on gender equality throughout her career. See Ulrike Schultz, Gisela Shaw, Margaret Thornton and Rosemary Auchmuty (eds), *Gender and Careers in the Legal Academy* (Hart, 2020).
2   Conversely, when referring to Deborah in a personal capacity, this collection will refer to her by her first name alone. This acknowledges the constant traversing of this book between the public and the private sphere, as well as Deborah's vibrancy in both of them.

later with a draft of her article in the *Melbourne University Law Review*, which Margaret Young's chapter in this collection discusses, and it was only then I realised she was a student.

Deborah's generosity of spirit and eagerness to steer people in the right direction was a hallmark of her personality. From that first meeting on, I was the beneficiary of her advice, support, insight, her friendship, her loyalty and her love. A highlight for me was moving her admission to legal practice in the Supreme Court of Victoria: I felt proud to be introducing a candidate of such integrity and creativity into the legal profession. We overlapped later at ANU in Canberra, where Deborah taught for almost four years. She was not only a superb colleague, a dedicated teacher and a great catalyst for ideas, but she also greatly improved the Law Faculty's fashion sense. Deborah indeed took me in hand in the style stakes, once observing that she could not determine whether my outfit was cool and retro or just plain frumpy.

Deborah was always practical – not for her woolly expressions of emotion; she would rather knit, bake or cook to show her interest and concern. Even when she was very ill, Deborah would turn the conversational tables around to check up on me, my parents and my family, and to offer insights and advice, or to recommend recipes and readings.

While devoting fine attention to the stuff of everyday life, Deborah Cass was also a brilliant scholar. Although the deep sense of loss and sadness at Deborah's death remains, it is wonderful to have her writings as a continuing source of inspiration and consolation. In them, we continue to hear Deborah's firm, clear voice, her appreciation of language, her seriousness, her curiosity, her sensitivity and her wry humour.

Reading her work, and recalling seminars and talks I heard Deborah Cass give over the years, I am reminded again of her penetrating, inquiring mind. She was not one for intellectual short cuts, and would reprimand me kindly but firmly when she found me doing this. As this collection shows, Deborah had broad academic interests. She was a gifted constitutional lawyer, a path-breaking international lawyer and a shrewd critic of legal theory. Within the field of international law, unlike many of us, Deborah Cass ranged over many areas, becoming an internationally recognised expert on areas as diverse as natural resources, self-determination, international institutions and international trade law.

Deborah Cass had a rare capacity to analyse the trajectories of legal ideas and movements. She could discern trends and contradictions without getting bogged down in the conventional legal fascination with particular instances. This talent is on elegant display in an article published in 1996, 'Navigating the Newstream: Recent Critical Scholarship in International Law'.[3] The article is a sympathetic but rigorous study of the critical school in international law – pioneered by David Kennedy at Harvard and Martti Koskenniemi at the University of Helsinki. Deborah Cass had encountered the 'New Approaches to International Law' (NAIL) school while a graduate student at Harvard and was friendly with many of its proponents. Her intellectual fearlessness did not allow her to pull her punches, however.

NAIL scholars positioned themselves as a Newstream challenging the mainstream of international law, primarily concerned with rules and institutions. The traditional account was that international law could deliver an objective answer to any international dispute through the application of legal rules. NAIL scholars challenged this claim in a variety of ways. Koskenniemi, for example, identified two contradictory tendencies in international legal practice. First, the understanding of legal practitioners that the doctrines of international law do not have a stable meaning, with the result that the prevailing rule or principle in any particular dispute is dependent on the preferences of the arbiter.[4] Second, the power of the utopian sensibility in international legal thinking, enshrined in concepts such as 'global justice'. Koskenniemi regarded international law as an essentially argumentative practice, and reasoned that the function of legal advisers to decision-makers in this context was 'to enable the retreat of the decision-maker from the existential *Angst* of the decision to the comforting structures of the law'.[5]

Deborah Cass took on the role of a supportive critic of NAIL in her article, explaining the movement's significance, but calling also on 'Newstreamers' to lift their game. Her article remains a valuable description of three techniques favoured by the Newstream: using polarities to construct arguments; invoking the device of a personal quest to explain

3   Deborah Cass, 'Navigating the Newstream: Recent Critical Scholarship in International Law' (1996) 65 *Nordic Journal of International Law* 341, doi.org/10.1163/15718109620294924.
4   Martti Koskenniemi, *From Apology to Utopia: The Structure of International Legal Argument* (Cambridge University Press, reissue, 2005) Epilogue, doi.org/10.1017/cbo9780511493713.011.
5   Koskenniemi (n 4) Preface. See also David Kennedy, 'A New Stream of International Legal scholarship' (1988) 7 *Wisconsin International Law Journal* 1, 6.

a disenchantment with international law; and a specific focus on language.[6] Deborah Cass observed the 'stultifying' nature of the disdain for critical approaches expressed by the international legal mainstream, and warned that it was preventing 'the development of a more nuanced and responsive international legal theory'.[7] At the same time, she castigated Newstream scholars for failing to exploit the potential of their critique by ducking out of 'explicit evaluative choices', and for conceiving of international law as nothing more than 'a variable set of argumentative possibilities'. A further critique was of the 'condescending and reductive tone' of Newstream writings, and 'its occasionally derivative and abstract theorizing'.[8]

Deborah Cass argued that the critical call for the integration of politics with law was not 'sufficiently problematised'. 'The call', she wrote reprovingly,

> is a commendable ambition but doubts remain. There is a tendency in some Newstream work for an apparently radical critique to conclude with a facile or reductive call for a move to politics, yet the political is as contested and enigmatic as the legal. While concepts such as sovereignty are being denigrated as too incoherent to underpin the legal system, a radically pluralistic politics seems an inauspicious place to find a new normative consensus.[9]

Deborah Cass placed her own critique at the borderline between the mainstream and the Newstream, 'in the hope that it will enable both sides to explore each other's territory'.[10] Over 20 years later, this article remains an astute account of NAIL: prescient about its journeys and current in its identification of the movement's strengths and weaknesses. The article highlights Deborah Cass's distinctive academic characteristics as a translator and communicator of legal thought, a bridge-builder between intellectual traditions, a generator of reconstructive ideas and a confident and generous traverser of divides.

This collection explores some of Deborah Cass's contributions to the fields of international and public law. It also includes reflections on Deborah, the person rather than the scholar, by family, friends and colleagues. As you will find, the range of topics covered in the book signal just how

---

6   Cass, 'Navigating the Newstream' (n 1) 362–77.
7   Ibid 343.
8   Ibid.
9   Ibid 379.
10   Ibid 343.

broad her interests were. The collection is also a cartography of Deborah's scholarly style and preoccupations. The pieces illustrate her interest in legal doctrine and her insightful and critical eye, celebrating her extraordinary ability to experiment with ideas in order to present a fresh perspective on familiar debates. These meditations on Deborah Cass's work remind us what a path-breaking scholar she was: everything she wrote helped shape an intellectual field. The title of this collection captures a particular quality of Deborah Cass's scholarship – her capacity to cross disciplinary and subject boundaries. Indeed, the title is borrowed from an article by Deborah Cass on the vexed relationship between international law and Australian constitutional law.[11]

Part 1 of the book deals with some of Deborah Cass's work in constitutional law. Kim Rubenstein revisits an article she and Deborah wrote jointly in 1995 on the representation of women in the Australian Constitution.[12] Deborah was passionate about equality for women and she addressed it in all aspects of her life, personally, politically and professionally. Kim recounts how the writing project came about and the way that the article was later used in advocacy about the representation of women in the 1998 Australian Constitutional Convention. Kim's chapter extends the analysis of the earlier article by considering how job-sharing for parliamentarians could enhance the system of representative democracy. She argues that this is a practical way in which the work of care could be made more equal, further enhancing the quality of our democracy.

Part 2 covers natural resources and the principle of self-determination, areas of international law in which Deborah Cass made important interventions. Margaret Young considers Deborah's first published academic article, on the impact in the Pacific of provisions of the 1982 Convention on the Law of the Sea (UNCLOS) relating to fisheries.[13] In that article, Deborah Cass had applauded what she saw as UNCLOS' grant of complete discretion to coastal states with respect to foreign access to fisheries, in what were termed their 'exclusive economic zones'. She suggested that this would be particularly significant in the Pacific, where predatory fishing practices by foreign fleets had diminished the fisheries

---

11   Deborah Cass, 'Traversing the Divide: International Law and Australian Constitutional Law' (1998) 20 *Adelaide Law Review* 73.
12   Deborah Cass and Kim Rubenstein, 'Representation/s of Women: Towards a Feminist Analysis of the Australian Constitutional System' (1995) 17 *Adelaide Law Review* 3.
13   Deborah Cass, 'A Quiet Revolution: The Exclusive Economic Zone and Foreign Fishing Access in the Pacific' (1987) 16 *Melbourne University Law Review* 83.

of island states. Margaret compares Deborah Cass's arguments about the likely impact of the exclusive economic zone provisions of the Convention with later judicial interpretations. She notes the prescience of Deborah Cass's observation of the significance of coastal states' rights, but suggests that she may have placed too much faith in the capacity and willingness of coastal states to achieve sustainable fisheries.

Deborah Cass worked with Tony Anghie on an international commission of inquiry into the worked-out phosphate lands of Nauru in the late 1980s. The government of Nauru had established this commission to investigate liability and compensation for the devastation of Nauru's environment by the states that had administered Nauru as a mandated territory under the League of Nations, and then as a trust territory under the United Nations, these states being Australia, New Zealand and the UK. The chair of the commission was a distinguished international lawyer, Professor Christopher Weeramantry, then at Monash University, and later a member of the International Court of Justice (ICJ). The report of the commission laid the foundation for a case Nauru brought against Australia in the ICJ. Tony's chapter in the book reflects on the principle of self-determination at the heart of Nauru's claim, and the subject of an article of Deborah Cass's, published in 1992.[14] He examines the legacy of the Nauru case both in international law and in Australia's complex imperial history. In Australia's understanding of Nauru as part of an Australian Empire, Tony examines the way that it deflected claims of self-determination. He also points to the situation of Nauru in 2018, perceptively observing how Australia is reproducing its own colonial origins as a penal colony there.

Part 3 turns to Deborah Cass's work on the World Trade Organization (WTO), the subject of her prize-winning book, *The Constitutionalization of the World Trade Organization* (Oxford University Press, 2005). Deborah challenged the prevailing wisdom that the WTO was engaged in constitutionalisation, or a process of developing structured constraints on institutional activity, through the separation of powers. While rejecting claims that traditional forms of constitutionalisation were emerging in the WTO, Deborah Cass did not want to give up on the notion itself. She ended the book calling for a radical rethinking of the concept of constitutionalisation to encompass 'trading democracy', which would entail economic development and redistribution. Kerry Rittich's chapter in

---

14   Deborah Z Cass, 'Re-Thinking Self-Determination: A Critical Analysis of Current International Law Theories' (1992) 18 *Syracuse Journal of International Law and Commerce* 31.

this book lucidly provides a context to appreciate the richness of Deborah Cass's work. Kerry emphasises in particular Deborah Cass's imaginative analysis and her focus on the network of beliefs and commitments that structured the WTO.

The book continues in Part 4 (before concluding with reproductions of Deborah Cass's original articles in Part 5) with reflections on Deborah by her brother, Daniel, and husband, Gerry Simpson. They remind us that, apart from being a brilliant academic, Deborah was a warm, funny, wise and compassionate person. She did not do anything by halves and forged an unconventional path into the law and academia. It is unsurprising that her and Gerry's two daughters, Hannah and Rosa, have inherited Deborah's sense of adventure and generosity of spirit.

PART 1

Constitutional Work

Introduction to 'Constitutional Work'

Jenny Morgan

Hilary and Kim have entitled the symposium 'Traversing Divides', and on re-reading the pieces that are to be discussed, or at least inspire the discussion in this coming session, I can see why.

Glancing at the papers to be examined by Jennifer Clarke, we see a traversing of the law–politics divide. In her work with Kim, and related work (and indeed in much of Deborah Cass's work), we see the law–feminism divide traversed. And in her work on campaign financing, we see a close and fascinating reading of the history of campaign financing law, crossing the law–history divide.

And I think what this particular part of Deborah Cass's work which is to be discussed in this session demonstrates is that the divide is not a divide: law cannot be read without politics, history and, I would say, feminism – or at least asking the 'woman question'. So I wonder whether it is traversing divides, or rejecting divides … However, I will leave that to my expert panel.

All three of our speakers were both colleagues and friends of Deborah's, as indeed was I. And thinking about chairing this session led me to reflect both on my own experience with constitutional law, and of course on Deborah Cass. I was taught constitutional law by Michael Coper, and it is terrific that he was able to join us for today's reflections. Michael used to share with us not only the reflections of others on the constitution – for example, PP McGuinness's quizzical suggestion that if section 92 was so fundamental why wasn't it section 1 – but also the errors of previous students. The one that sticks in my mind was the student who, Michael insisted, had referred in an exam context, to the founding fathers as the 'pounding panthers'. And the pounding panthers made me think of Deborah. You might well ask why. I mused that one might describe Deborah's work as pounding – as insistent, as persistent, as resolute. And a panther is always sleekly elegant – and Deborah was always elegant in her presentation to the world.

Jennifer Clarke, in an aside, suggested that such a comment could only be made by someone who had not shared a house with Deborah. This is a comment that illustrates what was so very special about the day Hilary and Kim organised in celebration of Deborah and Deborah's work, and again consistent with the title of the symposium: the constant traversing of the public–private divide. The day gave us an opportunity to reflect on our personal and our intellectual relationships with Deborah; it allowed the personal into the intellectual, and the scholarly into the intimate in a way that academia rarely encourages.

Returning to 'Representation/s of Women': Feminist analysis and job-sharing as core constitutional concerns

Kim Rubenstein

Introduction

I first met Deborah Cass when I began my undergraduate law studies at the University of Melbourne in 1984, after spending a 'gap year' overseas straight after high school, gathering 'worldly' experiences. We were fellow law students, although she had many more worldly experiences under her belt[1] and, more significantly through my eyes then, she became well known as one of the editors of the university student newspaper *Farrago* the following year. When I later became President of the Melbourne University Jewish Students' Society I didn't have much luck enticing Deborah to regular events but we enjoyed stimulating conversations, and

---

[1] Deborah's path to university was different to many at Melbourne law school at that time. She 'attended an experimental school and found its artistic chaos both intoxicating and disturbing. In her mid-teens she rebelled against her upbringing in an unusual way, leaving home to become a secretary and a sales representative living in the outer suburbs. As a result, she got to university five years later than her peers, but determined not to waste any time'. See James Button, 'Writer and Educator Saw Law as a Means to Better the World', *Obituary, The Age* (Melbourne, 2 August 2013), then published online: James Button, 'Writer and Educator Saw Law as a Means to Better the World', *The Sydney Morning Herald* (online, 2 August 2013) <https://www.smh.com.au/national/writer-and-educator-saw-law-as-a-means-to-better-the-world-20130801-2r1oj.html>. See a little more about Deborah at: Helen Irving, 'Vale: Deborah Zipporah Cass 15 February 1960', *A Woman's Constitution* (Blog Post, 22 July 2013) <http://web.archive.org/web/20190501064437/http://blogs.usyd.edu.au/womansconstitution/2013/07/vale_deborah_zipporah_cass.html>.

I have clear memories of talking with her while checking out books from the Law library back in the days when it was housed in the University of Melbourne's Old Quadrangle.

We followed similar styled paths to academia – the same year of articles in different law firms with practical work experience added in, before setting upon a professional life in academia. Mine with my graduate work first at Harvard before returning to the University of Melbourne, and Deborah starting at the University of Melbourne sooner and then moving to The Australian National University (ANU) before embarking on her graduate work at Harvard. It was during those early academic years that I reconnected with Deborah through her partnership with Gerry, who became my colleague at the University of Melbourne when Deborah was already up at ANU, and it was when Deborah was at Harvard that our academic collaboration emerged.

Deborah contacted me about joining her to write an article she had begun, as she had too much on her research plate to continue with it on her own. Indeed, it is a theme to which this chapter returns – the importance of shared work as a key to constitutional and societal strength. Deborah sent me a skeleton draft, with a clear structure and premise, of what became 'Representations of Women: Towards a Feminist Analysis of the Australian Constitutional System', and it is around that piece this contribution is based. The article was published in the *Adelaide Law Review*,[2] and then later reproduced in a modified manner as a chapter in Helen Irving's edited collection, *A Woman's Constitution?*,[3] and then further updated for a comparative constitutional law collection.[4] I am particularly grateful that Deborah invited me to collaborate with her on that article as it was important to my own public law scholarship around the relationship between the individual and the state. Some of that early thinking and our discussions have been central, too, to my work on citizenship, which grew alongside my work on gender and constitutional issues.

2   Deborah Cass and Kim Rubenstein, 'Representations of Women: Towards a Feminist Analysis of the Australian Constitutional System' (1995) 17 *Adelaide Law Review* 3.
3   Deborah Cass and Kim Rubenstein, 'From Federation Forward: The Representation of Women in the Australian Constitutional System' in Helen Irving (ed), *A Woman's Constitution? Gender and History in the Australian Commonwealth* (Hale and Iremonger, 1996) 108. The piece was also extracted in one of the early editions of T Blackshield and G Williams, *Australian Constitutional Law and Theory* (Federation Press, 1996) 98.
4   Kim Rubenstein and Christabel Richards Neville, 'Australia's Gendered Constitutional History and Future' in Susan H Williams (ed), *Social Difference and Constitutionalism in Pan-Asia* (Cambridge University Press, 2014), doi.org/10.1017/cbo9781139567312.015.

This chapter draws out some of the history around the article itself and the central aspects of that article's thesis. It then extends the discussion about the nature of representation, and the concept of shared representation as a means of improving representative democracy in Australia's constitutional system, by examining the court challenge in the UK in 2015 around their elections when two women, Sarah Cope and Claire Phipps, nominated for election to the UK Parliament on a joint job-sharing basis. Their nomination was declined by the acting returning officer and her decision was ultimately upheld by Justice Wilkie in *R (Cope) v Returning Officer for the Basingstoke Parliamentary Constituency* ('*Cope*').[5]

The issue has remained on the UK Green Party's agenda and has been discussed in a scholarly and practical way in the UK since that time.[6] It is time for it to be discussed more in Australian constitutional circles too, given the continued low numbers of women in the Parliament, and it is a discussion I am sure Deborah would have enjoyed engaging with.

Representations of Women in the Australian Constitutional System

History Around the Writing of and Impact of the Piece

Deborah had already begun writing our 1995 article when she approached me to continue working with her on it. Susan Marks wrote in her reflections, 'In Memoriam: Deborah Cass', that Deborah's 'writing was fresh and forthright and full of luminous, funny phrases'.[7] Deborah's attention to the ironic is seen beautifully in the opening of our piece, which she had already designed, with an extract from Sir Owen Dixon's judgment in *Re Foreman & Sons Pty Ltd; Uther v Federal Commissioner of Taxation*:

---

5   [2015] EWHC 3958 (Admin) ('*Cope*').

6   See Sarah Childs, *The Good Parliament* (Report to UK Parliament, July 2016) <https://www.bristol.ac.uk/media-library/sites/news/2016/july/20%20Jul%20Prof%20Sarah%20Childs%20The%20Good%20Parliament%20report.pdf>. See also Rosa Curling, 'The High Court Case' in *Open House? Reflections on the Possibility and Practice of MPs Job-Sharing* (Pamphlet, The Fawcett Society, 5 September 2017) 17.

7   See Susan Marks, 'In Memoriam: Deborah Cass' (2014) September *LSE Ratio: The Magazine of LSE Law* 22, 23.

> Like the goddess of wisdom the Commonwealth *uno ictu* sprang
> from the brain of its begetters armed and of full stature.[8]

She wrote: 'According to Sir Owen Dixon, the Commonwealth of Australia sprang, like the Goddess Athena, fully armed from the head of the States. Whether or not this is an apt metaphor from a classical perspective' (and here we cited some literature around that metaphor),[9] we continued:

> from the perspective of Australian women, it is a strange choice. Athena is one of the strongest female images of the Western literary tradition. In contrast, Australian women have not been represented with such vigour in Australian constitutional law. They appear rarely as litigants, occasionally as members of Parliament, sometimes as part of the Executive, and virtually never as judicial decision makers. Their presence in the Australian system could never be described as 'armed' or 'of full stature'. To this extent, the ascription of feminine strength to the entity which represented Australian nationhood is at odds with the reality; the historical exclusion of women from the constitutional arena.[10]

As for questions of choice, the idea behind placing our joint article into the *Adelaide Law Review* was timely and topical. Volume 17, 1995, included articles relevant to commemorating the centenary of the passing of the *Constitution Amendment Act 1894* in March 1895.[11] That Act was the final legal step in extending suffrage to women on equal terms with men in the state of South Australia. Much has been written around those steps and where it fits in the overall history of women's right to vote in the British Empire and internationally,[12] and it was also important ultimately to the development of section 41 of the Australian Constitution (which expresses a guarantee to the right to vote), given section 41 was inserted thanks to

---

8   (1947) 74 CLR 508, at 530.
9   Cass and Rubenstein, 'Representations of Women' (n 2) 3.
10 Ibid 4, footnotes omitted.
11 See 'Editorial' (1995) 17 *Adelaide Law Review* 1.
12 This was discussed in the article itself, and since then there has been further work. Dr Clare Wright has also made a film about this period of history, see *Utopia Girls* (2011) <https://www.clarewright.com.au/broadcaster>, in which she highlights how Adelaide was the first place where women got *both* the right to vote and to stand for office concurrently. There is some uncertainty about that latter claim, according to the introduction in the *Adelaide Law Review* where it is stated that 'up until 1916 when the Parliamentary Qualifications (Women) Bill was passed there was some doubt that women could stand for election despite having the vote. It was not until 1959 that two female candidates endorsed by the Liberal Country League were elected to the South Australian Parliament' ('Editorial' (1995) 17 *Adelaide Law Review* 1). Interestingly, Catherine Helen Spence stood for election to the 1897 Constitutional Convention, but some argue her failure to get sufficient votes was due to the uncertainty raised by her opponents of her eligibility to stand in a national arena.

those South Australian women's insistence that they did not want to lose their existing right to vote in the state when they were able to participate in Commonwealth elections after Federation occurred.[13]

Indeed, those women who had been campaigning their representatives to the Convention about the creation of a Commonwealth Constitution inspired me, with Deborah's support, to use the article not only in academic circles (where it was one of the first academic constitutional law pieces that had gender as a central focus) but practically also, and in 1998 I relied on our piece as a trigger to lobby government directly around the proposed 1998 Constitutional Convention.

The Howard Government had determined to hold a Constitutional Convention, 100 years on from the 1898 People's Convention, to discuss whether Australia should become a republic. It had been determined there were to be 152 delegates, drawn from each state and territory. Seventy-six of the delegates were to be elected by a voluntary postal ballot, held after the first 76 were appointed by the federal government.

The campaign I began with Susan Brennan (then Joint President of YWCA (Young Women's Christian Association) Australia and now Senior Counsel at the Victorian Bar) was to ensure that the 1998 Convention, 100 years on from the founding Convention, would involve equal numbers of men and women, given *no women* had been present at the 1890s Convention. Susan and I prepared a petition, which supporters around the country signed electronically, with many women's organisations also distributing it through their memberships and beyond. This was followed by a trip to Canberra to meet personally with Senator Nick Minchin, who had carriage of organising and running the Convention. We also met other members of Parliament. Deborah met us at Parliament House in advance of our meetings (then pregnant with Rosa), and she contributed to our presentation in Senator Minchin's office with her powerful and intellectually striking manner.

One can only imagine how *few* women might have been appointed *without* our campaign, for in spite of it, of the 76 appointed delegates, the government appointed 23 women (30 per cent). When the final composition of the complete 1998 Constitutional Convention (following

13   I have written about that separately in my 'Feminist Judgment' in E Arcioni and K Rubenstein, 'R v Pearson; Ex parte Sipka: Feminism and the Franchise' in Heather Douglas et al (eds), *Australian Feminist Judgments* (Hart Publishing, 2014) 55, doi.org/10.5040/9781474201292.ch-004.

the postal voting for the other half)[14] did not represent 'equal' numbers of women (there were ultimately 49 women out of 152 delegates – 32 per cent), a concerted effort to involve more women in the discussion around the move to a republic led to the organising of a dedicated Women's Constitutional Convention held in Parliament House itself, on the 29 and 30 January 1998 in advance of the Government's Convention. The slogan for the Women's Convention, highlighted on the website for the event, stated:

> One hundred years ago men gathered to draft the Australian Constitution. Now, for the first time, women from all sections of society will have the opportunity to contribute their perspective.[15]

Several women's organisations were instrumental in organising the Women's Convention with a Convening Committee including representatives from Australian Women Lawyers, the Constitutional Centenary Foundation (ACT Chapter), the National Women's Justice Coalition, the Women's Electoral Lobby, Women Into Politics and YWCA of Australia. Over 300 women, including all those appointed or elected to the Government's Convention, together with women as representatives of a range of organisations and individual women (all listed on the archived website)[16] participated, culminating in a communique delivered to the Constitutional Convention[17] held in Old Parliament House from 2 to 13 February 1998.

---

14 I was also involved in 'running' as an elected delegate in Victoria on a 'Women's Ticket' supported by the Victorian Women's Trust and a range of women's organisations, to make the point that more women needed to be elected in the elected section to ensure there were equal numbers, given only 30 per cent of the appointed delegates were women. That experience is worthy of its own article and while not being directly elected, I did attend the Convention as an 'adviser' to Misha Schubert who was elected on a Youth Ticket 'Republic4U'. Her biography at the time stated: 'at 24 years old she is the youngest elected delegate to the Constitutional Convention'. Misha is now the CEO of Science & Technology Australia, see 'STA Board and Executive', Science & Technology Australia (Web Page) <https://scienceandtechnologyaustralia.org.au/board-and-executive/>.

15 See the archived website from the event at 'Future Directions', *Women's Constitutional Convention* (Web Page, 1 October 1997) <http://purl.nla.gov.au/nla/pandora/womconv>, archived at: <http://pandora.nla.gov.au/nph-wb/19980901130000/http://www.womensconv.dynamite.com.au/index.html>.

16 'Attendees', *Women's Constitutional Convention* (Web Page, 26 May 1998) <http://pandora.nla.gov.au/nph-wb/19980901130000/http://www.womensconv.dynamite.com.au/dels.htm>.

17 'Outcomes', *Women's Constitutional Convention* (Web Page, 6 April 1998) <http://pandora.nla.gov.au/nph-wb/19980901130000/http://www.womensconv.dynamite.com.au/outcomes.htm>.

Before the communique was developed, many individuals delivered papers,[18] including Deborah Cass. Her paper was titled 'The Last Bastion: Does One Woman on the High Court Equal "Gender Balance"?',[19] and she provocatively began:

> Today I want to speak about an issue which is not on the agenda of the Constitutional Convention but which has a more frequent impact upon Australian democratic life than the identity of our head of state. I am talking about the composition of the High Court. I want to suggest to you that the health of the entire Australian constitutional democracy (regardless of whether we become a republic or not) is undermined by gender imbalance at the High Court.

In her paper, Deborah Cass developed an idea that she had stated in a different context in our original piece. In the context of the High Court and appointments she explained:

> I want to clarify something. Everything I am about to say operates regardless of whether one thinks that women judges would decide cases in a particular way, which is different to the way men judges decide. The jury is still out on that one. And I am not entirely sure of the answer myself. But what I am saying, is that regardless of whether women judges decide cases differently to men judges, they should be on the High Court. My argument is about equality of representation, nothing else. Women should be there because they comprise over 50 per cent of the population, are active in law, are affected by it, and because the absurdity of the current imbalance is illustrated by the fact that the reverse situation would never be tolerated by men. Imagine six women and one man. The mind boggles.[20]

---

18   'Programs and Papers', *Women's Constitutional Convention* (Web Page, 7 April 1998) <http://pandora.nla.gov.au/nph-wb/19980901130000/http://www.womensconv.dynamite.com.au/program5.htm>.
19   'The Last Bastion: Does One Woman on the High Court Equal "Gender Balance"?', *Women's Constitutional Convention* (Web Page, 7 April 1998) <http://pandora.nla.gov.au/nph-wb/19980901130000/http://www.womensconv.dynamite.com.au/cass.htm>. I might add, that Deborah was 'very' pregnant when she delivered this paper in Parliament House, as she delivered Rosa the following week!
20   This point reminds me of Ruth Bader Ginsburg's answer to the question, How many women should be on the US Supreme court? Ryan Lovelace, 'Ruth Bader Ginsburg: There will be Enough Women on the Supreme Court when there are Nine', *The Washington Examiner* (online, 12 September 2017) <https://www.washingtonexaminer.com/ruth-bader-ginsburg-there-will-be-enough-women-on-the-supreme-court-when-there-are-nine>.

This is one aspect of our discussion about representation raised in our 1995 article to which I will now turn – does it matter whether women act or represent their electorate 'differently' to men?

Themes of the Piece

The central focus of our 1995 piece was around the concept of representation. It examined women as representatives in government, women as they are represented by government and women in representations of government. The argument in the article was that, in 1995, at the level of doctrine, the High Court was moving to a position that emphasised the participatory aspect of representation, which we argued was consistent with a feminist critique of representative democracy. Our point, which is still important, is that low levels of participation by women undermines the representative nature of that concept.[21]

Moreover, we were of the view that in light of Australia's history and in light of Australia's practice at 1995, Australia's system lagged behind the theoretical insights suggested by feminist argument, and the conclusions which followed from High Court doctrine at that time. Our aim was to demonstrate the need for a synthesis of constitutional practice with theory and doctrine, by suggesting that increased participation of women is essential for Australia's constitutional system to conform with evolving standards of representative democracy.[22] The piece was structured around the following sections: 'Representative Democracy as a principle which underpins the Australian Constitutional system', 'Representative Democracy and the relevance of gender', 'The representation of women in the Australian Constitutional system', and 'Becoming a more Representative Democracy'. The first section's content, examining representative democracy as seen through the High Court analysis, was framed naturally around the jurisprudence at that point, and since that time, there is more to 'add' and 'subtract' to the Court's views on representative democracy. Some of that newer material was touched upon in my subsequent piece with Christabel Richards Neville,[23] and is further extended by Katrina Hall in her research in this area.[24] The points about

---

21 Cass and Rubenstein, 'Representations of Women' (n 2) 5–6.
22 Ibid.
23 Rubenstein and Neville, 'Australia's Gendered Constitutional History' (n 4).
24 Katrina Hall, 'A Case For Allowing MP Job-Sharing' (JD Paper, ANU Law School, 2018) on file with the author.

the relevance of gender are ongoing. One of the significant points in that section that still resonates in so many ways with my thinking about these issues more broadly was first made by our colleague Hilary Charlesworth, in the context of the United Nations (UN):

> How or whether women's equal participation in decision making would affect the quality of UN decisions is not yet certain. But whatever the evidence of a distinctive woman's influence in political decision-making, it is at least clear that the realities of women's lives under the present unbalanced system do not contribute in any significant way to the shaping of UN policy.[25]

We continued arguing that:

> the central insight suggested by the justification remains compelling, namely that women experience the world differently to men as an undeniable matter of practical reality. Moreover, regardless of how many different voices women may have, it does not mean that men can properly represent those different voices. The personal experience of some women representatives suggests that men cannot listen to women's views.[26]

Sadly, this is still a common problem.[27]

There have also been changes since 1995 to the issues we identified in 'The representation of women in the Australian Constitutional system': on one hand, the growth of women on the High Court has been positive;[28] on the other, there has not been significant change in relation to the proportion of women in Parliament in those 20-plus

---

25   Cass and Rubenstein, 'Representations of Women' (n 2) 22, quoting Hilary Charlesworth, 'Transforming the United Men's Club: Feminist Futures of the United Nations' (1994) 4 *Transnational Law and Contemporary Problems* 420.

26   Cass and Rubenstein, 'Representations of Women' (n 2) 22.

27   This is an issue that is not only related to democratic representation in Parliament, but in society more broadly, as seen through the '"me too" campaign' and the need for men to listen to women's experiences.

28   In 2018, there are three women on the High Court bench with the first woman as Chief Justice appointed in January 2017. See 'Susan Kiefel Sworn in as Australia's first Chief Justice of the High Court', *ABC News* (online, 30 January 2017) <http://www.abc.net.au/news/2017-01-30/susan-kiefel-sworn-in-as-first-female-high-court-chief-justice/8222868>. See also my commentary on her appointment, Kim Rubenstein, 'Kiefel Appointment is Refreshing, But Greater Diversity is an Ongoing Task', *The Sydney Morning Herald* (online, 30 November 2016) <https://www.smh.com.au/opinion/kiefel-appointment-is-refreshing-but-greater-diversity-is-an-ongoing-task-20161129-gt05g4.html>.

years.[29] The seesawing that has occurred of women in high office, which reached a high in 2011 when Australia had a woman as Governor-General (Quentin Bryce), Prime Minister (Julia Gillard) and Attorney-General (Nicola Roxon) concurrently,[30] has ultimately led to the result that within two years, none of those positions were still held by women, and only one woman was a member of Cabinet.[31] There are also further disappointing examples of the point we made around how women are represented in visual and textual descriptions of aspects of the constitutional process. As we wrote:

> historically, representations of women in the Australian constitutional system have been characterised by trivialisation, ambiguity, or complete absence. Women were either not there at all; there in the guise of men in drag; or there to be ridiculed.[32]

The experiences of Julia Gillard as prime minister provide further data to be included as an update to this issue.[33]

Returning to the point of having more women in Parliament to better reflect the diversity of life experiences of the community, it is relevant also to the broader argument and final part of our 1995 article, of how best to become a more representative democracy. For men and women are not, respectively, monolithic groups, and within those groups we need to also acknowledge the diversity of experience that impacts the way we each

---

29   As at May 2018, female members comprised just under 32 per cent of all parliamentarians at the federal level, and just under 35 per cent in the states and territories. See Anna Hough, 'Composition of Australian Parliaments by Party and Gender: A Quick Guide' (Research Paper Series 2018–19, Parliamentary Library, Parliament of Australia, 2018) Table 1.

30   A great visual image of women in public office is at 'Women of the New Gillard Ministry', *ABC News* (online, 14 December 2011) <http://www.abc.net.au/news/2011-12-14/women-of-the-new-gillard-ministry/3731528>, showing Julie Collins, Kate Ellis, Nicola Roxon, Julia Gillard, Quentin Bryce, Jenny Macklin and Tanya Plibersek after the swearing in, 2011.

31   See commentary available at Jonathan Pearlman, 'Tony Abbott Under Fire for Having Only One Woman in Cabinet', *The Telegraph* (online, 16 September 2013) <https://www.telegraph.co.uk/news/worldnews/australiaandthepacific/australia/10311885/Tony-Abbott-under-fire-for-having-only-one-woman-in-cabinet.html>.

32   Cass and Rubenstein, 'Representations of Women' (n 2) 42.

33   See Marian Sawer, 'Misogyny and Misrepresentation' (2013) 65(1) *Political Science* 105, doi.org/10.1177/0032318713488316; Marian Woodward, 'Ditch The Witch: Julia Gillard and Gender in Australian Public Discourse' (Honours Thesis, Sydney University, 18 October 2013) <https://ses.library.usyd.edu.au/bitstream/2123/9554/1/Woodward%2C%20M_GCST_HonoursThesis_2013.pdf>.

experience the world. This relates both to gender, and how gender impacts on one's life experience, as well as a range of other factors that influence how each person sees, views and experiences the world.[34]

It is that idea of intersectionality and diversity of experiences that becomes especially relevant to the next section on job-sharing, both in Parliament and beyond. But, to complete this section, which focuses on our joint article as a foundation to the next part of the paper, woven into the actual intellectual underpinning of the piece was the practical fact that we job-shared the writing of that 1995 article. The practice itself reflects an appreciation of shared work as an important and positive step around academic/work 'practice' and about our lived experiences, which is also relevant to becoming a more representative democracy.

My memory is that Deborah approached me to collaborate with her, knowing her own commitments to a balanced workload (she had been successful in receiving some research grants that extended her research work beyond this research), balancing her other academic responsibilities of teaching and university service, together with her personal life (starting a family, as Hannah was born in 1995). This meant she could not and should not have done everything on her own. Moreover, the practice of collaboration meant that we could engage with each other's ideas directly (and I could contribute from my life experience and thinking and research perspective at that point) and from that interaction we came to what I believe was a richer piece than if either of us had written it on our own.

These are principles that also apply to representative democracy and it is around the ideas and value of joint 'shared' work, in a constitutional setting, that I now turn.

---

34 This is often referred to as 'intersectionality', a term first coined by law professor Kimberlé Crenshaw and her work in the US around gender and race. See 'Kimberlé Crenshaw on Intersectionality, More than Two Decades Later', *Columbia Law School* (Web Page, 8 June 2017) <https://www.law. columbia.edu/pt-br/news/2017/06/kimberle-crenshaw-intersectionality>. The simple point from the idea behind it is that there are many aspects of our life experiences that influence how we engage with issues and how power is exercised, and they may be fluid and context-dependent.

Job-sharing as a Feminist Constitutional Contribution: The Queen on the application of Sarah Cope and Clare Phipps[35]

This volume developed from the series of 'evergreen' papers presented at the Centre for International and Public Law conference, 'Traversing Divides – A Symposium in Honour of Deborah Cass', at ANU on 14 August 2015, two years after Deborah's death. In the same year as the conference, on 9 April 2015, Sarah Cope and Clare Phipps had applied to the returning officer for Basingstoke to stand as joint candidates for the UK general election on 7 May 2015. Sarah Cope, a single mother of two young children, was unable to work full-time as she was the principal carer for her children, one of whom has an autistic spectrum disorder.[36] Clare Phipps could not work full-time due to suffering from idiopathic hypersomnia.[37] They had determined they wanted to represent the constituency of Basingstoke in a job-sharing arrangement and submitted a nomination paper naming them both as a single candidate for the Green Party. The returning officer determined their nomination was invalid because the particulars of the 'candidate' were not 'as required by law' and the paper not subscribed as required.[38] Sarah Cope and Clare Phipps were therefore unable to stand for election and the Green Party had no candidate for the Basingstoke constituency.[39] On application for judicial review of the returning officer's decision, they received a written refusal before renewing their request and seeking an oral hearing of the matter. Their application was ultimately heard before Justice Wilkie at the High Court in London on 28 July 2015.

---

35   I am grateful for the work of ANU Law student, Katrina Hall, around her graduate research under my supervision linked to this case and her insights on the decision. Her excellent 2018 ANU graduate paper, 'A Case For Allowing MP Job-Sharing', has contributed to my thinking and I have drawn from her descriptions around the case in this section. Her paper also discusses the earlier Scottish case, *Secretary of State for Scotland and the Advocate General for Scotland v Mann* [2000] EAT/56/00, discussed in Alice Belcher and Andrea Ross, 'The Case for Job-Sharing Elected Representatives' (2001) *Edinburgh Law Review* 380, 384, doi.org/10.3366/elr.2001.5.3.380.

36   *Cope* (n 5) [1].

37   This is a chronic condition resulting in her sleeping for approximately 12 hours per day. While the judgment explained the 'reasons' for their application to share, more about their situation is set out in Rosa Curling, 'The High Court Case' (n 6) 17.

38   *Cope* (n 5) [5].

39   Ibid [5].

In that hearing, they applied for a declaration that the returning officer's rejection of their joint nomination was unlawful. Their arguments drew from their rights under the *European Convention on Human Rights*, including their right to stand for election,[40] their right to be free from discrimination on the grounds of gender and disability,[41] and their right to respect for private and family life.[42] In their view, the refusal was inconsistent with the Convention, and in order to be consistent with the Convention the term 'member' in section 1 of the *Parliamentary Constituencies Act 1986* (UK) should be interpreted as including 'two or more members together representing the constituency carrying one vote'. Moreover, they argued the term 'candidate' in schedule 1 of the *Representation of the People Act 1983* (UK) should encompass a scenario in which two or more elected candidates would together represent a constituency and carry one vote.[43] Given section 6(c) of the *Interpretation Act 1968* (UK), entitled 'Gender and Number', indicates that 'words in the singular include the plural and words in the plural include the singular', they argued that if that interpretation is not permitted, the Court should make a declaration that the provisions of the 1983 and 1986 Acts are incompatible with the Convention by its powers under section 4 of the *Human Rights Act 1998* (UK).[44] While this latter approach would not affect the validity, operation or enforcement of the laws,[45] this would then be a trigger for Parliament to then decide whether it wished to amend the law so as to be compatible with the Convention.[46]

Justice Wilkie did not accept their arguments, and determined that the 1983 and 1986 Acts did not permit the nomination of two or more people as representative of single candidate:[47]

> [T]he language respectively of schedule 1 of the Representation of the People Act 1983, which sets out Parliamentary election rules, and the Parliamentary Constituencies Act 1986, on the face of it, describe a situation which parliamentary constituencies are represented by a single member and that the arrangements set out

---

40 *Convention for the Protection of Human Rights and Fundamental Freedoms*, opened for signature 4 November 1950, 213 UNTS 221 (entered into force 3 September 1953), art 3, protocol 1.
41 Ibid art 14.
42 Ibid art 8; see *Cope* (n 5) [3], [6].
43 *Cope* (n 5) [6].
44 Ibid [8].
45 *Human Rights Act 1998* (UK) section 4(6).
46 Curling, 'The High Court Case' (n 6) 20.
47 *Cope* (n 5) [12].

in the rules envisage one person standing as a single candidate and, on the face of it, give no more room to there being a job share in which two or more people put themselves forward as a single candidate.[48]

In his view, this conclusion was self-evident on the face of the legislation.[49] Under section 1(1) of the *Parliamentary Constituencies Act 1986* (UK), the Parliament provides:

> There shall for the purpose of parliamentary elections by the county and borough constituencies (or in Scotland and the county and borough constituencies), each returning a single member, which are described in Orders in Council made under this Act.

That did not stop him, however, from commenting on the principle of shared representation.

> There can be no doubt about the seriousness of the issue or the fact that the job share is, in many fields, a means whereby diversity may be increased in the makeup of particular professions or roles ... In my judgment the issue which the claimants raise is a fundamental one in relation to our parliamentary democracy.[50]

Yet, these were not issues for a judge to grapple with, because they raised

> a range of complex practical and conceptual questions with which the court is not remotely equipped to deal with and, in my judgment, insofar as the supposed amendment would require the court to consider those issues as germane to the issue of incompatibility, these are not proper issues for the court to debate and determine.[51]

As a judge, he was concerned that the decision would involve 'important practical repercussions' which the Court was not equipped to handle,[52] such as how job-sharing would work in practice regarding voting and provisions that would be made in the event of the death of a member.[53]

---

48   Ibid.
49   Ibid [13].
50   Ibid [26]–[27].
51   Ibid [30].
52   *Cope* (n 5) [20] (Wilkie J).
53   Ibid [23].

The idea that Parliament should take this issue on had been emphasised in the final report of the Speaker's Conference on Parliamentary Representation in 2010, which stated:

> Justice requires that there should be a place within the House of Commons for individuals from all sections of society. If anyone is prevented from standing for Parliament by reason of their gender, background, sexual orientation or a perceived disability, this is an injustice. The democratic right to stand for Parliament exists separately from any debate about the intellectual and behavioural merits of [individuals] as parliamentarians.[54]

Justice Wilkie's decision therefore squarely placed the issue back into the hands of the Parliament,[55] and it has been part of public discourse since, with no concrete changes at this point.

If job-sharing in Parliament is promoted, it could be a straightforward means to 'improve' systems of representative democracy, as hoped for in our 1995 article. For the same reasons raised by Sarah Cope and Clare Phipps, and as outlined further in Sarah Childs' report[56] and Rosa Curling's analysis,[57] job-sharing would enhance our system of representative democracy, both in terms of gender but also in terms of a diversity of life experiences of men and women that would be better accommodated through shared work frameworks.

There are various means for thinking through this approach in Australia, and Katrina Hall has outlined some of these in the Australian context. She has argued that the *Commonwealth Electoral Act 1918* (Cth) ('*Electoral Act*') could be interpreted to allow joint representation in the Commonwealth Parliament and that this approach is supported by the existing legal frameworks in the *Sex Discrimination Act 1984* (Cth) and *Fair Work Act 2009* (Cth). She explains that if section 163 of the *Electoral Act* was interpreted in a manner that would disallow joint nomination for election to Parliament, this would discriminate against women and all potential candidates who are unable to work full-time due to caring

---

54   *Cope* (n 5) [11].
55   *Cope* (n 5) [23].
56   Childs, *The Good Parliament* (n 6).
57   Curling, 'The High Court Case' (n 6) 17.

responsibilities or health requirements.[58] She also makes the argument that an interpretation disallowing joint representation would breach the constitutionally implied freedom of political communication.[59]

Beyond fulfilling the principles of representative democracy, there is also an argument that providing for job-sharing in Parliament would also provide a better foundation and institutional role model to society more broadly. Encouraging job-sharing more universally would enhance not only representative democracy, but the health and wellbeing of the community. This point is made by Professor Jennifer Nedelsky's work with Tom Malleson in their book, *Part Time for All*.[60] As Nedelsky and Malleson powerfully argue:

> Western societies face three critical problems that arise out of dysfunctional norms of work and care: unsustainable stress on families, persistent inequality for women and others who do care work, and policy makers who are ignorant about the care work that life requires.[61]

Rather than 'allowing' parliamentarians to choose to job share, their proposal in effect mandates it for everyone. Their proposal seeks to ensure that society comes to a position (whether legislatively or through changed norm expectations that would compel it) so that

> mature, competent adults are expected to be employed part time (what we now call part-time); no less than between 12 and 30 hours a week, and to do unpaid care work part time – also somewhere between 12 and 30 hours a week.[62]

The arguments in support of this proposal are extensive and significant around several issues, yet there is one argument that is particularly relevant to this article's proposition. Nedelsky and Malleson note, in thinking broadly about problems associated with care management in society, that 'the third problem is the least commented on in the now extensive literature on care'.[63] They call this 'the policy/care divide'.[64] This means

---

58 Hall (n 36).
59 Ibid.
60 Jennifer Nedelsky and Tom Malleson, *Part Time for All: A Care Manifesto* (Oxford University Press, forthcoming).
61 Ibid.
62 Ibid.
63 Ibid.
64 Ibid.

'that those in top policy making positions' (which of course includes lawmakers) 'are almost always people with very little experience of the demands, or satisfactions, or importance of care taking'.[65] In Nedelsky and Malleson's view, this means policymakers on the most part are 'ignorant of a core dimension of human life'[66] rendering them 'unfit for the job'.[67] They further argue:

> we should no more consider electing someone without substantial experience in caregiving to public office, or appointing them CEO of a corporation, than we would someone who had never held a job.[68]

Their claim is supported by the argument that 'knowledge of care is essential to good policy making, and the necessary knowledge can only be acquired by hands-on experience'.[69] In other words, caring for others is relevant and essential to being a good representative in Parliament in fulfilling one's role as a policy and lawmaker. Job-sharing (which may be necessary if more than the 12–30 hours of work are needed for what is recognised as one position), and a responsibility to undertake compulsory care work, is therefore fundamental to a society's fulfilment of representative democracy.

Regardless of whether one is as persuaded as I am by the universal expectation of Nedelsky and Malleson, the central point about policy and representation sits comfortably and powerfully with the concept of shared representation in Parliament, and introducing it and encouraging it would indeed provide a sound role model for job-sharing and could be helpful on the road to the more universal expectation around it, to enhance society more broadly.

Conclusion

In Deborah and my 1995 article, we identified a range of ideas that had been advocated to improve representation, specifically women's representation:

---

65   Ibid.
66   Ibid.
67   Ibid.
68   Ibid.
69   Ibid.

Some aim to alter the composition of parliament and the executive directly. These include: the introduction of voluntary or mandatory gender quotas for the party preselection of candidates, in major political parties; double sex parliamentary representation whereby the size of each electorate would be doubled and each would elect a male and a female representative; the introduction of constitutional quotas guaranteeing a certain percentage of seats to women; and the inclusion in Cabinet of the Minister responsible for women's affairs. A petition presented to a select committee of the New Zealand parliament calls for alteration of electoral legislation to ensure equality and parity of gender representation. Other methods of group representation include the use of functional constituencies in Hong Kong representing groups such as unions and industry within the Legislative Council. Other proposals aim to alter the political and legal culture in which the under-representation has occurred. 'Schooling' in parliamentary skills for women; using the Upper House to 'experiment' with representation for particular groups; reforming parliamentary working hours; and regular government reporting to international review bodies such as the CEDAW [Convention on the Elimination of all Forms of Discrimination Against Women] committee about percentages of women in parliamentary institutions, have all been suggested.[70]

None of those suggestions specifically identified job-sharing – although the idea of each electorate being doubled to elect a male and female representative has a sense of 'shared' representation, although that proposal would lead to two full-time individuals elected to a larger seat. The point behind that proposal, originally identified by the retired member of Parliament Jim Carlton and affirmed by his political adversary Robert Macklin, was, as Macklin wrote in the *Canberra Times*, not about affirmative action; 'it was about getting a more accurate reflection of society into Parliament'.[71] Shared representation, which enables an even more accurate reflection of society by including more people– those whose lives do not enable full-time work to be entertained – is another important way of achieving a more accurate reflection of society in Parliament.

---

70   Cass and Rubenstein, 'Representations of Women' (n 2) 45–46, footnotes omitted.
71   Robert Macklin, 'An Idea Whose Time has Come', *Canberra Times* (online, 22 October 1993) 11[2] <http://nla.gov.au/nla.news-article127513054>.

Is shared representation an idea we should be thinking about more seriously in Australia, to ensure true democratic representation in our Parliaments, and as a positive constitutional change? Will it be one way to ensuring a more effective and diverse representative body, to better reflect the Australian people? Moreover, might constitutional change also encourage a broader societal change to accepting and encouraging shared work as step towards a commitment legislatively, socially and normatively to the creation of a more balanced, healthy and fairer society (with shared work in many areas) for all?

I think so.

We will never know for sure, but I feel confident this is an idea that Deborah would have supported. She was certainly my first role model for job-sharing, and both the ideas and the practice have been part of my own scholarship since. Her inspiration for so many of us therefore continues strongly, in many and varied ways.

PART 2

Natural Resources and Self-Determination

Introduction to Professor Anghie

Catherine Hawkins

Good afternoon. I'd like to acknowledge the traditional owners of the land on which we meet, and pay my respects to their elders, past, present and emerging.

I acknowledge Deborah's family: her parents, Moss and Shirley, her brother Daniel, Gerry, her cousin Gina and her lovely daughters, Hannah and my fairy goddaughter Rosa.

I'd like to thank Kim, Hilary and all the organisers for putting this day together.

We are very lucky to have Professor Tony Anghie here to talk to us this afternoon all the way from the University of Utah. Tony crossed paths with Deborah way back in the days of the Nauru Commission of Inquiry. Their high-flying paths crossed again later in Harvard and other esteemed locales.

Tony has had a distinguished career. He has scored an academic Daily Double, to use a racing term. He has been honoured by his university both as Outstanding Teacher of the Year and Outstanding Scholar of the Year. In a room of academics that will resonate as a particularly impressive double act.

One usually starts such sessions noting that it is a pleasure to be here. But today that is not so much the case for me. Today is not at all an unequivocal pleasure.

In reading Deborah Cass's piece on rethinking self-determination in preparation to chair this session, all I wanted to do was engage in a spirited discussion with her about her piece and the ideas in it. I've been picturing that spirited conversation with Deborah nestled in a comfy, sunny corner of her beach house in Somers.

But, of course, that is not to be.

So. This is a tough day to engage with the divides Deborah traversed without having her here to debate them with us.

I must say that when Kim and Hilary mentioned the plans for today, I did wonder whether Deborah would have been aghast at the very idea of today's symposium. I can hear Deborah modestly telling us with a slightly dismissive shake of her head and her hand that her academic legal work was really nothing special and there were plenty of other people who were doing more significant work.

But Deborah did significant academic legal work in her public sphere days, and I am glad that we're here today to remember that aspect of her life.

I met Deborah as she was on the up in her career as a scholar. I had come to Canberra in 1993 to take up a graduate role in Attorney-General's Department. In 1993 she had of course just been awarded her Caltex scholarship. It was around then that I had the amazing good fortune to meet Deborah. And where did I meet her? Over the back fence in Nimbin Street, Narrabundah, where we both lived.

Throughout the late 1980s and early 90s at university I had been boring senseless all my family and many extended friends with my constant undergrad barrages about structural inequality in our society.

So. I could not believe my good luck when I met Deborah over the back fence. Being from Sydney, and therefore not as familiar with the Melbourne core of the Cass clan, my first overexcited question to Deborah was whether she was related to Bettina. I'd been imbibing Bettina Cass's work for feminist papers I'd written at uni. 'Get out. You're her niece?' And so our friendship began.

How lucky was I to meet a friend like Deborah. Someone with whom I could seamlessly move from Catharine McKinnon and Andrea Dworkin's work through to discussing, almost as energetically, important matters of fashion, arts and literature. Thank you, Nimbin Street, Narrabundah.

For me, Deborah's crowning achievements were not her public sphere academic works, important though they were.

For me, Deborah's crowning achievements were her friendship – one that I continue to treasure – and the gorgeous girls she brought in to this world: Hannah and my fairy goddaughter, Rosa.

So, personal reflections aside, let's get stuck in to the topic of this session: Deborah Cass's research contribution to Nauru and beyond. To self-determination.

The concept is of course complex and contested. But given the spoils of statehood: use of force, taxing and spending, shaping society for good and ill (and hopefully for more good than ill), it is no surprise that in the hallowed arena of international law, the concept of self-determination – who gets to be a state – is such a contested arena.

Deborah's paper asks whether the 'penumbra of uncertainty' surrounding the concept of self-determination is so pronounced that it obscures the term's settled meaning.

I'm not so convinced. But I'm no scholar. And the fact that Deborah was made me love our conversations all the more. My starting point is my position as a lawyer in the executive government. I work on international crime cooperation, where in international work we deal with grey concepts on a daily basis, but things work out. Yes, there is grey, but it works.

Maybe I'm too used to dealing in pragmatic outcomes. At the negotiations on the new Sustainable Development Goals – which will replace the Millennium Development Goals at Leaders Week in the UN New York in September 2015 – it was the wording on self-determination that was still being negotiated right down to the wire in an exceedingly long document, with 17 goals and 169 targets.

The enduring debate about the scope of self-determination shows us that Deborah was of course right in her focus on drilling in to this important concept, and to exhort us to make it make more sense.

So, Professor, please take the conch from me and share with us your thoughts on Deborah Cass's work on Nauru and beyond.

Self-Determination and Beyond: Reflections on the Aftermath of the Nauru Case

Antony Anghie[1]

Introduction

I first met Deborah sometime in 1987, on the 49th or 50th floor of what was then known as Nauru House. Located in Collins Street, Nauru House was one of the tallest buildings in Melbourne at that time, a prominent symbol of the almost legendary affluence of the people of Nauru. Deborah was a Research Officer to Barry Connell, Counsel Assisting the Nauru Commission of Inquiry.[2] The broad task of the Commission of Inquiry was to explore the history of the phosphate mining that had taken place on the island during the time it was administered by Australia, first under the Mandate System of the League of Nations, and then subsequently the Trusteeship System of the United Nations. The mining had devastated the island, and the commission was charged with the task of inquiring into two major issues. First, the feasibility of rehabilitating the island, and, second, the legal question of the responsibility of the three partner governments: Australia, the UK and New Zealand, who had been granted the Mandate and Trusteeship over Nauru, for the environmental damage suffered by the island during the relevant period.

1   My thanks to Kim Rubenstein and the other participants at the symposium 'Traversing Divides' held in memory of Deborah's work, at The Australian National University, Canberra, August 2015. My thanks also to Liz Thomas for her superb research assistance.
2   CG Weeramantry, *Commission of Inquiry into the Rehabilitation of the Worked-Out Phosphate Lands in Nauru* (Report, 1988) <http://asiapacific.anu.edu.au/pambu/catalogue/index.php/commission-of-inquiry-into-rehabilitation-of-worked-out-phosphate-lands-in-nauru;isaar> ('*Commission of Inquiry*').

Deborah had completed the massive task of scouring the archives in various places including London, Geneva, New York, New Zealand, Melbourne and Fiji, to gather and organise all the documents that were essential for the work of the commission. Deborah also had to initiate several Freedom of Information Actions in an effort to get access to documents that the Australian Government refused to provide, despite the fact that these were surely the property of Nauru. Australia had declined to participate in the commission. My own work consisted of serving as a research assistant to CG Weeramantry, the chair of the commission, who was responsible for writing up that part of the report which dealt with the history and complex legal issues relating to the phosphate mining.[3] The scientific part of the report which examined the feasibility of rehabilitation was completed by another commissioner, an engineer, Mr RH Challen. The final report ran to something like 10 volumes of text and documents. The commission felt under some pressure to provide a comprehensive and detailed report precisely because none of the partner governments involved had appeared before the commission.

We relied completely on the several filing cabinets full of documents that Deborah had so carefully compiled and catalogued – I should say, in a manner that demonstrated a clear and precise awareness of the legal issues that had to be addressed. It is a testament to the thoroughness and precision of Deborah's work that the case that was later argued in the International Court of Justice was based on the foundations that she had laid;[4] I am still unaware of any documents that were later added to Nauru's case. Deborah had provided all that was needed. It was not always easy working for the government of Nauru. It is a myth to believe that those who have somehow been at the receiving end of colonialism, however benevolently administered, would be ennobled by the experience. Despite all this, Deborah remain undeterred, driven on by her powerful sense of injustice to do all the work that was needed to give the people of Nauru a chance to articulate their grievance.

The theme of self-determination was central to Nauru's claims. Article 22 of the League of Nations, which created the Mandate System of the League, stipulated that the mandate power was to ensure the 'well being and development' of the native peoples unable to look after their own

---

3   Ibid.
4   *Certain Phosphate Lands in Nauru* (*Nauru v Australia*) (*Preliminary Objections*) [1992] ICJ Rep 240 (*'Certain Phosphate Lands'*).

interests.[5] The System in this way purported to prevent the colonial exploitation that had been such a prominent feature of international relations up to that time. In legal terms, the Nauru mandate was granted by the League of Nations to Australia, New Zealand and the UK; however, Australia administered Nauru on behalf of all the partner governments, a result of an internal arrangement among them.[6] It was unclear at this stage what the League envisaged as the ultimate status of Nauru and other territories placed under the Mandate System. The theme of self-determination, expressed somewhat uncertainly, tentatively and controversially in the time of the drafting of the League, had assumed a far more detailed character by the time Nauru was placed under the Trusteeship System of the United Nations. Under the Charter, Nauru was recognised as possessing the right to self-determination. Consequently, Nauru claimed that Australia had failed to meet its obligations to preserve the interests of the people of Nauru, by failing to facilitate their transition to a functioning and sustainable sovereign statehood, and thereby not protecting their right to self-determination.[7] Most immediately, the very physical territory of Nauru had been devastated by the mining and the partner governments were responsible for the rehabilitation of the lands.

Self-determination was a topic that Deborah Cass explored later in a far more wide-ranging and theoretically ambitious work, one of her first: 'Re-Thinking Self-Determination: A Critical Analysis of Current International Law Theories', which was published in 1992. Surveying all the claims to self-determination made in the late 1980s and early 1990s: the break-up of the Balkans, the war in Iraq, claims being made in Palestine, Moldava and Ukraine, Deborah Cass argued that what she termed the 'conventional' approach to self-determination – which stipulated that colonised peoples could exercise this right only once and within pre-existing boundaries – was outmoded, and that the right of self-determination should be reconceptualised to permit minorities and indigenous peoples to exercise it. As she puts it:

---

5   *The Covenant of the League of Nations*, League of Nations Members, opened for signature 28 June 1919 (entered into force 10 January 1920) art 22 ('*Covenant*').

6   League of Nations [including Australia, New Zealand and the UK], *Mandate for Nauru* (Miscellaneous No. 6, His Majesty's Stationery Office, London, 1921) <https://dl.wdl.org/468/service/468.pdf>.

7   See, eg, Mary Nazzal, 'Nauru: An Environment Destroyed and International Law' (Paper, lawanddevelopment.org, April 2005) <http://www.lawanddevelopment.org/docs/nauru.pdf>; M Rafiqul Islam, 'The Dispute between Nauru and Australia over Rehabilitation: A Test Case for Economic Self-Determination' (1992) 8 *Queensland University Technology Law Journal* 147, doi.org/10.5204/qutlr.v8i0.364.

> The challenge for international law is therefore not to exclude the ever-increasing list of claimants because they do not match precisely with an outmoded theory, but to find methods for assessing and evaluating the validity of claims according to realistic, functional and humanitarian measures.[8]

Self-determination is a topic that has haunted international law ever since the concept was first articulated, in different forms, by Lenin and Wilson. A massive amount of literature has focused on the subject. Deborah Cass's article remains a valuable contribution to this literature not only because the problems she discusses remain with us – who should be able to claim this right, and what is its content – but because of the incisive manner in which she sets out the problem and the many different analytic tools she employs to explore the problem. Such tools include classic positivist textualist analysis, leavened by a more critical jurisprudential approach which suggests how a new paradigm must be developed to accommodate developments in state practice and expectations. It is a striking feature of Deborah's brilliance that she made contributions to so many areas of law: international, domestic, constitutional, theoretical. She did not, as far as I know, return to the theme of self-determination. She proceeded instead to author one of the first analyses of 'New Approaches to International Law',[9] before then writing her pioneering book on constitutionalism and the World Trade Organization.[10] And yet, the Nauru experience had not completely disappeared from her thinking. She believed that the topic of trusteeship in international law required further exploration and was considering writing on this topic for her Doctor of Juridical Science (SJD) at Harvard. Her intuition, again, proved to be correct, as trusteeship, broadly conceived, is now being studied in far greater detail by numerous scholars whose works illuminate how this broad idea has engaged the discipline.

My purpose in this essay is not only to review Deborah Cass's important work for the Nauru Commission and her prescient thinking on self-determination, but to consider, in a reflective rather than analytic way, almost 25 years after the International Court of Justice handed down its

---

8   Deborah Z Cass, 'Re-Thinking Self-Determination: A Critical Analysis of Current International Law Theories' (1992) 18 *Syracuse Journal of International Law and Commerce* 31.

9   Deborah Z Cass, 'Navigating the Newstream: Recent Critical Scholarship in International Law' (1996) 65 *Nordic Journal of International Law* 341, doi.org/10.1163/15718109620294924.

10   Deborah Z Cass, *The Constitutionalization of the World Trade Organization: Legitimacy, Democracy, and Community in the International Trading System* (Oxford University Press, 2005).

decision on 'Certain Phosphate Lands of Nauru',[11] the aftermath of self-determination, and the subsequent history of Nauru and its relationship with Australia. I try then to suggest some of the more immediate legacies and possible reverberations of the Nauru case and the ways in which the Nauru experience might be considered within the broader context of both international law and Australia's foreign relations and engagement with international law. For these purposes, I sketch the outlines of a concept that has featured only occasionally and unevenly in Australian history: 'Australian Empire', and I consider Nauru as an example of that empire in operation.

The Aftermath of Self-Determination

Nauru is now, as a result of bipartisan policy of Liberal and Labor governments, a detention facility for people seeking asylum in Australia. Considerable controversy has followed. *The Guardian* reported on leaked documents which revealed that considerable violence was taking place in Nauru.[12] Detainees were being sexually and physically abused by guards. Many had attempted suicide. The Australian Minister of Immigration, Peter Dutton, accused detainees of sewing up their own lips and setting themselves on fire in an outrageous and flagrantly manipulative attempt to enter Australia.[13] However, thousands of Australians protested against their government's policies, and called for the closing of the camps and the transfer of all detainees to Australia.[14]

11　*Certain Phosphate Lands* (n 4). See also Antony Anghie, 'The Heart of My Home: Colonialism, Environmental Damage and the Nauru Case' (1993) 34(2) *Harvard International Law Journal* 445.

12　Paul Farrell, Nick Evershed and Helen Davidson, 'The Nauru Files: Cache of 2,000 Leaked Reports Reveal Scale of Abuse of Children in Australia Offshore Detention', *The Guardian* (online, 10 August 2016) <https://www.theguardian.com/australia-news/2016/aug/10/the-nauru-files-2000-leaked-reports-reveal-scale-of-abuse-of-children-in-australian-offshore-detention>.

13　Ben Doherty and Paul Farrell, '"People have Self-Immolated to Get to Australia" – Immigration Minister's Response to Nauru Files', *The Guardian* (online, 10 August 2016) <https://www.theguardian.com/news/2016/aug/11/labor-will-reintroduce-bill-to-force-mandatory-reporting-of-child-abuse-after-nauru-files>.

14　Isabella Kwai, 'Australia Revokes Medical Evacuations for Offshore Detainees', *The New York Times* (online, 4 December 2019) <https://www.nytimes.com/2019/12/04/world/australia/medevac-refugees-repeal.html>; on the Australian public's reaction to off-shore detention see further Helen Davidson, 'Thousands Call for Nauru and Manus Camps to Close in Rallies across Australia', *The Guardian* (online, 27 August 2016) <https://www.theguardian.com/australia-news/2016/aug/27/nauru-files-manus-island-close-the-camps-rallies-asylum-seeker>.

Whereas previously Nauru had supplied Australia with the phosphate it had so strenuously sought for its agricultural needs, it now serves a different function within the scheme of Australian foreign relations. In his book, based on the Nauru Report, Christopher Weeramantry wrote, 'Nauru presents in a microcosm an unusual variety of the great historical currents that have shaped the course of human affairs'.[15] He refers to the settlement of the Pacific, the emergence of a distinctive culture and way of life in Nauru, and the gradual expansion of the European presence in the remotest parts of the Pacific in search of land and minerals. The history of the European Empire in the Pacific could be told through the story of Nauru. It is, as these histories tend to be, marked by a strange dissonance; decisions made in Berlin and in Versailles have profound consequences for people living thousands of miles away who have very little idea of the people and factors deciding their fate. For instance, Nauru was placed in the German sphere of influence,[16] whereas the neighbouring island of Banaba (part of the Gilbert and Ellis chain of islands) was placed in the British sphere of influence, thanks to the Anglo–German Treaty of 1886. This agreement was reached during the aftermath of Berlin Conference of 1885, which had focused on European empires in Africa and that led to the Berlin Act of 1885, which regulated commerce in the Congo.[17] The Nauru case dealt with international legal doctrines relating to the exploitation of resources and the content of self-determination, and it also offered in its own way a graphic illustration of how entrenched systems of political economy are fundamentally inimical to environmental wellbeing and how environmental devastation could result in the destruction of sovereignty itself. Now of course, Nauru and the events occurring there are enmeshed in yet another set of international legal controversies and doctrines – relating not only to environmental damage, but refugee and asylum law and human rights. It is taken as exemplary of how environmental devastation – now caused by climate change – may endanger the existence of states,[18] and create 'environmental refugees'. The plight of Nauru also parallels in some ways the fate of the Chagos Islanders who were displaced from their land, and whose failed struggles for self-determination also

15   Christopher Weeramantry, *Nauru: Environmental Damage Under International Trusteeship* (Oxford University Press, 1994) 1.
16   The Commonwealth, *Nauru: History* (Web Page, 2019) <http://thecommonwealth.org/our-member-countries/nauru/history>.
17   See especially Katerina Martina Teaiwa, *Consuming Ocean Island: Stories of People and Phosphate from Banaba* (Indiana University Press, 2014).
18   Carl N McDaniel and John M Gowdy, *Paradise for Sale: A Parable of Nature* (University of California Press, 2000).

raised complex issues about the legacies of colonialism.[19] Further, the Nauru case is rich for reconsideration in the context of new developments in the history and theory of international law promise, which scrutinise the relationship, for instance, between colonialism, political economy and the environment.[20]

The Nauru case raises enduring questions about the meaning and content of self-determination. At the time art 22 of the League of Nations was drafted, self-determination was still a vague principle: its legal status was uncertain and its political ramifications worrying and unclear. The former Ottoman territories in the Middle East designated countries such as Iraq and Syria as mandate territories, which were classified as 'A' mandates that were developed to the point 'where their existence as independent nations can be provisionally recognized'.[21] Nauru, however, was characterised as a 'C' mandate that was to be administered 'under the laws of the Mandatory as integral portions of its territory'.[22] Crucially, such administration was to be 'subject to the safeguards above mentioned in the interests of the indigenous population'.[23] Clearly then, Nauru was to be administered in accordance with basic principles of trusteeship which ensured that all the

19   Stephen Allen, *The Chagos Islanders and International Law* (Oxford University Press, 2015); David Vine, *Island of Shame: The Secret History of the US Military Base on Diego Garcia* (Princeton University Press, 2009), doi.org/10.1515/9781400838509.

20   Stephen Humphreys and Yoriko Otomo, 'Theorizing International Environmental Law' in Anne Orford and Florian Hoffmann (eds), *Oxford Handbook of the Theory of International Law* (Oxford University Press, 2016), doi.org/10.1515/9781400838509. As Stephen Humphreys and Yoriko Otomo point out, 'European colonialism was premised on the exploitation of natural resources and on the maintenance of conditions of global trade in raw materials'. For recent scholarship on the issues that arise, see generally Ileana Porras, 'Binge Development in the Age of Fear: Scarcity, Consumption, Inequality, and the Environmental Crisis' (doi.org/10.1017/cbo9781107239357.002) and Karin Mickelson, 'International Law as a War Against Nature? Reflections on the Ambivalence of International Environmental Law' (doi.org/10.1017/CBO9781107239357.003) both in Barbara Stark (ed), *International Law and Its Discontents: Confronting Crises* (Cambridge University Press, 2015); Usha Natarajan and Kishan Khoday, 'Locating Nature: Making and Unmaking International Law' (2014) 27(3) *Leiden Journal of International Law* 573, doi.org/10.1017/s0922156514000211; Usha Natarajan and Kishan Khoday, 'Fairness and International Environmental Law from Below: Social Movements and Legal Transformation in India' (2012) 25(2) *Leiden Journal of International Law* 415, doi.org/10.1017/s0922156512000118. For particular studies of Nauru and the legacies of the phosphate mining see Katerina Teaiwa, 'Ruining Pacific Islands: Australia's Phosphate Imperialism' (2015) 46(3) *Australian Historical Studies* 374, doi.org/10.1080/1031461x.2015.1082609; Cait Storr, 'Islands and the South: Framing the Relationship between International Law and Environmental Crisis' (2016) 27(2) *European Journal of International Law* 519, doi.org/10.1093/ejil/chw026.

21   *Treaty of Peace Between the Allied and Associated Powers and Turkey,* opened for signature 10 August 1920, art 94 <https://wwi.lib.byu.edu/index.php/Section_I,_Articles_1_-_260>.

22   *Covenant* (n 5) art 22.

23   Ibid.

resources of the island were utilised or preserved for the benefit of its people. At the very least, the obligations of art 22 of the League of Nations Charter prohibited the destruction of the physical territory of Nauru.

The Mandate System was replaced by the Trusteeship System of the United Nations. The obligations undertaken by the Australia and the partner governments under that system were far more specific and detailed than those included in art 22. Article 76(b) of the United Nations Charter stipulated the purpose of the Trusteeship System:

> to promote the political, economic, social and educational advancement of the inhabitants of the trust territories and their progressive development towards self-government or independence as may be appropriate to the particular circumstances of each territory and its peoples and the freely expressed wishes of the peoples concerned, and as may be provided by the terms of each trusteeship agreement.[24]

The people of Nauru were desperate to continue their existence as an independent people, and art 76(b) in effect protected their right to self-determination, to emerge as a sovereign nation-state. It was clear however, from the beginning of the Australian Administration in 1919, that Australia wanted to mine out the island and then resettle the remaining Nauruans in Australia. The management of the island was effectively left in the hands of the British Phosphate Commissioners (BPC), the body which was established to conduct the mining operations. The Nauru Island Agreement between the partner governments which created this entity included the startling provision that prevented the administrator of the island from interfering with the mining operation.[25] The commissioners and the mining operation they were charged with managing governed the island, as many outsiders observed.[26] The Australian officials who were concerned about the impact of phosphate mining on the territory and people were thus legally disabled from controlling a system of governance essentially based on the exploitation of the phosphates.

---

24 *Charter of the United Nations* art 76(b).

25 *The Nauru Island Agreement Act (No 8) 1919* (Cth) art 13, 'There shall be no interference by any of the three Governments with the direction, management, or control of the business of working, shipping or selling the phosphates …'.

26 See Weeramantry, *Commission of Inquiry* (n 2) 128. Mr Rolz Bennett of Guatemala stated that 'every aspect of life on Nauru depended on a single activity, the exploitation of the phosphate deposits': *Trusteeship Council, 18th Session: Verbatim Record of the 741st Meeting Held at Headquarters, New York, on Thursday, 9 August 1956*, UN Doc T/PV.741 (9 August 1956) 153 <https://digitallibrary.un.org/record/3844199?ln=en> ('*Trusteeship Council, 18th session*').

The Nauru Case was settled in 1993 by Australia's payment (the other partner government later contributed) of something like A$107 million for the rehabilitation of the phosphate lands damaged by the mining.[27] Since then, Nauru has lurched from crisis to crisis as it struggles to survive: it suffers major financial problems and most its major assets have been sold, and it has practiced all the manoeuvres available to 'bare sovereignty', for Nauru's resources do not seem to amount to very much more than its legal status as a sovereign state.[28] It extended recognition to entities seeking statehood and was compensated for doing so, and defended Australia's infamous 'Pacific Solution', which provides Nauru with the millions of dollars it desperately needs from the Australian Government.[29] Previously Australia's policies were effectively destroying the sovereignty of Nauru – not out of any particular malice towards its people, whom it viewed generally with affectionate but devastating condescension – but because it was intent on exploiting all the phosphates available. Now, however, Australia would prefer to insist on Nauru's sovereignty: it is Nauru that must protect the human rights of the many unfortunate people housed on the island. Nauru represents a complex and anomalous sort of sovereignty. Nauru, like Guantanamo – another product of a colonial relationship – has been termed a 'legal black hole'.[30]

For those who are somewhat familiar with the history of Nauru, it was apparent from the outset that even the success of the Nauruan campaign for compensation was a decidedly ambivalent victory. Nauru itself should not be exonerated of the consequences of the many bad decisions it made following independence. But given the history of the relationship between Australia and Nauru, it was obvious that the odds were very much against the people of the tiny island. Indeed, it was astonishing that Nauru was able to achieve independence at all, given implacable Australian policies concerning Nauru, and the unrelenting determination of Australia to

---

27   US Department of State, 'Nauru (04/08)' (Background Note), archived at <https://2009-2017.state.gov/outofdate/bgn/nauru/111187.htm>: 'Australia settled the case out of court in 1993, agreeing to pay a lump sum settlement of A$107 million (U.S.$85.6 million) and an annual stipend of the equivalent of A$2.5 million in 1993 dollars toward environmental rehabilitation'.

28   'Nauru: Paradise Well and Truly Lost', *The Economist* (online, 20 December 2001) <https://www.economist.com/christmas-specials/2001/12/20/paradise-well-and-truly-lost>.

29   Ariane Rummery, 'Australia's "Pacific Solution" Draws to a Close', *United Nations High Commissioner for Refugees* (Web Page, 11 February 2008) <https://www.unhcr.org/en-au/news/latest/2008/2/47b04d074/australias-pacific-solution-draws-close.html>.

30   See George Williams, 'Asylum Seekers on Nauru are in a Legal Black Hole', *Sydney Morning Herald* (online, 3 February 2016) <http://www.smh.com.au/comment/nauru-a-legal-black-hole-for-asylum-seekers-20160203-gmklf8.html>.

exploit a completely unequal relationship. It is telling for instance, that Australia prevented the Nauruans access to expert advice when it came to the extraordinarily complex and crucial negotiations with the BPC and government prior to independence.[31] Australia on the other hand, was able to draw on the brilliance of eminent lawyers to justify its position. It was only through the courage and determination of the Nauruan leader, the heroic Hammer DeRoburt, and the supervision of the Trusteeship Council in continuously questioning Australia's policies in Nauru, that the island survived.[32]

Self-determination, as granted by Australia, consisted in handing over a devastated landscape to a people that were deliberately neglected and subordinated, whatever the funds supposedly available to them. Mining was the only industry that Australia fostered on the island, and so Nauru was faced with the predicament whereby its only means of economic development was the continuation of the mining that was so damaging to the island. Further, intent on protecting the phosphate industry, the Australian Government made little effort to educate the Nauruans and prepare them for self-government, despite the talent the Nauruans demonstrated. Dedicated Australian officials sought to make good on Australia's obligations under the mandate, but these initiatives were defeated by the imperatives of the mining operation. As far back as 1928, the first Australian administrator of Nauru had planned to educate Nauruans to manage their own affairs and had instituted a training program for Nauruans in Geelong. As a result, a group of concerned citizens from Geelong became involved in the development of the island, and arranged for Nauruans to be trained in Geelong in various trades. The program was a great success, and both the organisers and sympathetic Australian administrators believed that the 'Geelong Boys', as they came to be known, could gradually assume responsibility for many aspects of the administration of the island. This did not occur. Trained Nauruans were a threat to the continuing operation of the phosphate industry and the Geelong program was condemned for producing 'malcontents'.[33]

---

31 See generally Teaiwa, 'Ruining Pacific Islands' (n 20), speaking to the inequality of the Australia–Nauru relationship especially in relation to phosphate.

32 'Hammer DeRoburt: Nauruan Politician', *Encyclopaedia Britannica* (online, last updated 21 September 2019) <https://www.britannica.com/biography/Hammer-DeRoburt>.

33 Weeramantry, *Nauru: Environmental Damage* (n 15) 113.

Over time, the Australians who took an interest in the welfare of the Nauruans and became familiar with their affairs were greatly disturbed by Australian policies in Nauru. They formed an organisation, based in Geelong, the Pacific Island Natives Welfare Association (PINWA) which took up the Nauruan cause, for by the 1940s, it was obvious that the continuation of phosphate mining would have completely devastated the island. Several members of PINWA were very well acquainted with the plight of the Nauruans as they had worked on Nauru and had also supported the 'Geelong Boys'. PINWA, after much effort, met with the Minister of External Territories to express their concerns, but were disappointed in the government's response. Many years later, HE Hurst, a member of PINWA who had also earlier been involved in the Geelong training program, set out what he saw as the desperate plight of the Nauruans in an article titled, 'Australia Seeks to Destroy Nauruans as a People'.[34] Much earlier, William Groves, who had served as a Director of Education in Nauru, noted the failure of Australia to promote education for self-governance, pleading that the Nauruans should not become 'what I fear our Australian aborigines have become, a despised and dying race'.[35] The Trusteeship Council too, continuously questioned Australia and its failure to promote self-government. Australia had responded that no Nauruans were capable of assuming real responsibilities.[36] Thus, having deprived the Nauruans of a proper education system, the Australian Government then proclaimed them to be incapable of assuming any administrative responsibilities. It seemed that Australia was intent on keeping Nauruans in a permanently subordinate position. It was not until 1965, three years before independence, that Nauruans were given even limited legislative powers, and even then, they never exercised any sort of powers with respect to the phosphate mining, despite their protests. It is uncertain how meaningful self-determination could have followed, or how Nauru could have sustained itself politically and economically, given this history. Article 76(b) of the UN Charter outlines self-determination as ensuring, not simply political independence, but the promotion of the economic, social and cultural advancement of the peoples under trusteeship. Australia, in its efforts to protect the mining of phosphates, failed in all these areas.

---

34   Ibid 390.
35   Ibid 113.
36   Ibid 141, citing *Trusteeship Council, 18th session* UN Doc T/PV.741 (n 26) 151.

The people of Nauru, almost from the beginning of their relationship with Australia, have been treated with a level of condescension that was entirely demeaning and ignorant, even if supposedly benevolent. In the course of the pre-independence talks, the Nauruan representatives made this point:

> We feel the Australian people have an image of Nauruans which is quite wrong ... Australians seem to have a picture of an absurdly small people who want too much from Australia, who want complete sovereign independence, and who are not as grateful as they should be for what Australia is generously offering them.[37]

Nauru continues, of course, to be the subject of Australian belittlement and derision. Most infamously Alexander Downer described Nauru as being the worst place he had ever visited.[38] Given Australia's responsibility for the situation of Nauru, and indeed, the actions of Downer's predecessors as Australia's Minister for Foreign Affairs, the denunciation is ironic and tragic while reflecting an unfortunate ignorance of Australia's role in creating the dereliction that the Minister now condemns. Phosphate was crucial for Australian agriculture, and Nauru had supplied thousands of tons of the fertiliser to Australian farmers at cost price.[39] Apart from the environmental damage it caused, Australia had benefited enormously from the whole relationship: the Commission of Inquiry provided some plausible figures suggesting the extent of the massive sums involved.[40] What is also perhaps most telling is that the people who presciently saw, warned against, and protested the destruction of the island of Nauru and its effects on its people were conscientious Australian administrators and citizens, people such as Griffith and HE Hurst who had a deep knowledge of the situation in Nauru, and who sincerely attempted to ensure that Australia fulfilled its obligations under the Mandate and Trusteeship arrangements.

---

37 Weeramantry, *Nauru: Environmental Damage* (n 15) 290.
38 See Tony Wheeler, 'Letter From ... Nauru: The Worst Place in the World?', *Crikey* (Online, 5 April 2011) <https://www.crikey.com.au/2011/04/05/letter-from-nauru-the-worst-place-in-the-world/>.
39 'Nauru – Overview of Economy', *Nations Encyclopedia* (Web Page, 2019) <http://www.nations encyclopedia.com/economies/Asia-and-the-Pacific/Nauru-OVERVIEW-OF-ECONOMY.html# ixzz4N7Wqx948>: 'Phosphate has been exported mainly to Australia and New Zealand, where it improved the poor soils in those countries'.
40 *Certain Phosphate Lands* (n 4) [233].

Papua New Guinea: Mining and the Postcolonial state

We might consider the Nauru case not just in terms of its legacy for the people of Nauru, but as exemplifying a set of practices and policies that Australia chose to adopt more widely in the Pacific.

In her important article, Katerina Teaiwa analyses Nauru in the context of what she terms 'Australia's Phosphate Imperialism', an imperialism which extended to other Pacific islands, such as Banaba, which were equally devastated.[41] Here I focus on another territory that was under Australian Mandate and later Trusteeship administration: Papua New Guinea (PNG). The situation in the two territories was somewhat different. Whereas in the case of Nauru, the phosphates were mined by the BPC as explicit representatives of the partner governments, the resources of PNG that were discovered in the 1960s were handed over to private entities. In the case of the massive Bougainville mine, these included the Australian mining company Rio Tinto.[42] In the 1960s, it was hardly acceptable, under trusteeship, for the partner governments discharging that trusteeship to follow the procedures that were more redolent of the nineteenth century and establish a monopoly over the phosphates, even if indirectly, to a body which it effectively controlled. Private rights, however, were better protected from any sort of governmental or international interference.[43]

A cursory glance at some of the Trusteeship Council proceedings regarding the mining concessions in PNG raise various questions. The 'development discourse', which had begun at the time of the League of Nations itself, had reached a further stage and the Special Representative for Australia noted that, '[l]ike all developing countries, the Territory needed an established policy on outside investment to ensure that the interests of the people were safeguarded'.[44] The World Bank had visited PNG and written an influential report on how development was to be achieved, and mining became crucial for this project. Various local bodies had been consulted about the need for such investment, and the House of Assembly

41   See Teaiwa, 'Ruining Pacific Islands' (n 20).
42   See, eg, Australian Department of Foreign Affairs, *Documents on Australian Foreign Policy: Australia and Papua New Guinea 1966–1969*, ed Stuart Dora (Commonwealth of Australia, 2006) (*'Australia and Papua New Guinea'*), detailing the interactions of Rio Tinto in Papua New Guinea during the 1960s.
43   See James Gathii, *War, Commerce and International Law* (Oxford University Press, 2010).
44   *Report of the Trusteeship Council*, UN TCOR, 24th sess, UN Doc A/7604 (2 June – 6 August 1969) [170] (*'Report of the Trusteeship Council'*).

had 'adopted a formal declaration on development capital, providing for various guarantees for investors: that declaration had been reaffirmed on 3 September 1968'.[45] Information was given about the benefits that would accrue to the local population, and how the processing of raw materials within the territory could add value. Furthermore, plans were made to provide the local populations with equity in the mining operations. The Trusteeship Council monitored these arrangements, which were lauded by the representatives of the UK and France. The Soviet representative, however, demurred and stated:

> [T]he Bougainville Copper Company would be set up in such a way that two thirds of the shares would belong to Riotinto Zinc, a company known for its activities in the southern part of Africa, which was an international monopoly. One third of the shares would belong to the New Broken Hill Company which had its headquarters in London. They would exploit the extremely rich deposits of copper of Bougainville Island. He said that from the statement of the Special Representative it was quite obvious that the lion's share of this project would go to Bougainville Copper and not to the indigenous population. And there was no reason to doubt that if the project went forward Bougainville island would really become the patrimony of the company'.[46]

The Russian response might be interpreted as a predictable and ideologically motivated criticism in the context of the ongoing Cold War. Notably, for instance, a detailed study of the conflict in Bougainville conflict states that '[b]y the standards of the time, Bougainville Copper Limited (BCL), whose principal investor was Conzinc Riotinto Australia (CRA), had a comparatively advanced sense of corporate social responsibility'.[47] This policy was based on enlightened self-interest: BCL provided scholarships to indigenous students, funded agricultural extensions and paid for all the infrastructure needed to operate the mine, such as roads, electricity, water, telecommunications, ports, airstrips and housing.[48] The Australian Administration of PNG exercised its right to acquire 20 per cent of the equity of the mine, and many shares were purchased by indigenous individuals. The mining companies paid very high taxes on their profits, and these increased even further after independence when

---

45   Ibid.
46   Ibid [246].
47   See John Braithwaite et al, *Reconciliation and Architectures of Commitment: Sequencing Peace in Bougainville* (ANU E Press, 2010) 12, doi.org/10.22459/RAC.09.2010.
48   Ibid.

the new government of PNG entered into negotiations.[49] The Australian Government believed that the exploitation of the mine was central to the development of PNG, in doubling the territory's export income:

> The Administration believes that the Bougainville Copper project offers a most important opportunity for the Territory to take a significant step forward toward economic self-reliance. Because of this the project is seen as of national rather than local importance, and it is seen as a unit in the mining industry rather than a single mine.[50]

However generous the mining companies were according to the standards of the time, the Russian warning in this sense became a reality. The mine was central to achieving not merely political sovereignty, but 'economic self-reliance', and thus the mine became one of the central institutions of the political life of PNG.

The conflict in Bougainville has been the subject of study for many institutions, and enormous effort and resources have been devoted to peace building and conflict resolution in the island.[51] It is unclear as to how the history and origins of the conflict have been understood, or even whether these things matter. Perhaps the most important issue is to address the immediate demand of the parties involved: put simply, to stop the violence.

What is absolutely clear to me, however, is that Australian officials would have been aware that mining, without adequate regulations, could cause massive environmental damage which would have catastrophic consequences for the welfare of the indigenous population, the native peoples whose interests were to be protected by the trusteeship arrangement. It was in the early 1960s, precisely, that the desperate Nauruans were making this very point, and the scarred landscape of

---

49   Braithwaite et al, *Reconciliation and Architectures* (n 47) 12.

50   See *Australia and Papua New Guinea* (n 42) xxxix, this is a statement by Newman to the House of Assembly, Port Moresby Memorandum of 16 June 1969, 'White Paper on Bougainville'. This was an attempt to persuade the Papuan House of Assembly of the benefits of the mining. But it seemed that the administration was prepared to do whatever was necessary in Bougainville, including use force 'subject to humanity and standing field orders', if the administration's explanations were rejected. There had been fierce local opposition to CRA's activities by the locals in Bougainville, and as early as 1969 there were dangers of Bougainville seceding.

51   See, eg, Anthony Regan, 'Causes and Course of the Bougainville Conflict' (1998) 33(3) *The Journal of Pacific History* 269; Volker Boege, *Bougainville and the Discovery of Slowness: An Unhurried Approach to State-Building in the Pacific* (Australian Centre for Peace and Conflict Studies, 2006); Benjamin Reilly, 'State Functioning and State Failure in the South Pacific' (2004) 58(4) *Australian Journal of International Affairs* 479, doi.org/10.1080/1035771042000304742.

the island offered its own eloquent story. The Australian Department of Territories – under the Ministership of Sir Paul Hasluck at the time – was busy battling the Nauru protests and claims arising from mining, while at the same time formalising the Bougainville concession agreements to two major Australian mining companies.[52] There was, however, at least one significant difference between the two situations. In the case of PNG, the community that suffered most as a result of the mining, the people of Bougainville, were not the community that had been able to engage directly and decisively with the Australian Administration, even if local communities were paid royalties. The government of PNG and its antecedent had no particular concern for the wellbeing of the people of Bougainville, who it seems had always seen themselves and been viewed as a different community. The situation is a familiar one in postcolonial states. The Nigerian government was indifferent to the wellbeing and concerns of the Ogoni people – namely that their lands were being destroyed by oil drilling – as this activity benefited both the Nigerian state and the different ethnic group that were dominant within it.[53] Secessionist wars have been fuelled by the volatile combination of ethnic differences, which have been compounded by uneven economic development. In another variation on this theme, European powers have attempted to foster secession in countries in the hope of getting or retaining access to mineral-rich areas; thus Belgium encouraged the secession of Katanga from the Congo in order to protect the interests of its mining companies.[54] Many mining companies, such as Rio Tinto, had interests in several different colonial territories, and their strategies for advancing and protecting those interests were international in character. A global history could be written then, of the relations between colonial governments and the private mining companies with which they were intimately connected – it is telling, after all, that BHP, one of the concessionaires of Bougainville, was famously known as 'The Big Australian'.[55]

---

52   See, eg, Russell McGregor, 'Wards, Words and Citizens: AP Elkin and Paul Hasluck on Assimilation' (1999) 69(4) *Oceania* 243, doi.org/10.1002/j.1834-4461.1999.tb00372.x, detailing the interactions of Paul Hasluck and the Aboriginal community in the 1960s.

53   For further information on the Ogoni people in Nigeria, see, eg, Steven Cayford, 'The Ogoni Uprising: Oil, Human Rights, and a Democratic Alternative in Nigeria' (1996) *Africa Today* 183.

54   'Congo in Crisis: The Rise and Fall of Katangan Secession', *Association for Diplomatic Studies and Training* (Web Page, 8 September 2015) <http://adst.org/2015/09/congo-in-crisis-the-rise-and-fall-of-katangan-secession/>.

55   Even the *Sydney Morning Herald* occasionally still refers to BHP as the 'Big Australian', see, eg, Clin Kruger, 'BHP Reject South32 Beats the "Big Australian" on Share Price and CEO Pay', *The Sydney Morning Herald* (online, 11 September 2016) <http://www.smh.com.au/business/cbd/bhp-reject-south32-beats-the-big-australian-on-share-price-and-ceo-pay-20160908-grc0gz.html>.

Furthermore, the manner in which the governments attempted to protect the companies against the threat of self-determination is a complex and compelling theme. The independence of PNG would not necessarily have helped local communities. Here, ironically and tragically, the postcolonial state of independent PNG continued in some respects to reproduce the role of the colonial state, because it was indifferent to the needs of the local communities and because it needed the expertise and capital offered by the mining companies. As far as these local communities were concerned, the postcolonial state, invariably obsessed by the imperatives of 'development', was no better, and perhaps much worse, than the colonial state. It is important to note that, right from the outset, local communities in Bougainville protested against the mining.[56] Scholars of nationalism have elaborated on this crucial problem confronting multiethnic states where one ethnic group took control over the formidable apparatus of the state.

Extensive litigation has followed over the years. Residents of Bougainville unsuccessfully sued Rio Tinto in the US under the *Alien Tort Claims Act*, alleging it had committed crimes against humanity, war crimes and racial discrimination.[57]

Conclusion

Self-determination was the revolutionary doctrine that was the foundation of the anti-colonial movement. Initially articulated by former US President Woodrow Wilson, and intended by him to apply only to what he regarded as the suppressed nations of Europe, self-determination became a central feature of the United Nations era. It is mentioned in the UN Charter, and is the subject of several foundational General Assembly Resolutions. Nauru and PNG, however, suggest some of the unfortunate legacies of self-determination, and raise crucial questions about the limitations of self-determination. In the case of Nauru, self-determination

---

56 Anthony J Regan and Helga-Maria Griffin (eds), *Bougainville Before the Conflict* (ANU E Press, 2005) 131–2, doi.org/10.22459/BBC.08.2015.

57 See *Sarei v Rio Tinto plc*, 671 F 3d 736 (9th Cir, 2011), cert. granted, judgment vacated, 133 1995, 185 L Ed 2d 863 (2013); see also Jonathan Stempel, 'Rio Tinto Wins End to Human Rights Abuse Lawsuit in US', *Reuters* (online, 29 June 2013) <http://www.reuters.com/article/riotinto-abuse-lawsuit-idUSL2N0F41AD20130628>. The *Sarei* decision followed the US Supreme Court decision in *Kiobel v Royal Dutch Petroleum Co*, 569 US 108 (2013) which decisively limited the application of the Alien Tort Claims Act in in the US.

ultimately took the form of returning a territory scarred by mining to its people: a people who had been denied a meaningful education or any significant engagement in running their own affairs. No steps had been taken, further, to develop an economy based on anything other than mining. At independence, Nauru was one of the richest nations in the world per capita. However, in the absence of any sort of preparation for self-government, noting again here that the Trusteeship System envisaged and required such training, the combination of wealth and inexperience in the management of political and international affairs has proven to be disastrous. No rehabilitation of phosphate lands had commenced as yet. Nauru has been prone to making extremely expensive financial mistakes, and is now suffering an ongoing crisis. Indeed, new forms of dependency between Australia and Nauru have emerged. The payment it receives from Australia by serving as a detention centre is now crucial to its economy.[58] What this means, however, is that Nauru has become complicit in the many human rights violations that have taken place in those centres. It is surely tragic that Nauru, itself a victim in many respects of colonial abuse, has now itself allied with its former colonial power to inflict such violations on asylum seekers, people who have presented no threat to Nauru itself. The hard-won sovereignty of Nauru has now been deployed in the interests of Australia to enable it to further a highly questionable policy, one that has been severely criticised by many human rights organisations and the United Nations itself.[59]

In PNG, where Australia made concerted efforts as the administering power to further education and facilitate self-governance, self-determination confronted a different set of difficulties. Developing countries had recognised that political self-determination would be gravely limited if it was not accompanied by economic self-determination. As such, developing states, seeking to make decolonisation an effective reality, combined their demands for political self-determination with a campaign for economic self-determination that involved asserting claims of 'permanent sovereignty over natural resources'. Re-establishing control over their natural resources thus became a central concern for the new states, as for many, their nationalised resource industries were owned by

---

58   'How Nauru Threw It All Away', *ABC News* (online, 11 March 2014) <https://www.abc.net.au/radionational/programs/rearvision/how-nauru-threw-it-all-away/5312714>.

59   Ravina Shamdasani, 'Press Briefing Notes on Nauru, Yemen and Democratic Republic of the Congo', *United Nations Human Rights Office of the High Commissioner* (Press Briefing Notes, 12 August 2016) <https://www.ohchr.org/en/NewsEvents/Pages/DisplayNews.aspx?NewsID=20368&LangID=E>.

corporations affiliated with the former colonial power. In the case of PNG, the Bougainville mine was viewed as crucial for the economic future, the sovereignty, of PNG. The nascent government of PNG, the Australian Administration and the experts of the World Bank were all unanimous that the mine would ensure the prosperity and development that was essential for the new state of PNG. The protests of the native peoples of Bougainville were disregarded or placated. Here, tragically, the mine that was the key to PNG's wellbeing has instead become a threat to its very existence. Conflict has haunted the mining operation, and the people of Bougainville themselves are asserting their right of self-determination in precisely the manner feared by all the newly independent states, who were always concerned that their ethnically divided state could fall apart. In both Nauru and PNG, their abundant natural resources have proven to undermine rather than further self-determination, due to the potential for gross exploitation. The logic of their exploitation, different in each case, led to political fracture and disempowerment.

The ambiguities of self-determination revealed by these cases support arguments that the doctrine is incoherent and indeed, injurious. And yet, for many communities, self-determination offers a means, perhaps the only means, of achieving some degree of autonomy and empowerment. Thus it is hardly surprising, after Aboriginal and Torres Strait Islanders have long campaigned for self-determination, that this idea lies at the heart of the Uluru Statement.[60] This is a development that Deborah herself pointed to more than 25 years ago. In her article she raised the issue of self-determination, not only in relation to distant Pacific islands, but to Australia itself, asking the question of whether self-determination could translate into 'forms of power redistribution being experimented with in relation to indigenous peoples in Canada, New Zealand and to a lesser extent Australia'.[61] Deborah was sensitive to injustice wherever she perceived it; her life was animated by her sense of fairness. We miss her incisive, uncompromising and compassionate voice.

---

60   See Referendum Council, 'Uluru Statement from the Heart' <https://www.referendumcouncil. org.au/sites/default/files/2017-05/Uluru_Statement_From_The_Heart_0.PDF>; see further Natassia Chrysanthos, 'Journey from the Heart: What is the Uluru Statement from the Heart?', *Sydney Morning Herald* (online, 27 May 2019) <https://www.smh.com.au/national/what-is-the-uluru-statement-from-the-heart-20190523-p51qlj.html> for an overview of the significance of the Statement and the Indigenous voice envisioned by the document, biographies of crucial advocates and leaders involved and an explanation of the creation stories forming the artwork around the Statement.
61   Cass, 'Re-Thinking Self-Determination' (n 8) 39.

A Quiet Revolution: The Exclusivity of Exclusive Economic Zones

Margaret A Young[1]

Introduction

The allocation of sovereignty and sovereign rights is international law's driving force. In lawmaking and dispute resolution, international law not only distributes resources, but shapes power, knowledge and ideas. This is an ongoing feature of treaty negotiations, both of multilateral packages, such as an agreement on marine biological diversity in the high seas,[2] and of smaller, regional endeavours, such as a Pacific-based trade agreement.[3] It is also present in the resolution of disputes by international courts and tribunals, of which the *South China Sea Award* is a leading example.[4] When pronouncements are made on which countries can access which markets or jurisdictional zones (and which tribunals can compulsorily hear claims arising from those rights), the implications can be revolutionary.

1   With thanks for helpful comments to Katharine Young, Camille Goodman and the participants at The Australian National University symposium, especially Hilary Charlesworth and Kim Rubenstein.
2   See, eg, negotiations for an anticipated binding instrument to protect marine biological diversity in areas outside national jurisdiction: *International Legally Binding Instrument Under the United Nations Convention on the Law of the Sea on the Conservation and Sustainable Use of Marine Biological Diversity of Areas Beyond National Jurisdiction*, GA Res 72/249, 72nd sess, Agenda Item 77, UN Doc A/RES/72/249 (adopted 24 December 2017); the fourth and final session of the Intergovernmental Conference has been postponed by decision 74/543 of 11 March 2020.
3   *Comprehensive and Progressive Agreement for Trans-Pacific Partnership (CPTPP)*, signed by 11 countries, 8 March 2018, [2018] ATS 23 (entered into force 30 December 2018).
4   *In the Matter of the South China Sea Arbitration before an Arbitral Tribunal Constituted under Annex VII to the 1982 United Nations Convention on the Law of the Sea (Philippines v China) (Award)* (Permanent Court of Arbitration, Case No 2013-19, 12 July 2016) ('*South China Sea Award*'), available at: <https://pca-cpa.org/en/cases/7/>.

In 1987, Deborah Cass foresaw a quiet revolution in the developments of maritime zones[5] within the recently concluded United Nations Convention on the Law of the Sea (UNCLOS).[6] Hers was an early intervention when UNCLOS was still yet to enter into force, but when countries around the world had already devoted nine years of their time and international advocacy in order to agree on a 'package deal' for the oceans. The UNCLOS negotiations – a third in a series of historic negotiations and known by the acronym UNCLOS III – took place during the late 1970s and 1980s, when decolonised developing countries sought to challenge historic arrangements which had allowed strong maritime powers to exploit the distant waters surrounding weaker states. Concepts such as 'permanent sovereignty over natural resources', 'preferential rights' and the 'common heritage of mankind' were debated. An exclusive economic zone, or EEZ, was the newly recognised zone beyond and adjacent to the territorial sea, extending 200 nautical miles from a coastal state. UNCLOS entrenched the sovereign rights of those coastal states to the resources of the zone, thus limiting the size and concept of traditional notions of freedom of fishing on the high seas.[7]

Deborah Cass's analysis – her first legal publication in a series of engagements with matters of international and constitutional law – heralded an ongoing intuition for issues of disciplinary significance. Fisheries is the international law problem par excellence: one of the earliest examples of interstate cooperation seemingly driven by material facts, such as migratory species crossing borders of states, but also infused with ephemeral concepts like justice and fairness. The earliest international law texts are devoted to it,[8] and the ministries of foreign affairs of most states remain occupied with it.[9] Understanding the patterns of behaviour, reasons for cooperation and precursors to normative development in fisheries allows one to make sense of international law's subsequent response to concerns that only latterly have been conceived as global.

---

5   Deborah Cass, 'The Quiet Revolution: The Development of the Exclusive Economic Zone and Implications for Foreign Fishing Access in the Pacific' (1987) 16 *Melbourne University Law Review* 83.
6   *United Nations Convention on the Law of the Sea*, opened for signature 4 June 1992, 1833 UNTS 396 (entered into force 16 November 1994) ('UNCLOS').
7   UNCLOS (n 6) pt V ('Exclusive Economic Zone').
8   David Armitage, *The Free Sea: With William Welwod's Critique & Grotius's Reply* (Liberty Fund Inc, 2004), which includes Hugo Grotius's *Mare Liberum,* first published 1609.
9   One could cite current examples from all regions, from the skirmishes between French and British scallop fishermen, the reluctance of distant water fishing nations to agree to conservation and management measures in the Pacific islands, and the ongoing fisheries disputes in the South China Sea.

Indeed, I suspect I may share at least one affinity with Deborah Cass:[10] a professional conviction that some of the greatest social and legal problems of our time can be understood through the lens of fisheries. Even though I met her but a few times, I am confident that Deborah Cass would be in complete agreement with that conviction, and would similarly enjoy the incredulous reactions of others to it.

This chapter is structured in three parts. First, I draw attention to the high political and ideological stakes in UNCLOS's recognition of maritime zones. Deborah Cass was interested in the geopolitics behind the changing economic relationships between the Pacific island states and the distant water fishing nations such as the Soviet Union and the US. The first part of this chapter reflects upon her arguments in the context of a very different environment from the Cold War–inspired era in which she wrote. In the second part, I move to some relevant provisions of UNCLOS relating to the EEZ, particularly art 56's provision for rights, jurisdiction and duties of the coastal state in the EEZ. I engage with Deborah Cass's hypothesis that art 56 provided for full discretion for coastal states in denying access to foreign fishing nations, comparing this analysis with later interpretations from international tribunals such as the International Tribunal for the Law of the Sea (ITLOS) and ad hoc tribunals. I show that though her fishery study was extremely perceptive, it did not account for some emerging issues relating to unfettered coastal state discretion. These issues are examined in the third part of the chapter, which examines the need for coastal states to cooperate and give 'due regard' to others while practicing 'due diligence' with respect to the resources within the EEZ.

The High Stakes of the Maritime Zones

The geopolitical and ideological aspects of the newly formed EEZs have changed drastically since Deborah Cass's writing, but the high stakes behind the allocation of jurisdictional zones in UNCLOS have not diminished. Indeed, with the ecological pressures on fishing now leading to recommendations to close the remaining areas outside of the EEZs

---

10 Another might be a recently discovered intercultural appreciation for a hand-written family recipe for borscht; see Deborah's creative writing piece, Deborah Cass, 'Her Beauty as a Sword' (2011) 10 *Etchings* 5–12.

(the high seas) to extractive fishing as a precautionary measure,[11] the stakes have risen even higher. Deborah Cass's insights foreshadow the struggle for power and legitimacy that currently dominates the law of the sea, especially in the Pacific. Her reflections on the ability of foreign fishing nations to access the EEZs of coastal states in the Pacific combined technical analysis of state practice and custom as well as broader reflections on geopolitical and ideological implications. She went further than interpretation of the treaty text and delved into media interviews and ministerial statements, a method that provided excellent sources for her perspectives on contemporary ideas about 'creeping jurisdiction' and the global economic order. This part adopts a similar method to re-examine UNCLOS's imposition of law amid changing patterns of sovereign power.

Curbing the Distant Water Fishing Nations

UNCLOS signalled a major change in fishing access, because the concept of the EEZ allowed smaller, less sophisticated states to deny access to their fishing zones to the larger and exploitative 'distant water fishing nations'.[12] Those large maritime nations had been sailing the world for centuries to plunder living resources in faraway places. The two distant water fishing nations that possessed the largest fleets, the Soviet Union and Japan, sought a preservation of the status quo at UNCLOS III, with the granting of mere 'preferential rights' to the coastal states.[13] Instead, the finalised EEZ regime was more closely aligned with the demands of Latin American and African states, who had been seeking greater control over coastal resources even before UNCLOS III, especially in the face of the growing

---

11   U Rashid Sumaila et al, 'Fisheries Subsidies and Potential Catch Loss in SIDS Exclusive Economic Zones: Food Security Implications (2013) 18(4) *Environmental and Development Economics* 427, doi.org/10.1017/s1355770x13000156; see also Cassandra M Brooks et al, 'Challenging the "Right to Fish" in a Fast-Changing Ocean' (2014) 33 *Stanford Environmental Law Journal* 289.

12   Although this term dominates the secondary literature, UNCLOS refers instead to 'States whose nationals have habitually fished in the zone or which have made substantial efforts in research and identification of stocks': arts 62, 69. Part V of UNCLOS also refers variously to 'developed land-locked States', 'geographically disadvantaged States' and 'developing States'. In negotiations, states had used various language, for example the Chinese representative referred to '[t]he super-Powers [that] had for years wantonly plundered the offshore resources of developing coastal States, thereby seriously damaging their interests': *Summary Records of Meetings of the Second Committee*, 24th mtg, UN Doc A/CONF.62/C.2/SR.24 (1 August 1974) [2]; *Official Records of the Third United Nations Conference on the Law of the Sea, Volume II (Summary Records of Meetings of the First, Second and Third Committees, Second Session)* 187, <https://legal.un.org/diplomaticconferences/1973_los/vol2.shtml>, cited in *South China Sea Award* (n 4) para 251.

13   *South China Sea Award* (n 4) [248]–[254].

technological capacity of the distant water fishing nations.[14] It has been commented that 'the evolution of the exclusive economic zone concept took place in the developing world'.[15] By recognising sovereign rights of coastal states, UNCLOS shifted the resource base and opportunities of those coastal nations; now, 35 per cent of the oceans and 75–80 per cent of fish stock would be subject to EEZ jurisdiction.[16]

But Deborah Cass was not content to mark this as a simple shift in resource allocation. She argued that the 'dramatic' jurisdictional change 'has brought with it the fear of a revolution of a more sweeping kind'.[17] The emergence of the EEZ doctrine and its associated increase in economic autonomy was a sign for Deborah Cass of more fundamental transformations. The Pacific island state of Kiribati had just used its coastal jurisdiction to negotiate access rights for fishing nations to its EEZ: instead of allowing the US boats that had traditionally fished in the area to procure access for a fee, Kiribati sold the rights to the highest bidder, which happened to be the Soviets. Quoting a news report headed 'Soviets Get New Pacific Toehold', Deborah Cass argued that 'fishing rights have suddenly become the battleground for global ideological conflict'.[18] In references to Australian parliamentary debates and diplomatic correspondence, she showed that the link between fishing, economic changes and national security was being made in Australia and abroad. The Pacific states were seen by Australia's Secretary of the Department of Foreign Affairs as 'inevitably open to exploitation or infiltration from outside'.[19]

Global Ideological Conflict

In tracing the shifts in fishing rights represented by UNCLOS's EEZ regime to global ideological conflict during the last years of the Cold War, Deborah Cass demonstrated how international law is shaped by and generates power relations which, for some proponents, are used in ideological narratives. Her work was referenced in David Caron's

---

14 Ibid.
15 Satya Nandan, 'The Exclusive Economic Zone: A Historic Perspective' in Food and Agriculture Organization (ed), *The Law and the Sea: Essays in Memory of Jean Carroz* (Food and Agriculture Organization, 1987) <http://www.fao.org/docrep/s5280T/s5280t00.htm>.
16 MH Belsky, 'Management of Large Marine Ecosystems: Developing a New Rule of Customary International Law' (1985) 22 *San Diego Law Review* 733, 759, cited in Cass 'The Quiet Revolution' (n 5) 83.
17 Cass, 'The Quiet Revolution' (n 5) 83.
18 Ibid.
19 Ibid 101.

examination of the US's use of sanctions as an instrument of foreign policy, which considered historic denials of access for fishing privileges, including to the Soviet Union in the late 1970s and Poland in the early 1980s, as well as a number of whaling nations.[20]

Similar issues were relevant to the negotiations of other parts of UNCLOS, particularly the negotiations over rights to the deep seabed, and the contestation over the concept of 'common heritage of mankind', which had been proposed by Maltese diplomat, Arvid Pardo, to the United Nations General Assembly in 1967, and which promised to ensure equitable sharing of projected seabed mining.[21] By instituting a regime in which 'the Area and its resources are the common heritage of mankind'[22] (Part XI), the Convention entrenched universal aspirations observed by Philip Allott to be 'the new wine of communitarianism spilling over from the old bottle of legal formalism'.[23] It was this allocation of rights within the deep seabed mining regime – and not UNCLOS's provisions regarding highly migratory species, as Deborah Cass argued[24] – that is said to have proved the most significant impediment to ratification of the UNCLOS by the US.[25]

Of course, given the trajectory of the Cold War, the framing of issues of access to fishing resources as a contestation between capitalism and communism did not last long. The Pacific islands built their bargaining power against distant water fishing nations within a number of regional cooperatives.[26] Soon after the publication of Deborah Cass's article,

20   David D Caron, 'International Sanctions, Ocean Management, and the Law of the Sea: A Study of Denial of Access to Fisheries' (1989) 16 *Ecology Law Quarterly* 311.

21   Arvid Pardo, 'Who Will Control the Seabed?' (1968–1969) 47 *Foreign Affairs* 123; Arvid Pardo, 'Address to the American Society of International Law' (1968) 62 *ASIL Proceedings* 216; Arvid Pardo, 'Sovereignty under the Sea' (1968) 58 *Commonwealth Journal of International Affairs* 341; see generally Surabhi Ranganathan, 'Global Commons' (2016) 27 *European Journal of International Law* 693.

22   UNCLOS (n 6) art 136.

23   Philip Allott, '*Mare Nostrum:* A New International Law of the Sea' (1992) 86 *American Journal of International Law* 764, 785, doi.org/10.1017/s0002930000010927.

24   Cass, 'The Quiet Revolution' (n 5) 94.

25   John R Stevenson and Bernard H Oxman, 'The Future of the United Nations Convention on the Law of the Sea' (1994) 88 *American Journal of International Law* 477, 477, doi.org/10.2307/2203716.

26   The Forum Fisheries Agency was first established in 1979: *South Pacific Forum Fisheries Agency Convention,* opened for signature on 10 July 1979, 1579 UNTS 315 (entered into force 9 August 1979). Eight of the members of this Forum with adjoining exclusive economic zones formed a subregional group known as Parties to the Nauru Agreement (PNA) in 1982: *Nauru Agreement Concerning Cooperation in the Management of Fisheries of Common Interest,* opened for signature 11 February 1982 (entered into force 4 December 1982) <http://www.pnatuna.com/sites/default/files/Nauru%20Agreement_0.pdf>. The members of the PNA are the Federated States of Micronesia, Kiribati, Marshall Islands, Nauru, Palau, Papua New Guinea, Solomon Islands and Tuvalu.

US fishing boats returned to the region.[27] The controversial issue of highly migratory species in the western and central Pacific Ocean was directly addressed by the establishment of a new commission.[28] The imperative of coastal states and other states to cooperate within this commission was given impetus by the 1994 *Fish Stocks Agreement*, which the US was one of the first countries to ratify.[29] Pacific states have sought a range of enforcement measures to assist in policing their areas and ensuring they receive a commercial return from the foreign states to which they have permitted access.[30] Some have even closed their fishing zones due to environmental concerns,[31] amid a more general awareness that agreed access rights to EEZs can be exploitative and unsustainable.[32]

These developments were not relevant solely to the law of the sea. Other treaty regimes recorded agreements and fostered expectations, some of which diverged from UNCLOS III. For many developing countries, a legal interest in access to fishing zones was overshadowed by a legal interest in access to fishing markets: developing countries challenged the legal compatibility of attempts by developed countries to restrict

---

27   Cass, 'The Quiet Revolution' (n 5) 102.

28   *Convention on the Conservation and Management of Highly Migratory Fish Stocks in the Central and Western Pacific Ocean*, opened for signature 5 September 2000, 2275 UNTS 43 (entered into force 19 June 2004), <https://www.wcpfc.int/about-wcpfc>, establishing the Western and Central Pacific Fisheries Commission. Current members of the Commission are Australia, China, Canada, Cook Islands, European Union, Federated States of Micronesia, Fiji, France, Indonesia, Japan, Kiribati, Republic of Korea, Republic of Marshall Islands, Nauru, New Zealand, Niue, Palau, Papua New Guinea, Philippines, Samoa, Solomon Islands, Chinese Taipei, Tonga, Tuvalu, United States of America and Vanuatu.

29   *United Nations Agreement for the Implementation of the Provisions of the United Nations Convention on the Law of the Sea of 10 December 1982 relating to the Conservation and Management of Straddling Fish Stocks and Highly Migratory Fish Stocks*, opened for signature 4 December 1995, 2167 UNTS 88 (entered into force 11 December 2001) ('*Fish Stocks Agreement*'). The US was the third state to ratify the *Fish Stocks Agreement* (on 24 August 1996). See further Tore Henriksen and Alf Håkon Hoel, 'Determining Allocation: From Paper to Practice in the Distribution of Fishing Rights Between Countries Determining Allocation' (2011) 42 *Ocean Development & International Law* 66, doi.org/10.1080/00908320.2011.542106.

30   See generally Camille Goodman, 'The Cooperative Use of Coastal State Jurisdiction with Respect to Highly Migratory Stocks: Insights from the Western and Central Pacific Region' in Lawrence Martin, Constantinos Salonidis and Christina Hioureas (eds), *Natural Resources and the Law of the Sea: Exploration, Allocation, Exploitation of Natural Resources in Areas under National Jurisdiction and Beyond* (JurisNet, 2017) 215.

31   For a list of closed areas within the jurisdiction of countries of the Pacific Islands Forum Fisheries Agency, see 'PIP Closed Areas', *Pacific Islands Forum Fisheries Agency (FFA)* (Web Page, 23 November 2016) <https://www.ffa.int/us_mtreaty_closed_areas>.

32   For one example on access agreements with the EU leading to adverse effects on the sustainability of Senegal's coastal fisheries, see Emma Witbooi, 'The Infusion of Sustainability into Bilateral Fisheries Agreements with Developing Countries: The European Union Example' (2008) 32 *Marine Policy* 669, 674, doi.org/10.1016/j.marpol.2007.11.008.

access to their markets on environmental grounds.[33] Part XI on the deep seabed regime was renegotiated; the resulting new agreement of 1994[34] was said to represent a 'mutilated' regime.[35] Overcapacity of the entire fishing fleet was increasingly recognised as a problem for conservation and management. Alongside the subsidy programs of distant water fishing nations, who had built up their fleets in order to enhance their competitive advantages, coastal states began to allocate more resources to their fishing industries in order to better exploit their expanded EEZ rights.[36] Subsidies of states to their fishing fleets became a focus for reform at the World Trade Organization (WTO) in 2001.[37] Members agreed to seek to clarify disciplines on fisheries subsidies for both economic and ecological objectives.[38] Meanwhile, for many developing countries the economic gains of an increased EEZ have been gouged by rampant illegal, unreported and unregulated (IUU) fishing.[39] As well as threatening revenues of coastal states – estimated at over US$600 million annually for the Pacific island states alone[40] – IUU fishing has caused social dislocation and environmental degradation.[41] The allocation of resources to enhance capacity, which is planned by the state, driven by private capital or sourced from a combination of both, shows that jurisdictional zones under the law of the sea are not the only influence on practices of exploitation and overexploitation.

---

33   See also Margaret A Young, *Trading Fish, Saving Fish: The Interaction between Regimes in International Law* (Cambridge University Press, 2011), doi.org/10.1017/s2047102512000167.

34   *Agreement Relating to the Implementation of Part XI of the Convention of 10 December 1982*, 48th sess, Agenda Item 36, UN Doc A/RES/48/263 (entered into force 28 July 1966).

35   As Ranganathan has shown, the strong language came from RP Anand, an earlier contributor to Third World approaches to international law in his *Studies in International Law and History: An Asian Perspective* (Springer, 2004) 188, cited in Ranganathan (n 21) 712.

36   J Samuel Barkin and Elizabeth R DeSombre, *Saving Global Fisheries: Reducing Fishing Capacity to Promote Sustainability* (MIT Press, 2013) 106–7, doi.org/10.1162/glep_r_00233.

37   See *Doha Ministerial Declaration*, WTO Doc WT/MIN(01)/DEC/1 (14 November 2001) para 28.

38   Margaret A Young, 'Fragmentation or Interaction: The WTO, Fisheries Subsidies, and International Law' (2009) 8 *World Trade Review* 477, doi.org/10.1017/s1474745609990140. For the latest draft working text for a new agreement, see WTO Doc TN/RL/W274R5 (Working Documents, 26 July 2018).

39   For estimates of global losses, see David J Agnew et al, 'Estimating the Worldwide Extent of Illegal Fishing' (2009) 4(2) *PLoS ONE* e4570, doi.org/10.1371/journal.pone.0004570.

40   The estimated annual value of IUU fish harvested or transhipped in the region is around US$616.11 million: Duncan Souter et al, *Towards the Quantification of Illegal, Unreported and Unregulated (IUU) Fishing in the Pacific Islands Region* (Report, MRAG Asia Pacific, February 2016) i.

41   The growth in illegal fishing is even thought to have spurred the European migration crisis: 'Illicit Migration to Europe: Consequences of Illegal Fishing and Overfishing in West Africa', *The Global Initiative Against Transnational Organized Crime* (Web Page, 8 May 2015) <www.globalinitiative.net/illicit-migration-to-europe-consequences-of-illegal-fishing-and-overfishing-in-west-africa/>.

Emerging Powers and the South China Sea

Deborah Cass revealed much about how international law was seen to be facilitating political intrigue and legal wrangling. This has become most apparent since, in the context of the dispute over the South China Sea brought by the Philippines against China. The EEZ concept had itself spurred already existing expansionist tendencies within the South China Sea, the region comprising the western Pacific Ocean spanning an area of almost 3.5 million square kilometres to the south of China, to the west of the Philippines, to the east of Vietnam and to the north of Malaysia, Brunei, Singapore and Indonesia.[42] At the end of the Cold War, these countries (as well as Taiwan) sought title to sovereignty over the islands in order to take advantage of the 200-nautical-mile zone and its security and economic benefits. Christopher Joyner wrote:

> Were all claimants to declare exclusive economic zones or continental shelf delimitations seaward from points fixed by islands over which they now assert sovereignty, nearly the entire ocean and sea-bed in the South China Sea would be subjected to various degrees of national jurisdiction. An ocean region legally comprised of high seas and international sea-bed would be rendered into a semi-enclosed sea.[43]

The hope of Joyner was that China would agree to dispute settlement and that the claimant states would find solutions based on regional cooperation and joint resource development.

When Philippines sought arbitration against China pursuant to Part XV of UNCLOS in 2013, China neither accepted nor participated in the proceedings. The tribunal found that it had jurisdiction in 2015.[44] China consistently rejected the Philippines' recourse to arbitration,[45] which

---

42   *South China Sea Award* (n 4) [3].

43   Christopher C Joyner, 'The Spratly Islands Dispute: Rethinking the Interplay of Law, Diplomacy, and Geo-politics in the South China Sea' (1998) 13 *International Journal of Marine and Coastal Law* 193, 199, doi.org/10.1163/15718089820491980, footnotes omitted.

44   *In the Matter of the South China Sea Arbitration before an Arbitral Tribunal constituted under Annex VII to the 1982 United Nations Convention on the Law of the Sea (Philippines v China) (Award on Jurisdiction and Admissibility)* (Permanent Court of Arbitration, Case No 2013-19, 29 October 2015) *('Award on Jurisdiction and Admissibility')*.

45   *South China Sea Award* (n 4) [11].

was conducted at the Permanent Court of Arbitration in the Hague.[46] The tribunal gave its substantive findings in the absence of Chinese counsel or submissions, although it sought to ascertain China's position via public statements and it noted that its responsibility was to satisfy itself 'not only that it has jurisdiction over the dispute but also that the claim is well founded in fact and law'.[47]

While the case most notoriously centred on disputes between the Philippines and China regarding the legal basis of maritime rights and entitlements in the South China Sea (and especially the status of certain geographic features artificially constructed by China), it also related to the lawfulness of certain actions taken by China within a part of the South China Sea that constituted the Philippines' EEZ. As such, the tribunal made a number of findings relating to the interpretation of UNCLOS and art 56. The tribunal's reasons are discussed in the following section but for the purposes of the present part it is sufficient to note that the rise in economic might of one maritime nation did not prevent the tribunal from ruling in favour of the coastal state: the Philippines' sovereign rights in its EEZ were upheld.

In addition to engaging in emerging sovereign claims, Deborah Cass may be said to have foretold current narratives of a clandestine takeover of sovereign control through access and investment arrangements, especially in the South Pacific. Almost three decades after her article documented reports of the Soviets getting a 'new Pacific toehold', a news report was headed 'Kiribati Deal Shocks Fishing World'![48] The narrative was familiar, but the proponents had changed: Kiribati had decided against granting fishing rights to US boats and instead granted rights to a higher bidder: this time, China and Taiwan. An industry leader was quoted as saying, '[w]ith this China is now taking over the South Pacific and there will be no sustainability: this will rip the guts out of the American tuna fleet'.[49]

46　The Tribunal found that there was a dispute within the terms of UNCLOS art 288, and that resolution of the dispute would not require an implicit determination of sovereignty (which would have been outside of the jurisdiction of UNCLOS). The Tribunal noted it was 'fully conscious of the limits on the Claims submitted to it and, to the extent that it reaches the merits of any of the Philippines' Submissions, intends to ensure that its decision neither advances nor detracts from either Party's claims to land sovereignty in the South China Sea': *Award on Jurisdiction and Admissibility* (n 44) [153].

47　*South China Sea Award* (n 4) [12]. In addition to the Philippines legal team, observers to the proceedings included Australia, the Republic of Indonesia, Japan, Malaysia, Singapore, the Kingdom of Thailand and the Socialist Republic of Viet Nam: see para 15.

48　Michael Field, 'Kiribati Deal Shocks Fishing World' *Stuff* (Web Page, 10 October 2014) <http://www.stuff.co.nz/business/industries/10603447/Kiribati-deal-shocks-fishing-world>.

49　Ibid.

The sentiments have similarities with a commonly heard narrative of an Asian takeover of Australian assets. When a proposed investment by China and Chinese investors into Australia's energy infrastructure was blocked by the Australian treasurer in 2016, the reason given was national security.[50] The law of the sea emerged as a key concern. Alongside cyber hacking, some commentators linked the Australian decision to Chinese military actions in the South China Sea.[51] Australia's alliance with the US was a dominant theme, especially in the context of the US's support for the Philippines' initiation of the arbitration leading to the *South China Sea Award*.

In summary, Deborah Cass's keen observations of changing sovereign power structures could be replicated today, notwithstanding the rotating roles of some of the main protagonists. The US and China are asserting their global status (and differences) via oceans policy, focusing on military, strategic and fishing concerns. While regional disputes over the South China Sea existed well before UNCLOS III, the recent practices of China in asserting its rights and power – including through land reclamations – have been documented by the arbitral tribunal constituted under UNCLOS Annex VII. Meanwhile, Australia's aid to the South Pacific faces competition from China, the US, Europe and Japan – and much of the aid from these latter countries is linked expressly or impliedly with fisheries. The retreat of Soviet fleets in the Pacific is now over, with a newly empowered Russia seeking influence in fisheries and security.[52] Even among drastic geopolitical change since the publication of Deborah Cass's article in 1987, her insight of a quiet revolution over fishing rights (for her, in a bipolar Cold War environment) continues to apply in the multipolar expansions that are undergirded by global capitalism.

---

50 See former Australian treasurer Scott Morrison, '[The foreign investment review process] has not enabled us to identify suitable mitigations to protect against the national security issues in this case': Paul Karp, 'Scott Morrison Blocks Ausgrid Sale on National Security Grounds', *The Guardian* (online, 11 August 2016) <https://www.theguardian.com/australia-news/2016/aug/11/scott-morrison-blocks-ausgrid-sale-on-national-security-grounds>.

51 See Peter Jennings of the Australian Strategic Policy Institute cited in: 'China Ramps Up Pressure over Blocked Ausgrid Bid', *SBS News* (online, 18 August 2016) <http://www.sbs.com.au/news/article/2016/08/18/china-ramps-pressure-over-blocked-ausgrid-bid>.

52 Olga Krasnyak, 'Russia Vying for Power in the South Pacific', *The Vanuatu Independent* (online, 22 November 2017) <http://web.archive.org/web/20181203092156/https://vanuatuindependent.com/2017/11/22/russia-vying-for-power-in-the-south-pacific/>.

Article 56 and the Discretion of Coastal States

One of the preoccupations of Deborah Cass's analysis was the relative power and discretion of the coastal states granted by the new EEZ provisions in Part V of UNCLOS. The legal provisions achieved a shift in economic and geopolitical interests by allocating sovereign rights and duties and setting out specific grounds for cooperation and the granting of access. At the time of Deborah Cass's article, important questions were unanswered about the common intentions of the parties and the wording they adopted. Her arguments relating to these provisions have proved remarkably accurate, as this part demonstrates.

Interpreting Art 56

The legal provision at the heart of the newly entrenched EEZ regime is art 56 of UNCLOS, which sets out the rights, jurisdiction and duties of the coastal state in the EEZ. It provides:

> *Article 56*
>
> 1. In the exclusive economic zone, the coastal State has:
>
>   (a) sovereign rights for the purpose of exploring and exploiting, conserving and managing the natural resources, whether living or non-living, of the waters superjacent to the seabed and of the seabed and its subsoil, and with regard to other activities for the economic exploitation and exploration of the zone, such as the production of energy from the water, currents and winds;
>
>   (b) jurisdiction as provided for in the relevant provisions of this Convention with regard to:
>
>   (i) the establishment and use of artificial islands, installations and structures;
>
>   (ii) marine scientific research;
>
>   (iii) the protection and preservation of the marine environment;
>
>   (c) other rights and duties provided for in this Convention.

2. In exercising its rights and performing its duties under this Convention in the exclusive economic zone, the coastal State shall have due regard to the rights and duties of other States and shall act in a manner compatible with the provisions of this Convention.

3. The rights set out in this article with respect to the seabed and subsoil shall be exercised in accordance with Part VI.

The rights and duties of other states in the EEZ are set out in art 58; these are limited to freedoms of navigation and overflight and the laying of submarine cables and pipelines, 'and other internationally lawful uses of the sea related to those freedoms, such as those associated with the operation of ships, aircraft and submarine cables'. In art 62, the states 'whose nationals have habitually fished in the zone' are mentioned in the context of coastal states that lack the capacity to harvest the entire allowable catch within their EEZ. States aside from the coastal states may vie for access so as to fish for the surplus. In granting access, the coastal states are expected to take into account 'the need to minimize economic dislocation in States whose nationals have habitually fished in the zone or which have made substantial efforts in research and identification of stocks', in addition to the needs of developing countries, the overarching need to conserve living resources and other factors.[53]

The question that was occupying many commentators at the conclusion of UNCLOS III was whether this allocation of sovereign rights would lead coastal states to exclude all foreign fishing. The question of access to fishing zones had implications economically, politically and ideologically, as set out in the first part of this chapter. Daniel O'Connell, for example, was concerned that by granting sovereign rights to coastal states, UNCLOS marks the 'triumph of individualism over collectivism'.[54] Lawrence Juda was warning of the 'creeping jurisdiction' of the EEZ,[55] an issue that continues to be a 'siren song'.[56]

---

53   UNCLOS (n 6) arts 61–62.
54   Daniel P O'Connell, *The International Law of the Sea*, ed IA Shearer (Oxford University Press, 1982) vol 1, 552, cited in Cass, 'The Quiet Revolution' (n 5) 96.
55   Lawrence Juda, 'The Exclusive Economic Zone: Compatibility of National Claims and the UN Convention on the Law of the Sea' (1986) 16 *Ocean Development and International Law* 44, doi.org/10.1080/00908328609545784, cited in Cass, 'The Quiet Revolution' (n 5) 84.
56   See, eg, Bernard Oxman, 'The Territorial Temptation: A Siren Song at Sea' (2006) 100 *American Journal of International Law* 830.

Deborah Cass was rightly preoccupied by ambiguities in the text. She stated:

> It is not at all clear what 'due regard' means in this context. Does it mean that the coastal state *must* take into account the interests of other states or is it just a mechanism to encourage discussion between the parties in the event of a conflict?[57]

She concluded, '[i]t is likely to be the latter, given the wide-ranging scope of coastal state authority defined by article 56'.[58]

This conclusion is the position reached by the recent arbitral tribunal in the South China Sea dispute. China had asserted jurisdiction over maritime areas of the South China Sea encompassed by the so-called 'nine-dash line', due in part to 'historic rights'. The Philippines submitted that these claims were contrary to UNCLOS and without lawful effect (the case did not extend to sovereignty claims, which would have been outside of the jurisdiction of the tribunal). The tribunal accepted the Philippines' arguments, concluding that UNCLOS superseded any historic rights or other sovereign rights or jurisdiction in excess of the limits imposed therein.[59] The tribunal reasoned:[60]

> As a matter of the text alone, the Tribunal considers that the Convention is clear in according sovereign rights to the living and non-living resources of the exclusive economic zone to the coastal State alone. The notion of sovereign rights over living and non-living resources is generally incompatible with another State having historic rights to the same resources, in particular if such historic rights are considered exclusive, as China's claim to historic rights appears to be. Furthermore, the Tribunal considers that, as a matter of ordinary interpretation, the (a) express inclusion of an article setting out the rights of other States and (b) attention given to the rights of other States in the allocation of any excess catch preclude the possibility that the Convention intended for other States to have rights in the exclusive economic zone in excess of those specified.

---

57 Cass, 'The Quiet Revolution' (n 5) 88.
58 Ibid.
59 *South China Sea Award* (n 4) [278].
60 Ibid [243].

The tribunal further found that China had breached art 56 with respect to the Philippines' sovereign rights by promulgating a moratorium on fishing in the South China Sea (which it had done in 2012 without exception for the Philippines' EEZ and without limiting the moratorium to Chinese flagged vessels).[61] China was found to have breached art 58 by failing to prevent its nationals from unlawfully fishing in the EEZ.[62] China was also found to have violated other UNCLOS provisions, including inter alia those related to the protection and preservation of the marine environment, and requirements to 'protect and preserve rare or fragile ecosystems as well as the habitat of depleted, threatened or endangered species and other forms of marine life'.[63]

The decision in the *South China Sea Award* came after an ITLOS decision which upheld certain contingent rights of coastal states in assuming regulatory competence over bunkering activities of foreign vessels operating near their EEZ.[64] The decision, which related to the arrest by a coastal state of a vessel that was providing fuel for fishing vessels within the EEZ, included the following statement, in a passage that is consistent with Deborah Cass's reading of art 56:

> The term 'sovereign rights' in the view of the Tribunal encompasses all rights necessary for and connected with the exploration, exploitation, conservation and management of the natural resources, including the right to take the necessary enforcement measures.[65]

Institutional Aspects

Aside from interpreting the treaty text, there are other reasons for Deborah Cass's conclusion of a wholesale power of coastal states in deciding on questions of access to their EEZs. At least part of her argument seems to be based on a nuanced appreciation of the institutional aspects of the law of the sea regime. Decisions on coastal state access are not part of the compulsory dispute settlement system that is otherwise a hallmark

---

61 Ibid [716].
62 Ibid [757].
63 Ibid [992].
64 *M/V 'Virginia G' (Panama/Guinea-Bissau) (Judgment)* (2014) ITLOS Rep 4.
65 Ibid, para 211.

of UNCLOS and its far-reaching Part XV.[66] The discretion of states to decide whether or not to give access to other states to their surplus fisheries is not open to conflict resolution, and Deborah Cass argues that this increases the likelihood that coastal states will have total discretion in access matters. I see this insight to be a precursor to her analysis, almost two decades later, of the way in which the compulsory dispute settlement system of the World Trade Organization has affected the substance of trade norms. Even in this early piece she recognises that international laws are shaped by their institutional context: here, in the EEZ regime, the lack of an enforceable provision means that the power is left to the discretion-holding state; there, the compulsory dispute settlement of the WTO means that discretionary trade liberalisation rules have been interpreted to contain procedural and substantive obligations that are not written in the text. The special place occupied by the WTO Appellate Body, due partly to the *ex ante* consent to its jurisdiction by WTO members, means it was the perfect candidate for Deborah Cass's masterful treatment in her book, *The Constitutionalization of the World Trade Organization*, which features in another chapter in this collection.[67]

Deborah Cass's arguments contrast heavily with the reception that UNCLOS received from other quarters: for Philip Allott, for example, the revolution of UNCLOS was of quite a different kind. Allott celebrates the diminishing concepts of territorial exclusivity within the Convention, demonstrated primarily but not solely in the entrenchment of the ideal of 'common heritage of mankind' in Part XI.[68] He compares changes in notions of exclusive political control over land territory (especially given international society's direct interest in all that happens within state systems, manifested, for example, by human rights law) and predicts that '[p]reconceptions of exclusive political control over naturally communal sea areas must tend to become anomalous to the same extent'.[69] He also celebrates the requirement that disputes over access to EEZs should be resolved

---

66   UNCLOS (n 6) art 297(3). On limits to the compulsory dispute settlement system of UNCLOS, see generally Natalie Klein, *Dispute Settlement in the UN Convention on the Law of the Sea* (Cambridge University Press, 2005).

67   Kerry Rittich, 'Deborah Cass, *The Constitutionalization of the World Trade Organization*: A Reading in Time', this volume.

68   Allott, '*Mare Nostrum*' (n 23) 785.

69   Ibid 768.

on the basis of equity and in the light of all the relevant circumstances, taking into account the respective importance of the interests involved to the parties as well as to the international community as a whole.[70]

For Allott, this clause was intended to construct a social process where contracting parties would be required to achieve, 'in their future interactive social behaviour, equal treatment, equitable sharing, regard for legitimate interests ... effective protection for the marine environment', and so on.[71] Allott writes:

> [E]very sea area, whatever its conceptual articulation in terms of property relations, is conceived in [UNCLOS] as being, not incidentally but inherently, an area of power and interest shared by two or more state systems. The exercise of the supposed property right is, in all cases, actually a process of decision making within procedural and substantive constraints.[72]

Deborah Cass is right that the lack of compulsory dispute settlement might eviscerate the processes that Allott saw so idealistically, and yet after 30 years we have seen legal issues of the EEZ regime litigated by a number of parties at different tribunals, including via advisory opinions. While these have confirmed that coastal states have sole discretion on questions of access – as exemplified by the *South China Sea* arbitral award – they have also provided a stronger sense of the obligations to 'give due regard to the needs of other states'. International law contains procedural duties of states to be 'other-regarding' in their decisions, as I argue below. Recent cases have also shown that the holders of discretion under the EEZ regime are not always the weaker party in traditional power relations, and that the risk of overexploitation of resources within the EEZ by the holders of sovereign rights – the coastal states – should not go unchecked.

---

70 UNCLOS (n 6) art 59.
71 Allott, *'Mare Nostrum'* (n 23) 785.
72 Ibid 785.

'Due Regard', 'Due Diligence', and the 'Duty to Cooperate'

Experience, new law, state practice and changing ideas in international law have led to a richer sense of rights and duties, in the context of fisheries and beyond. Although there has not been a direct challenge to the allocation of access according to the EEZ regime (in accordance with Deborah Cass's expectations), there have been a number of disputes that have applied UNCLOS art 56 directly or indirectly. Moreover, decisions from the International Court of Justice (ICJ), ITLOS and other tribunals serve to demonstrate the duties of coastal states, while new laws for straddling fish stocks[73] and lawmaking for areas beyond national jurisdiction[74] impose broader duties on all states. This part examines the jurisprudence and situates it within broader normative developments in international law.

The Duties of Coastal States

A challenge to the designation by a coastal state of a marine protected area (MPA) provides new perspectives on Deborah Cass's thesis on unfettered coastal state discretions. In 2010, the UK, as part of its asserted sovereignty over the British Indian Ocean Territory, established an MPA within the EEZ of the Chagos Archipelago. Mauritius, the long-suffering former colony and neighbour, had relied on access to the relevant EEZ for fishing and economic interests, and challenged the UK using the dispute settlement provisions of UNCLOS. An arbitral tribunal constituted under Annex VII of UNCLOS handed down its decision in 2015.[75] Its claim was in part a claim about the substance of art 56: whether the UK should have had 'due regard' to the interests of Mauritius in deciding on the MPA.

---

73   See especially *Fish Stocks Agreement* (n 29) and accompanying text; see also Rosemary Rayfuse, 'The United Nations Agreement on Straddling and Highly Migratory Fish Stocks as an Objective Regime: A Case of Wishful Thinking?' (1999) 20 *Australian Year Book of International Law* 253.

74   Margaret A Young and Andrew Friedman, 'Biodiversity Beyond National Jurisdiction: Regimes and Their Interaction' (2018) 112 *AJIL Unbound* 123, doi.org/10.1017/aju.2018.47.

75   *Chagos Marine Protected Area Arbitration (Mauritius v United Kingdom) (Award)* (Permanent Court of Arbitration, Case No 2011-03,18 March 2015) ('*Chagos*'), see further: <https://pca-cpa.org/en/cases/11>. The members of the Tribunal were Ivan Shearer, Christopher Greenwood, Albert Hoffmann, James Kateka and Rüdiger Wolfrum.

The UK sought to give a restrictive meaning to its obligations, submitting that 'the meaning of "due regard" in art 56 does not mean to give effect to the rights of other States'.[76] The UK also stated that its public consultations with Mauritius had satisfied the relevant obligations.

The tribunal declined to find 'any universal rule of conduct' in the obligation to give 'due regard', but drawing on the ordinary meaning of the terms found that the obligation required the UK to have 'such regard for the rights of Mauritius as is called for by the circumstances and by the nature of those rights'.[77] The degree of 'due regard' was high given the significant effect that the establishment of the MPA would have on Mauritius's rights.[78] After reviewing the UK's efforts at consultation, the tribunal found that it did not have sufficient 'due regard',[79] and concluded that the proclamation of the MPA was incompatible with UNCLOS.[80]

The joint dissenting and concurring opinion of Judges Wolfrum and Kateka give additional content to the standard required of 'due regard'. The judges expressed doubts that the UK had not acted under an ulterior motive in establishing the MPA, and found that it violated the standard of good faith.[81] Citing the *Nuclear Tests Case*,[82] they emphasised that '[t]rust and confidence are inherent in international co-operation'.[83] The implications of the case are wide-ranging, both for the question of marine environmental protection,[84] and for the ongoing quest by Mauritius to set right historic failures of the UK during the decolonisation process, which was considered by the ICJ in its Advisory Opinion in 2019.[85]

---

76 *Chagos* (n 75) [458].
77 Ibid [519].
78 Ibid [521].
79 Ibid [524].
80 Ibid [536].
81 *Chagos* (n 75) [90] (Judges Wolfrum and Kateka).
82 *Nuclear Tests (Australia v France) (Judgment)* [1974] ICJ Rep 253, 269 [46].
83 *Chagos* (n 75) [90] (Judges Wolfrum and Kateka).
84 David Ong, 'Implications of the Chagos Marine Protected Area Arbitral Tribunal Award for the Balance Between Natural Environmental Protection and Traditional Maritime Freedoms' in Stephen Allen and Chris Monaghan (eds), *Fifty Years of the British Indian Ocean Territory: Legal Perspectives* (Sprinter, 2018) 263, doi.org/10.1007/978-3-319-78541-7_11.
85 *Legal Consequences of the Separation of the Chagos Archipelago from Mauritius in 1965 (Advisory Opinion)* [2019] ICJ Rep 95. This opinion was delivered after the completion of the writing of the present chapter and is not considered further here.

The content of coastal states' duties was given separate consideration by ITLOS in one of its first advisory opinions.[86] The request for an advisory opinion was brought by Cape Verde, Gambia, Guinea, Guinea-Bissau, Mauritania, Senegal and Sierra Leone, acting as the 'Subregional Fisheries Commission', to determine the context of legal responsibilities to take necessary measures to prevent, deter and eliminate IUU fishing. The tribunal reviewed the emphasis given in UNCLOS to the coastal states' management of natural resources (art 56(1)) and their role in determining the allowable catch (art 61), allocating any surplus (art 62) and enforcing domestic laws to meet their obligations. In the light of these 'special rights and responsibilities given to the coastal states', the primary duty to take measures with respect to IUU fishing was found to rest with coastal states.[87]

These primary responsibilities did not release other states from obligations, however.[88] Flag states, or those that license or register the vessels fishing in the relevant zones, had to have duties 'to take the necessary measures to ensure that their nationals and vessels flying their flag are not engaged in IUU fishing activities'.[89] The tribunal noted:

> [T]he obligation of a flag State … to ensure that vessels flying its flag are not involved in IUU fishing is also an obligation 'of conduct' … as an obligation 'of conduct' this is a 'due diligence obligation', not an obligation 'of result' … The flag State is under the 'due diligence obligation' to take all necessary measures to ensure compliance and to prevent IUU fishing by fishing vessels flying its flag.[90]

These comments were cited with approval in the *South China Sea Award*,[91] and were used to ground that tribunal's conclusions that China had failed to exercise due diligence in preventing fishing by Chinese flagged vessels

---

86 *Request for an Advisory Opinion Submitted by the Sub-Regional Fisheries Commission (SRFC) (Advisory Opinion)* (International Tribunal for the Law of the Sea, Case No 21, 2 April 2015) ('*SRFC request*'), archived at <http://perma.cc/KY5V-EMXP>.

87 Ibid [106].

88 Ibid [108].

89 Ibid [124]. The tribunal noted that its findings were restricted to flag states that were not members of the relevant cooperative convention: [89].

90 Ibid [129]. For further exposition of the due diligence concept, see *Pulp Mills on the River Uruguay (Argentina v Uruguay)* [2010] ICJ Rep 425 [187] ('*Pulp Mills*'); *Responsibilities and Obligations of States Sponsoring Persons and Entities with Respect to Activities in the Area (Advisory Opinion)* (International Tribunal for the Law of the Sea, Case No 17, 1 February 2011) 10 ('*Responsibilities and Obligations of States*').

91 *South China Sea Award* (n 4) [744].

in various locations in the South China Sea, and thus failed to exhibit due regard for the Philippines' sovereign rights with respect to fisheries in its EEZ. Accordingly, China was found to have breached its obligations under art 58(3) of the Convention.[92]

The tribunal in *South China Sea* also quoted the oft-cited passage from *Mox Plant* that 'the duty to cooperate is a fundamental principle in the prevention of pollution of the marine environment under Part XII of the Convention and general international law'.[93] This was important for its finding that China had, through its toleration and protection of, and failure to prevent, Chinese fishing vessels engaging in harmful harvesting activities of endangered species, breached arts 192 and 194(5) of the Convention.[94]

A 'duty to cooperate' was also important for the reasoning of the ICJ in *Whaling in the Antarctic,* when Japan was found to have breached its obligations under the Whaling Convention.[95] As is well known, the Court agreed with Australia that Japan failed to meet the appropriate standard of conduct required of parties to the Whaling Convention when undertaking scientific research into whaling. A key deficiency in Japan's conduct was its failure to give due regard to decisions of the International Whaling Commission (IWC).

The Court's articulation of a duty of states to cooperate with the IWC can be traced to the terms of the Whaling Convention[96] itself, and the reporting and monitoring functions of the IWC. Judge ad hoc Charlesworth also observed that the concept of a duty of cooperation 'is the foundation of legal regimes dealing (*inter alia*) with shared resources and with the environment'.[97] As I have argued elsewhere,[98] the ICJ judgment is heavy with consequences for the future conduct of states, and for the ability of tribunals to allow for evolution of the law in applying treaties. While the Court refused to take an overt 'evolutionary' interpretation of the Whaling Convention, it established a duty to give reasons when states

92   Ibid [757].
93   *MOX Plant (Ireland v United Kingdom) (Provisional Measures)* (2001) ITLOS Rep 89, para 82.
94   *South China Sea Award* (n 4) [992].
95   *Whaling in the Antarctic (Australia v Japan: New Zealand Intervening) (Judgment)* (International Court of Justice, General List No 148, 31 March 2014) ('*Whaling in the Antarctic*').
96   *International Convention for the Regulation of Whaling,* opened for signature 2 December 1946, 161 UNTS 74 (entered into force 10 November 1948) art VIII.
97   *Whaling in the Antarctic* (n 95) [13] (Judge Charlesworth).
98   See generally Margaret A Young and Sebastián Rioseco Sullivan, 'Evolution Through the Duty to Cooperate: Implications of the *Whaling* Case at the International Court of Justice' (2015) 16 *Melbourne Journal of International Law* 310.

divert from established practices, even if those practices are not binding.[99] A reviewable obligation of states parties to 'give due regard' is likely to lead to a more responsive and adaptive system of law, and a different conception of sovereignty and responsibility.[100]

'Due Regard' in Public International Law and the Needs of Conservation

Quite aside from these recent cases, one could argue that the seeds for a fuller conception of an obligation to give 'due regard' were sown much earlier, predating UNCLOS III and the precise wording of art 56. In the *Fisheries Jurisdiction Case* of 1974 (between Iceland and Germany), the ICJ held that:

> It is one of the advances in maritime international law, resulting from the intensification of fishing, that the former laissez-faire treatment of the living resources of the sea in the high seas has been replaced by a recognition of a duty to have due regard to the rights of other States and the needs of conservation for the benefit of all.[101]

In addition to this jurisprudence, we see an embrace of concepts such as duties of cooperation across a vast range of scholarship. Indeed, we are now familiar with the preoccupation of reason-giving and procedural obligations that scholars of global administrative law such as Benedict Kingsbury, Richard Stewart and Nico Krisch would advance.[102] There are at least some similarities with the work of Elinor Ostrom, who found that the tragedy of the commons could be averted by cooperative systems rather than enclosure.[103] Localised, cooperative accounts of monitoring

---

99   Ibid 318. Even though Japan had voted against key resolutions of the IWC, it was required to 'give due regard' to those resolutions, including in providing adequate justification for its scientific methodologies and practices.

100   Ibid.

101   *Fisheries Jurisdiction (Germany v Iceland) (Judgment)* [1973] ICJ Rep 49 [64]. Rather than dwell on this case, Deborah Cass prefers to rely on the earlier *Fisheries Jurisdiction* case between Iceland and the UK, which was important in recognising the concept of coastal states possessing 'preferential rights' in the fishing zones adjacent to their coasts; 'Application Instituting Proceedings', *Fisheries Jurisdiction (United Kingdom v Iceland)* [1972] ICJ Pleadings 1. She may have passed over the Court's comments here due to their focus on the high seas.

102   Benedict Kingsbury, Nico Krisch and Richard B Stewart, 'The Emergence of Global Administrative Law' (2005) 68 *Law and Contemporary Problems* 15.

103   Elinor Ostrom, *Governing the Commons: The Evolution of Institutions for Collective Action* (Cambridge University Press, 1990), doi.org/10.1007/978-3-531-90400-9_93. See further Margaret A Young, 'International Adjudication and the Commons' (2019) 41 *University of Hawai'i Law Review* 353.

and peer review also feature in the New Governance literature of Joanne Scott, among others.[104] Reporting and review mechanisms have become established in new multilateral agreements, including the Paris Agreement, as well as human rights regimes. To return to fisheries, the poor conservation and management record of coastal states has led to direct calls for the institution of these types of mechanisms.[105]

Some would go even further; writing in 2013, Eyal Benvenisti provides a Rawlsian account of states as trustees of humanity.[106] Benvenisti argues that international law contains obligations for states to 'take other-regarding considerations seriously into account in formulating and implementing policies, even absent specific treaty obligations'.[107] Benvenisti argues:

> The sovereign as trustee must ensure meaningful opportunities to have the voices of affected stakeholders – both foreign governments and individuals – heard and considered, and must offer them reasons for its policy choices.[108]

These normative arguments have parallels, once again, in the fisheries context. The public trust doctrine has been argued as the appropriate legal concept to apply to the EEZ.[109] Moreover, the duty to cooperate has been emphasised to apply to the fishing states who participate within regional fisheries management organisations as well as to new entrants seeking access to fishing areas,[110] with distributional and ecological consequences that have not yet been satisfactorily resolved in fisheries.

---

104 Gráinne de Búrca and Joanne Scott (eds), *Law and New Governance in the EU and US* (Hart Publishing, 2006).
105 Richard Barnes, 'The Convention on the Law of the Sea: An Effective Framework for Domestic Fisheries Conservation' in David Freestone, Richard Barnes and David M Ong (eds), *The Law of the Sea: Progress and Prospects* (Oxford University Press, 2006) 233, 259–60, doi.org/10.1093/acprof:oso/9780199299614.003.0013.
106 Eyal Benvenisti, 'Sovereigns as Trustees of Humanity: On the Accountability of States to Foreign Stakeholders' (2013) 107 *American Journal of International Law* 295, 318, doi.org/10.5305/amerjintelaw.107.2.0295.
107 Ibid 300.
108 Ibid 318.
109 Mary Turnipseed et al, 'The Silver Anniversary of the United States' Exclusive Economic Zone: Twenty-Five Years of Ocean Use and Abuse, and the Possibility of a Blue Water Public Trust Doctrine' (2009) 36 *Ecology Law Quarterly* 1.
110 Andrew Serdy, '*Pacta Tertiis* and Regional Fisheries Management Mechanisms: The IUU Fishing Concept as an Illegitimate Short-Cut to a Legitimate Goal' (2018) 48 *Ocean Development and International Law* 345, doi.org/10.1080/00908320.2017.1349525.

Deborah Cass was more reticent about the content of states' duties to have regard to others in international law. While she recognised conservation imperatives, she also noted that many of the smaller developing states would not have capacity to determine issues such as the effect of their actions on ecosystems.[111] She considered the obligation of coastal states to take into account the effects of fishing on associated and dependent species to be 'probably not enforceable'.[112] The final section of this chapter seeks to account for the scepticism she exhibited in the context of fisheries access, and demonstrates that the issues continue to be important for the future of the law of the sea.

Inbuilt Restrictions on Sovereignty Over Natural Resources

Deborah Cass's argument that coastal states have total discretion in deciding upon access to their fishing zones might be said to be underpinned by a regard for the developing states whose interests were so central to the advancement of the EEZ concept.[113] She was advocating for justice and an equitable allocation that would enable those weaker states to finally have some control over their economic future under globalisation. Deborah Cass's work at the time as research assistant to the Commission of Inquiry into the Rehabilitation of Nauru might have contributed to this perspective.[114] Indeed, it is difficult not to have sympathy for the argument, especially when historically many of those states had ensured sustainable fishing within their region, as opposed to the rapacious attitudes of the distant water fishing nations. Yet Deborah Cass perhaps was too accommodating in her belief that the sovereign equality of states could serve to equalise an international legal order that, after years of war and colonialism, had given rise to this very system of developing countries. Third World approaches to international law would

---

111 Cass, 'The Quiet Revolution' (n 5) 92, writing in the context of the coastal state's determination of the maximum sustainable yield and its need to take into account associated and dependent species, see UNCLOS (n 6) art 61.
112 Cass, 'The Quiet Revolution' (n 5) 92.
113 See Nandan, 'The Exclusive Economic Zone' (n 15).
114 See Anthony Anghie in this volume: Tony Anghie, 'Self-Determination and Beyond: Reflections on the Aftermath of the Nauru Case'.

subsequently show a different side to these issues.[115] Deborah Cass herself was perhaps aware of the need for caution in drawing conclusions about the Pacific nations, stating upfront that her analysis was not conclusive given the lack of primary material available. She observed that the island states 'do not possess the kind of bureaucracies to which we are accustomed to produce the data required'.[116]

Thirty years after UNCLOS III, we now know that enclosure of the EEZ has not led to sustainability. The responsibility for this must rest with coastal states, alongside other states and actors. The idea that coastal states are the best stewards for their total allowable catch has not been supported by state practice since the EEZ concept was codified, with many domestic fisheries in a deplorable state.[117] Many states are unable to monitor or police their areas of EEZ, leading to a burgeoning and organised criminal focus on illegal fishing. Fishing activities that follow agreed access rights within EEZs can be appallingly exploitative and unsustainable. In return for financial assistance, trade concessions and aid programs, the small coastal states surrounded by vast areas of the ocean have allowed vessels to wreak havoc on their resources: to cite just one set of examples, early access agreements with the EU led to adverse effects on the sustainability of Senegal's coastal fisheries.[118] In part, the collapse of many domestic fisheries lies with deficiencies within UNCLOS's EEZ framework, and an absence of more direct and coherent obligations on coastal states.[119]

In her review of UNCLOS Part V, Deborah Cass was perhaps too restrictive in her analysis of the content of coastal states' obligations to give 'due regard'. In addition to the obligation of the coastal state to ensure that the maintenance of living resources in the EEZ is not endangered by overexploitation,[120] there are general environmental obligations with respect to pollution, rare and fragile ecosystems and the habitat of threatened species, both in the high seas and within the EEZ to which she may have referred, and which have progressed since the publication of her

---

115 Ibid. See also in this volume, Kerry Rittich, 'Deborah Cass, *The Constitutionalization of the World Trade Organization*: A Reading in Time'; Deborah Cass, 'Navigating the Newstream: Recent Critical Scholarship in International Law' (1996) 65 *Nordic Journal of International Law* 341, doi.org/10.1163/15718109620294924; see further below n 128.

116 Cass, 'The Quiet Revolution' (n 5) 85.

117 Barnes, 'An Effective Framework' (n 105) 233.

118 Witbooi, 'The Infusion of Sustainability' (n 32) 674.

119 Barnes, 'An Effective Framework' (n 105).

120 UNCLOS (n 6) art 61(2).

article.[121] Tribunals have given increased attention to concepts such as the 'duty to cooperate' and the need to undertake 'due diligence',[122] and these concepts pertain not just to coastal states but to flag states and others. UNCLOS has evolved, aided especially by the proliferation of a range of instruments from within and outside the law of the sea that have helped to give content to emerging notions.[123] This evolution in obligations, as well as rights, is essential if international law is to address modern environmental challenges, especially those like climate change that are both caused and manifested outside of bounded areas such as EEZs.[124]

It should be remembered, too, that it is often the powerful states who hold coastal rights, rather than the developing states – a fact that Deborah Cass also acknowledged.[125] In the Chagos arbitration, the issue was not whether the holders of sovereign rights in the EEZ could enjoy discretion in selling off the resources, but whether the rich state could enjoy discretion in closing the zone. As discussed above, two of the judges were extremely concerned by the behaviour of the rights-holder in denying access: they saw in the UK's conduct a continual disregard of Mauritius's rights carried on from colonial times. In contrast, the *South China Sea* case involved questions about an emerging economic power: China, which had hitherto been on the side of the developing countries,[126] and was now seeking unlawful access to the weaker state's EEZ.

Perhaps instead of idealism about coastal states, Deborah Cass's views are underpinned by a deep scepticism about the potential, and even appropriateness, of international law in giving content to duties and obligations. As we have heard in the context of international criminal law,[127] one needs to ask what international society needs to *be* to host

---

121 See especially UNCLOS (n 6) art 192, 'States have the obligation to protect and preserve the marine environment'. See also *South China Sea Award* (n 4) [945].

122 See *Pulp Mills* (n 90) [187]; *Responsibilities and Obligations of States* (n 90) 10.

123 Alan Boyle, 'Further Development of the Law of the Sea Convention: Mechanisms for Change' (2005) 54 *International and Comparative Law Quarterly* 54, doi.org/10.1093/iclq/lei018. See also Irina Buga, 'Between Stability and Change in the Law of the Sea Convention: Subsequent Practice, Treaty Modification and Regime Interaction' in Donald R Rothwell et al (eds), *The Oxford Handbook of the Law of the Sea* (Oxford University Press, 2015) 46, doi.org/10.1093/law/9780198715481.003.0003.

124 For reflection on the territorially bounded notions of duties in the face of global warming, see Joanne Scott, 'The Geographical Scope of the EU's Climate Responsibilities' (2015) 17 *Cambridge Yearbook of European Legal Studies* 1, doi.org/10.1017/cel.2015.4.

125 Cass, 'The Quiet Revolution' (n 5) 90.

126 China's position during the UNCLOS III negotiations 'as one of the foremost defenders of the rights of developing States' was remarked upon by the Tribunal in the South China Sea dispute, see *South China Sea Award* (n 4) [251].

127 See Gerry Simpson in this volume, 'Concluding Remarks'.

a form of law: for Simpson, retributive justice might not yet enjoy its needed social foundation, while for Deborah Cass, normative content to the duties with respect to the EEZs was not justified. It might be that Deborah Cass held greater confidence in the scope of domestic law to provide the necessary content to ethical, cultural, social or environmental obligations. Her critique of the notion of obligations of coastal states under international law may indeed have sustained her interest in domestic constitutional law and her academic pursuits demonstrated that the two disciplinary fields have never been anything but closely intertwined.

The answer to the question posed by Deborah Cass's expansive interpretation of the rights of coastal states perhaps comes from Deborah Cass herself, writing 10 years after 'Quiet Revolution' was published. When engaging with a range of critical legal theories and methods in 1996, she suggested some potential research projects that would ensure such theories and methods could be deployed usefully, to effect lasting transformation after international law's repeated injustices. She posed as one example the examination of:

> [W]hether there are inbuilt restrictions upon the application of [the] principle of permanent sovereignty over natural resources and, if there are, whether these internal limits ought to be reassessed in the light of current understandings of equality and disadvantage.[128]

International law has demonstrated that it is possible to place restrictions over the principle of coastal states' sovereign rights to their EEZ. The obligations of 'due regard' and 'due diligence' are examples of such restrictions. Arguably the *Chagos* arbitration has signalled a preparedness of international tribunals to take into account equality and disadvantage in developing these norms, at least in the joint dissenting and concurring opinion. Perhaps it is this set of issues that will require the next revolution.

Conclusion

This chapter has considered the revolutionary aspects of the entrenchment of an exclusive economic zone in the United Nations Convention on the Law of the Sea. It shows that Deborah Cass's insights about the high stakes

---

128 Cass, 'Navigating the Newstream' (n 115).

of the maritime zones – which covered contested territory including the EEZ, the high seas and the deep seabed mining area – have continued relevance, even as some of the early defenders of the rights of developing states have now assumed the role of traditional maritime powers.

For Deborah Cass in 1987, the quiet revolution of UNCLOS lay in the empowerment of coastal island states against the exploitative and destructive tendencies of the distant water fishing nations and their constructed ideological battles. Over 30 years later, her political, legal and critical insights continue to push international lawyers, enriching our understanding, practice and tools for change. Her core argument – that the newly entrenched EEZ regime provided total discretion to coastal states with respect to which states would access the resources – has been vindicated. In the *South China Sea Award*, for example, China's historic rights were found to have been extinguished by the creation of the EEZ regime in UNCLOS, meaning that the Philippines is free to decide upon issues of access and control with respect to its EEZ. Yet there are other issues that cannot be separated from the issue of the rights of coastal states: these relate to the duties of coastal states to give 'due regard' to the needs of others and to practice due diligence. This has become a major preoccupation, and tribunals have found in the law of the sea an evolving set of duties since the publication of Deborah Cass's analysis.

The law of the sea is a precursor to much of the evolution and development of public international law. Deborah Cass's preoccupation with the content and institutional structure of art 56's requirement for states to give due regard to the interests of others demonstrates broader tensions in the substance, procedure and even *idea* of international law. Her interest in the position of developing states in the Pacific reminds us to be cautious about the institutional capacities and technical resources some states have in exercising their rights. Her work also suggests that the discharge of duties of coastal states needs to acknowledge historical inequality and disadvantage in order to be just. Cooperative arrangements rest on this substantive engagement as well as the procedural guarantees developed by treaties and jurisprudence. An awareness of the broader ideological and geopolitical aspects of these issues necessarily complicates a neat division between community and exclusivity in public international law.

PART 3

**International Law and the
World Trade Organization**

Introduction to International Law and the World Trade Organization

Rosanne Kennedy

Thanks to Kim and Hilary for organising this wonderful event and to the Cass family and Deborah's friends for being here.

I am honoured to have been invited to participate in this memorial symposium for my friend and colleague Deborah Cass. I teach in literary studies and gender studies in the College of Arts and Social Sciences at The Australian National University (ANU).

I first met Deborah in 1992 when we were both newly arrived at ANU, and we quickly discovered that we had a shared interest in gender and feminist legal theory. I was excited to meet this vibrant, engaging and energetic new colleague. She invited me to speak to her legal theory class. I envied her sense of style, and although I don't remember her doing so, she probably wanted to give me fashion advice! The next thing I knew she had won the Caltex award and was off to Harvard. When we met again a couple of years later, it was at the University Child Care Centre across the street from here, so it's particularly nice to be meeting in this location today – which used to be the staff club before it had its reincarnation as the Crawford School. Hannah and my son Benjamin became good friends, and not long after Deborah had Rosa and I had Isobel, and they too became friends. Many of my and Deborah's subsequent conversations took place in the hectic circumstances of the playground, birthday parties and picnics, although I do remember a lively night out at a Canberra restaurant to celebrate Deborah's 40th birthday. Our conversations dealt with the issues of everyday life: mothering, parenting, feminism, being a woman in the academy, among other intellectual topics.

When the family moved to London, we stayed in touch. I visited them in their London house and went walking with Deborah in the local park. She seemed to love the London life. One of my fondest memories of Deborah was when the family visited us for Christmas at the beach (Bermagui). The kids made a Christmas tree out of driftwood and decorations out of tinfoil and Hannah received a surf board! I have lovely pictures and funny stories from those years, but I'll spare Hannah and Rosa the embarrassment. One thing that I remember with considerable nostalgia was the frequent conversations I had with Deborah and Gerry about literature. Somehow, despite the demands of careers, families and international travel, we found time to read. We often discussed novels and writers, and traded novels. That, as well as her own creative writing, was such an important part of Deborah's life.

Speaking of books, my task today is to chair a session on Deborah Cass's book, *The Constitutionalization of the World Trade Organization: Legitimacy, Democracy, and Community in the International Trading System*, which was published by Oxford University Press in 2005. It won the Certificate of Merit from the American Society for International Law. The book has been praised by eminent scholars as 'that rare thing: An account which is sophisticated at both a theoretical and a doctrinal level' and as setting 'a benchmark for all future writing on this theme'. Described as 'build[ing] important bridges between political philosophy and international law' this book is central to today's discussion of how Deborah Cass's scholarship 'traverses divides'.

Deborah Cass, *The Constitutionalization of the World Trade Organization*: A Reading in Time

Kerry Rittich

Introduction

Any occasion to reflect on Deborah Cass's *The Constitutionalization of the World Trade Organization* (*CWTO*),[1] serves immediately as a call to internationalists to revisit the moment and the context in which it was conceived. How to characterise that moment? At the time, it felt like a moment of not just substantial but of permanent, epochal change. The mid-1990s saw, in light of the birth of the World Trade Organization (WTO), the inauguration of a new system of multilateral trade relations, one that reposed an unusual degree of confidence in the possibility that legal rules, institutional forms and technocratic processes of adjudication might be used both to create a more fully integrated global market and to successfully regulate trade disputes within the international economic order. Other developments accompanying the birth of the WTO, however, were just as consequential to the new international order and, ultimately, to the context and manner in which the WTO operated, even if in ways not evident at its inception.

---

1   Deborah Z Cass, *The Constitutionalization of the World Trade Organization* (Oxford University Press, 2005).

The mid-nineties was also the high-water mark of market fundamentalism. It was a moment of pervasive belief, at least among elites, in the primacy of the markets, one which saw a resurgent hope in market processes simpliciter as the source of welfare gains, as well as economic growth.[2] The apparent supremacy of market ordering extended to the political realm, leading to a fusion of markets and democracy in the liberal imaginary, what Susan Marks has called the 'end of ideology' ideology that market-centred democracy represented the 'end of history'.[3]

As market fundamentalism became established as normative across the international order and international institutions and economic technocrats began to give pride of place to the efficient facilitation of investment and transactions across borders in the order of concerns, they also consolidated a consensus view about good governance supporting that venture, successfully disseminating templates for domestic institutional and regulatory reform in its supposed image.[4] The ascendance of market fundamentalism and its associated governance priorities and projects marked an important waypoint in the decline and disintegration of the embedded liberal compromise,[5] the severance of two projects that had been imagined as indissoluble parts of the postwar economic order: liberalised trade at the global level, accompanied by protection against the destabilising social and political consequences that economic integration and restructuring inevitably entail at the national level, realised through some combination of domestic monetary, fiscal, social and industrial policies.[6]

2　Joseph E Stiglitz, 'Is There a Post Washington Consensus Consensus?' in Narcís Serra and Joseph E Stiglitz (eds), *The Washington Consensus Reconsidered: Towards a New Global Governance* (Oxford University Press, 2008) 41, doi.org/10.1093/acprof:oso/9780199534081.003.0001.

3　Susan Marks, *The Riddle of All Constitutions: International Law, Democracy, and the Critique of Ideology* (Oxford University Press, 2000), doi.org/10.1093/acprof:oso/9780199264131.001.0001; Francis Fukuyama, 'The End of History?' (1989) 16 *The National Interest* 3; Francis Fukuyama, *The End of History and the Last Man* (Avon Books, 1992).

4　John Williamson, 'Democracy and the "Washington Consensus"' (1993) 21 *World Development* 1329.

5　John G Ruggie, 'International Regimes, Transactions, and Change: Embedded Liberalism in the Postwar Economic Order' (1982) 36 *International Organization* 379, doi.org/10.1017/s00208183 00018993.

6　See Robert Howse, 'From Politics to Technocracy ... and Back Again: The Fate of the Multilateral Trading Regime' (2002) 96 *Am. Journal of International Law* 94; A Lang, *World Trade Law After Neoliberalism* (Oxford University Press, 2011), doi.org/10.2307/2686127.

The mid-1990s was also a time of growing challenges to the autonomy and power of the state and, indeed, to the Westphalian international order itself. The sources of these challenges were varied, and they clustered at the infra- and transnational as well as the supranational level. Some disruptions emanated from the proliferation of new international regimes and tribunals, of which the WTO itself was a prime exemplar. The sheer variety and number of normative regimes along with the burgeoning institutions that had emerged to support them on the international plane provoked worries about legal 'fragmentation'.[7] They ensured, at minimum, that there would be competing perspectives and determinations on central international legal questions; at maximum, there would be unresolved conflict that seemed to threaten the authority of law itself. But challenges to the authority of the state, as well as to the international legal order, also came from new forms – and greater usage – of transnational law and non-state norms promulgated by private parties.[8] Indeed, the fragmentation and destabilisation of international law was itself linked to the emergence of 'new governance' – broadly speaking, alternatives to classic, top-down forms of governance and regulation promulgated by the state or through interstate agreement – to manage problems and processes of global and regional economic integration for which traditional state-based approaches were, it was often claimed, ill-suited or simply inadequate.[9]

Yet a third destabilising dimension or development also reared its head: the problem of empire, ensuing from the singular role the US was then in a position to play as the sole hegemonic power remaining after the end of the Cold War.[10] That position enabled the US both to use international legal institutions as mechanisms to further its interests and projects, but equally to ignore international law when it suited its purposes.

---

7 For a discussion, see International Law Commission, *Fragmentation of International Law: Difficulties Arising from the Diversification and Expansion of International Law*, UN Doc A/CN.4/L.682 (13 April 2006) ('the Koskenniemi Report'); Andreas Fischer-Lescano and Gunther Teubner, 'Regime-Collisions: The Vain Search for Legal Unity in the Fragmentation of Global Law' (2004) 25 *Michigan Journal of International Law* 999.
8 Philip Jessup, *Transnational Law* (Yale University Press, 1956); Peer Zumbansen, 'Transnational Law', in J Smits (ed), *Encyclopaedia of Comparative Law* (Edward Elgar Publishing, 2006).
9 Gráinne de Búrca and Joanne Scott (eds), *Law and New Governance in the EU and the US* (Hart, 2006).
10 Martti Koskenniemi, 'Constitutionalism as Mindset: Reflections on Kantian Themes about International Law and Globalization' (2007) 8 *Theoretical Inquiries in Law* 9, doi.org/10.2202/1565-3404.1141.

If only because its birth was so deeply interconnected with these changes, the WTO seemed to provide a convenient, even inevitable, point of departure for the examination of myriad associated questions of governance. The Uruguay round negotiations out of which the WTO emerged had already pushed established boundaries on the settlement between the national and international, for example in debates about non-tariff barriers to trade, intellectual property rights and trade in services. Thus, debates about the uses and efficacy of the WTO were immediately entangled in debates about where and how to conduct political debate over matters of policy as well as justice, transnational as well as domestic, and how to ensure democratic input and control over these matters in a dynamic international order in which many of the ordinary channels for democratic deliberation seemed blocked, destabilised, missing or simply unclear.

If at this point the WTO seemed the centre of global governance debates *tout court*, viewed in retrospect, the picture looks quite different. At a time when multilateralism is in decline and regionalism on the rise in trade relations, central organs of the WTO like the Appellate Body are in crisis, and trade negotiations are once again sites for the assertion of national interest and competing geopolitical projects, that moment seems less the dawn of a new 'universal' era organised through rules-based global commerce than the beginning of a highly differentiated world, one paradoxically furthered by a commitment to the universalising possibilities of market ordering itself. The sentiment of hopefulness that the WTO represented concerning the political possibilities of law appear now to be not only transitory but even aberrational.[11] And whatever their putative relationship within liberal theory, the connections between democracy, liberalism and markets are now frayed, evident in the rising number of authoritarian leaders and regimes as well as the many strains on the most famously successful market integration project, the EU, emanating from states as disparate as Greece and Britain.

But as crucial as the broad international context indisputably was to the project, it seems important to flag the highly local one too. At the time *CWTO* began to take shape, its author was part of a cohort of graduate students at Harvard Law School, one that, at least by previous standards, was both unusually diverse in its composition and distinctly

---

11 Lang, *World Trade Law* (n 6); see below n 21 R Wai, 'Normal Trade Law'.

heterodox and expansive in its approach to legal scholarship. Both in collective discussions and within their individual projects, these scholars were reflecting on the conceptual, legal and political conundrums which these interlinked developments on the international horizon threw up and puzzling through their implications for international law, justice and politics. Questions of development, South–North relations and histories of colonialism were all central to the inquiry, but so was consideration of received disciplinary traditions and institutional forms. Debates invariably engaged innovations in social and political theory that transcended the discipline of law as well. In short, within this community, it was common ground that a vastly expanded lens and a wide array of analytic tools were critical to assessing the trajectory and import of the emerging international legal order as well as to comprehending its past.

As the scholarly writing generated by those scholars' documents, that community proved to be an immensely fertile laboratory for new – even revolutionary – forms of critical scholarship in the field.[12] As her writing from this period attests, Deborah was a central interlocutor in the key intellectual debates,[13] and their imprint remains visible throughout *CWTO*.

Setting the Stage: The International Context

What follows is an admittedly motivated reading of *CWTO*, one animated by a desire to surface its engagement and continuing connections with debates about law and development on the one hand and global governance and democracy on the other. There are three reasons that make it seem defensible to read *CWTO* in this way. The first is that the analysis itself overlaps so much with those scholarly debates that we could now safely place *CWTO* within these literatures. The second is that questions of development and global governance and their impact on the aspirations of democratic governance are where *CWTO* itself ends up; by the end of the analysis, we get very clear indications that these concerns

---

12   Along with *The Constitutionalization of the World Trade Organization,* among the texts that emerged from that period were Antony Anghie's *Imperialism, Sovereignty and the Making of International Law* (Cambridge University Press, 2004) and Balakrishnan Rajagopal, *International Law from Below* (Cambridge University Press, 2003), doi.org/10.1017/CBO9780511494079.
13   Deborah Cass, 'Navigating the Newstream' (1996) 65(3) *Nordic Journal of International Law* 341.

are where the author's heart lies, and where if it had been at all possible, her scholarly and analytic attention would next have gone. The third is, of course, that these questions lie at the heart of the political conundrums in which we now find ourselves.

The WTO and Global Economic Transformation

Like many other writings of its time, *CWTO* is suffused with the widely shared understanding that something big was afoot with the creation of the WTO. Put simply, everyone perceived that its emergence represented a signal change in the international order, something beyond simply the outcome of the latest round of negotiations that had formed the ordinary business of international trade law since the end of World War II. Rather, the creation of the WTO represented a new settlement in the international economic order, one that went a long distance to displace trade relations based primarily on the political management of interstate conflict with those more closely tethered to the technocratic processes of dispute resolution that gave enhanced role to rules-based adjudication. In the process, the new trade regime opened up new avenues to alter the balance of power between the domestic and the international.

When *CWTO* was written, the WTO sat at the apex of the international economic order. The WTO had a number of features that made it seem both powerful and effective as an institution and as a regulatory regime, particularly in comparison to those elsewhere in the international order. These features, in turn, caused people to think that the WTO might serve as a prototype for future institutional development in the international arena; for some, the WTO could even be imagined as a vehicle for global governance writ large.[14] The WTO housed the pre-eminent international dispute resolution tribunal, the new Appellate Body, that was empowered to judicially review the decisions of panels of first instance and thereby authoritatively pronounce on the conformity of policy decisions of national legislatures and executive bodies with global trade rules. At the same time, the institution of the new reverse-consensus rule concerning the adoption of panel decisions moved the management of trade disputes out of the realm of diplomacy and more decisively into the realm of technical, rules-based adjudication. These changes gave the panels and

---

14   Marco Bronckers, 'More Power to the WTO?' (2001) 4 *Journal of International Economic Law* 41, 44.

bodies charged with adjudication enhanced power and importance. These features made the WTO seem not only like an effective institution for rule enforcement and thus a compelling model in other areas of international economic law: as the burgeoning literature on 'trade linkage' during this period of time confirms, they induced scholars and activists working in areas such as labour, the environment and human rights to devise ways to attach their normative and regulatory agendas to the WTO's laws and enforcement mechanisms.[15]

All of these developments generated enthusiasm, but they provoked deep unease in equal measure. The subtitle of *CWTO* says it all: *Legitimacy, Democracy and Community in the International Trading System* is a concise encapsulation of the concerns around which debates about trade law and global economic governance were beginning to congeal. As the controversies around the 'mega-regional' trade agreements such as the recently concluded Comprehensive and Progressive Transpacific Partnership (CPTPP) and the proposed Transatlantic Trade and Investment Partnership (TTIP) between the US and the EU confirm, it remains a remarkably well-targeted statement of the preoccupations around which they continue to revolve.[16]

We might style the large question that *CWTO* is grappling with as follows: how to analyse and assess the organisation of global economic and political order, once the settled understanding about the respective roles and competences of nation-states and international institutions has become disrupted; when the conventional disciplinary narrative within international law about the sovereign equality of states in the Westphalian order no longer persuades at either the descriptive or programmatic levels; and when it has become evident that ever-deeper market integration has become, by design and by default, both the engine reconstituting global political and economic relations and the very problem to be managed. Thus, we can think of *CWTO* as a point of entry into a broad range of issues – normative, institutional, political – connected to the governance of the international economic order writ large.

---

15   Robert Howse and Makau Mutua, *Protecting Human Rights in a Global Economy: Challenges for the World Trade Organization* (International Centre for Human Rights and Democratic Development, 2000), doi.org/10.1163/221160800x00037.
16   See for example, Eyal Benvenisti, 'Democracy Captured: The Mega-Regional Agreements and the Future of Public Law' (Working Paper No 2/2016, Institute for International Law and Justice, New York University School of Law, 2016).

CWTO is in constant conversation with the developments – legal, social and political – in the international order that were coterminous with the creation of the WTO and which helped cement its status as the pre-eminent international economic institution. One is the mainstream consensus about the benefits of trade liberalisation and extensive market integration; another is the changing normative landscape against which the WTO itself operates, from the move to 'regulation' to the embrace of a constellation of private as well as public mechanisms to address governance and policy concerns. At its heart, however, is a systematic engagement with the principal interlocutors on what are still broadly recognised as the 'big questions' of international economic law. These include: John Jackson, Ernst-Ulrich Petersmann, Robert Howse and Armin von Bogdandy on the perils and possibilities of the emerging regional and multilateral trade and market integration projects;[17] Joseph Weiler, Neil Walker and Guenter Frankenberg on the conundrums of constructing responsible and responsive political community beyond the nation-state;[18] Dan Tarullo and Brian Langille on the 'baseline' problem that besets all efforts to establish the legal parameters of a free market;[19] and Robert Wai on the significance of private law and private ordering to the conduct of international economic transactions, something that trade law, as a branch of public law, leaves out of view.[20]

---

17 John H Jackson, *The World Trade Organization: Constitution and Jurisprudence* (Royal Institute of International Affairs, 1998); Ernst-Ulrich Petersmann, *Constitutional Functions and Constitutional Problems of International Economic Law* (University Press, 1991); Robert Howse (ed), *The World Trading System: Critical Perspectives on The World Economy* (Routledge, 1998); Armin von Bogdandy, 'Law and Politics in the WTO – Strategies to Cope with a Deficient Relationship' in JA Frowein and R Wolfrum (eds.), *Max Planck Yearbook of United Nations Law* (Kluwer Law International, 2001) vol 5, 609, doi.org/10.1163/187574101x00169.

18 Joseph HH Weiler, *The Constitution of Europe* (Cambridge University Press, 1999); Neil Walker, 'The EU and the WTO: Constitutionalism in a New Key' in Gráinne de Búrca and Joanne Scott (eds), *The EU and the WTO: Legal and Constitutional Issues* (Hart Publishing, 2001) 31, doi.org/10.5040/9781472562630.ch-002; Guenter Frankenberg, 'The Return of the Contract: Problems and Pitfalls of European Constitutionalism' (2000) 6 *European Law Journal* 257, doi.org/10.1111/1468-0386.00107.

19 Dan K Tarullo, 'Beyond Normalcy in the Regulation of International Trade' (1987) 100 *Harvard Law Review* 546, doi.org/10.2307/1341113; Brian Langille, 'General Reflections on the Relationship of Trade and Labor (Or: Fair Trade is Free Trade's Destiny)' in Jagdish Bhagwati and Robert Hudec (eds), *Fair Trade and Harmonization: Prerequisites for Free Trade? Vol 2: Legal Analysis* (MIT Press, 1996) 231.

20 Robert Wai, 'Transnational Liftoff and Juridical Touchdown: The Regulatory Function of Private International Law in an Era of Globalization' (2002) 40 *Columbia Journal of Transnational Law* 209.

It is clear in retrospect that, as an institution, the WTO has had its own rise and fall narrative.[21] International economic law no longer pivots exclusively around the WTO; even within trade law, the centre of gravity when it comes to political negotiation and institutional innovation has shifted from multilateral trade to bilateral and regional trade and investment regimes. Yet in all these new arenas, there are the immense unresolved struggles about how to both conceptualise and manage the legal, institutional and normative concerns that have been central to the WTO since its inception. Fortunately for us, it is these very matters that lie at the heart of *CWTO*.

The WTO and Constitutionalism

It is worth emphasising that *CWTO* is as much a study of constitutionalism as it is an analysis of trade law or international economic law. There are good reasons to think about the WTO – and other projects of global legal transformation – through the lens of constitutionalism. Even those attempting to come to grips with the governing structures of networks and social systems now employ constitutionalism as a heuristic.[22] In short, constitutional norms, values and discourse have been embraced to assess the workings of private power and the manner in which non-state entities as well as states effectively 'rule'.

One compelling reason for this expanded use is that constitutionalism is the framework which liberal theory and polities conventionally use to design and evaluate basic matters of the allocation of power and competences. Within the ambit of constitutionalism fall the distribution of powers as between different governing entities, the state and its citizens, as well as the institutions and processes by which disputes about these powers are disposed of. But constitutionalism, of course, serves wider normative and discursive functions concerning matters of political, economic and social organisation and coexistence. Constitutionalism is the language in which legal and political scholars conventionally conduct debates about foundational questions of representation, participation and democracy. Constitutionalism and constitutional rights are, of course, also part of the popular vernacular, a mechanism for voicing concerns about the exercise and legitimacy of power, both private and public.

---

21   R Wai, 'Normal Trade Law', draft on file with the author; Lang, *World Trade Law* (n 6).
22   See, eg, Gunther Teubner, *Constitutional Fragments: Societal Constitutionalism and Globalization* (Oxford University Press, 2012).

As it turns out, controversies about all of these issues surround the WTO. Constitutional norms and values were widely used in the early years to celebrate the WTO; as Deborah Cass noted, constitutional challenges to the basic structure of the WTO were few, due to what she rightly identifies as 'the pervasive consensus about the benefits of trade liberalization'.[23] Indeed, many scholars cited the institutional features most familiar from liberal constitutional orders as conclusive evidence of the new trade regime's superiority over the old. Yet over time, constitutionalism's value as a means of challenging, even impugning, these very institutional features has become more evident. Deborah Cass's signal contribution was to recognise early on that the rise of the discourse of constitutionalism in *respect* of the WTO was related to the challenges that the WTO posed *to* international law and to the international order, particularly in respect of norms of democratic choice and participation. Thus, she perceived that constitutionalism could be used not merely in its most familiar mode or guise, as a means to defend and advance the WTO, but productively, as a heuristic to reveal much about what might be normatively problematic – even pathological – about its governance structures. Above all, constitutionalism provided a means to critically consider perhaps the most significant aspect of the WTO: the immensely expanded scope it seems to provide both to international technocrats and to private actors to challenge domestic rules and policy decisions, and the troubling constraints on democracy that thereby ensue.[24]

The WTO, Ideas and Knowledge Practices

CWTO is perhaps most fundamentally a work about the role and power of ideas and ideational frameworks in the governance of international economic relations. It seems important to stress how novel and important a contribution it made for this reason alone. At the time that *CWTO* was being written, scholars were producing myriad doctrinal and institutional analyses of the new WTO; for international economic lawyers during the 1990s, engaging in that enterprise was arguably the only game in town. Any review of the relevant journals during that time will disclose article after article parsing the new rules of the regime, examining the scope of the powers of the new Appellate Body, and/or taking sides in the decisions it was beginning to render.

---

23 Cass, *The Constitutionalization of the World Trade Organization* (n 1) 79.
24 For a sophisticated analysis of the multiple factors and forces that lie behind the widened scope of the trade regime, see Lang, *World Trade Law* (n 6).

Deborah Cass, however, was one of the first people to seriously consider that the *idea* of the WTO – how it was conceived as an institution, how it imagined the community of states and other actors engaged in trade relations, and the ethos and values that organised these relations and informed the operation of the regime as a whole – was an independently significant field of inquiry. It is the deep and systematic inquiry of *CWTO* into the structures of thought organising the new trade regime, as well as the beliefs and claims about constitutionalism, liberal values and human rights to which the institution quickly became attached, that ultimately make it of such enduring value. For in the intervening period, it has become abundantly clear that when it comes to international economic law, institutions rule the world. It is in the realm of ideas, and the knowledge practices through which people and institutions give life and substance to those ideas, that the big battles are fought, large transformations are affected, and significant stakes, political as well as economic, for particular parties disposed.[25]

Deborah Cass was unusually alert to the fact that the emergence of the discourse of constitutionalism in and around the WTO was bound up in a host of aspirations intimately connected to a broader project of global economic and political transformation. As she noted, constitutionalism served as a form of wish fulfilment, a means of marking fundamental change in the global order, of separating the past from the present, and creating new legal obligations even – perhaps especially – where it was far from clear what intentions and circumstances warranted.[26] In short, the discourse of constitutionalism was *itself* doing a huge amount of transformative work, work that promised – or threatened – to take international trade law well beyond where trade negotiations had themselves taken it, even given the momentous results of the Uruguay round.

The Strategy

How to tackle such a mammoth task? Here is how the author takes up the challenge.

After a brief outline of the origins of the constitutionalisation debate surrounding the WTO, *CWTO* proceeds directly to a 'received account' of constitutionalism itself. This account first distils and then arrays the

---

25   Lang, *World Trade Law* (n 6); David Kennedy, *A World of Struggle: How Power, Law, and Expertise Shape Global Political Economy* (Princeton University Press, 2016).
26   Cass, *The Constitutionalization of the World Trade Organization* (n 1) 69.

essential elements of constitutionalism as a mode of conceptualising legal, political and institutional relations, with the aim of providing a means to assess the status and transformation of the fundamental relations of the trade regime. The function of this account, the author emphasises, is less to crystallise a conception of constitutionalism in any essential or absolute sense, than to provide a set of yardsticks with which to measure various claims and accounts of constitutionalism as they are applied to the WTO.

To this end, Deborah Cass identifies six elements or features of constitutionalism, unfolding an idea about to how think about each of them. She then moves on to link debates about the constitutionalisation of the WTO to developments within international economic law scholarship.

The six identified elements of constitutionalism are constraints on social, political and economic behaviour; *Grundnorm* change; community; deliberation; realignment of relationships; and legitimacy. I will only note in passing the immense command of constitutional theory and scholarship that the construction of this compelling 'received account' required, as well as the significance of that mastery to the project at hand. Only someone with deep knowledge of public law norms, institutions and doctrines at the domestic level could have detected so many gaps and slippages in the efforts to transpose constitutional norms and heuristics onto the international plane in the first place. And only a person so situated could have fully explored and displayed the manner in which that transposition then enabled an immense and divergent range of claims and aspirations to be projected onto the WTO.

Deborah Cass has a specific argument about how that scholarship, in her words, 'fueled the promotion of the constitutionalization of the WTO'.[27] The first step is the discipline's preoccupation *with* and characterisation *of* the WTO as an institution as such, as opposed to a mere treaty or set of rules. The second, highly consequential step, is the elision between institution and constitution. As against this characterisation, Deborah Cass insists on a distinction. Even if we are prepared to characterise the WTO as an institution, in the absence of the attributes of constitutionalism already outlined, an institution, she points out, cannot 'simply metamorphose' into a higher order institution or constitution.[28] For the apparent success of this conflation or metamorphosis, the belief and acceptance within the

---

27 Cass, *The Constitutionalization of the World Trade Organization* (n 1) 62.
28 Ibid 60.

discipline in 'the WTO as a thing in itself, a regime, a concept which is more than the sum of its parts',[29] has everything to do with the conferral of enhanced legitimacy and authority on the WTO. As she notes, this is a highly problematic move: it immediately imports a set of powerful ideas into the trade regime, some of which are fundamentally alien to it. One is the belief that non-discrimination rights concerning market access, long a part of multilateral trade law, are *human* rights, rights moreover that domestic courts can apply and that 'citizens can rely on ... to challenge state action'.[30] Constitutionalism can also serve what she describes as a 'door-closing' function, insulating the WTO from critique to which it would otherwise be subject and thereby reifying its particular institutional features.[31] International economic law scholarship operating in the mode of constitutionalism also fosters an easy linkage between the WTO and developments that might otherwise only be contingently associated with neoliberal globalisation. That risk or possibility is, in her assessment, especially live, given the detachment of disciplinary debates within international economic law from earlier calls for a New International Economic Order. Although there are still dissident voices, the critical tradition within international economic law is, in her estimation, 'small in number and low in profile'.[32] The community of international legal scholars, then, has a lot to answer for.

CWTO then proceeds to examine three basic variants of constitutionalism associated with the WTO, analysing them through the claims of the scholars and personages with whom they are most prominently identified. It is worth noting that all of these variants circulate as central pillars of the mainstream support and defence of the WTO, and all are in some sense interrelated. The three variants are institutional managerialism; rights-based approaches; and judicial norm determination.

This constitutional typology proves to be immensely successful, and the analysis of these variants is really the heart of the book. As a heuristic, it not only allows us to examine in a systematic way what otherwise might appear to be a quite chaotic set of issues, themes, trends and arguments: it also permits us to grasp the distinct social and political visions that

---

29   Ibid 101.
30   Ibid 69.
31   Ibid.
32   Ibid 81.

animate different claims, and to do so, moreover, in a way that helps reveal precisely how and why those visions might *also* be such a cause of worry for the WTO's critics.

Institutional Managerialism

Institutional managerialism, identified foremost with the work of John Jackson, involves not just the juridification of trade disputes and the move to the management of trade by rules as opposed to diplomacy: it also enabled the WTO to manifest as an institution, 'a thing in itself', something more than the sum of its parts. This, in turn, made the project of trade law seem vested with unity and coherence; it also provoked an association between the WTO and democracy. After the appearance of Jackson's *The World Trade Organization: Constitution and Jurisprudence*, 'the symbiotic relationship between institutionalism and constitutionalism was cemented once and for all',[33] despite the fact that it had never been 'through the process of democratic authorization by a defined constitutional community'.[34]

How did this chain of associations unfold or 'work', and with what consequences? The superiority of rules-based trade relations over trade diplomacy was a bedrock assumption at the creation of the WTO.[35] But as the term 'managerialism' is intended to suggest, the adoption of a more stringently rules-based regime brought with it governance by technocratic expertise, a process that empowered trade bureaucrats at the expense of other regime actors in a variety of ways. What was less obvious, at least until the new regime really got going, was how much rule application informed principally by the value of progressive liberalisation of trade might become a way to tilt *other* values, those associated with democracy and the rule of law in particular, off their axis at the same time.

As many trade scholars have noted, trade law has always operated through and against a background consensus on the proper domain and reach of the regime itself.[36] The optimism, expressed by Jackson and others, that a practical, pragmatic spirit, along with a few small tweaks to the system, could satisfactorily address any new challenges and conflicts

---

33 Ibid 101.
34 Cass, *The Constitutionalization of the World Trade Organization* (n 1) 106.
35 Ibid 115; Lang, *World Trade Law* (n 6).
36 Lang, *World Trade Law* (n 6).

about this fundamental issue generated by the new regime, soon proved unwarranted. For it turns out that there was no logical end point to the claims touching on domestic law and policy that might be advanced in the name of liberalised trade; absent explicit mechanisms of politics and diplomacy, there was also no easy way to limit to the regime's capacity to penetrate domestic legal systems in novel and capacious ways. This tendency was to be powerfully – indeed deliberately – reinforced by the next pillar of trade constitutionalism.

Rights-Based Approaches

Rights-based approaches are prescriptive calls for a radical transformation of the trade regime. Based on a combination of strategic and normative rationales[37] and more openly values-based than institutional managerialism, the constitutional innovation of rights-based approaches is to represent the WTO as 'a system of protection for individual economic rights beyond national borders'.[38] Beginning life as a means 'to facilitate the direct effect of WTO law into national legal systems' and going further through the door that had already been opened under the North America Free Trade Agreement's Chapter 11 provisions, rights-based approaches rest the legitimacy of the WTO on the extent to which it allows the voice and interests of private actors a direct role in the instigation and management of trade disputes.

Rights-based approaches are what Deborah Cass calls frankly ideological, even 'messianic' approaches to the world economic order. Here, we encounter not (just) a world of order and agreement among states, but a vision of a transnational community of rights-bearing citizen-consumers marching into a future of trans-border economic deals, all under the banner of private rights. Like institutional managerialism, the recognition of private rights, too, facilitates the use of WTO as a constraint on the reach and interpretation of domestic law by, for example, providing a basis on which to subject national legislation to judicial review based on WTO agreements.[39]

---

37   Cass, *The Constitutionalization of the World Trade Organization* (n 1) 162.
38   Ibid 146.
39   Ibid 148.

The resuscitation and advancement of a private right to trade,[40] cast not just in the language of rights but in the language of *human* rights is, in the author's assessment, a powerful legitimating move. This is surely correct: once transmuted into the language of human rights, rights-based approaches become an effective mode of self-legitimation as well as a source of enhanced authority for the WTO.[41] Replacing open political contestation over competing aims and values with claims rooted in fundamental moral and ethical precepts, rights-based approaches enable their proponents to bootstrap the status of a radical reconceptualisation of trade law, one that would fundamentally alter its reception into national legal systems and give private actors privileged status in international law to boot,[42] by linking it – normatively and semantically – with Kantian liberal political theory and highly individualist ideas about human freedom and human dignity.

Setting aside entirely the fact that the claimed 'right to trade' can charitably be described as obscure (no reference to any such right can be located in any human rights treaty, for example), it turns out that moralising about free trade is a bad idea for other reasons. For one, hanging the case for free trade on individual moral rights has proved to be an effective way to delink free trade from the broader welfare goals on which the postwar multilateral trade regime found much of its original justification. For another, it provides a means to insulate trade rules from any accounting of consequences or trade-offs with *other* rights. It forms no part of the rights-based approach, for example, that losses to some are not just an unintended side effect of liberalised trade; they are how the gains of trade are realised.[43] For both reasons, absolutist approaches to private rights undercut the normative and analytic basis on which states might try to temper the destabilising effects of liberalised trade on their populations.

It was surely correct on Deborah Cass's part to mark the significance of rights-based approaches to trade; indeed, it now looks prescient. Although inchoate and still aspirational when she wrote, efforts to give enhanced status to private rights at the level of process and substance have become only more muscular and well-developed in the international

---

40 The right to trade had long been invoked in international law; see, eg, Hugo Grotius, *The Rights of War and Peace*, tr AC Campbell (M Walter Dunne, 1901) <http://oll.libertyfund.org/titles/grotius-the-rights-of-war-and-peace-1901-ed>.

41 Cass, *The Constitutionalization of the World Trade Organization* (n 1) 151.

42 Cass, *The Constitutionalization of the World Trade Organization* (n 1) 153.

43 Howse, 'From Politics to Technocracy' (n 6).

economic order in the intervening time. For example, private investor-state dispute resolution provisions have been a key feature – and major source of contention – of many of the trade and investment regimes now under negotiation, in particular the 'mega-regional' trade and investment treaties like the TTIP and the CPTPP that have taken centre stage as multilateral negotiations have stalled or been abandoned.

The standardisation of private rights to trade and transact is arguably even more central to other initiatives in the international economic order, especially those designed to set normative benchmarks for economic rules and institutions. For example, the extent to which states grant adequate, or enhanced, protection for private rights serves as a key metric of many of the regulatory reform programs that the World Bank, including its flagship *Doing Business*, project.[44] The same objective arguably animates the OECD's projects on regulatory quality and regulatory coherence, evident in the extent to which it, on the one hand, privileges the goals of efficiency and on the other, avoids discussion of welfare objectives.[45] Indeed, the chapter on regulatory coherence within the CPTPP is designed to further such goals, at the same time as it normalises the objective of reducing regulatory differences.[46] In short, the broader world of international economic law is now suffused with the same constitution-like vision of transnational private rights.

Judicial Norm Development

The third approach, judicial norm development, locates the engine of the regime's constitutionalisation in the new institutional innovation, the WTO Appellate Body. Like reviewing courts in common law jurisdictions, the Appellate Body operates in constitutional mode by reflecting the governing norms of the institution, and through the accumulation of case law, by building those norms at the same time.[47]

In a layered, nuanced account, Deborah Cass takes the opportunity to point out the deficiencies of judicial norm generation within the WTO as measured by constitutional yardsticks, the obvious model and predecessor

---

44 World Bank, 'Doing Business 2020', *Doing Business* (Web Page, 2020) <https://www.doing business.org/>.
45 See for example, OECD, *Regulatory Policy and the Road to Sustainable Growth* (OECD, 2010).
46 See Government of Canada, *Global Affairs Canada* (Web Page, 9 November 2019) <https://www.international.gc.ca/gac-amc/index.aspx?lang=eng>.
47 Cass, *The Constitutionalization of the World Trade Organization* (n 1) 178.

being Joseph Weiler on the role of the European Court of Justice on the transformation of the European Community.[48] Following von Bogdandy, her emphasis is on the constitutional inadequacies that follow from the introduction of a system of judicial review that operates on its own, not counterbalanced by anything like an adequate political branch or legislature. As she describes, democratic values are compromised by the absence of a deliberative body, while the outsourcing of rule-making to standard-setting bodies risks subjecting those rules to capture by private actors. Moreover, the introduction of judicial review turns out to alter the relationships between the central actors in the trade regime in fundamental ways. Among the consequences is the erosion of the longstanding international law rule that the state is the ultimate arbiter of how international obligations are implemented. Appellate review, too, boosts the role of technocratic trade-biased decision-makers over political decision-makers, for example, by compelling states to advance a scientific rationale when assessing questions of risk and defending their legislative choices, even though such rationales are, on their own, an inadequate means of resolving the political and economic controversies that invariably underpin policy and regulatory decisions.

On Constitutionalism and the Trade Regime: Costs and Benefits

The cumulative effect of these different constitutional lenses is both impressive and so revealing as to be transformative. By the time the analysis is finished, we have in full view a deep conundrum: although the language of constitutionalism is everywhere to be found in respect of the WTO, on almost any angle the regime seems constitutionally deficient. All three approaches to the defence and explication of the WTO, it turns out, come up short when measured against normal expectations about constitutional orders, whether it concerns matters of form, content or process.

Above all, through the discourse of constitutionalism, *CWTO* suggests the immense stakes of trade regimes that threaten to slip the expectations, and even the grasp, of their creators.

---

48   See, eg, Weiler, *The Constitution of Europe* (n 18).

To recapitulate, *CWTO* makes clear the risky, unstable settlement between the domestic and the international when it comes to foundational decisions about social and economic priorities that the new regime has imported and inaugurated. Here, the crucial issue is the constraints on policy space faced by states when it comes to implementing any rule or decision that might have an effect on the allocation of risk or the costs and benefits of trade. This is now arguably the central theoretical and political question for trade negotiations as a whole. In so doing, *CWTO* also foregrounds the shifting balance of power between the domains of politics and technocracy, and the declining role of diplomacy in favour of expertise in the trade regime. *CWTO* marks the rising status of the individual or corporate actor vis-a-vis nation-states within the trade regime enabled by the mechanism of private rights, now transposed into 'human rights', and the deep challenge to democratic values posed by that ascendancy. As a consequence of the previous three moves, *CWTO* also highlights the uncertain and imperilled status of non-economic or social concerns – here, read distributive equity and social justice – in the current trade law calculus. Finally, *CWTO* focuses our attention on the vexed problems of constructing institutions and rules for representation and deliberation in a post-Westphalian world, where whether at the descriptive or normative level, states are manifestly no longer the only actors in town.[49]

CWTO makes equally clear the mechanisms and vectors of this transformational change. Here, we need to return to the role of ideas and recall the leitmotif running throughout *CWTO*, the independent significance of using constitutionalism as the frame in which to reflect on and measure such concerns. Throughout, the author draws our attention to the discursive function of constitutionalism, the fact that in applying the language of constitutionalism to the WTO, we have *already* made a significant move to import a host of legitimating assumptions and operations into the regime. Here she notes the 'door-closing' function of constitutionalism: its capacity to reify features that we might well have reason to question, but also its opposite – the possibility that constitutional discourse will facilitate the extension of the WTO into so many areas in which its authority is both uncertain and contentious. In describing the easy slippage from the apparent 'fact' of a new trade institution to the claim that that institution has, or should be endowed with, enhanced

---

49   Nancy Fraser, *Scales of Justice: Reimagining Political Space in a Globalizing World* (Columbia University Press, 2009).

status, Deborah Cass displays a remarkably good ear for the false note: for example, the way that constitutionalism both constructs and fuels a false antinomy between the individual and an all-powerful state, paradoxically in an era when private actors and entities have unprecedented reach and power.

The Constitutionalisation of the WTO: Signposting the future

CWTO is relentlessly analytic and taxonomic; it is also exhaustively – and at moments exhaustingly – even-handed in its treatment of the merits of different constitutional arguments. Yet an undercurrent of normative energy and disquiet threads its way throughout the analysis nonetheless; by the last chapter, that undercurrent finally bubbles up in full view. If Deborah Cass has not changed her mind about the value of the constitutional inquiry *tout court*, then by the end she is very clear about two interconnected problems.

The first problem concerns the limits of transposing the discourse of constitutionalism from the nation-state to the international sphere. Deborah Cass's systematic inquiry into the WTO throws into sharp relief the inadequacies that attend the projection of norms, assumptions and practices of domestic constitutionalism onto the international level. Here, we might read her as a critic, engaging in the exercise of foregrounding the background. As the exercise in reversal reveals, a host of institutions and practices associated with the nation-state operating in normal, liberal mode turn out to be crucial to the defence – and even the intelligibility – of constitutional norms, although many form no part of the conversation about constitutionalism and the WTO. If some or many of those practices and institutions are absent, weak or distorted, then constitutionalism will both mean and do very different things than we ordinarily understand it to mean and do. This is, of course, precisely what she has demonstrated with respect to the various models of constitutional engagement with the WTO.

The second problem concerns not just the limits but the pathologies of such exercises in projection, as it becomes clear that dominant ideas of constitutionalism so often work to further those aspects of the WTO that are most problematic. Here, Deborah Cass identifies problems with constitutionalism at both the descriptive and the normative levels. Not only are existing models for analysing the WTO 'deeply unsatisfying', but in her view, 'the ascendancy of these particular models of constitutionalism is related to (these) perceived deformities of democracy, sovereignty and economic and political organization in the international order'.[50] These are tough words. If modes of political and institutional analysis developed within and premised upon the nation-state are not easily transposed into the supranational register, if the use of constitutionalism in the international sphere can even perform a sort of reverse alchemy, turning the gold of cherished political values into leaden constraints against democratically responsive modes of governance, then what comes next?

The final, quite short but powerful, indicative chapter gives us a pretty good idea of where she, and we, might go. For *CWTO* ends with a normative/reconstructive project; Deborah being always unhappy with intellectual ventures that stopped short of reform, 'what is to be done' being very much part of her orientation both as a scholar and as a human being.

In an earlier venture, 'Navigating the Newstream: Recent Critical Scholarship in International Law', Deborah Cass took stock of a loosely consolidating, though still nascent, critical engagement with 'mainstream' international law. While crediting critical scholars with crucially important insights into the discipline, she also took them to task for failing to adequately take those insights forward. Here's how she saw the promise, and limits, of critical scholarship:

> as pedagogical tools, the Newstream writings are invaluable because they offer plausible explanations of international lawmaking, interpretation and application, at a point in time in which traditional understandings about law have been questioned by (post)modern insights into cultural fragmentation, the making of history and the role of language in law.[51]

Yet 'while these Newstream challenges could be transformative tools of changing law their potential is largely unrealized';[52] '[n]ewstream critiques frequently seem to pull back from the brink of affecting real change in international dialogue'.[53] For example, while analyses of the culture of international law are

---

50 Cass, *The Constitutionalization of the World Trade Organization* (n 1) 245.
51 Cass, 'Navigating the Newstream' (n 13) 343.
52 Ibid 345.
53 Ibid 378.

> partially persuasive, they ... leave unanswered the question of
> how international law can be loosened from the particular cultural
> moorings it has acquired over time and which are now represented
> in Mainstream literature.[54]

It was already clear long before *CWTO*, then, that deeply probing and sceptical inquiry into the conceptual scaffolding of mainstream legal scholarship, however necessary, could only ever, in Deborah's view, be part of the enterprise; no adequate account of the trade regime would stop there. To avoid these deficiencies, Deborah Cass has a quite specific suggestion: that constitutionalism debates in the WTO should be refocused on the ends of democracy and development. This should be done by effecting a merger of a transformationalist mindset with respect to constitutionalism with many of the anti-constitutional critiques already in circulation. We have a very good foretaste of the character of this imagined merger, moreover, having encountered many of these critiques in the course of her analysis of the mainstream constitutional models.

Such a merger would require going well beyond the received accounts of constitutionalism that have been in play so far. For their effect, as the reader can now fully appreciate, has been to inhibit rather than advance the very thinking about the WTO and its place within international economic law that, now as then, is so evidently necessary.[55] Surfacing not only the question of constitutional forms but also the substantive aims or goals of constitutionalism, this merger would compel us to revisit foundational questions about the distribution of powers among public and private actors and the hierarchy of goals and values in the international order, questions that the debate over constitutionalism has paradoxically foreclosed.

Having performed what is in effect a monumental constitutional ground-clearing exercise, Deborah Cass was poised to delve deeply and directly into these foundational normative and political controversies. The contemporary reader of *CWTO* might well want to hear much more on precisely these points, if only because they have become *the* central questions about the international economic law in the intervening time. Yet even as it stops at precisely this point, *CWTO* remains a brilliant and far-sighted analysis, one infused with highly attuned political intuition that shines continued light on the path on which we now find ourselves.

---

54   Ibid 350.
55   Cass, *The Constitutionalization of the World Trade Organization* (n 1) 245.

PART 4

Personal Reflection and Conclusions

Traversing Divides:
My 'Integrated' Sister

Dan Cass

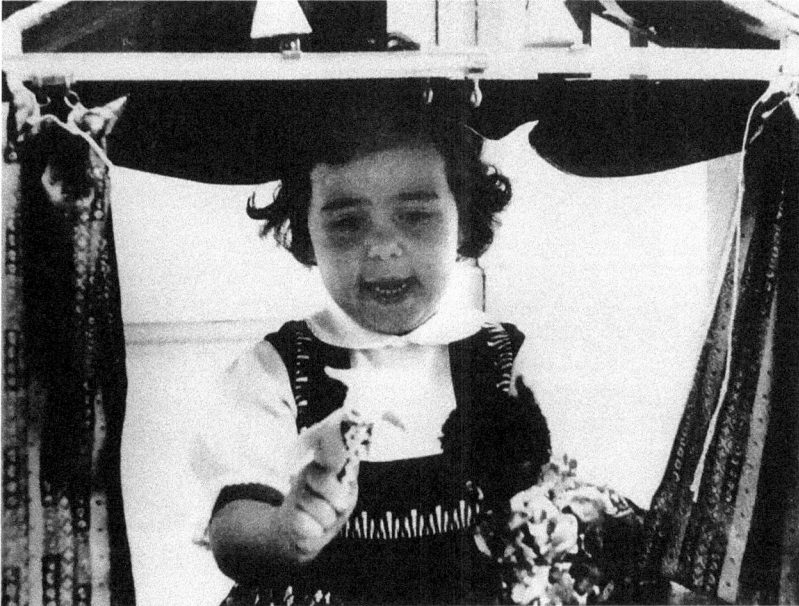

Deborah and her finger puppets, circa 1964.
Source: Photo provided by Dan Cass.

Deborah Cass was my sister and I want to share some of what I know about her. I think it is easy to connect her personal story with her scholarship or politics, because she was such a clear, integrated person. Everyone has contradictions; many people have commented to me that Deborah was so much *her*self: teaching law, cooking dinner, meditating while in intensive care, writing *that* book-with-the-long-title, mothering her daughters, listening to friends.

I am not the only one who wishes Deborah was beside us. In her introduction to this volume, her dear friend and mentor Hilary Charlesworth writes, 'it is wonderful to have her writings as a continuing source of inspiration and consolation'. Hilary writes of 'Deborah's firm, clear voice, her appreciation of language, her seriousness, her curiosity, her sensitivity and her wry humour'.[1]

If you had ever lost an argument with Deborah you would be surprised to know she was shy once. Our parents, Shirley and Moss, made her a theatre to help build her confidence. Dad constructed a wooden stage. Mum sewed a curtain on it and fashioned a troupe of finger puppets. The photo in this chapter shows Deborah, circa 1964, acting out a little play, literally trying on different characters, to find her own voice. Her ability to listen to the stories of the world and tell better ones is a clue to her power.

Stories and Change

Deborah reinvented herself many times in her life: hippie child of the 1960s, a stint in Melbourne's outer suburbs in the late 1970s, student politician at the University of Melbourne in the 1980s, rising scholar in the 1990s, aspiring author and thorough seeker of health and spiritual truth, from her cancer diagnosis in 2003 until her death in 2013.

Deborah's love of stories blossomed when she learned to read. I inherited some of her childhood favourites, paperback editions of *The Chronicles of Narnia* by CS Lewis and some of the Moomintroll series by Finnish artist and writer Tove Jansson. As a teenager Deborah read and reread the Greek myths and held them close to her through her life. When she spoke of one of the myths, her eyes brightened with wonder.

She built a strong story of self but never lost her tenderness. For as long as I can remember, she would sometimes grab my head in both hands and say, 'I used to change your nappies!', then shake her head, with a theatrical frown, 'How is that possible?' When she was in year seven she walked home from school at lunchtimes to see baby me. If I find life hard now, I imagine talking to her and I feel comforted.

---

1   See in this volume, Hilary Charlesworth, 'Traversing the Divides: Remembering Deborah Cass'.

Deborah came of age in Melbourne and Canberra in the heady days of 1970s. At the end of the 1960s Deborah and our sister Naomi joined the world's oldest socialist-Zionist youth movement, Hashomer Hatzair, or Hushy. As in so many things, I followed them, a decade later. We all went on the camps with other children of left-wing Jews, sung Israeli songs and danced and debated peace in the Middle East and other political and even philosophical issues around the campfire. Hushy was the place I first heard about postmodernism, in about 1985, when one of our university-age leaders read us some of Italo Calvino's *If on a Winters Night a Traveller.*

I don't think I have ever experienced such a loving and ethical community as Hushy, and I know it was a big part of Deborah's life. Her daughter Rosa spent her own gap year in Israel, on a program with the progressive Zionist group, Netzer.

My parents sent Deborah and our oldest sister, Naomi – who she was very close to – to an experimental high school, Brinsley Road Community School, in Camberwell. Deborah soaked up the counterculture and she never became cynical about its aspirations for a peaceful, ecological, dare we say it, 'paradigm shift'. She made friendships that lasted her whole life, such as filmmakers Sharon Connolly and Trevor Graham. At the end of the second term of her final school year she dropped out.

Deborah grew her beautiful hair down to the waist. Deborah and Naomi ran barefoot around the sand dunes at Somers where our parents had a diminutive beach house, built from a shipping container. Deborah, or 'Dood' as we called her, loved the music of her time, from Pink Floyd's spaced-out *Ummagumma*, to those nice Jewish boys Simon & Garfunkel.

She never forgave my parents for refusing to let her go to Sunbury Rock Festival, Australia's answer to Woodstock, when she was about 14. In more recent years she went to see Leonard Cohen multiple times and could be heard yelling over the stage barriers, 'I love you, Lennie!'

After Brinsley Road, Deborah reinvented herself around a conventional life. She left home and moved to Melbourne's outer eastern suburbs with a man who worked in TV. She taught herself to bake – including her famed pavlova and sachertorte – and sold cakes to a shop. They played doubles tennis and bet on horses. They had a personal computer and she drove a sports car with a sun roof. I was so proud! She read novels and learned to touch-type and supported herself working as a medical secretary.

When she finally decided to change again, it was because of a conversation. A wise friend of the family told her that she didn't need a destination, rather a path. He told her that she should study, because learning is like a bus: you just get on and it takes you to new places.

When Deborah finally returned to do her final year of school, her ambition and her exam results steered her to law at the University of Melbourne. She never looked back. She graduated with honours, won five prizes including the scholarship that paid for her to do her Master of Laws (LLM) at Harvard University, and then topped it off with Harvard's prestigious legal doctorate, the Doctor of Juridical Science, or SJD.

Deborah threw herself into campus life, studying arts/law at the University of Melbourne. She lived in a share house on Rathdowne Street in North Carlton, and walked or cycled the dozen blocks to campus. She dyed her hair pink. One Monday morning I told my incredulous friends at the boys' school I went to that on the weekend I had been at my sister's party and saw two women passionately kissing each other.

Deborah was a successful political organiser. She came to university life as a very adult radical; a builder, not a smasher, articulate and confident. She helped form the Labour Club which displaced the ALP Club in elections to the student council. She won the role as editor of *Farrago*, the University of Melbourne student newspaper, with Tania Patston and James Button, two of her close, lifelong friends.

She took me to see Talking Heads. I followed her to a protest at a joint US–Australian military base in the northern Melbourne suburb of Watsonia where her comrades were all dressed as spies, in trench coats and dashing hats and silly glasses.

Deborah never did finish the arts degree, or make a career in politics, but both these sides of her are integral to understanding who she was. For her, the law was always a practical endeavour, to make the world better. She loved stories and was masterful at making them, and this talent gave her the resilience she needed later in life.

Law or Literature

If the law was the great love of Deborah's hard-working intellect, then her first love was literature. She loved debating books, including with her friends who were successful authors.

After falling ill in 2003 Deborah retired from the law, to get healthy and care for her darling daughters. After her first operation, she took to writing fiction. This was a surreptitious enterprise at first, but later she spoke of it to friends and studied writing at RMIT (formerly the Royal Melbourne Institute of Technology). She had some short stories published and started on her novel.

When Deborah died, it was our mother who came up with the idea of commemorating her through a literary prize. By Shirley's design, the Deborah Cass Prize for Writing goes to early-career authors, who have a migrant background (a writer is eligible if they or one of their parents migrated to Australia). It is optimistic and a tribute to our grandparents, European Jews who migrated to Australia early last century, as a safe haven from anti-Semitism.

The Prize is also a tribute to her loving friendships. Her two coeditors from *Farrago*, James Button and Tania Patston, manage the judging and fundraising and with other friends and family, raised the funds to establish the Prize in 2015. Of the three esteemed, inaugural judges, two were close friends she made at uni: Christos Tsiolkas and Tony Ayers. (Alice Pung was the third inaugural judge, and like Tony and Christos, has drawn on the migrant experience in her work.)

A translator whose family migrated from Tuscany, Moreno Giovannoni, won the first Prize in 2015 and his beautiful book, *The Fireflies of Autumn*, was published in July 2018, by Black Inc.

The Prize is for literature, but in an era of resurgent nationalism, it has a broader impact, because literature is an antidote to bigotry. David Kidd and Emanuele Castano at the New School for Social Research have presented experimental evidence that literary fiction improves 'theory of mind'. The theory of mind is our brain's ability to detect the emotional states of others, understand these emotions and represent their intentions and beliefs in our own minds. It is a scientific model of what is generally known as empathy.[2]

Deborah had great empathy and knew the power of stories. For her, there had to be a point to an argument, even on an obscure topic. Deborah was driven to find the world meaningful and just.

Slow Politics

Deborah steered away from student politics and towards the law, and brought her values with her. She was patient and practical. She believed in intellectual achievement and was very proud of hers, but she was not a snob. She knew that change has to happen through democracy.

I think that her years in suburbia had a big impact on Deborah. In between Brinsley Road and her return study, she worked as a sales representative for JM Dent & Sons. Dent published the *Everyman Library* of classics and *Everyman Encyclopaedia*, using modern printing press technologies to make books cheap enough to be read by a broad audience.

One of the great things about America, until relatively recently, was a respect for learning and a desire for rationality.[3] Middle-class and working-class readers educated themselves. America had a multiplicity of middlebrow magazines that were fierce cheerleaders for nature, rationality, science and technology: *National Geographic, Reader's Digest, Popular Science, Discovery, Popular Mechanics.*

Even when Deborah moved to highbrow Harvard and then the London School of Economics, she expressed no disdain for her past in the suburbs. She knew that middlebrow readers are still intelligent readers who should be taken seriously; indeed, that our democracy depends on it. She loved mastering complexity but knew change comes from big ideas, expressed simply.

---

2   David Kidd and Emanuele Castano, 'Reading Literary Fiction Improves Theory of Mind' [2013] (342) *Science* 377, doi.org/10.1126/science.1239918.
3   See for example, Susan Jacoby, *The Age of American Unreason in a Culture of Lies* (Vintage Books, 2018).

Deborah's big idea was 'trading democracy'. This meant that rather than trying to maximise the freeness of trade, or protesting for its fairness, we painstakingly build the institutions to enable its democratisation. Her big work in this area was *The Constitutionalization of the World Trade Organization* (*CWTO*), which was originally her SJD thesis at Harvard.

Deborah gave copies of her book to all her family, including our paternal grandfather, Ben Cass, who was 103 at the time. Papa was only just easing up on his long-held habit of reading *The Economist* every week, marking the important points in all the key articles and sometimes posting them to Deborah and his other grandchildren, according to their areas of professional interest. Deborah wasn't the first person in the family to see the highlighting pen as a civilisational triumph.

In Kerry Rittich's chapter on CWTO she writes that Deborah was 'always unhappy with intellectual ventures that stopped short of reform, "what is to be done" being very much part of her orientation both as a scholar and as a human being'.[4]

Unfortunately, we know almost nothing about Deborah's vision for a synthesis of trade liberalisation and international economic democratisation. Rittich says that Deborah's book was a 'constitutional ground-clearing exercise'.[5] It mastered the field, schematising previous schools of thought but only teasing us with the merest outline of her alternative.

For those who want to explore the possibilities Deborah was uncovering, Rittich offers thoughts from an earlier essay that Deborah wrote, in which she looked at the debate between the accepted, or 'Mainstream', view in international law and the 'Newstream' critique. As Hilary Charlesworth also notes, Rittich says Deborah was critical of the conservativism of orthodoxy but also the inability of the rebels to effect real change.

I think this is a key point about her philosophy. She had the courage to make the radical critique but the modesty to know it had to make an impact on the world as it is.

---

4   See in this volume, Kerry Rittich, 'Deborah Cass, *The Constitutionalization of the World Trade Organization*: A Reading in Time' 15.
5   Ibid 16.

Deborah's politics was always practical as well as intellectual. While she was at the University of Melbourne, a judge ruled that a sex worker who had been raped had suffered less because of her profession, so Deborah organised a protest and condemned the judgment on the evening TV news. Before she went back to study in the 1980s, Deborah won a considerable sum in the lottery and donated a significant amount to the African National Congress to support its struggle against apartheid in South Africa.

In our family we often discussed politics, sometimes a little too monotonously. Our father, Moss, had been a Cabinet Minister in a short-lived but energetically reforming left-wing Australian Government.[6] Deborah had a rare confidence in the political process.

Deborah saw the law as deeply political and a vehicle for change. She agreed with Jenny Morgan, one of her closest friends and a colleague in the law, who writes that Deborah's work demonstrates that 'law cannot be read without politics, history and, I would say, feminism'.[7]

I admired Deborah's patience and rigour. I remember when she deferred from her studies to be a research assistant to counsel at the Nauru Commission of Inquiry into the Rehabilitation of Phosphate Lands in Nauru.

The tiny island of Nauru, in the western Pacific, had been covered with deposits of calcium phosphate, as pure and valuable as any in the world. This industrial-grade fertiliser was in the faeces of sea birds over at least 80,000 and perhaps as long as 300,000 years.[8] While Nauru was administered by Australia, the phosphate was taken for Western industrial agriculture and was vital to the economic development of Australia and New Zealand.

Although Deborah had the commission's most junior legal role, she left a big mark. Tony Anghie recalls that she had the 'massive task of scouring the archives in various places including London, Geneva, New York, New Zealand, Melbourne and Fiji'. He writes:

---

6   Moss Cass, Vivien Encel and Anthony O'Donnell, *Moss Cass and the Greening of the Australian Labor Party* (Australian Scholarly Publishing, 2017).
7   See in this volume, Jenny Morgan, 'Introduction to "Constitutional Work"'.
8   SJ Gale, 'The Mined-out Phosphate Lands of Nauru, Equatorial Western Pacific' (2016) 63(3) *Australian Journal of Earth Sciences* 334, doi.org/10.1080/08120099.2016.1206621.

We relied completely on the several filing cabinets full of documents that Deborah had so carefully compiled and catalogued … It is a testament to the thoroughness and precision of Deborah's work that the case that was later argued in the International Court of Justice was based on the foundations that she had laid … Deborah had provided all that was needed.[9]

This diligence was a matter of her character. She wanted to change the world and knew, as Max Weber wrote, that '[p]olitics is a strong and slow boring of hard boards'.[10]

The Healthy Self

If politics is a struggle against chaos, then so too is having a body. Cancer brought chaos to Deborah's body and her family. She had multiple operations over a decade, in London and then at Melbourne's excellent Peter MacCallum Cancer Centre. I think that two of her important sources of strength during this period were her diligence and her storytelling.

When Deborah realised that the cancer was truly serious and ongoing, she moved her family back to Melbourne. I moved soon after from Sydney and so for several years our family of origin lived in the same city. The closeness forged with Deborah over those years and the experience of getting to really know Gerry, Hannah and Rosa is a highlight of my life.

Deborah responded to mortality and suffering with courage and focus. She became an expert, bringing a notebook to all her medical meetings. She worked hard at being as healthy as possible. She redirected her brilliant mind from the law to the big philosophical questions about life and death. Again, she reinvented herself, telling herself the story that would open up new horizons.

She truly did defy the odds. At one meeting with her team in 2012 they said Deborah was doing so well that she was, statistically speaking, 'off the graph'. She had survived years longer than any of the surgeons or oncologists had predicted. Even then, in her last year, they were optimistic about what she could achieve, in her remarkable way.

---

9   See in this volume, Tony Anghie, 'Self-Determination and Beyond: Reflections on the Aftermath of the Nauru Case'.

10   Scott Horton, 'Weber on the Political Vocation', *Harper's Magazine* (Web Page, 8 June 2008) <https://harpers.org/blog/2008/06/weber-on-the-political-vocation/>.

Every day she was able, Deborah went for a long walk. She made her own fresh juices. She bought a vast range of healthy foods and supplements. She read about Buddhism, meditation, spirituality, cognitive science, conventional medicine and alternative therapies. She continued to enjoy poetry, novels, and the papers, including the *London Review of Books* and Melbourne's *Age*.

At one point in the latter years, Deborah was readmitted to hospital. I was the one spending time by her bed that week. (Naomi, our sister, often slept in the hospital room and tended to Deborah there and when she was at home, with incredible dedication.) On this particular occasion I entered Deborah's hospital room to find her bed empty.

After gathering courage, I went to the nurses' station to ask what had happened. There was silence until a young nurse said Deborah had raised her weak and pained body and was walking around the ward, leaning on the infusion pump. The nurse said, 'she's like the Terminator'.

Like many people, I had always avoided thinking about death, before Deborah fell ill. A good friend recommended I read Elisabeth Kübler-Ross (1926–2004), the Swiss-American psychologist who founded the clinical study of how Western people face mortality. *On Death and Dying*, published in 1969 (Simon & Schuster), proposes that we are unable to really comprehend our own death. She observed we try to 'bargain' with fate. We think that if we are morally worthy, then God will heal us. Or, for the atheists, we think that if we work hard (at meditation or positive thinking or consuming healthy foods and supplements), then our bodies will heal us.

In her last couple of years, I used to go around every second weekend to help her make a vast volume of freshly squeezed vegetable and fruit juice, which she believed was holding the cancer at bay. These were lovely times, when we would talk for hours about everything under the sun. We often went for a coffee – a dandelion brew for her – to Me & Julio, the café on her street in North Fitzroy, opposite the school yard. One day she suddenly faced me and said, 'It's not fair that I am going to die and you are going to still be here'. We cried and I held her tight.

Gerry and their girls were amazingly strong through these years. Gerry supported Deborah and her choices, even when her path took her to realms they could not share. The girls and Gerry gave all their love to her. Their home was a happy one, full of all the normal joys and dramas that come with two children growing up.

Over that last difficult and amazing decade, Deborah worked hard to tell the best story she could about herself, the cancer and the meaning of her life. I think that the creativity of the storyteller in her sustained her life for so many years longer than the doctors gave her. In her early life she fell in love with stories and the power they have to remake us. She never gave up on that little Deborah inside.

She studied Buddhism and practiced meditation, at times for several hours a day. She went on retreats. When she died in 2013, Sogyal Rinpoche sent an email to followers around the world asking them to meditate for her.

Deborah also turned to Judaism. She found a teacher to instruct her in the foundations of the Kabbalah and spoke of it with close friends like Kim Rubenstein in Canberra and Jon Turner QC in London.

This part of her journey was an unusual one for our family. Our parents had brought us up as atheists, or at least rationalist and agnostic. As children we went to the synagogue together for the big days in the religious calendar: Rosh Hashana (New Year) and Yom Kippur (the Day of Atonement). This was more for connection to a shared culture and history than connection to God.

The one body of the Jewish canon which we all could recite was the comedy. Shirley, our mum, has a particularly wicked sense of the absurd. During times of difficulty – or indeed any time – she would lob a grenade of bitter-sweet pathos and blow up any solemnity. I can see Deborah holding her sides, crying with laughter.

We loved the films of the Marx Brothers and Woody Allen, and the family record and cassette collections included Tom Lehrer and Lenny Bruce.

The family favourite was the 1965 classic, 'You Don't Have to Be Jewish'. One sketch we all loved was the supposed reading of the will of a Samuel B Cohen, of Long Island, New York.

The sketch consists of Cohen's executor reciting the will, to squeals of admiration and sotto voce commentary. There is one million dollars to 'my beautiful boy Sheldon' and the same amount to 'my beautiful daughter', 'who has been a little too particular or she'd be married already'. Cohen's wife gets two million and 'the Picasso from the back of the store'. To his brother-in-law Louis, 'who lived with us all his life' and 'who never had to do a day's work' and 'always smoked the best cigars; mine' and 'who all his life said I'd never remember him in my will; hello Louis!'

I loved walking and talking with Deborah. Wherever she lived in that big last decade, she took long walks, swinging her arms vigorously and holding herself erect. She was convinced that this gave vitality to her immune system. She experienced the clarity it brought to her mind. In Melbourne and at her Somers beach house she brought along trusty Angus, her little Scottish Highland Terrier.

I shared Deborah's fascination with neuroscience. We loved Norman Doige's bestseller, *The Brain that Changes Itself* (Penguin, 2007), and I gave her Daniel J Siegel's *Mindsight* (Random House, 2010). The promise of this new generation of neuroscientists is the idea that we can use our thoughts to change our brains.

This appealed very much to Deborah's sense that we can use the power of the stories we tell to shape ourselves and our societies, as moral agents. Neuroplasticity provides a scientific approach to practice of meditation and an empirical account of its positive impacts. If we can use the software of our thoughts to repeatedly think in more mentally healthy ways, then our brain will, over time, rewire into more mentally healthy hardware.

Daniel Siegel is a clinical neuroscientist who has expanded this vision of neuroplasticity into the social realm. He theorises that wellbeing is a function of three factors: brain, mind and relationships. If our relationships carry some of the content of our mind, then they influence our brains.

On our walks together, Deborah discussed her hope that a unified theory of brain and self was emerging. She enjoyed thinking that science and spirituality could find a deep connection through concepts of mind.

Deborah did not need to read neuroscience to know how to love and be loved. Even when sick, she was often busy with friendships: writing aerograms, making cakes, talking through problems. She used to advise, 'I water my friends better than you do'.

Deborah wanted to know everything. She also wanted to be in the thrall of becoming, of mystery. I love the story of her playing with finger puppets on her little stage as a girl, but her strength was a mysterious force, rising from her unconscious.

On 25 June 2014, Natalia Schiffrin, Philippe Sands QC and other of Deborah's London friends put on a beautiful memorial for her at Burgh House, near Hampstead Heath. Maria Aristodemou spoke rather intensely about the exhilarating and sometimes confronting sense of being in the moment with Deborah.

Maria said that Deborah had something she wanted for herself: an honesty that was fundamental. Deborah was, in psychoanalytic terms, the 'Ego' that Maria wanted to become, 'the ethical subject for whom there's no distance between the "saying" and "the said" … [who can] speak their desire without fear and without lying'.[11]

As you might hope, I think there is a valuable political lesson for us in Deborah's personal struggle. The biggest challenge facing the world is global warming and it is something that I have worked on, and cried about, since 1991. When people ask me, 'is there any hope left?', I now reply that it is not the most useful question.

After doing my part to help Deborah struggle for health, I learned that hope is not the point. Her struggle made our lives bigger, because we lived it fully with her. She may have hoped for a cure and bargained for the impossible, but she got up each day and lived meaningfully.

We live in a real world of objectively knowable truths, but we relate to them through the stories we tell and the courage we have to face things as they are.

I recall Deborah's friendships, mindfulness, singing to Leonard Cohen, long walks with Angus the terrier, afternoons listening to radio broadcasts of summer test cricket, weekends at her Somers beach haven, fearless and tender cultivation of her daughters and love of her husband, and they all remind me how to live well. She knew her story would have the ending she did not want, but she kept telling better stories about herself and the world, each day.

---

11   Email from Maria Aristodemou to Dan Cass, 31 January 2017.

Concluding Remarks

Gerry Simpson

On the 7th of June, 2012, Hannah, Rosa and I attended the launch of the then-latest edition of the fiction magazine, *Etchings*, held in Readings bookstore in St Kilda, just opposite the site where the famous Jewish café Scheherazade had stood. Deborah's grandfather, Benjamin Cass, had been a regular at Scheherazade for 20 years (more or less until his death at 104, almost twice the age Deborah was when she died).

Four writers were there to read from recently published work. Two women recited passages from their own worthy memoirs and were followed by a booming man recounting some hugely unerotic 'erotic adventures'. He clearly imagined himself to be the star speaker that evening. Right up until the point when Deborah began reading. She read – with such charm, poise and authority – a passage from her short story, 'Her Beauty as a Sword' (about her grandmother, Eva Shulman).[1] The room was captivated.

It was the last time Deborah spoke in public, and the story was the last work she published.

But Deborah and her work have had such powerful afterlives. I still see references to her *Nordic Journal* essay, 'Navigating the Newstream' (a brilliantly clever title, if I may say so), her superb *tour d'horizon* of the Newstream movement in international law.[2] Meanwhile the constitutionalisation of trade law book is a standard reference (discussed recently at an American Society event) and her other work pops up very

---

1   Deborah Cass, 'Her Beauty as a Sword' (2011) 10 *Etchings* 5–12.
2   Deborah Cass, 'Navigating the Newstream: Recent Critical Scholarship in International Law' (1996) 65 *Nordic Journal of International Law* 341, doi.org/10.1163/15718109620294924.

frequently. Cait Storr was kind enough to reference Deborah recently in Tbilisi when she spoke about Nauru. My students continue to quote her. They probably have no idea that I was married to her for 20 years.

Deborah left so much behind: friends (she had the best friends, as Catriona Drew once told me), ideas, ways of seeing and being, cousins, nieces, nephews, a brother, a sister, a mother, a father, a husband and two daughters. And now, this book can be added to Deborah's afterlife.

So, I could not be more grateful to Kim and Hilary (two of Deborah's dear friends and hugely admired colleagues), for organising the conference from which this book arises, and to Deborah's friends and colleagues (and brother, Dan). They write so beautifully about her public life and her private world or both; Catherine Hawkins describes talking feminist politics over the back fence in Narrabundah with Deborah, and Dan's piece is a fluent and moving tribute to the various private and public Deborahs we knew and didn't know.

Deborah told me, shortly after I met her, that she had *published* her undergraduate essay in public international law. We were both international law tyros at this point so I felt vaguely disturbed by this news. At that point, I had published nothing (unless we count a poem about John Lennon in the 1980 edition of *Thor*, the Thurso High School Magazine). Worse still, she was merely a tutor whereas I had ascended to the heady heights of 'lecturer in law (continuing)' at Melbourne University. After professing a total lack of interest in this news, I searched out her essay immediately. It had an irredeemably boring title (something like 'The Quiet Revolution: International Law and Fishing on the High Seas') but, disappointingly, it was, like Margaret Young's return to that subject in these pages, rather good.[3]

A few months later, still in the midst of a faltering campaign to win her heart, I took her to Jimmy Watson's Wine Bar in Carlton where she dropped another bombshell: her essay on self-determination (celebrated here in Tony Anghie's affectionate tribute to her work on Nauru) had been accepted by *The Syracuse Journal of International Law*.[4] I muttered something about not having a clue where Syracuse was but I knew then

---

3   Deborah Cass, 'A Quiet Revolution: The Exclusive Economic Zone and Foreign Fishing Access in the Pacific' (1987) 16 *Melbourne University Law Review* 83.
4   Deborah Z Cass, 'Re-Thinking Self-Determination: A Critical Analysis of Current International Law Theories' (1992) 18 *Syracuse Journal of International Law and Commerce* 31.

that the die was cast. Deborah was on the move, and quickly. I hastily knocked off an essay on some recent international law case and then, in imitation of Deborah, I rehashed my Master's thesis on self-determination and persuaded the *Stanford Journal of International Law* to publish it.

It was a breathless and prolix retread of Deborah's elegant dissection of the same subject.

By the time it was published, Deborah had published our first daughter, Hannah, and the battle was over.

Deborah always seemed to be one step ahead, not just of me, but of nearly everyone. Feminist constitutional law (with Kim), the revival of trusteeship as an international legal doctrine, the turn to histories of the discipline, the emergence of trade law, the constitutionalisation of trade law: Deborah was there first or a close second.

But the book on trade law was, really, what Kerry Rittich calls a 'ground-clearing exercise'.[5] Further books would follow: on trade and democracy, on campaign finance, a critical study of Nauru and trusteeship. There would be a magnum opus on international law and redistribution, then a (first) novel called *A History of Boyfriends*. Each of them 'fresh and forthright and full of luminous, funny phrases', in the words Susan Marks used to describe Deborah's writing.

But none of this happened. Life got in the way. Then death.

Or maybe it did happen (some of it at least) but was carried out by others in their own distinctive and distinguished way. When I read these essays I feel Deborah's spirit and intelligence in the pages. When Tony Anghie speaks of Nauru and Australia's various imperialisms, Deborah's archival research and thinking is so very evident (not least in Tony's generous acknowledgments).

Margaret Young's conviction, expressed in her wide-ranging retrospective, that fisheries law is a way into understanding not just important aspects of the law of the sea but also what she calls the 'allocation of sovereignties' at the heart of international law, is a conviction that Margaret is right to say would be shared by Deborah.

---

5   See in this volume, Kerry Rittich, 'Deborah Cass, *The Constitutionalization of the World Trade Organization*: A Reading in Time'.

Deborah did not collaborate often in her academic career but the fruits of a rare and important collective effort are discussed by Kim Rubenstein in her essay on representations of women in Australian constitutional life and politics. Here, Kim returns to an essay she and Deborah published in the *Adelaide Law Review* in 1995.[6] I think what Deborah appreciated most about this prescient essay was its potential to inspire change beyond the academy. It is to Kim's enormous credit that the article has had such a powerful afterlife in Australian constitutional thought and that Kim and others are prepared to use the essay and recent English jurisprudence (*Cope*[7]) as a departure point for thinking of job-sharing (a subject to which Deborah's illness made her highly attuned) as a constitutional issue. One of Deborah's great friends from her Harvard days and beyond, Kerry Rittich, has offered here a wonderfully creative reading of Deborah's prize-winning book on *The Constitutionalization of the World Trade Organization*. As she puts it:

> Deborah … was one of the first people to seriously consider the idea that the *idea* of the WTO – how it was conceived as an institution, how it imagined the community of states and other actors engaged in trade relations, and the ethos and values that organised these relations and informed the operation of the regime as a whole – was an independently significant field of inquiry.[8]

How we wish that such work could have been continued by Deborah; how grateful we are that this work is being pursued with such rigour and imagination by those close to her.

Deborah's friends have done her an enormous service in these pages. When this book is launched; when we pick it up and read these sparkling essays, we will experience both Deborah's powerful presence, and her absence.

---

6   Deborah Cass and Kim Rubenstein, 'Representations of Women: Towards a Feminist Analysis of the Australian Constitutional System' (1995) 17 *Adelaide Law Review* 3.

7   *R (Cope) v Returning Officer for the Basingstoke Parliamentary Constituency* [2015] EWHC 3958 (Admin).

8   See in this volume, Kerry Rittich, 'Deborah Cass, *The Constitutionalization of the World Trade Organization*: A Reading in Time'.

PART 5

**Reproductions of
Articles Discussed**

The Quiet Revolution: The Development of the Exclusive Economic Zone and Implications for Foreign Fishing Access in the Pacific

Deborah Cass

Deborah Cass, 'The Quiet Revolution: The Development of the Exclusive Economic Zone and Implications for Foreign Fishing Access in the Pacific' (1987) 16 *Melbourne University Law Review* 83, 83–102 <http://www5.austlii.edu.au/au/journals/MelbULawRw/1987/5.html>.

THE QUIET REVOLUTION:
THE DEVELOPMENT OF THE EXCLUSIVE ECONOMIC ZONE AND IMPLICATIONS FOR FOREIGN FISHING ACCESS IN THE PACIFIC

BY DEBORAH CASS*

[*The exclusive economic zone, established under the 1982 Convention on the Law of the Sea, represents a significant incursion on traditional fishing rights on the high seas and has caused some commentators to view it with suspicion. Under the regime, coastal states have sovereign rights over resources within a 200 mile limit. This article examines the historical development of the zone, rights and responsibilities within it, and its relevance to Australia. It then focuses on the question of how coastal states determine the right of access to the zone of foreign fishing powers. A detailed discussion of the provisions with regard to access follows. The author concludes that the decision to grant access is entirely within the discretion of the coastal state, and that the determination will be made predominantly on the basis of economic considerations. This proposition is then illustrated with examples of the practice of states, including Australia, in the South Pacific region.*]

INTRODUCTION

Nations have been arguing over fishing rights since Jonah and the whale. Such disputes hardly seem the basis for a revolution. But that is exactly what is happening in the Pacific, with the introduction of the 1982 U.N. Convention on the Law of the Sea.[1] The once common practice of large nations exploiting the waters of smaller, less sophisticated states is no longer acceptable at international law. Large nations now must pay for the right to fish in someone else's backyard.

This dramatic change has brought with it the fear of a revolution of a more sweeping kind. 'Soviets get new Pacific toehold' was the headline of a front page news report when the Soviets outbid the U.S. for fishing rights in Kiribati.[2] Fishing rights have suddenly become the battleground for global ideological conflict.

The vehicle of this change is a new doctrine of international law — the exclusive economic zone (E.E.Z.). Ostensibly it is an innocuous enough doctrine which aims to conserve and manage the living resources within its area. However, these objectives gain in significance because of the enormous area and fish stocks covered by the Zones. With over 35% of ocean and 75-80% of stock within the E.E.Z. jurisdiction,[3] the new doctrine is vital to the world economy.

As far as international law is concerned, the evolution of the concept of the exclusive economic zone is important for two main reasons. First, it represents a significant incursion on traditional notions of freedom of the high seas. Secondly, its evolution is an excellent example of the complex interplay of forces which affect the development of a new rule at international law.

* Arts/Law student, University of Melbourne. Research Assistant to Commission of Inquiry into Rehabilitation of the Worked Out Phosphate Land in Nauru. The author wishes to thank Dr Gillian Triggs for her support, encouragement and advice.
1 U.N. Doc. A/CONF. 62/122 (1982) — hereafter cited as U.N.C.L.O.S. III.
2 *Age* (Melbourne) 1 April 1986.
3 Belsky, M. H., 'Management of Large Marine Ecosystems: Developing a New Rule of Customary International Law' (1985)22 *San Diego Law Review* 733, 759.

This paper will attempt to illustrate these reasons by focussing on the most crucial aspect of the exclusive economic zone — the right of the third parties to have access to the living resources of the E.E.Z. A number of problems have arisen in this area, including the interpretation of key clauses such as total allowable catch. Another issue concerns the type of factors for consideration by the coastal state in granting access. The paper will conclude that the rights of the coastal state to determine the right of third parties to have access are completely discretionary. This causes some legal commentators to view the new doctrine with suspicion. Yet, economic considerations will be shown to be the determining factor in calculations between coastal states and distant water fishing nations in the South West Pacific region.

At the outset it should be noted that the question of access is extremely contentious in both legal and political terms. The advance on customary international law in the area of access has led one legal commentator to remark that the United Nations Law of the Sea Convention (1982) represents the 'triumph of individualism over collectivism',[4] implying that the individual coastal state will benefit at the expense of the international community. Similarly, Juda describes the E.E.Z. as representing the danger of 'creeping jurisdiction', because E.E.Z. claims may become the precursors of claims to extend the territorial sea.[5] Political responses, particularly from the United States, have also been forceful.

These warnings are particularly relevant to Australia which is currently taking a spectator's role in the negotiations between the United States and the South Pacific nations over the question of U.S. access to tuna stocks in the Pacific. The Soviet Union has just purchased access to fishing rights in Kiribati for $2.4 million for the next 12 months.[6] For these reasons, it is important that Australia understands the impact of the development of the E.E.Z. on the region.

For ease of exposition this paper will be divided into two parts: Part A, the exclusive economic zone, and Part B, fishing rights focussing on access in particular. The first part will look at the historical background to the E.E.Z., the rights and responsibilities of nations generally within the zone, and the position of Australia.

The second part will be divided into four sections and will detail the general articles of U.N.C.L.O.S. III which regulate fishing rights in the zone, and then focus on the particular problem of access. Following these two sections will be a discussion of the relationship between state practice in the area of access and the evolution of customary international law.

The final part of the second section will take up the discussion with particular application to the South West Pacific region. It will look at state practice evidenced by the incorporation of the U. N. C. L. O. S. III provisions in domestic legislation and in multilateral agreements, and conclude with a comparison of the South West Pacific experience with Australia's fishing zone.

4 O'Connell, D. P., *The International Law of the Sea*. Vol. 1 (1982) 552.
5 Juda, L., 'The E.E.Z.: Compatibility of National Claims and the U.N. Convention on the Law of the Sea' (1986)16 *Ocean Development and International Law* 44.
6 Doulman, D. J., *Round Six of the Pacific Tuna Treaty Talks*, Pacific Islands Development Program, unpublished, 5.

It should be noted that primary material in this latter part of the paper is scarce because the island states concerned do not possess the kind of bureaucracies to which we are accustomed to produce the data required. It should not be assumed therefore that this paper is conclusive, rather on the limited information available it is hoped that it will raise some of the problems of intepretation and look at how States in the region have dealt with these issues.

A. *THE EXCLUSIVE ECONOMIC ZONE*

1. *Historical background*

Until recently, international law assumed international waters were *res nullius*: totally free and belonging to any nation. Nation states which had the technology and capital to support lengthy fishing expeditions were free to exploit the resources of seas adjacent to other States.[7]

This freedom initially existed because territorial boundaries extended no further than the low water mark of the physical terrain. However, by the mid nineteenth century a new rule had evolved: the notion of the three mile territorial sea. This rule had its antecedents in the concept of the canon shot limit, which held that a nation's sovereignty extended as far as it could protect itself — hence the canon shot measure. The existence of a new rule was confirmed by the Anglo-French Fishing Convention of 1839 which recognised that the three mile area of sea beyond the low water mark formed part of the territory of the State, although traditional interests still thrived beyond.

It was not until the end of the 19th century that the emphasis began to shift from the economic merits of maintaining traditional rights to the conservation of stocks by the coastal state.[8] It was part of an overall movement to re-evaluate outmoded colonial values which had condoned the rights of distant water fishing nations to exploit the resources of other states. But international law still lagged behind concern over exhausting resources of the seas.

The process of recognizing adjacent state sovereignty received a major fillip in 1951. In that year Chile declared national sovereignty over its continental shelf and areas adjacent to its coastline to the extent necessary to protect its natural resources up to a 200 nautical mile limit. The scientific basis of the Chilean claim was clearly demonstrable, a fact which was not always present in later claims.[9]

The next significant step towards recognizing coastal state sovereignty beyond the territorial sea occurred at the 1958 United Nations Conference on the Law of the Sea (U.N.C.L.O.S. I) with the introduction of the continental shelf regime. While the Continental Shelf Convention did not provide the coastal state with any rights in the water column above the shelf area it did create the significant precedent of extending state sovereignty beyond contemporary limits.

---

[7] According to Beslky, *op. cit.* 744, the history of the law of the sea has been to strike a balance between a broad interpretation of the freedom of the seas and a narrower interpretation of the notion of adjacent state sovereignty. The result had been to tip the balance almost completely toward the view that freedom of the high seas was immutable and included the 'right' to overfish.

[8] O'Connell, *op. cit.* 524.

[9] The rationalization was the peculiar geography of the area and the vicissitudes of the Humboldt current.

A number of Latin American claims later followed the 1951 Declaration of Santiago, including the Montevideo Declaration of the Law of the Sea in 1970[10] and the Declaration of Santa Domingo on the Patrimonial Sea in 1972. They also had the effect of extending coastal state control over adjacent waters. The Latin American claims marked the beginning of the concern that the delimitation of high seas was at risk of being encroached upon. The United States repeatedly protested against these assertions of jurisdiction.[11]

The next step occurred with the landmark *Fisheries Jurisdiction Case (U.K. v. Iceland)* in 1974.[12] The background to the case was a longstanding dispute between the two countries over the rights of British trawlers to fish in Icelandic waters. In 1951 Iceland unilaterally declared a 12 mile territorial sea which resulted in concerted protest from the United Kingdom. In 1961, through an exchange of notes, the U.K. agreed to recognize Iceland's zone on the condition that the phasing out of Britain's fishing interests be gradual and that notice be given if the zone was to be further extended. Iceland responded in 1971 by extending the zone to 50 miles. The U.K. protested again. Iceland ignored the protests and in 1972 legislated to enforce the new zone. The U.K. challenged the validity of Iceland's legislation in the International Court of Justice.

The result was mixed. The Court found that two trends in international law had emerged since 1958: one, the acceptance of a 12 mile territorial sea and two, the concept that the coastal state has preferential rights in adjacent waters particularly if the coastal state is dependent on these waters, but that these rights were not to be exercised to the exclusion of historic rights. Iceland's 50 mile fishing zone was held to be invalid, but in the course of the judgment the Court recognized the concept of coastal states possessing 'preferential rights' in adjacent waters. The Court's recommendation was that the parties return to the negotiating table to sort out an equitable solution.

The case is significant in terms of the development of the E.E.Z. concept because it was the first time that the Court had recognized that coastal states had the right to exercise some form of control (although only preferential) over the fishing resources of the area adjacent to its territorial sea. It was also significant that this decision was made despite the failure of the second Law of the Sea Conference in 1960 to agree to an extension of the territorial sea to the 12 mile limit.

By the time of the Third Law of the Sea Conference in 1982 most states had declared an adjacent fishery zone, although the form and content of that zone varied greatly between states.

At U.N.C.L.O.S. III a number of different solutions were proposed. The Latin American states favoured seabed and fisheries jurisdiction combined to 200

---

[10] The Montevideo Declaration does list amongst its criteria the 'right to establish the limits of maritime sovereignty and jurisdiction . . .' in its 200 mile zone. The use of the word 'sovereignty' would tend to support O'Connell's statement. In contrast the Santa Domingo Declaration talks in terms only of 'sovereign rights'. In any event both claims were part of a general movement towards the recognition of the coastal state's rights over the resources in the waters superjacent to its continental shelf.

[11] O'Connell, *op. cit.* 557 expresses some reservations about the scientific basis of these later claims and concludes that 'they were in practice indistinguishable from territorial waters claims'.

[12] I.C.J. Reports 1974, 3.

miles; the African states sought to stress the 'economic' nature of the zone; Australia and New Zealand advocated a limited fisheries management zone and the distant water fishing nations (D.W.F.N.s), such as the United States and Japan, argued that as they were best equipped to ensure that the maximum yield was taken, they should be free to continue fishing in the traditional manner.[13] The actual text of the provisions resembles the position put by the developing states. The cornerstone article (article 56) provides that the coastal state in the E.E.Z. has 'sovereign rights for the purpose of exploring and exploiting, conserving and managing the natural resources . . . of the waters superjacent to the sea-bed'.[14]

One final aspect of interest to the history of the E.E.Z. is the innovative method of decision-making used to approve U.N.C.L.O.S. III. No votes were taken on separate provisions, instead the Convention was treated as a 'package' with states compromising on one provision in order to get another one accepted. By using this method of consensus decision-making it was hoped to speed up the ratification process and to ensure the immediate acceptance of U.N.C.L.O.S. III as customary international law. However a number of writers are sceptical of the effectiveness of this process. Harris remarks that 'it must be borne in mind that the consensus favouring the inclusion of a particular rule *as a part of the overall package* may mask opposition to the rule taken by itself.'[15] On the other hand it could be argued that, given the painstaking process of negotiation and the time it took to negotiate (nine years), the third Law of the Sea Convention is the most representative piece of legislation that the international community has produced.

What is certain is that the E.E.Z. provisions of U.N.C.L.O.S. III did reflect state practice. By 1982 a majority of states had already declared an adjacent zone over which they had some rights over the living resources. To this extent the provisions were merely declaratory of existing law, although there are particular aspects of the E.E.Z. regime which arguably represent an extension on customary international law (the provisions with regard to highly migratory species beyond the E.E.Z. for instance[16]). In this respect they are a mixture of what Harris calls 'codification and progressive development'.[17]

Whether or not U.N.C.L.O.S. III does come into force — and at this stage this is arguably doubtful with only 28 ratifications of the 60 required — the E.E.Z. has acquired sufficient status to have become part of international law. What this actually means in terms of rights and obligations of nations will be discussed generally in the following section.[18]

[13] O'Connell, *op. cit.* ch. 15.
[14] A number of other relevant changes were also made in 1982. They included the extension of the territorial sea to 12 miles, increased rights for archipelagic and land-locked states, improved marine pollution control, changes to the continental shelf regime, the development of a regulatory mechanism for deep sea-bed mining, the establishment of an International L.O.S. Tribunal in Hamburg and the introduction of compulsory judicial arbitration and settlement of most disputes.
[15] Harris, D. J., *Cases and Materials on International Law* (3rd ed. 1983) 286.
[16] See *Infra*.
[17] Harris, *op. cit.* 284.
[18] Even if the Convention is not ratified by all signatories, there is an obligation for non-signatories not to defeat or frustrate the purpose of the treaty. Art. 18 of the Vienna Convention on the Law of Treaties states that if a state has signed the treaty or has expressed its consent to be bound by the treaty pending entry into force of the treaty, 'a State is obliged to refrain from acts which would defeat the object and purpose of a treaty.'

2. Rights and Responsibilities in the E.E.Z.

The main article of the E.E.Z. provisions is article 56 which provides that the coastal state has 'sovereign rights for the purpose of exploring and exploiting, conserving and managing the natural resources, whether living or non-living, of the waters superjacent to the seabed and of the sea-bed and its subsoil . . .'

The Convention continues to list the breadth of the zone (article 57), the rights and duties of other states (article 58), and the basis for the resolution of conflicts (article 59). It then further elaborates on the requirements of article 56. Articles 61 and 62 deal with conservation and utilization of the living resources respectively, article 63 looks at the problem of shared stocks and article 64 focuses on highly migratory species. The rights of land-locked and geographically disadvantaged states are also dealt with in articles 69 and 70.

There are a number of points to note about these general articles. First, article 56 accords the coastal state 'sovereign rights' and not sovereignty. This wording was deliberate. It will be recalled that prior to U.N.C.L.O.S. III many states had already declared adjacent zones of control. Juda commented in an article on the compatibility of national claims and the Convention that many states had (possibly unwittingly) claimed 'sovereignty' over their Zones. The Convention therefore sets a limit on coastal states' rights while still according them control sufficient to carry out the duties set out in the provisions. In O'Connell's view, the term 'sovereign rights' underscores the limited authority of the coastal state.[19]

The E.E.Z. is therefore a transitional zone between the freedom of the high seas and the sovereignty of the territorial sea[20] and has been labelled a zone *sui generis* by a number of writers.

The second area of interpretative difficulty occurs in the provisions dealing with the general rights and duties of other states. Paragraph 2 of article 56 says that the coastal state 'shall have due regard to the rights and duties of other states'. It is not at all clear what 'due regard' means in this context. Does it mean that the coastal state *must* take into account the interests of other states or is it just a mechanism to encourage discussion between the parties in the event of a conflict? It is likely to be the latter, given the wide-ranging scope of coastal state authority defined by article 56.

The authority of the coastal state is subject to some limits. The freedoms of navigation and overflight and the laying of submarine cables and pipelines are all recognized by article 58. (Juda's survey of legislation found that less than half explicitly recognized these freedoms.) Other provisions dealing with access do not limit coastal authority as such, but they do place an obligation upon the coastal state at least to consider the allocation of any fishing surplus. These will be discussed later.

---

[19] Although it should also be pointed out that the language of art. 56 is not permissive — the coastal state 'has' certain rights, not 'may claim'. This usage stresses the mandatory element of their control.

[20] Juda, *op. cit.* 2.

The third area of potential difficulty is article 59 dealing with the resolution of conflicts regarding the attribution of rights and jurisdiction in the exclusive economic zone. It says that 'the conflict should be resolved on the basis of equity and in respective importance of the interests involved to the parties as well as to the international community as a whole'. This appears to be one of those provisions to which Harris referred to earlier in which the attempt to achieve consensus has masked opposition below. The provision tries to strike a balance which is commendable but perhaps unrealistic. The interests of the parties may not always be compatible with the interests of the international community, and furthermore it may be that neither of these is necessarily reconcilable with 'equity'.[21]

The significance of these ambiguities is increased by the fact that rights and jurisdictional conflicts are specifically exempted from the generally compulsory dispute resolution procedures of article 297(3).[22] In other words the discretion of coastal states to decide whether or not to allocate their surplus is not open to dispute except according to the limited procedures of article 59.

There is possibly one other area of uncertainty and that is in the relationship between the E.E.Z. and the continental shelf. As already mentioned the rights attached to the sea-bed and subsoil must be exercised in accordance with Part VI dealing with the continental shelf. O'Connell believes that this dual legislative approach hides a basic contradiction in the Convention whereby access to mineral resources is exclusive under Part VI, but access to fishing resources is only preferential under Part V. The meaning of 'exclusive' is thus qualified in this context. O'Connell continues,

There is . . . a fundamental legal instability in this doctrine which can only be productive of grave difficulties of interpretation.[23]

O'Connell does not elaborate on this point. However, one theme of this paper will be to show on the basis of this research and limited primary sources that the coastal state has total discretion with regard to access. It follows that while the zone may not be 'exclusive', it is certainly much more than 'preferential'. 'Preferential' implies that other factors may direct the coastal state decision with regard to access, but as has already been noted with regard to dispute resolution alone, this is not the case. Third parties have only a limited right to challenge any decision. Thus the legal instability which O'Connell rightly perceived may have turned out to be more apparent than real. It appears that while there are certain responsibilities put on coastal states to consider the interests of third parties, once that consideration has been made the coastal state may decide in its own best interests. In practice then there may be little difference between this authority and that exercised by the coastal state with regard to its continental shelf.

---

[21] Does this provision refer to equity as a body of law or does it merely foresee the use of 'equitable' solutions? As the provision is quite explicit it appears that it requires reference to the particular rules of equity.

[22] This article provides that disputes over coastal state authority are not subject to the general dispute resolution procedures. The only exceptions are the arbitrary acts of the coastal state with regard to determining its total catch or the consideration of allocation of its surplus. And even though these exceptions can be arbitrated upon the decisions are not binding.

[23] O'Connell, *op. cit.* 553.

3. *Position of Australia generally*

The countries which benefit most from the campaign led by the developing countries are the developed countries,[24] including Australia, New Zealand and the United States, which have the largest 200 mile zones.

Another factor which underscores the benefits of the E.E.Z. campaign for Australia is that it is not a long distance fishing industry.[25] Therefore Australia had nothing to lose and everything to gain by supporting the proposal at U.N.C.L.O.S. III.

Prior to the Convention in 1978, the Department of Foreign Affairs was called upon to produce a paper assessing the situation and put forward a favoured position. At the time that the 'L.O.S. Australia Maritime Boundaries' Report[26] was produced Australia claimed a 3 mile territorial sea and a 12 mile contiguous zone. The package eventually proposed by Australia called for a zone where the coastal state had exclusive responsibility for the maintenance and conservation of fishing resources, but also had an obligation to allow others to take the surplus on terms and conditions defined by the coastal state. A position very similar to this was finally accepted by the Conference.

A reflection of this position can be seen in the legislation declaring Australia's fishing zone (A.F.Z.). There are no criteria restraining the government's choices with regard to access except that of 'optimum utilization' which, as shall be seen later, is hardly an onerous requirement. In contrast the legislation of Fiji does include the criteria of 'the benefit that other nations provide . . . in terms of research, identification of stocks, and the conservation and management of fishing resources'.[27]

Australia played a kind of mediating role in negotiations at U.N.C.L.O.S. III. This role was a reflection of Australia's political role in the region — as both a close associate of the island states in the Pacific and an ally of the United States. For instance, Australia's compromise proposal on highly migratory species (H.M.S.) — which was eventually rejected — gave the coastal state special rights with regard to H.M.S. but these rights were to be regulated by an international organization.[28]

Another Australian compromise, which was successful, was one concerning the marine environment. It allowed coastal states to unilaterally legislate on pollution controls, as long as that legislation was 'reasonable'.[29] Obviously Australia's interest in the Barrier Reef was relevant to this position.

Having now considered the background to the evolution of the E.E.Z. the general rights envisaged by the Convention and the role played by Australia at the Conference, we are now in a position to review the particular problem of access.

---

[24] *Ibid.* 557.
[25] Phillips, J. C., 'The Economic Resources Zone and the Southwest Pacific' (1982) 16 *International Lawyer* 265, 266.
[26] Greig, D. W., (ed.) *Australia Year Book of International Law* 315 ff.
[27] Marine Spaces Act 1977 (Fiji) s. 11; Phillips, *op. cit.* 269.
[28] Phillips, *op. cit.* 270.
[29] *Ibid.* 272.

B. *FISHING RIGHTS: ACCESS*

1. *General responsibility*

It will be recalled that the coastal state has sovereign rights for the purpose of exploring, exploiting, conserving and managing the natural resources of the waters superjacent to the sea-bed under article 56. It must also have due regard to the interests of other states in determining its rights and duties. Thus the question of access is firstly determinable by the coastal state limited only by regard for other states' interests.

The process of how this determination will actually occur is outlined in the subsequent provisions, which deal with conservation, utilization, shared stocks, highly migratory species, and land-locked and geographically disadvantaged states (L.L.G.D.S.).[30]

The following section will discuss the relevant provisions dealing with access by attempting to answer a number of questions: it will look at the actual wording of the provision, discuss any limits or ambiguities, define any legal problems with the provision, and discuss how these have been interpreted.

2. *Fishing provisions*

(a) *Total allowable catch*

The central feature of the conservation and management requirement is that under article 61 the coastal state shall determine the allowable catch of the living resources in its E.E.Z. It should be done by taking into account the 'best scientific evidence' to ensure that the living resources are not 'endangered by over-exploitation'.

The determination of the allowable catch is a discretionary decision, not to the extent as to whether it can be made, but as to how it can be made. While the Convention goes to great lengths to define the process, it also contains many qualifications which allow the coastal state to make the determination at its own discretion.

The first of these qualifications can be seen in paragraph 2 of article 61 which requires the coastal state to use the 'best scientific evidence available to it'. The problems here are twofold. First, 'best' implies that the coastal state is not required to find the most accurate scientific data but only the best that it can manage. This impression is reinforced by the latter part of the phrase, 'available to it,' which again suggests that the coastal state may not have a positive duty to seek out the data.[31]

---

[30] Burke, W. T., 'The Law of the Sea Conventions Provisions on Conditions of Access to Fisheries Subject to National Jurisdiction' (1984) 63 *Oregon Law Review* 73, 77 outlines this process as comprising five stages: a) determining the total allowable catch b) calculating the restrictions on harvesting capacity c) making a decision as to how much the coastal state can harvest d) deciding what other nations may have access to harvesting and on what terms and e) negotiating arrangements on the basis of these decisions. This is a convenient structure in which to consider the issues, but it is by no means conclusive.

[31] However, the lack of compulsion in this article is to a large extent alleviated by the requirement in para. 5 to contribute and exchange any relevant information through international organizations.

The maintenance or restoration of the maximum sustainable yield (M.S.Y.) is also open to interpretation. The Convention provides that this is to be ascertained 'as qualified by relevant environmental and economic factors' and then goes on to list a number of factors. The inclusion of the broad delineations 'environmental and economic' suggest that the coastal state may use any number of references to qualify its determination of the M.S.Y. This interpretation is supported by the generous range of factors which are listed subsequently. They are 'the economic needs of coastal fishing communities and special requirements of developing States, and taking into account fishing patterns, the interdependence of stocks'. Thus if the particular fishing community is entirely dependent on fishing for its livelihood, the coastal state may adjust its M.S.Y. accordingly. The implication which can be drawn from the language of the treaty is therefore significant — that M.S.Y. is, to an extent, a discretionary measure.[32]

(b) Optimum Utilization

Article 62 forms the basis of the access decision following on from the determination in article 61. It provides that the coastal state should 'promote the objective of optimum utilization'. The coastal state should firstly determine its own harvesting capacity. Where its capacity does not exceed the allowable catch it should give other states access to its surplus, having regard to the land-locked and developing states of articles 69 and 70 and certain other criteria of assessment in paragraph 4.

The wording of the first paragraph again indicates the discretionary nature of the obligation on coastal states. It is required only to 'promote' the 'objective' of optimum utilization; there is no compulsion upon the coastal state to achieve a quantifiable standard — this is reflected in the use of the word 'optimum' rather than 'maximum'.

(c) Harvesting capacity

The concept of harvesting capacity is critical to the equation and yet is also loosely defined. The decision to allocate to other nations is taken by subtracting the coastal states' harvesting capacity from the allowable catch (article 62(2)). Yet if, as Burke notes, the harvesting capacity is dependent on the allowable catch, and, this can be decided by considering whether the coastal states' interests are best served by determining the allowable catch at a level equal to or less than its harvesting capacity, the requirement in article 62(2) places no 'meaningful obligation'[33] upon the coastal states. In practice this will mean that the coastal

---

[32] The effects on associated and dependent species by harvesting further broadens the equation the coastal state must make in order to determine the allowable catch. This widening of responsibility is one which is welcomed by some writers (e.g. Belsky, op. cit.), but will bring with it its own attendant problems. It means that the coastal state must also now have the capacity to research the effects of its actions on the eco-system of which it is a part. This facility will not be available to many of the smaller developing states and is therefore probably not an enforceable obligation.

[33] Burke, op. cit. 90.

state has the authority to make a choice with regard to harvesting capacity that suits its own best interests.[34]

(d) *Dispute settlement*

Under article 297, there is no obligation upon the coastal state to submit to compulsory dispute settlement procedures on an issue arising out of the exercise of its sovereign rights to fisheries. Thus a coastal state's refusal to set an allowable catch or harvesting capacity, which would result in the allocation of its surplus, cannot be challenged. Only if the decision is 'arbitrary' can it be pursued through compulsory 'conciliation', but even this is not binding. Therefore the exclusion of this factor from the dispute procedure leads to the conclusion that 'C.L.O.S. contains virtually no restriction on coastal state authority to forbid access to foreign fishing'.[35]

(e) *Access*

The actual determination of access is to be made according to the last 3 paragraphs of article 62(2). On the basis of the above mentioned calculation the surplus will be allocated, by agreement, paying due regard to the interests of L.L.G.D.S., and taking into account certain other criteria.

This is not to say that the coastal state will necessarily refuse foreign fishing powers the right of access to their surplus. The opposite is often true. Most coastal states will be more than willing to facilitate access to their Zones because they can charge considerable fees for this right. (There is no restriction on licensing fees in article 62(4)(a)). The economic gains will therefore usually mean that the coastal state will allocate. But under the Convention the terms and conditions of that access are now in the sphere of coastal state authority. This aspect is what is causing the most practical problems, because it means that any access accorded must be paid for on terms which are to the satisfaction of the coastal state.

(f) *Land-locked and geographically disadvantaged states*

Some of the constraints on coastal state authority to allocate its surplus are listed in articles 69 and 70 which deal with the rights of land-locked and geographically disadvantaged states respectively. The provisions give the L.L.G.D.S. the right to participate in an 'appropriate part of the surplus' on an 'equitable basis'. While this does give them some right of access, it is limited. Again the words 'appropriate' and 'equitable' imply that the discretion lies with the coastal state making the determination.

There are also limits on the rights of L.L.G.D.S. The right to participate must 'take into account the relevant economic and geographical circumstances of all

---

[34] One other minor problem with the concept of harvesting capacity being determinative is the fact that the coastal state could feasibly increase its own harvesting capacity by authorizing foreign vessels to fish under its flag. This would preclude other states legitimately exercising their rights to access under the Convention.

[35] Burke, *op. cit.* 91.

the states concerned' and it must be 'in conformity with the . . . provisions of article 61 and 62'. This means that the coastal state's 'circumstances' may override the other state's claim.

Furthermore the obligation is limited to one merely of 'co-operation' to achieve an 'equitable arrangement' (articles 69(3) and 70(4)). It appears that there is a duty upon the coastal state, but the use of these terms indicates that it is not an onerous one.[36] Once the coastal state has given consideration to its duty by engaging in negotiations with the L.L.G.D.S. its duty will be fulfilled.[37]

Finally, it should be noted here that developed L.L.G.D.S. are restricted to participating in the surplus of another developed state.

Overall, the provisions of articles 69 and 70 are a constraint on coastal state discretion as to access, but this constraint is limited. The author agrees with Burke's view that these articles 'give the L.L.G.D.S or developing L.L.G.D.S. a claim to secure access to the surplus. However, realization of this claim requires negotiating with the coastal state, each bilateral, subregional, and regional agreement, on terms and conditions satisfactory to the coastal state.'[38] In this respect the duty upon the coastal state with regard to L.L.G.D.S. is not significantly different to its duty to other states.

(g) *Highly migratory species*

Highly migratory species are singled out by the Convention because they pose a particular problem of conservation and management. The issue concerns who has responsibility for stocks which do not stay within the same area during their lifetime. The stock include tuna, which has presented the most problems for the Pacific region. Article 61 places an obligation on all states whose nationals fish H.M.S. to co-operate to ensure that both conservation and optimum utilization of the species occurs.

There is considerable disagreement as to the meaning of this article. Does it override the earlier provisions which give coastal states exclusive authority, or is it an additional obligation to co-operate which does not take away from their sovereign rights under article 56? The United States believes that the inclusion of a separate article means that H.M.S. do not come under general coastal state authority and has legislated to give effect to this view. The Fishery Conservation and Management Act of 1976[39] proclaims a fishing zone of 200 miles which does not include jurisdiction over tuna and provides that the U.S. will embargo any state which prevents U.S. vessels fishing for H.M.S. in their zone. This provision was applied when the Solomon Islands confiscated the U.S. tuna boat, the Jeanette Diana, in 1984. This area of the Convention is the main obstacle to U.S. acceptance of the E.E.Z. as outlined in U.N.C.L.O.S. III.[40]

---

[36] Burke, *op. cit.* 95-101 discusses at length what constitutes co-operation in this context and what consequences would flow from a failure to co-operate.

[37] Additionally, a breakdown in communication will not constitute a failure to co-operate to the extent that the coastal state has not fulfilled its duty.

[38] Burke, *op. cit.* 100.

[39] Pub. Law 94-265, 94th Cong., ss 101, 102, 103, 201 (c).

[40] The U.S. has been unwilling to recognize the E.E.Z. in other contexts. For instance, when negotiating the *South Pacific Regional Environmental Treaty*, the U.S. refused to discuss dumping restrictions unless the area was defined as a general region rather than the E.E.Z.s of coastal states.

The U.S. position is rejected by most writers on the subject and all other D.W.F.N.s. Australia has stated that the U.S. juridical position is 'inconsistent with international law'.[41] There is nothing in the wording of the article which suggests paramountcy over the earlier provisions.

It would also be against the intention of the Convention to vary coastal state general sovereignty with regard to H.M.S. when the aim was to give coastal state authority over all stocks within its E.E.Z. All this provision does is to require the coastal state to exercise this control by means of a particular co-operative process established in article 64.[42]

The only area of potential difficulty is whether or not the coastal state's authority over H.M.S. extends beyond the E.E.Z. If it does then it represents a significant advance in customary international law in broadening coastal state control into the high seas. It appears that in order to discharge its obligation to conserve and manage these stock, the coastal state would have to exercise its authority within the high seas beyond the E.E.Z.

(h) *Fishing in the high seas*

Although article 64 places an obligation upon D.W.F.N.s to consider the effects on coastal states of H.M.S. fishing in the high seas, the coastal states do not possess any enforcement authority beyond the limits of the E.E.Z. Likewise there is no authority to take into account high seas stocks in determining the total allowable catch.

On the other hand if, as Belsky argues, the E.E.Z. regime provides an opportunity for states to participate in total eco-system management, high seas stocks may be taken into account. The requirement in article 61(4) to take account of the effects of fishing on associated or dependent species strengthens Belsky's argument.

3. *Access assessed*

A detailed examination of the provisions relating to access therefore reveals that the decision to allocate surplus to third parties rests almost entirely within the domain of coastal state authority. This is because the determinative factors which go toward affecting the decision are all within the control of the coastal state. Allowable catch, harvesting capacity and optimum utilization can all be determined according to the best interests of the coastal state. Subsequent criteria to be used to decide which state can have access are also within coastal control. Even states which are singled out for special consideration, like the L.L.G.D.S, only establish a claim to secure access, not a right to do so. Likewise, stock such as H.M.S., although accorded particular notice, still come within the general authority of the coastal state outlined in the major articles.

---

41 Australian Foreign Affairs Record, Vol. 56, Sept. 1985, 824.
42 The argument against the U.S. position is further reinforced by the repetition of the words 'conservation' and 'optimum utilization', concepts which are only explicable by reference back to the general provisions of arts 61 and 62. However, given the present inability of the world community in total to agree on the limited regime within the E.E.Z., it is unlikely that enforcement of similar rights will occur beyond the Zone.

The latter section of this part of the paper will illustrate these conclusions by reference to documentary material in legislation and agreements and by reports of state practice. It will also show that while coastal state authority may be total in theory, in practice it is very rarely exercised to completely exclude all foreign fishing. O'Connell's concern that the Convention marks the 'triumph of individualism over collectivism'[43] is unfounded in this respect. Likewise is Juda's suspicion of the 'creeping jurisdiction' of the E.E.Z.[44] In practice, access is usually accorded for foreign fishing vessels. As Burke comments,

> CLOS contains virtually no restriction on coastal state authority to forbid access to foreign fishing. For practical legal purposes, the Convention provides no effective remedy even for arbitrary denials of access . . . However, it must also be emphasized that *most coastal States will exercise their discretion to find that a surplus exists and that some foreign access is desirable.*[45]

However, what the Convention does is to establish a list of criteria and a process on which to make the judgment as to who is entitled to access. In this way it may provide ready-made reasons for refusing access to states. And in turn this authority may enable states to give access to whichever foreign state is prepared to pay the most for that right. For example, the Soviet Union recently acquired fishing rights to the E.E.Z. of Kiribati to the exclusion of the United States, which had traditionally fished the area. The basis of this decision was purely economic.[46] The United States refused to pay the $2.4 million which Kiribati demanded as the value of its stocks. This example accords with Burke's prediction that a 'decision to maximise revenue from a surplus resource is a reasonable one'.[47] He continues that 'all conceivable interests that might bear on fisheries, including political, military, educational, ecological, cultural, religious or ideological interests'[48] may be considered in making this determination. The discretion of the coastal state is virtually unlimited.

4. *Evolution of customary international law*

There are two questions to be answered: one, has customary international law evolved in this area, and two, which particular aspects have evolved?

First, it is clear that while U.N.C.L.O.S. III as a whole was a mixture of what Harris calls 'progressive development' and 'codification',[49] the provisions relating to the E.E.Z. were, in general, merely codifying existing international law. Prior to the Convention, over 95 countries had already claimed management jurisdiction over adjacent Zones.

Furthermore, the *Fisheries Jurisdiction* case (*U.K. v. Iceland*)[50] indicated that customary international law had evolved at least to the point of recognizing preferential rights for coastal states in adjacent waters. This position has been confirmed by the Mexican Foreign Minister Mr Castenada in an address to the

---

[43] O'Connell, *op. cit.* 552.
[44] Juda, *op. cit.*
[45] Burke, *op. cit.* 91. Author's italics.
[46] The Soviet fleet is not permitted to operate within the territorial waters, nor does it have port privileges in Kiribati. Doulman, *op. cit.* 6.
[47] Burke, *op. cit.* 103.
[48] *Ibid.*
[49] Harris, *op. cit.* 284.
[50] I.C.J. Reports 1974, 3.

U.N. General Assembly, where he stated that customary international law had evolved to the point that 'failure of some countries to sign [the Convention] . . . does not mean, that the world can go back to . . . the 1958 Geneva Convention as if nothing has happened'.[51]

The particular aspects of the law of the sea which have evolved are less easy to identify. Certainly there is general acceptance of the concept of coastal state authority within a zone. It is also clear that, despite the United State's assertion to the contrary, most writers believe that coastal state authority extends to H.M.S., at least when those stock are within the E.E.Z., and possibly even when they are beyond in the high seas. It has to be pointed out that the United States accepts this position with regard to all other H.M.S. except tuna. One writer comments that:

> The purpose of maintaining the U.S. position on jurisdiction is to give the tuna industry some leverage in negotiations . . . there is no matter of principle at stake . . . because the United States itself also claims jurisdiction over HMS, [in its own Zone] only for somewhat different species which have, nonetheless, precisely the same management needs.[52]

Thus the United States' aim to shape evolving customary international law has not succeeded and H.M.S. are included within the stock over which the coastal state has authority.

However, one area in the Convention which does represent an advance on customary international law regards H.M.S. outside the E.E.Z. In this respect it does appear that the traditional freedom of high seas fishing has been altered to the extent that this right is now subject to a limited form of coastal state control.

The role of state practice in assessing the evolution of customary international law cannot be underestimated. The doctrine of the E.E.Z. has no theoretical antecedents, unlike that of the continental shelf which is based on the concept of local authority over the terrain.[53] The status of the E.E.Z. therefore depends greatly for its viability upon state practice.

5. *State practice*

(a) *Incorporation and interpretation of E.E.Z. provisions in agreements in the South West Pacific region.*

Having considered the effects of the provisions of the Convention in theory, it is now necessary to look at the practical result of their incorporation in agreements relevant to Australia.

First, to return to the question of access, what have been the preconditions for making such agreements? As pointed out earlier, the criteria for assessing access is extremely broad and economic considerations may be the determining factor. For example, the President of Kiribati, Ieremia Tabai, stated that the decision to allow the Soviet Union to fish in Kiribati's E.E.Z. was 'purely economic'.[54] He

---

[51] Lee, R. S., 'The New Law of the Sea and the Pacific Basin' (1983) 12 *Ocean Development and International Law Journal* 247, 253.

[52] Burke, W. T., 'Highly Migratory Species in the New Law of the Sea' (1984)14 *Ocean Development and International Law* 273, 307.

[53] O'Connell, *op. cit.* 570.

[54] *Age* (Melbourne) 24 July 1985.

also said that the Kiribati government would only deal with the United States if it was prepared to pay a 'fair price'.[55] Both these comments illustrate the discretion of the coastal state under article 62.

Many of the provisions of the Convention are embodied in the agreements between South Pacific States to establish the South Pacific Forum Fisheries Agency,(S.P.F.F.A.) and in the arrangements that agency has subsequently negotiated. The S.P.F.F.A. was set up in 1979. Its functions include the harmonization of fishing policies, encouragement of co-operation with D.W.F.N.s, co-operation with regard to surveillance and enforcement, and co-operation in the determination of access. The agency was in existence before the 1982 Convention and has had to adjust its functions since then.[56]

It acts as a negotiating conduit for discussions between coastal states and D.W.F.N.s. At present it is presiding over discussions to establish a multilateral treaty between the United States and Pacific nations on the question of access to tuna stocks in the Pacific.[56a] The outcome of these negotiations is not yet known, and yet is extremely important to the evolution of future practice and consequent custom in the Pacific. According to Doulman, a research fellow with the Pacific Islands Development Program, the United States is still unwilling to pay the S.P.F.F.A.'s licensing fee.[57] It should be noted that the reference to the United States actually refers to the American Tunaboat Association, not the U.S. government, although generally their position has been the same.

Closer to home, Australia has negotiated a number of agreements pursuant to its legislation. The statements of Australian government officials and the language of various agreements aim to implement the Convention's objectives of conservation and management of the natural resources of the region. One such agreement is the Japan/Australia Fisheries Agreement, which is renewed annually through a subsidiary agreement. It ensures the 'close co-operation with regard to the conservation and optimum utilization' of the living resources within Australia's fishing zone.

The criteria which Australia uses to determine access under this agreement is, more often than not, economic. Two illustrations follow. The first can be seen in a statement to the Parliament by Senator Grimes in October 1984. He said:

> . . . in response to earlier concerns by game fishing interests, Japanese longliners have already been excluded from areas off the east coast where direct competition with Australian fishermen was evident.[58]

In September of the same year the Minister for Primary Industry, Mr John Kerin, announced a new agreement with Korea for squid jigging within the A.F.Z. He said that Korean vessels would 'not be permitted to fish in any areas where

---

[55] *Age* (Melbourne) 11 April 1986.

[56] Carroz comments that this 'Institutional adjustment' has not been given sufficient consideration. He believes that now that conservation and management regimes are enforceable under the Convention, the role of institutions have, to an extent, been superseded, although in the case of the S.P.F.F.A. this is not the case. See Carroz, J. E., 'Institutional Aspects of Fishery Management Under the New Regime of Oceans' (1984)21 *San Diego Law Review* 513.

[56a] See postscript.

[57] Doulman, *op. cit.* 5. See p. 9 for the American Tunaboat Association's 'special case'.

[58] *Australian Foreign Affairs Record*, Vol. 55, Oct. 1984, No. 10, 1117.

interference with Australian fishermen would occur'.[59] Both these statements would come under article 62(3) which allows 'the significance of the living resources of the area to the economy of the coastal State concerned' to be taken into account in granting access.

However, as indicated earlier, 'other national interests' (article 62(3)) is extremely broad, and, in the case of Australia, has included the refusal of foreign states to co-operate with local catch limits. The Minister for Primary Industry was prepared to ban access when stocks were threatened. In October 1984 he stated that:

> . . . under a new agreement Japan tuna vessels would not be able to operate in the A.F.Z. where they could take Southern Bluefin Tuna (S.B.T.) because they would not accept controls Australia put on its own fishermen.[60]

However, the fact that broad discretion has been given to the coastal state and a certain decision has been made excluding another state from participating in its surplus, does not mean that the decision cannot be reviewed. Once the Japanese industry was prepared to limit its global catch, new tuna agreements were negotiated.[61] The role of the Convention in this example was to provide the Australian government with the authority necessary to enforce certain obligations on a foreign fishing power in order to conserve its depleted stock.

Thus the wording of the various agreements is similar to that in the Convention. It repeats the requirements of conservation, optimum utilization, allowable catch and the determination of allocation of surplus. Additionally, the Pacific agreements also specify the management of tuna stocks pursuant to article 64 of the Convention.

(b) Incorporation of the E.E.Z provisions in Domestic Legislation

The incorporation of the E.E.Z. objectives in legislation does not always reflect the language of the Convention. Juda found that much domestic legislation does not mention optimum utilization or the right of third party access to the Zones.[62]

Even when domestic legislation does refer to foreign access, only a small number provide any explicit indicia for determining such access.[63] Australia leaves the decision entirely up to governmental discretion. New Zealand refers to the benefits given to the industry by the foreign fishing state in terms of the identification of stocks.

(c) The Pacific region compared with Australia

The former Minister for Foreign Affairs, Mr Andrew Peacock, distinguished Australia's Zone in October 1979 as a fishing zone. While there is little difference in practical effect, it is worth noting why this distinction was made as it may also explain why Australia has had little of the difficulties experienced by other developed nations.

---

[59] *Australian Foreign Affairs Record* Vol. 55, Sept. 1984, 1006.
[60] *Australian Foreign Affairs Record* Vol. 55, No. 10, Oct. 1984., 1132.
[61] *Australian Foreign Affairs Record* Vol. 55, No. 9, Sept. 1984, 1006.
[62] Juda, *op. cit.* 12ff, 23.
[63] *Ibid.*

First, as pointed out, earlier, Australia has made enormous gains by proclaiming a Zone, whether it be fishing or economic, in accordance with the Convention. The sea area it now controls greatly outstrips its former area of authority (12 miles).

Secondly, Australia does not engage in distant water fishing so that its interests could not be jeopardized by the proclamation of such a Zone.

Thirdly, Australia only possesses minimal stocks in any event and this means that it is economically unfeasible for many fishing nations to finance operations in Australian waters. The few countries which do fish within these waters often fish for stocks which do not form part of the Australian fishing industry anyway — stocks such as squid, which the Japanese require. Therefore, the history of fishing agreements between Australia and foreign fishing nations has generally been amicable. The preponderance of the phrase 'joint venture' reflects this co-operation. There is, then, no need for Australia to extend its authority beyond that provided by a fishing Zone. The economic needs of the Australian community are not dependent upon the fishing industry, unlike a country like Fiji which relies on fishing for 8% of its export income.[64]

CONCLUSIONS: STATUS OF THE E.E.Z. AND IMPLICATIONS FOR FOREIGN FISHING AND SECURITY IN THE PACIFIC

The concept of the E.E.Z. is crucial to the conservation and management of the living resources of the ocean given that over three-quarters of the world's fishing stocks are included within E.E.Z.s.

Nowhere is this more apparent than in the Pacific region. There are very few enclaves between Zones. This factor alone led the Australian Ambassador to the U.S., Mr F. Rawdon Dalrymple, to comment that the map of the South Pacific had undergone a 'striking transformation . . . that was going to change . . . [the South Pacific's] political importance and its strategic importance'.[65]

Fishing is crucial to the industry of the South West Pacific, forming a significant part of the G.D.P. of many island economies. Additionally, other benefits accrue to the coastal state under the E.E.Z. proclamation, inlcuding research and marine environment control.[66]

The concept is now part of customary international law. The most significant element of the doctrine is that coastal states can exercise their discretionary control in determining whether or not to grant access to third parties who wish to fish within the E. E. Z. This has led to some writers claiming that there are dangers associated with it.

This paper has argued that while determination of access is entirely discretionary, there are no necessary dangers attached to this authority. Burkes' view is correct when he argues that the economic benefits to be gained from granting access will usually result in access being granted.[67] Most small coastal states do not possess the financial or technical capacity to harvest the allowable catch and

---

[64] *Fiji Today 1984-5* Department of Information Publication, Fiji, 1985, 21.
[65] *Australian Foreign Affairs Record*, Vol. 56, Sept. 1985, 818.
[66] Phillips, *op. cit.* 278.
[67] Burke, *op. cit.*

are only too willing to accommodate the needs of foreign fishing powers. In the case of Australia, it is illustrated by a statement of Senator Grimes in the Parliament in October 1984. He said:

> . . . in the absence of clear evidence that our marlin industry or resource is being significantly affected, the imposition of a total ban on the taking of marlin . . . would undoubtedly bring a strong reaction from Japan, *especially in view of our international obligations to permit foreign vessel access to those resources of our Zone which are excess to our harvesting capacity.*[68]

Clearly the decision to refuse access will not be taken lightly.

It may be that there is another factor underlying the comments of writers such as O'Connell and Juda. This is the fear that 'unfriendly' countries may now get access to fishing resources which were traditionally refused to them. This economic access, it is thought, will provide some sort of leverage for these countries, notably the Soviet Union, to infiltrate other areas of the coastal states' domestic jurisdiction. The link between economic structural changes and security is perceived as a potential concern. Dr Stuart Harris, Secretary of the Department of Foreign Affairs, in an address to the National Defence University Symposium in February 1986 remarked that Pacific States

> . . . are inevitably open to exploitation or infiltration from outside and concern has been expressed both about the U. S. industry's exploitation of tuna and the Soviet moves with Kiribati and other South Pacific nations.[69]

It appears from this statement that while Australian officials share some concerns about the ramifications of the E.E.Z. in the Pacific, they are taking a fairly evenhanded approach to the problem. They clearly believe that the problem does not lie with the doctrine itself, as spelled out in the Convention, but with its erroneous interpretation. The Australian Ambassador to the U.S., in a strongly worded speech to the Asian Society in 1985, urged the U.S. to reverse its policy of placing embargoes on countries which confiscate U.S. vessels fishing without licences for H.M.S. within their Zones. These actions threaten the island economies of small states and force them to negotiate with the Soviet Union. He continued,

> if it is not satisfactorily resolved and resolved soon to the satisfaction of the South Pacific countries then I think it too will constitute in effect a gratuitous contribution towards making a hospitable climate for the Soviet Union, Libya, Cuba and others who would seek to radicalise and change the present political alignment of the region.[70]

This element has been further emphasized by the attitude of the Australian press.

Whatever the cause of the suspicion of the E.E.Z. doctrine it is now apparent that it forms part of international law and will serve as a mechanism to control the resources of the marine environment. It may also, as Belsky suggests, translate 'moral support' for the management of the eco-system into legal practice. At a time when the global environment is threatened by unregulated exploitation, the concept of the E.E.Z. is unparalleled in international law. The 'revolution' has already begun.

---

[68] *Australian Foreign Affairs Record* Vol. 55, Oct. 1984, 1117. Author's italics.
[69] *Australian Foreign Affairs Record* Vol. 57, Feb. 1986, 53.
[70] *Australian Foreign Affairs Record* Vol. 56, Sept. 1985, 818.

Postscript

On 1 April 1987, after exhaustive negotiations between the United States and the South Pacific Forum Fisheries Agency, an agreement was reached on fishing rights in the South Pacific region. Under the new arrangements the United States agreed to pay to the S.P.F.F.A. $U.S.10 million a year for 5 years for the right to seek licences within the region. A further $U.S.2 million is payable for the licences themselves and provision has also been made for the enforcement of the licences.

Rethinking Self-Determination: A Critical Analysis of Current International Law Theories

Deborah Z Cass

Deborah Z Cass, 'Rethinking Self-Determination: A Critical Analysis of Current International Law Theories' (1992) 18 *Syracuse Journal of International Law and Commerce* 21, 21–40 <https://surface.syr.edu/jilc/vol18/iss1/4/>.

RE-THINKING SELF-DETERMINATION: A CRITICAL ANALYSIS OF CURRENT INTERNATIONAL LAW THEORIES

Deborah Z. Cass*

TABLE OF CONTENTS

I. Introduction... 21
II. Self-Determination - A Brief History................... 23
   A. What is Self-Determination? 23
   B. History and Status 24
III. Scope and Content of the Concept 29
   A. The "Conventional" View........................... 29
   B. The "Controversial" View.......................... 30
   C. Analysis: Which Approach to Self-Determination is
      Appropriate?...................................... 31
      1. State Practice and Opinio Juris 31
      2. Textual Issues.................................. 36
      3. Jurisprudential Issues 37
   D. Issues for the Future 38
IV. Conclusion 40

I. INTRODUCTION

The year 1991 marked the thirtieth anniversary of the United Nations Declaration on the Granting of Independence to Colonial Countries and Peoples,[1] and the beginning of the Decade for the Eradication of Colonialism. It was also the year in which the fragmentation of the Soviet Union became irreversible. And it was the year in which independence movements worldwide, in Croatia, Slovenia, Eritrea and East Timor, accelerated promotion of their claims. The catalyst for all these developments is the principle of self-determination. One could expect therefore that a principle so readily utilized in the international arena would possess a definite meaning. This is not the case. Current international law theory regarding self-determi-

* L.L.B with Honors Melbourne University; Senior Tutor in Law, Melbourne University; and Research Fellow, Centre for Comparative Constitutional Studies Melbourne University; formerly Research Officer to Counsel Assisting the Nauru Commission of Inquiry. An earlier version of this paper was delivered in a joint seminar with Mr. Gerry Simpson at Melbourne University in September 1991. The author gratefully acknowledges the advice and assistance of Dr. Hilary Charlesworth.
1. G.A. Res. 1514, U.N. GAOR, 15th Sess., Supp. No. 16, at 66, U.N. Doc. A/L323 (1960).

nation is in a state of uncertainty and confusion. It is inconsistent within itself, and it does not accord with state practice.

The aim of this paper is to demonstrate the need to re-think the principle of self-determination by establishing that an undesirable level of uncertainty exists regarding the usage of the term, and to show that a major cause of the confusion is due to the inadequacy of conventional approaches. These objectives will be achieved by identifying and evaluating conflicting approaches toward the meaning of self-determination, proposing an explanation for why the debate has evolved and suggesting which approach best serves the needs of the international community.

Before analyzing the history of self-determination and how it evolved to encompass the current view, it is important to consider why it has become necessary to re-evaluate the term. As the paper will focus on interpretations of what constitutes self-determination, it is worth commenting at the outset that interpreting words, whether legal or not, is by its nature an imprecise process. One method of analyzing inconsistencies of meaning which arise in legal interpretation was proposed by Professor H.L.A. Hart.[2] Hart developed the distinction between the "core" meaning of a legal concept, and its "penumbra of uncertainty." Self-determination is a term which has a wide penumbra of uncertainty. A number of inconsistent meanings have been ascribed to the term.

The reason this confusion is critical is that it promotes an unstable international environment by failing to provide a consistent measure upon which groups can rely. In this volatile period so ubiquitous a term should possess greater certainty than it presently does. Furthermore, what was once a nice academic debate threatens to jeopardize the potential the concept has for aiding international law dispute resolution. In other words, the functional utility of the term is being undercut by a confusion in the theory. International law is becoming hamstrung by its own limitations. When President Bush hesitates before recognizing as legitimate a call to independence by the people of Lithuania, (a claim framed initially as a right to self-determination), his equivocation is based on the confusions and shortcomings of international law theory. The point has been reached where, borrowing from Hart, the "penumbra of uncertainty" surrounding the con-

---

2. The distinction between a 'core of settled meaning' and a 'penumbra of cases' was referred to in H.L.A. Hart, *Separation of Law and Morals*, 71 HARV. L. REV. 593, 607 (1958), and subsequently developed in H.L.A. HART, THE CONCEPT OF LAW 129 - 50 (1st ed. 1961).

cept of self-determination is so pronounced that it obscures the term's "core of settled meaning."

This problem assumes greater importance in the light of the increased reliance on the concept by indigenous peoples and ethnic minorities in a variety of unsettled political situations. The Commonwealth of Independent States, bargaining over nuclear stockpiles and struggling to suppress the dormant nationalist fervor of approximately 140 minority groups, probably represents the worst danger. The threat of the breakup of the Canadian federal system presents another. The civil war in Yugoslavia yet another.

It will be argued here that conventional theoretical approaches to self-determination are inadequate insofar as they provide neither a description of, nor a prescription for, the behavior of states in international relations. At a time when an increasing number of claims are being made by indigenous peoples and ethnic minorities, not enclosed within the parameter of classical, colonial boundaries, the disjunction between theory and practice becomes critical.

It is not within the scope of this paper to provide a complete history of self-determination or a complete discussion of its status, which have been comprehensively covered elsewhere.[3] The following two sections will, however, define self-determination in general terms and provide a brief overview of the concept's status. Part III will discuss the scope and content of self-determination. Specifically, the conventional and controversial views of its scope will be set out. State practices, opinio juris and textual and jurisprudential issues will be examined to determine which view appropriately defines self-determination. This paper concludes with a proposal to avoid the uncertainty created by the dissonance between state practice and the conventional view of self-determination.

II.   SELF-DETERMINATION - A BRIEF HISTORY

A.   What Is Self-Determination?

President Woodrow Wilson, introducing the concept to the League of Nations in 1919, described self-determination as "the right of every people to choose the sovereign under which they live, to be free of alien masters, and not to be handed about from sovereign to

---

3. *See, e.g.*, MICHLA POMERANCE, SELF-DETERMINATION IN LAW AND PRACTICE (1982); A. RIGO-SUREDA, THE EVOLUTION OF THE RIGHT OF SELF-DETERMINATION: A STUDY OF UNITED NATIONS PRACTICE (1973); U. UMOZURIKE, SELF-DETERMINATION IN INTERNATIONAL LAW (1972).

sovereign as if they were property."[4]

Subsequently, other writers described self-determination as a right which arises when there is "international recognition of the rights of the inhabitants of a colony to choose freely their independence or association with another state"[5] or when there is a "collective right of a people sharing similar objective characteristics to freely determine their own form of government while further developing their economic, social and cultural status."[6]

The definition was further elaborated regarding the manner in which the right could be implemented. The right to self-determination can be exercised in one of three ways - integration, free association or independence - but whichever method is chosen, it is clear that it is the *process* itself which is the "essential feature."[7]

According to Judge Dillard, in a separate opinion in the *Western Sahara Case*, "It is for people to determine the destiny of the territory and not the territory the destiny of the people."[8] It will be demonstrated therefore that self-determination encapsulates three basic ideas: 1) there has to be a group; 2) that group has to be concerned about its political status; and 3) that group must be able to exercise its own *choice* with regard to its political future.

Having reduced the concept for present purposes to these three elements the next step is to identify areas of inconsistency in relation to the term. Uncertainty exists at two levels. First, there is uncertainty surrounding the status of the concept of self-determination at international law. Is it a principle of politics, a tool of secessionist rhetoric, or has self-determination crystallized into a norm of international law? The second issue relates to the question of how to define the group. To whom does a right of self-determination apply? Does it apply only to groups within colonial boundaries, or all minorities however encased? In other words, what exactly is the scope of the term? The aim of this paper is to concentrate on the latter problem.

B. History and Status

Self-determination, as a principle of international law, originated

---

4. *Quoted in* Eric M. Amberg, *Self-Determination in Hong Kong: A New Challenge to an Old Doctrine*, 22 SAN DIEGO L. REV. 839, 842 (1985).

5. *Id.* at 840 (quoting Professor Louis Henkin).

6. John A. Collins, *Self Determination in International Law: The Palestinians*, 12 CASE W. RES. J. INT'L L. 137, 138 (1980).

7. Western Sahara Case, 1975 I.C.J. 12, para. 57 (Oct. 16).

8. *Id.* at 114 (separate opinion of Judge Dillard).

following World War I with the development of the mandate[9] system.[10] According to Quincy Wright, the eventual aim of the mandate system was to lead the territory under control to self-determination.[11] In the following two decades, the acceptance of the principle of self-determination was reflected by, inter alia, its incorporation into the Soviet Constitution[12] and, most significantly, into article 1 of the Charter of the United Nations.[13]

In subsequent years, the United Nations' largest representative body, the General Assembly, regularly invoked the concept in a series of resolutions, the most important of which were passed in 1960[14] and 1970.[15] With the emergence of the Group of 77 during the mid-seventies, the concept of self-determination was elevated further on the agenda of the United Nations.[16]

> Seeking to secure permanent sovereignty over their natural wealth and resources in a new international economic order, the third world countries emphasized self-determination, anti-colonialism, sovereign equality, non-intervention, and the invalidity of unequal treaties in their international affairs.[17]

---

9. The mandate derived from Roman law notions under which property of certain peoples unable to manage their own affairs was placed under the control of a guardian. Sovereignty over the property remained with the ward. Grotius describes this situation as a separation between "lordship" and "ownership." *See* 2 HUGO GROTIUS, ON THE LAW OF WAR AND PEACE, Book I, 207.

10. The mandate system was devised by the League of Nations after the first World War, as a humanitarian method of administering former colonies of the defeated powers. In 1947, most colonies still under mandate were transferred to U.N. control as trust territories. Collins notes a number of other factors which led to the emergence of the mandate concept including: 19th century nationalism; the American and French revolutions; World War I; and the formation of the League of Nations. *See* Collins, *supra* note 6, at 138 - 40.

11. QUINCY WRIGHT, MANDATES UNDER THE LEAGUE OF NATIONS 231 (1930).

12. Article 29 of the Constitution of the Union of Soviet Socialist Republics, adopted in 1917, stated that the USSR's relations with other states were based on, inter alia, "the equal rights of peoples and their right to decide their own destiny." Collins, *supra* note 6, at 140 (citing KONST. SSSR art. 29 (1917)).

13. U.N. CHARTER art. 1.

14. *Declaration on the Granting of Independence to Colonial Countries and Peoples*, G.A. Res. 1514, U.N. GAOR, 15th Sess., Supp. No. 16, at 66, U.N. Doc. A/L323 (1960); G.A. Res. 1541, U.N. GAOR, 15th Sess., Supp. No. 16, at 29, U.N. Doc. A/4684 (1966).

15. *Declaration on Principles of International Law Concerning Friendly Relations and Co-operation among States in Accordance with the Charter of the United Nations*, G.A. Res. 2625, U.N. GAOR, 25th Sess., Supp. No. 28, at 121 (1970).

16. The Group called on the international community to establish a New International Economic Order (N.I.E.O.). The combined influence of the developing, third world and Soviet interests, acting as a bloc, altered voting patterns in the U.N. General Assembly and, at a more important structural level, changed the agenda of the Assembly. *See generally* ROBERT F. MEAGHER, AN INTERNATIONAL REDISTRIBUTION OF WEALTH AND POWER: A STUDY OF THE CHARTER OF ECONOMIC RIGHTS AND DUTIES OF STATES (1979).

17. Amberg, *supra* note 4, at 840 - 41.

The signing of two major Covenants of international law in 1966,[18] and subsequent decisions of the International Court of Justice[19] (ICJ) further endorsed the concept. As a result, self-determination became, according to some, *"the* pre-emptory norm of international law."[20]

At the same time, the concept itself remained "highly controversial."[21] The nature of the controversy revolved around two inter-related issues - what was the status of the concept, and what did it include within its scope? This section will concentrate on the former point, but in order to do so, it is first necessary to identify three methods of approaching the status issue. This clarification is required because assumptions regarding status clearly inform the discussion as to what is included within the concept of self-determination. The definition of the term self-determination will depend, to an extent, on the status ascribed to it. If the notion is viewed as *lex ferenda*, it may be acceptable to tolerate some uncertainties of meaning. If, however, self-determination is *lex lata*, some suggest that it may be only a limited concept which has achieved this status. This paper is based on the premise that the concept is *lex lata*, but that a narrow definition of self-determination is inappropriate. In other words, the notion of self-determination has achieved the status of a norm of international law, and furthermore, the scope of its application is broadening.

There are, broadly, three ways to view the question of status. The first approach attacks the very notion of self-determination. It claims that the concept is vague, ill-defined and lacking in legal content - a concept of "policy and morality"[22] rather than positive law.

---

18. *International Covenant on Civil and Political Rights*, Dec. 16, 1966, 999 U.N.T.S. 171; *International Covenant on Economic, Social and Cultural Rights*, Dec. 16, 1966, 993 U.N.T.S. 3 [hereinafter *Covenants*].

19. Legal Consequences for States of the Continued Presence of South Africa in Namibia (South West Africa) Notwithstanding Security Council Resolution 276 (1970), 1971 I.C.J. 16 (June 21) (advisory opinion) [hereinafter Namibia Case]; Western Sahara Case, *supra* note 7. Compare these decisions with the decision of the Permanent Court of International Justice, some fifty years earlier, in the Asland Islands Case, L.N.O.J. Special Supp. No. 3, 3 (1920), where it held that positive international law did not recognize the right of national groups to separate themselves from the state of which they formed a part by a simple expression of a wish, any more than it recognized the right of other states to claim such a separation.

20. POMERANCE, *supra* note 3, at 1 (emphasis added).

21. HEATHER A. WILSON, INTERNATIONAL LAW AND THE USE OF FORCE BY NATIONAL LIBERATION MOVEMENTS 88 (1988).

22. *See* IAN BROWNLIE, PRINCIPLES OF PUBLIC INTERNATIONAL LAW 593 (3d ed. 1979). Brownlie notes that this approach, which he does not share, was assumed by western scholars. Collins states that this school of thought views the concept as "legally intangible, ambiguous, problematical, and only partially applicable . . . self-determination is in practice unnecessary and invalid." Collins, *supra* note 6, at 145.

A second group, characterized by Schwarzenberger, says, "self-determination has great potency, but [is] not part and parcel of international customary law."[23]

The third school assumes that self-determination is part of international law, but considers there to be disagreement as to the content of the concept. Thus, Brownlie in 1979 stated, "The present position is that self-determination is a legal principle . . . . Its precise ramifications in other contexts are not yet worked out."[24]

For present purposes, the view put forward by Brownlie is adopted on the basis of the sources of international law as listed in article 38 of the Statute of the ICJ[25] and interpreted by the court in the *Nicaragua Case*.[26] In the court's view, "the material of customary international law is to be looked for primarily in the actual practice and opinio juris of States."[27]

Evidence of state practice can be found in a range of sources. This includes: 1) the decolonization process of over seventy states since 1946; 2) explicit recognition by the member states of the U.N. of the right to self-determination by particular groups such as the Namibian and Palestinian people; and 3) a growing number of statements by the international community encouraging the acceptance of the validity of claims by peoples ranging from the Yugoslav republics,[28] to the Baltics,[29] to East Timor.[30] Examples of state practice are more comprehensively examined in the context of the scope of self-

---

23. *Quoted in* DAVID J. HARRIS, CASES AND MATERIALS ON INTERNATIONAL LAW 95 (3d ed. 1983).

24. BROWNLIE, *supra* note 22, at 595.

25. Article 38 provides that the ICJ shall apply international conventions, international custom as evidence of general practice, general principles of law, and, as a subsidiary means, judicial decisions and teachings of qualified publicists. *See* Statute of the International Court of Justice, art. 38 appended to the U.N. CHARTER, 59 Stat. 1031, T.S. No. 993 (1945).

26. Military and Paramilitary Activities in and Against Nicaragua (Nicar. v U.S.), 1986 I.C.J. 14 (June 27) [hereinafter Nicaragua Case].

27. *Id.* para. 183.

28. As of this writing, the United States (*The Age*, July 4, 1991), Britain (*The Age*, July 5, 1991), Germany (*The Age*, July 5, 1991), the European Community (*The Age*, July 4, 1991) and Australia (*The Age*, July 5, 1991) have indicated their readiness to accept the Slovenian and Croatian claims. *See also* Mary Curtius, *US, Allies Eye Halting Arms to Yugoslavia; Discuss Recognizing Republics if Federal Army Won't Withdraw*, BOSTON GLOBE, July 4, 1991, at 1.

29. See for example statements by the United States and Australia calling on the former Soviet Union to recognize the Lithuanian Parliament's declaration of independence. *The Age*, March 3, 1991. *See also* Warren Strobel, *Bush Bolsters Ties to Baltics*, WASH. TIMES, May 13, 1991, at A7.

30. *Question of East Timor*, G.A. Res. 3730, U.N. GAOR, 37th Sess., Agenda Item 97, U.N. Doc. A/RES/37/30 (1982).

determination,[31] their purpose here being merely to demonstrate that such evidence exists.

Since the *Nicaragua Case*, it is clear that the second element of the test from that case, evidence of opinio juris, may be deduced from U.N. General Assembly resolutions.[32] Resolutions 1514, 1541 and 2625 indicate a belief within the international community that self-determination is a part of customary international law.[33]

Treaties, a further source of law under the Statute of the ICJ, also confirm the existence of a legal right. The most representative treaties of all time, the U.N. Charter (1947),[34] the Universal Declaration of Human Rights (1948),[35] and the 1966 International Cove-

---

31. *See* discussion *infra* part III. A. 1.

32. HARRIS, *supra* note 23, at 99 (quoting the separate opinion of Judge Dillard in the Western Sahara Case, *supra* note 7); Nicaragua Case, *supra* note 26, para. 188.

33. General Assembly Resolution 1514 (1960), 1541 (1966) and 2625 (1970) all contain passages similar in wording to article 1 of the International Covenants of 1966. G.A. Res. 1514, *supra* note 14; G.A. Res. 1541, *supra* note 14; G.A. Res. 2625, *supra* note 15. The first of these, the *Declaration on the Granting of Independence to Colonial Territories and Peoples*, begins with the general proposition that the subjection of peoples to alien subjugation, domination and exploitation constituted a "denial of fundamental human rights" and is "contrary to the Charter of the United Nations." *See* G.A. Res. 1514, *supra* note 14. It then states in paragraph two that "all peoples have the right to self-determination" and that "immediate steps" should be taken in Trust, Non-Self-Governing, and all other territories which have not attained independence, to "transfer all powers to the peoples of those territories." *Id.* para. 5. General Assembly Resolution 1541 outlines three possible methods of implementation: 1) independence; 2) free association; and 3) integration. *See* G.A. Res. 1541, *supra* note 14. The third General Assembly Resolution, the 1970 *Declaration on The Principles of International Law Concerning Friendly Relations and Co-operation Among States*, re-asserted the primacy of the principle of self-determination. *See supra* note 15. It stated that "all peoples have the right to freely determine without external interference, their political status." *Id.*

34. One of the purposes of the United Nations under article 1 of the Charter is to "develop friendly relations among nations based on respect for the principle of equal rights and *self-determination* of peoples . . . ." U.N. CHARTER art. 1(2) (emphasis added). The content of the term was developed in article 55 which promoted, inter alia, higher standards of living, respect for human rights and fundamental freedoms based on the principle of self-determination. *Id.* art. 55. The use of the term self-determination in the Charter at articles 1 and 55 is persuasive evidence for recognizing that such a right existed at international law, although, John Humphrey, the first head of the Human Rights Commission of the United Nations, argues that in 1947 self-determination in the Charter was merely a "political principle" and later it became "something else." *See* HUMAN RIGHTS IN INTERNATIONAL LAW: LEGAL AND POLICY ISSUES 194 (Theodore Meron ed., 1984). The majority in the *Western Sahara Case* disagreed and held that the inclusion of the principle in the Charter was indicative of its status as law. *See* Western Sahara Case, *supra* note 7.

35. G.A. Res. 217, U.N. GAOR, 3d Sess., pt. 1, 183d plen. mtg., U.N. Doc. A/777 (1948). One of the first actions of the newly created United Nations in 1948 was to begin drafting a Universal Declaration of Human Rights. Although self-determination is not specifically mentioned in that Declaration, many of the rights listed could be interpreted as being elements of a right of self-determination. For instance, under the Declaration everyone has the right to own property (art. 17), to freedom of thought, conscience and religion (art. 18) and to take part in the government of their country (art. 21). More specifically, article 15 provides

nants,[36] whether viewed as a source of obligation derived from mutually binding promises, or as methods of developing law, indicate an acceptance of the concept. The inclusion of self-determination in customary international law is reflected also in two major decisions of the ICJ.[37]

III. SCOPE AND CONTENT OF THE CONCEPT

Turning now to the question which is the subject of this paper, the major issue to be addressed is, which groups are entitled to exercise a right to self-determination? The critical uncertainty here is whether the right of self-determination attaches to all "peoples,"[38] in a literal sense, or only to those peoples within existing colonial boundaries.

A. The "Conventional" View

Broadly speaking, two views can be identified in the literature. Harris, for example, believes that General Assembly Resolution 1514, the first to deal comprehensively with self-determination, contemplates self-determination within existing boundaries. He argues, pragmatically, that this limitation is necessary in the interests of international harmony.[39] Accordingly, ethnic minorities, not within definite colonial boundaries, are not entitled to exercise a right of self-

---

that everyone has the right "to a nationality" and that no one shall be "arbitrarily deprived" of their nationality - two elements implicit in a right of self-determination. *Id.*

36. *See Covenants, supra* note 18. The Covenants are the work of the U.N. Commission on Human Rights, whose brief was to translate the principles embodied in the Universal Declaration into treaty law. These then form the basis of the major international obligation in relation to self-determination. The Covenants came into force in 1976 and ratifications to date number over 90 including Great Britain, the U.S.S.R., the Federal Republic of Germany, the German Democratic Republic and Japan. The United States is a signatory to both Covenants.

37. *See* Collins, *supra* note 6, at 145. In its Advisory Opinion in the *Namibia Case,* the ICJ referred to the development of the law since 1920 as encapsulated in the U.N. Charter and the General Assembly Resolutions of 1960 and noted that its interpretation of the principles of law could not be "unaffected" by the "supervening half century." Namibia Case, *supra* note 19, para. 31. It concluded that in order to "faithfully discharge its functions" it could not ignore these developments which left "little doubt that the ultimate objective of the sacred trust was the self-determination and independence of the peoples concerned." *Id.* In the *Western Sahara Case,* the ICJ endorsed the abovementioned statements from the *Namibia Case* and referred to Resolution 1541 of 1966, which it said "gave effect to the essential feature of the right of self-determination." Western Sahara Case, *supra* note 7, para. 57.

38. The major U.N. instruments on self-determination, including the human rights Covenants and the resolutions of the General Assembly, provide that the right is possessed by all "peoples." *See supra* notes 14, 15, and 18.

39. Harris states that "[t]he post-colonial states in particular have taken the view that it would be too disruptive of international stability to allow self-determination within those boundaries for minorities." HARRIS, *supra* note 23, at 96. *See also* JAMES CRAWFORD, THE

determination. Presumably therefore, under a strict reading utilizing this approach many recent claims would fail. These would include for example, claims by the peoples of the republics of the former Soviet Union[40] against Moscow, by Croatia,[41] Slovenia[42] and Macedonia[43] against Yugoslavia, by the Serbian minority of Krajina against Croatia,[44] the Bouganville claim against Papua New Guinea;[45] and the list goes on. Query whether, according to this view, the claims of the peoples of Baltic states who are arguably resident within pre-existing but dormant colonial boundaries would have any validity under this approach.

In Australia, the view which strictly delimits the instances in which self-determination can apply was adopted by the Australian Law Reform Commission (A.L.R.C.), when it reported in 1986 on Aboriginal Customary Law. The A.L.R.C. stated:

> [A]dvocates for ethnic, indigenous or linguistic minorities sometimes rely upon the principle or right of self-determination in international law as a basis for claims to political or legal recognition. So far however, the principle has been confined in international practice to situations involving separate ('colonial') territories politically and legally subordinate to an administering power.[46]

The view espoused by the A.L.R.C. will be termed, for present purposes, the "conventional" view.

B. The "Controversial" View

A different, and more controversial perspective is adopted by, among others, Collins and Nanda. Professor Nanda's thesis is that

---

CREATION OF STATES AT INTERNATIONAL LAW 91 - 93 (1979); WILSON, *supra* note 21; POMERANCE, *supra* note 3, at 3; Amberg, *supra* note 4, at 853.

40. For example, 98.3% of the 90.5% of Georgians who voted in a recent referendum supported independence from Moscow. *See* THE AGE, Apr. 3, 1991. *See also* Elizabeth Shogren, *Soviet Georgians Flock to Polls to Vote for Secession*, L.A. TIMES, Apr. 1, 1991, at A1.

41. THE AGE, May 31, 1991. *See also* Andrew Borowiec, *Serbia Plans to Form Small Federation*, WASH. TIMES, Aug. 14, 1991, at A8.

42. THE AGE, Apr. 29, 1991. *See also* Borowiec, *supra* note 41.

43. THE AGE, Jan. 27, 1991. *See also* Borowiec, *supra* note 41.

44. THE AGE, Apr. 3, 1991. *See also* Balkan Woes, CHRISTIAN SCI. MONITOR, Apr. 8, 1991, at 20.

45. For a discussion of the Origins of the Bouganville claim *see* THE AUSTRALIAN, Sept. 4, 1990. *See also Papau New Guinea Prime Minister Namaliu on Bouganville Disturbances*, Xinhua General Overseas Newswire Service, Apr. 11, 1989, *available in* LEXIS, ASIAPC Library, ALLASI File.

46. A.L.R.C., REPORT NO. 31 RECOGNITION OF ABORIGINAL CUSTOMARY LAW 128 (1986).

the right of self-determination extends beyond the colonial context.[47] Although in order for the group to qualify for the right, they must first satisfy a formal set of criteria. Moreover, Collins states it is only political exigencies which have focused the right of self-determination onto colonial territories. He argues that:

> although political events have concentrated the UN's focus on colonial territories and the UN stands firm on the concept of territorial integrity, the principle of self-determination should not be considered strictly as a colonial right.[48]

C. Analysis: Which Approach to Self-Determination Is Appropriate?

It should be clear then that these two approaches, which have been labelled conventional and controversial, are inconsistent. It will be argued here that the latter is preferable; that in certain circumstances, the right to self-determination should be made available to minority groups, as well as states, trusts and non-self governing territories. This proposition is based on the view that the controversial theory of self-determination provides a more accurate explanation of the shift in international state practice, as well as a workable prescription for the future. The discussion in this section will show that state practice and the belief of states regarding that practice is in accordance with the controversial view. Moreover, the conventional view is premised on an inherent logical inconsistency, and is unsustainable from a jurisprudential perspective. The challenge for international law is therefore not to exclude the ever-increasing list of claimants because they do not match precisely with an outmoded theory, but to find methods for assessing and evaluating the validity of claims according to realistic, functional and humanitarian measures.

1. State Practice and Opinio Juris

The aim in this part of the paper is to outline the lack of correspondence between international legal theory and state practice and consequently show that the exclusion of non-colonially based claims is confusing and no longer appropriate.

Regardless of recent events in Europe and Asia, it is clear that during the last fifty years there has already been a marked alteration in the international community's perception of when the right to self-determination arises. A former head of the Human Rights section of

---

47. Ved P. Nanda, *Self-Determination Under International Law: Validity of Claims to Secede*, 13 CASE W. RES. J. INT'L L. 257, 266 (1981).

48. Collins, *supra* note 6, at 153.

the U.N., John Humphrey, argues that when self-determination was introduced into the U.N. Charter, at the behest of the former Soviet Union, ironically enough, it was clearly with colonial and mandated territories in mind.[49] The 1960 Declaration is in accord with that interpretation, and this, he says, was also the prevailing view in the U.N.[50] Humphrey then goes on, however, to acknowledge that the General Assembly had no such limitation in mind when it sanctioned the International Covenants in 1966. In his view, the General Assembly intended the word 'peoples' to extend beyond the colonial context.[51]

It is important to recall that colonial boundaries were the result of specific historical circumstances. The desire for territorial or economic gain led to the establishment of arbitrary boundaries which often cut across traditional spheres, although as Wilson notes, post-colonial states have in some cases come to accept these boundaries.[52] In many cases, the rearrangement of peoples into newer colonial units produced an alliance of groups which had no reason, other than colonialism, for existing. Currently these alliances, which often take the form of federations, are coming under increasing pressure from resurgent nationalism. Yugoslavia is clearly one of the more tragic illustrations of this problem, where years after redrawing the physical boundaries of the state, the psychological boundaries which define various groups remain as strong as ever. Boundaries, therefore, although "legal" in one sense, did not always reflect "practice," in the sense of what peoples within those artificial parameters continued to value. And whether or not post-colonial states accepted the imposed boundaries, it still begs the question of whether these limitations should be the critical yardstick by which to determine the validity of a self-determination claim.

More significantly, from the perspective of international law the-

---

49. Other commentators take a different view. For example, it has been suggested that when the U.N. Charter was drawn up the U.N. Secretariat defined peoples as groups who may or may not comprise states or nations. *See* J. Matthews, *Revision of ILO Convention No. 107* (May 1988) (unpublished manuscript delivered at International Law Association Conference, Australian National University).

50. J.P. Humphrey, *Political and Related Rights, in* HUMAN RIGHTS IN INTERNATIONAL LAW - LEGAL AND POLICY ISSUES 196 (Theodore Meron ed., 1984).

51. *Id.*

52. Wilson says, in 1968, the Organization for African Unity supported the territorial integrity of Nigeria against the Biafran secessionist movement, because to do otherwise "would set a dangerous precedent for the political unity of every African country." WILSON, *supra* note 21, at 87. *See also* the discussion of the *uti possidetis* doctrine, which prevents the stability of the new regime's borders being endangered in Frontier Dispute (Burkina Faso/Mali), 1986 I.C.J. Y.B. No. 40, at 161.

ory, is the confusion or disjunction between law and current events which is demonstrated by the fact that a blanket prohibition on the rights of minorities seeking self-determination does not accord with state practice. Certain minorities have either achieved self-determination, or are in the process of seeking it, often with international sanction and recognition, in spite of the conventional view. In recent times, the instances of groups seeking and sometimes exercising their right to determine their own future are rapidly increasing. International recognition for the claims of the Palestinians,[53] growing support for the recognition of the right to secede[54] by Slovenia and Croatia,[55] the Baltic states and perhaps even world response to the plight of the Kurds indicate that state practice is slowly building to support a shift in view, regardless of the fact that these examples are usually rationalized as exceptions to the general rule.[56] For example, President George Bush has referred to recognition of independence of the Baltic States as being a "special case."[57]

Events in Yugoslavia illustrate the changed state practice with regard to recognized acts of self-determination, even prior to the appearance of the elements which normally constitute statehood.[58] Although it is impossible to be precise about the state of events in Yugoslavia, it appears that as of this writing the U.S.,[59] Britain,[60]

---

53. *See, e.g.,* Res. ES-7/2: Question of Palestine (1980), *reprinted in* 18 DUSAN J. DJONOVITCH, UNITED NATIONS RESOLUTIONS: SERIES 1: GENERAL ASSEMBLY 479 (1979 - 80).

54. A right which extends beyond the right simply of self-determination.

55. THE AGE, July 5, 1991. *See also* Stephen Kinzer, *Europe, Backing Germans, Accepts Yugoslav Breakup,* N.Y. TIMES, Jan. 16, 1992, at A10.

56. For an example see the view expressed in Richard N. Kiwanuka, *The Meaning of 'People' in the African Charter on Humanitarian and Peoples' Rights,* 82 AM. J. INT'L L. 80, 90 (1988), that international recognition for Bangladesh only occurred because of "a set of circumstances that lent a cloak of legitimacy to what would otherwise be impermissible at international law."

57. David Hoffman, *Baker Vows Aid for Soviets, Lists Five Principles for Dealings,* WASH. POST, Sept. 5, 1991, at A34.

58. The 7th International Conference of American States - Convention on Rights and duties of States, Dec. 3 - 26, 1933, art. 1, 28 AM. J. INT'L L. SUPP. 75 (1934). Article 1 lists 4 elements: permanent population, defined territory, government and capacity to enter into relations with other States. Recognition also has an effect on statehood although controversy remains as to whether its role is "constitutive" or "declaratory." *See* JOSEPH M. SWEENEY ET AL., THE INTERNATIONAL LEGAL SYSTEM (3d ed. 1988).

59. *See* THE AGE, July 4, 1991. *See also* John Mashek, *Bush Edges Toward Recognizing Baltics,* BOSTON GLOBE, Aug. 27, 1991, at 12.

60. The British Prime Minister John Major was reported as saying, "it may no longer be possible to hold the country together." THE AGE, July 5, 1991. *See also* William Drozdiak, *Conflicts Over Yugoslav Crisis Surface in Europe; Debate Pits Principle of Self-Determination Against Preserving National Boundaries,* WASH. POST, July 5, 1991, at A15.

Germany,[61] the European Community,[62] and Australia[63] have indicated their readiness to recognize the declarations of independence by Slovenia and Croatia.[64]

The Baltics provide another example of the practice of states shifting to support claims by minorities for self-determination. What has been the response of the international community to their claims of independence from Moscow? Events have moved with startling rapidity. Just over one year ago one state only, Iceland, had formally recognized Lithuania's claim for independence.[65] Now recognition of independence has been accorded by at least eighteen countries including Australia, plus the U.S. and the European Community. The President of the Russian Republic has issued a decree recognizing the Baltic republics, as did the President of the defunct Soviet Union.[66]

Even prior to these events Lithuania's claim had already attained a certain degree of legitimacy from the international community. The U.S. and Australia, among others, were reported as attempting to pressure the Soviet Union into accepting Lithuania's declaration.[67] The U.S., adopting diplomatic means, postponed an important summit it had planned to hold with the Soviet Union.[68] The Soviet Union's military response to the Lithuanian movement was condemned by the U.S.,[69] Japan,[70] the European Community[71] and Australia,[72] and threats were made to suspend aid.[73] It is clear, therefore, that while Lithuania's right to self-determination had been recognized

---

61. See THE AGE, July 5, 1991. See also Drozdiak, supra note 60.

62. The European Community was reported to be ready to consider recognition if Belgrade refused to stop hostilities. THE AGE, July 4, 1991. See also Curtius, supra note 28.

63. See THE AGE, July 5, 1991.

64. The European Community formally recognized Croatia and Slovenia on January 16, 1992. See THE AGE, Jan. 16, 1992. See also Stephen Kinzer, Europe, Backing Germans, Accepts Yugoslav Breakup, N.Y. TIMES, Jan. 16, 1992, at A10. It has also recognized Bosnia and Herzegovina. See EC Grants Recognition to Bosnia and Herzegovina, THE WEEK IN GERMANY, Apr. 10, 1992, available in LEXIS, NEXIS Library, CURRNT File.

65. See GUARDIAN WEEKLY, Feb. 17, 1991. See also Debran Rowland, Lithuanians Mark Independence Day, CHI. TRIB., Feb. 18, 1991, at 7.

66. See Martin Sieff, Yeltsin Now Calls the Shots, WASH. TIMES, Aug. 26, 1991, at A1.

67. See THE AGE, Mar. 3, 1991. See also Daniel Sneider, Gorbachev Woos and Assails West, CHRISTIAN SCI. MONITOR, May 9, 1991, at 3.

68. See THE AGE, Jan. 30, 1991. See also Don Oberdorfer & Ann Devroy, Bush and Gorbachev Postpone Summit, WASH. POST, Jan. 29, 1991, at A1.

69. See THE AGE, Mar. 17, 1991. See also U.S. on Secession: Maybe, N.Y. TIMES, June 28, 1991, A8.

70. See THE AUSTRALIAN, Jan. 22, 1991. See also Martin Seiff, Violence Laid to Gorbachev's Foes,WASH. TIMES, May, 3, 1991, at A8.

71. See THE AGE, Jan. 23, 1991. See also Seiff, supra note 70.

72. See THE AGE, Jan. 16, 1991. See also Seiff, supra note 70.

73. See THE AUSTRALIAN, Jan. 22, 1991. See also Seiff, supra note 70.

by only one state, many others have implicitly indicated that, at the very least, they did not accept the Soviet Union's outright rejection of the Lithuanian claim. At the most, the negative response of these states can be interpreted as tacit approval of Lithuania's claim. If so, further support is lent to the argument that examples of state practice are incrementally building toward a re-examination of traditional theory.

The proposal for the establishment of a safe haven for Kurdish refugees from the Iraqi regime, regardless of whether it succeeds or not, also lends support to a change in practice. The territorial integrity of Iraq was affected by the allies' action in establishing the enclave and subsequent recognition of the Kurdish claim for full autonomy by the allies further confirms the allies' support of Kurdish claims for self-determination. Although it is clear that protection of the Kurds does not translate automatically into support for their right to self-determination, the allied intervention ensures that the Kurdish claim is kept alive, and may be a preliminary step necessary for the attainment of that goal. In addition, a U.S. Military Report specifically recognized as an objective the attainment of a permanent, secure and autonomous Kurdish region.[74] The Kurdish example indicates that a "people," subject to alien domination not within defined colonial borders, have been allocated, with the sanction and active contrivance of three significant powers and the U.N., a safe haven or enclave within the territory of another state.[75] A safe haven is clearly one important element towards achieving a successful claim for self-determination.

In principle, acceptance of a right to limited self-government for the Palestinian people has been recognized by Israel.[76] In view of the fact that self-determination is about the process of allowing a group to determine their political future, rather than any one particular result, Israel's acceptance is significant.

Two final examples of the shift in state practice concern the Czech and Slovak Federal Republic (C.S.F.R.) and Eritrea. C.S.F.R. President Vaclav Havel has indicated that the Slovakian people have a

---

74. *See* THE AUSTRALIAN, May 5, 1991. *See also Paper: U.S. May Seek Autonomous Kurdish Region*, CHI. TRIB., May 5, 1991, at 19.

75. *See* GUARDIAN WEEKLY, Apr. 28, 1991. *See also Paper: U.S. May Seek Autonomous Kurdish Region*, CHI. TRIB., May 5, 1991, at 19.

76. *See* THE AGE, Jan. 16, 1992. *See also* Norman Kempster & Daniel Williams, *Israel OKs Talks on Arab Self-Rule*, L.A. TIMES, Jan. 15, 1992, at A1.

right to secede, as long as it is done in a constitutional manner.[77] Similarly, the new Ethiopian government has reportedly adopted a charter recognizing the right of self-determination for all its nationalities, as long as the appropriate referendum is held, and has affirmed the right of the Eritreans in the north of the state to secede.[78]

The aforementioned examples do not confuse the political principle of self-determination with the legal right of self-determination, but recognize the *facts* of self-determination. There is a large and growing body of evidence indicating that the attitudes of the international community towards the right of minorities to assert a claim for self-determination are changing. As the ICJ stated in the *Nicaragua Case*, these facts constitute the most potent evidence of the state of customary international law.[79] If self-determination is to have any contemporary relevance, then, it must be taken to include the situation where ethnic minorities may exercise this right.

2. Textual Issues

An analysis of the texts which represent the conventional view of self-determination also reveals that it is based on a circular argument. It asserts that apart from States, trusts and non-self-governing territories or categories listed in Chapter XI of the U.N. Charter, the right is available only to those territories which possess a status similar to that of a non-self-governing territory. Crawford, for example, offers an additional rather vague category of situations, apart from the standard ones, where self-determination may also be relevant:

> [Possibly] other territories forming distinct political geographical areas, whose inhabitants do not share in the government either of the region or of the State to which the region belongs, *with the result that the territory becomes in effect . . . non-self-governing.*[80]

Similarly, Wilson believes that the right does not entail a right of secession from a self-governing state, "unless a part of that State has become effectively non-self-governing with respect to the whole."[81]

These arguments beg the critical question. Nowhere do they define *how* or *when* the territory in question becomes non-self-governing. They merely answer the problems by restating it. What does becom-

---

77. *See* THE AGE, July 9, 1991. *See also* Mary Battiata, *Separatist Slovaks Becoming More Vocal in 'Family Feud' with Czechs*, WASH. POST, Mar. 19, 1991, at A21.

78. *See* THE AGE, July 5, 1991. *See also* Robert M. Press, *Ethiopians Opt for Transition to Democracy*, CHRISTIAN SCI. MONITOR, July 5, 1991, at 1.

79. *See* Nicaragua Case, *supra* note 26.

80. Crawford, *supra* note 39, at 101 (emphasis added).

81. WILSON, *supra* note 21, at 87.

ing "in effect non-self-governing" or "effectively non-self-governing" mean? This is the crux of the whole self-determination issue, the need to formulate a legal method for determining when a particular entity has become "non-self-governing."

The deficiency of the conventional view is that by failing to formulate specific principles with which to assess a claim, it avoids the most controversial aspect of the right to self-determination. This is not an attack merely on the lack of clarity of the traditional view; the "legality" of a right is not diminished or increased by the uncertainty of its content. The conventional view is clear enough within a limited scope, but it does not provide an explanation or guide for when the right does arise beyond the traditional categories, categories which no longer cover the varieties of groups seeking to exercise the right.

3. Jurisprudential Issues

Assuming then that the conventional view of self-determination theory is no longer appropriate, on the basis both of developing state practice and inherent logical inconsistencies, it is interesting to consider how and why it has for so long been accepted. Furthermore, why has that acceptance been accompanied by continual academic controversy? The confusion of international opinion in this area is an example of what one jurisprudential approach would call a "crisis" in the "interpretive" community's "structure of beliefs."[82] This theory asserts that change in law comes about when the exceptions to a general rule are too numerous to rationalize. A "crisis" in the law results which can only be resolved by the reconciliation of the exceptions under a new rule, which thus moderates or changes the original rule. This reconciliation can only occur through an alteration in the community's belief structure and this happens when a sufficiently persuasive argument is formulated to explain the exceptions. In this manner, the law gradually evolves and retains the illusion (often fostered in law schools) of being simultaneously "static and yet dynamic." For example, Katz explains the process by reference to Thomas Kuhn's theory of scientific change:

Discovery commences with the awareness of an anomaly .... It then continues with a more or less extended exploration of the area of the anomaly. And it closes only when the paradigm theory has been ad-

---

82. *See, e.g.*, M.F. Katz, *After the Deconstruction: Law in the Age of Post-Structuralism*, 24 U. W. ONTARIO L. REV. 51, 57 - 58 (1986).

justed so that the anomalous has become the expected.[83]

Academic opinion regarding self-determination is currently in a state of "crisis." The profusion of debate reflects a period in which there is an "extended exploration of the anomaly." Berman refers to aspects of the debate as "the paradox of self-determination."[84] The mass of writing on the subject is evidence of the unsettled state of the law. Crawford's usage of the word "possibly" to qualify the application of self-determination to territories outside conventional theories only highlights the uncertainties. The recapitulation of the general rule, and attempts to explain or rationalize exceptions under the general rule, are unconvincing. They do not accord with either legal *or* political reality. There is a growing list of examples where a right to self-determination has been recognized regardless of its failure to fit conventional theoretical requirements. This list of examples includes the Baltic States, Croatia and Slovenia, and recent Israeli statements regarding a Palestinian right to limited self-government, to name a few. At this stage, it is sufficient to point out that politically and legally certain entities have successfully asserted their right to self-determination while others continue to do so. What is needed in order to resolve the "crisis" is a reformulation of the original rule. Otherwise, the factual exceptions cannot be reconciled.

It has been suggested here that there is an uncertainty in international law theory regarding when the right of self-determination applies; that this confusion has rendered the term incapable of application to the wide variety of situations it is being called upon to mediate; and, that reformulation of the conventional approach is necessary to reconcile factual exceptions. The controversial approach to the interpretation of self-determination more accurately reflects current state practice, and should therefore be formally recognized as the appropriate international law standard.

D. Issues for the Future

Adoption of the controversial approach to self-determination will undoubtedly be accompanied by a range of new and complex issues. For example, the most serious of these problems is the potential effect a successful bid for self-determination by a group in one state, may have on a neighboring state which also contains the same grouping.

---

83. *See id.* at 56 (citing THOMAS KUHN, THE STRUCTURE OF SCIENTIFIC REVOLUTIONS 90 (1967)).

84. N. Berman, *Sovereignty in Abeyance: Self-Determination and International Law*, 7 WIS. INT'L L.J. 51, 52 (1988).

In this context, the Chinese have expressed concern over the effect that independence for Kazakhstan may have over the large Kazakh minority in the Xinjiang province.[85] Serbs in the Croatian region of Krajina will also pose a problem for any independent Croatian state.[86]

Inter-ethnic rivalries *within* newly independent Soviet republics also create serious problems for international stability. It is difficult to keep abreast of the ever burgeoning list of minorities claiming rights, often against an entity which itself has just successfully asserted its right to self-determination. The Ossetians in Georgia, the self-proclaimed Dnieper Republic in Moldava and the Crimean autonomous republic in the Southern Ukraine[87] are examples of just a few claims by minorities within former minority entities.

Apart from a proliferation of claims which could result from the adoption of the controversial view, the other major issue concerns the area of implementation. How quickly and effectively can international and domestic constitutional law theory respond to the urgent need to construct new forms of power sharing to accommodate the proliferation of demands? Remembering that self-determination is not necessarily synonymous with complete independence, the "shape" of new forms of federal structures will be extremely important. The formation of the Union of Soviet Socialist Republics and its rapid replacement by the Commonwealth of Independent States with as yet undefined responsibilities in significant areas of economic and defense control illustrates the need for some creative legal thinking on the effect of self-determination on the constitutional structure of states.

Or will self-determination translate into the forms of power redistribution being experimented with in relation to indigenous peoples in Canada, New Zealand and to a lesser extent Australia? For example, will Canada proceed with a proposal by the notedly conservative Canadian Bar Association to introduce a separate system of justice for native Canadians? Will the New Zealand experience of placing land claims in a separate tribunal and allowing first offenders in the criminal justice system to be punished in consultation with Maori leaders constitute new forms of effective self-government?

These and a host of other issues accompany a shift in international law to the more controversial approach to self-determination.

---

85. *See* Lena H. Sun, *China Fears that Fever of Soviet Ethnic Conflicts Could Cross Border*, WASH. POST, Sept. 20, 1991, at A16.

86. *See* Laura Silber et al., *Serbian Leaders' Dispute Threatens UN Peace Plans*, FINANCIAL TIMES, Feb. 4, 1992, at 2.

87. *See* THE AGE, Sept. 7, 1991. *See also* Walter Laqueur, *Independence May Enslave Millions*, L.A. TIMES, Sept. 8, 1991, at M5.

It is suggested here, however, that these questions should be incorporated into the criteria to be applied in assessing a claim, or resolved at the domestic level, rather than automatically preventing the right from being exercised. Otherwise, the term self-determination is in danger of losing any useful currency it may have once possessed as a principle of international law.

IV. Conclusion

It has been argued here that conventional theoretical approaches to self-determination are inadequate insofar as they provide neither a description of, nor a prescription for, the behavior of states in international relations. To be useful to the field of international dispute resolution, international law theory should be functional, as well as analytical. This is particularly true when we are witnessing an increasing number of claims by indigenous peoples and ethnic minorities, not enclosed within the parameter of colonial boundaries, but who nevertheless wish to exercise their right to self-determination, a right which is part of international customary law. To date, the right is denied on the basis that the group does not "fit" the theory. The resulting dissonance between state practice and the conventional law on self-determination has led to an unacceptable level of uncertainty in the application of the law. A way out of this uncertainty has been proposed, utilizing existing tools of the discourse, to improve and refine the current paradigm.

Representation/s of Women in the Australian Constitutional System

Deborah Cass and Kim Rubenstein

Deborah Cass and Kim Rubenstein, 'Representation/s of Women in the Australian Constitutional System' (1995) 17 *Adelaide Law Review* 3, 3–48 <http://www.austlii.edu.au/au/journals/AdelLawRw/1995/2.html>

ARTICLES

Cass * *and Rubenstein***

REPRESENTATION/S OF WOMEN IN THE AUSTRALIAN CONSTITUTIONAL SYSTEM

INTRODUCTION

Like the goddess of wisdom the Commonwealth uno ictu sprang from the brain of its begetters armed and of full stature.[1]

ACCORDING to Sir Owen Dixon, the Commonwealth of Australia sprang, like the Goddess Athena, fully armed from the head of the States. Whether or not this is an apt metaphor from a classical perspective,[2] from the perspective of Australian

*   LLB (Hons) (Melb); Lecturer, Australian National University. LLM Candidate 1995, Harvard University.
** BA, LLB (Hons)(Melb), LLM (Harvard); Lecturer, University of Melbourne. We would like to thank Bridget Gilmour Walsh for her excellent research assistance, and for her contributions to ideas, which we have, wherever possible, acknowledged. We are grateful for the comments of Hilary Charlesworth, Jenny Morgan, Margaret Thornton, Geoff Lindell, Lisa Sarmas, Garry Sturgess and an anonymous referee.

1   *In Re Foreman & Sons Pty Ltd; Uther v Federal Commissioner of Taxation* (1947) 74 CLR 508 at 530 per Dixon J.
2   According to Greek mythology, Athena, the Goddess of Wisdom, was born from the head of her father, Zeus, the King of the Gods. See Harvey, (ed) *The Oxford Companion to English Literature* (Clarendon Press, Oxford, 3rd ed 1946) p46. Gatens points out that an often neglected part of the myth is that Zeus "gave

women, it is a strange choice. Athena is one of the strongest female images of the Western literary tradition. In contrast, Australian women have not been represented with such vigour in Australian constitutional law. They appear rarely as litigants,[3] occasionally as members of Parliament,[4] sometimes as part of the Executive,[5] and virtually never as judicial decision makers.[6] Their presence in the Australian system could never be described as "armed" or "of full stature". To this extent, the ascription of feminine strength to the entity which represented Australian nationhood is at odds with the reality; the historical exclusion of women from the constitutional arena.

However, with the coming of the centenary of Australian federation, discussion of constitutional change is commonplace and reform may be imminent. Academic issues are being debated in the public arena.[7] The question of how best to redress the historical constitutional imbalance between men and women and to incorporate the interests and concerns of women has been raised. Suggestions have been made to examine barriers

---

birth" to Athena only after he had swallowed whole the body of his pregnant wife. See Gatens, "Corporal representation in/and the body politic" in Diprose and Ferrell (ed) *Cartographies:Poststructuralism and the Mapping of Bodies and Spaces* (Allen & Unwin, Sydney 1991) 79 at 81

3   As Australia does not possess a Bill of Rights, most constitutional litigation has concerned the division of powers between the States and the Commonwealth. However even in relation to the small number of claims by individuals, women are unlikely to feature.

4   Statistics are presented in the Australian Law Reform Commission, *Equality Before the Law* (Discussion Paper No. 54) (1993) 59 [hereafter "ALRC Discussion Paper No 54"] and Sawer & Simms, *A Woman's Place:Women and politics in Australia* (Allen & Unwin, St Leonards, 2nd ed 1993) p58.

5   Women have been successful in entering the bureaucracy but they have not been rewarded with advancement to the highest policy levels: ALRC Discussion Paper No 54 at 63.

6   The first appointment of a woman to the High Court of Australia, Mary Gaudron, was made in February 1987. For one of the earliest discussions of the entry of women into the legal profession generally see Greig, "The Law as a Profession for Women" (1909) 6 *Commonwealth Law Review* 145. The absence of women from the judiciary has become a concern for government. See, for example: Aust, Attorney General's Dept, *Judicial Appointments* (Discussion Paper, September 1993). When the ALRC reported in 1993, only 12 out of 233 senior federal State and Territory judges were women. There are 3 women among the 136 State and Territory Supreme Court judges: ALRC Discussion Paper No 54 at 81.

7   The Constitutional Centenary Foundation has produced material which has received public attention. The Republican Advisory Committee which reported to the Commonwealth Parliament has also received public scrutiny.

to participation of women in public and political life;[8] to consider the inclusion of an equality right in any Bill of Rights;[9] and to review the history of women's struggle for the right to vote.[10]

None of these suggestions directly focus on the principles which underlie Australia's current constitutional system and the way those principles operate. None of them ask whether the system, in practice, meets or even aspires to meet, the theories or assumptions encapsulated by the principles. Nor do they deal with the related question of increasing importance; what it means to be a citizen within a representative democracy.[11]

The Australian Law Reform Commission's 1993 Discussion Paper, *Equality Before the Law*, stated that women should be able to "share equally in political power and in the formation of policy", "feel confident that their views are adequately represented ... and taken fully into account in policy formulation", and know that their views are being taken into account by the Parliament.[12] These statements reflect three principles fundamental to constitutional law: *representation, accountability and the sharing of power.*[13]

The focus of this article is representation. It examines women as *representatives in government; women as they are represented by government*; and women *in representations of government.*[14] The argument in this article is that at the level of doctrine, the High Court is moving to a position which emphasises the participatory aspect of representation. This position is consistent with a feminist critique of

---

8   ALRC Discussion Paper No 54 Ch 6 "Equal Participation in Political and Public Life".

9   Marquis, "A Feminist Republic? A Feminist Constitution?" [1993] *Spring Australian Quarterley* 29.

10   "Women's Suffrage Centenary Issue" (1994) 3 *Constitutional Centenary Foundation Newsletter*.

11   For some recent discussions of this question see Blackburn (ed) *Rights of Citizenship* (Mansell Publishing, London 1993); Thornton, "Embodying the Citizen" in Thornton (ed.) *Fragile Frontiers: Feminist Debates Around Public and Private* (forthcoming).

12   ALRC Discussion Paper No 54 at 57.

13   This paper is part of a larger project which questions the underlying assumptions of the Australian Constitution. Its thesis is that, despite its claims to representative democracy, accountability and the sharing of power, the practice of the Australian constitutional system, on all three accounts, has failed to meet the evolving standards of each of the principles.

14   This later sense means the visual and textual descriptions of government, primarily through the media.

representative democracy which demonstrates that low levels of participation by women undermine the representative nature of that concept. In history and current practice, Australia's system lags behind the theoretical insights suggested by feminist argument, and the conclusions which follow from High Court doctrine. The aim of this article is to demonstrate the need for a synthesis of constitutional practice with theory and doctrine, by suggesting that increased participation of women is essential for Australia's constitutional system to conform with evolving standards of representative democracy.

One part of the background to this discussion occurs in the international arena. In light of Australia's international obligations and the growing international focus on the under representation of women in public life, any deficiency in the Australian constitutional system of representative democracy is unsatisfactory. Australia is a signatory to the *Convention on the Elimination of All Forms of Discrimination Against Women* (CEDAW). This obliges State parties to take all appropriate measures to eliminate discrimination against women in the political and public life of the country, to ensure women's participation in the formulation of government policy, and to provide them with the opportunity to represent government internationally.[15] The United Nations committee established to review compliance with CEDAW has decided to make these provisions the focus of its forthcoming deliberations.[16] Under-representation of women was also a focus at the 1993 Vienna World Conference on Human Rights. In the lead up to the United Nations sponsored World Conference on Women to be held in Beijing in 1995, it is one of three areas designated for action in the Asia-Pacific region.[17] The regional preparatory conference held in Jakarta in June 1994 called for the achievement of full and equal participation of women in government and the strengthening of institutions to support women's full and active participation in community and national decision-making.[18] At the international level, representation of women has clearly emerged as a major issue.

---

15   Articles 7 and 8. This followed the *Convention on the Political Rights of Women*, July 7 1954, TIAS No 8289, 193 UNTS 135.
16   Arvonne Fraser, *International Women's Rights Action Watch, Women and Public Life, Articles 7 and 8 of the Women's Convention and the Importatnce of Non-Govermental Organizations in Creating Civil Societies* (Humphrey Institute of Public Affairs, University of Minnesota 1993).
17   Aust, Dept of Foreign Affairs and Trade, (1994) 3(9) *Insight* 6.
18   Aust, Dept of Foreign Affairs and Trade, "Draft Plan of Action for the Advancement of Women in Asia and the Pacific" (6 June 1994) 3(9) *Insight* 6. Note the inconsistency between these aims and the Australian goverment statement that as the provision for women of food, shelter, income, employment,

Moreover, Australia has take an active role on these issues in the lead up to Beijing, by claiming that it is a "leader" in the region with a history of "innovative government" which took "proactive, creative measures" for raising the status of women.[19] Further, the governing Australian Labor Party (at its 1994 National Conference) committed itself to preselecting women in 35 per cent of winnable seats by the year 2002.[20] Scrutiny of Australia's constitutional system is thus critical at this time.[21]

This article asks whether, *according to its own internal principles* of representation, the Australian constitutional system is deficient when it comes to women. Does the Australian constitutional system represent women in a manner consistent with an evolving standard of representative democracy?[22]

---

basic education and health-care are "non-controversial", they may be "implemented to a large extent by men making decisions on behalf of women": Aust, Dept of Foreign Affairs and Trade, (6 June 1994) 3(9) *Insight* 6 at 6.

19 The Australian government claims that in international fora on the status of women, "Australia is a leader": Aust, Dept of Foreign Affairs and Trade, (1994) 3(9) *Insight* 5.

20 See "Historic win for ALP women" *The Australian*, September 28 1994, 1.

21 The notion that women should be better represented in society is not, of course, limited to the constitutional and political spheres. For example, the Commonwealth government is reviewing selection procedures for judicial appointments because the present process has resulted in an "unrepresentative" judiciary. See Aust, Attorney General's Discussion Paper, *Judicial Appointments - Procedure and Criteria* (1993) at 3. Work is being conducted on the representation of women in a variety of other fields including commerce and health. In the field of health the United States' *Public Health Service Act* was amended in 1993 to ensure "clinical research equity" by requiring the National Institute of Health to take steps to ensure that women and members of minority groups are, where appropriate, included in the NIH clinical research projects. We would like to thank Natasha Cica for this observation.

22 Only tangentially does the project explore the claim made by some feminist theorists that the structure of constitutional theory itself fails to take account of women's concerns. In so limiting the argument we acknowledge that we may fall, albeit knowingly, into the critique referred to by Gatens, which is concerned with how the content of theories oppress women rather than challenging the neutrality of the framework, discussed in Phillips, *Engendering Democracy*, (Polity Press, Oxford 1991) p38. For a summary of different feminist critiques of the State see Rhode, "Feminism and the State" (1994) 107 *Harvard Law Review* 1181. MacKinnon argues that the law, and constitutional law in particular, sees and treats women in the way men see and treat women. So, according to MacKinnon, the "state is male". Constitutional theory is thus designed to suppress any consideration of gender. And, because the pre-constitutional social order assumes gender is not a status category, then constitutional cases in relation to issues such as pornography and abortion, will inevitably protect male

Rather than revisit debates which have been extensively canvassed elsewhere, this article seeks to examine gender inequality in the context of constitutional principles of representation which structure the Australian system of government.[23]

REPRESENTATIVE DEMOCRACY AS A PRINCIPLE WHICH UNDERPINS THE AUSTRALIAN CONSTITUTIONAL SYSTEM

Underlying the Australian constitutional system are four principles or concepts, namely federalism, responsible government, representative democracy and the separation of powers.[24] These four principles can be found in a variety of sources, including the text of the Constitution, constitutional conventions,[25] case law, and lesser tools of interpretation.[26]

Federalism, for example, is expressed in the Constitution by the division of legislative power between State and Commonwealth legislatures;[27] the saving of State constitutions,[28] and State laws,[29] the supremacy of federal law in the case of any inconsistency between State and Commonwealth laws,[30] and in representation of the States in the Senate.[31] Responsible government is implicit in that Ministers must be members of either the House of Representatives or the Senate,[32] and ensures that those who

---

power: MacKinnon, *Towards a Feminist Theory of the State* (Harvard University Press, Cambridge Ma 1989) pp157-170. Also see Pateman who argues that the status of women in marriage is related to their political status and that liberal democratic theory, and thus constitutional theory, is built around gendered assumptions based on male identity: Pateman, *The Sexual Contract* (Polity, Cambridge 1988).

23   We do not address issues of gender inequality in constitutional law through the insertion into the Constitution of a right to equality.

24   *Nationwide News Pty Ltd v Wills* (1992) 177 CLR 1 at 69-70 per Deane and Toohey JJ.

25   Jennings, *The Law and the Constitution* (University of London Press, London, 5th ed 1959).

26   For example the High Court has relied on constitutional debates in *Cole v Whitfield* (1988) 165 CLR 360.

27   The Constitution vests a small number of powers exclusively in the Commonwealth (eg ss52, 90). The remainder of listed powers are exercised concurrently with the States, (s51) except in the case of inconsistency when Commonwealth laws prevail (s109). Those powers that are not set out in the Constitution remain exclusively with the States (s107).

28   *Commonwealth Constitution* s106.

29   Section 108.

30   Section 109.

31   Section 7.

32   Section 64.

administer the Departments of State are also responsible to Parliament. The separation of powers doctrine can be discerned in the division of the Constitution into three chapters covering the legislature, the executive and the judiciary;[33] and the vesting of relevant power in each branch respectively.[34] This paper focuses on the fourth principle of representative democracy.

The Constitution and Representative Democracy

The Constitution creates a system where people are chosen to be members of Parliament. Sections 7, 24 and 29 each refer to members being "chosen". In addition there are references to "elections" and "electors" in a variety of sections.[35] Furthermore, s41 appears to protect the right to vote.

The interpretation of these sections has been determined by the High Court on several occasions. The more recent cases of *Nationwide News v Wills*,[36] and *Australian Capital Television v Commonwealth*[37] have held that representative democracy is fundamental to the Constitution.[38] But what representative democracy actually entails has not been clearly determined.

Matters of representative democracy arising before the High Court have ranged from compulsory voting,[39] to the right to vote,[40] to the value of the vote,[41] to the representation of the Territories[42] and to the nature of speech and participation.[43] Each of these matters will be analysed in order to

---

33   Chapter 1 is headed "The Parliament", Chapter II "The Executive Government" and Chapter III "The Judicature".
34   Section 51 (legislative power); s61 (executive power); s71 (judicial power).
35   Sections 8, 9, 10, 12, 30, 31, 32, 41 and 47. See also Zines, "A Judicially Created Bill of Rights?" (1994) 16 *Sydney Law Review* 166 at 175 and his discussion of rights based on representative government.
36   (1992) 177 CLR 1.
37   (1992) 177 CLR 106.
38   This has been affirmed in *Theophanous v The Herald & Weekly Times Limited* (1994) 124 ALR 1; *Stephens v West Australian Newspapers Limited* (1994) 124 ALR 80; and *Cunliffe v Commonwealth of Australia* (1994) 68 ALJR 791.
39   *Judd v McKeon* (1926) 38 CLR 380.
40   *R v Pearson; Ex parte Sipka* (1983) 152 CLR 254.
41   *A-G (Cth); Ex rel McKinlay v Cth* (1975) 135 CLR 1; *A-G (NSW); Ex rel McKellar v Cth* (1977) 139 CLR 527.
42   *Western Australia v The Cth* (the Territorial Senators' Case) (1975) 134 CLR 201.
43   *Nationwide News Pty Ltd v Wills* (1992) 177 CLR 1 and *Australian Capital Television v The Commonwealth* (1992) 177 CLR 106.

assess the standards of representative democracy that have been developed so far by the High Court.

Voting and Notions of Representative Democracy

One of the early cases which could have raised the constitutional requirements underlying our democratic system was *Judd v McKeon*.[44] Ernest Judd failed to vote at an election of members of the Senate for NSW. Voting was compulsory. Judd sought special leave to review the Divisional returning officer's determination that he had failed to provide a "sufficient reason" for not voting, on the ground that the right to vote implies a right *not* to vote, and that the *Electoral Act* (Cth) 1918-1925, which prescribed the compulsory voting, was not a valid exercise of power under s9 of the Constitution.

The opportunity therefore existed for the Court to explain some of the principles upon which the constitutional system was based. Knox CJ, Gavan Duffy and Starke JJ held that the only constitutional restriction within s9 was that the method of choosing senators had to be uniform for all the States. The closest general statement about the democratic system was made by Isaacs J. He stated that the franchise was to be regarded as a right and referred to the fact that s41 spoke of the right to vote.[45] Yet this did not extend to a right not to vote. No further elaboration of the principle of representative democracy was made. Parliament's prescription validly included compulsory voting.

This case reflected the view that Parliament was entitled to define the franchise. The Court did not develop constitutional principles associated with representative democracy. The only conclusion which can be drawn for our purpose is that women, like men, could potentially rely on a "right to vote" according to Issacs' statement. The meaning of representative democracy, however, remained undetermined by the Court.

A Right to Vote?

Section 41 of the Constitution prescribes that

> no adult person who has or acquires a right to vote at elections for the more numerous House of the Parliament of a State shall, while the right continues, be prevented by any

---

44   (1926) 38 CLR 380.
45   As above at 385.

law of the Commonwealth, from voting at elections for either House of the Parliament of the Commonwealth.

This "right to vote", if it was one, was to be short lived. Courts interpreted the provision in a narrow manner, and in a manner that gives us insight into the historical under-representation of women in our constitutional system.

The decision of *R v Pearson; Ex parte Sipka*[46] interpreted the guarantee in s41 as a transitional guarantee only. That guarantee ceased to exist after 12 June 1902, the date on which the *Commonwealth Franchise Act* 1902 (Cth) came into force.[47] In *Sipka*, the majority of the Court relied upon the historical context in which s41 was framed. At Federation, the qualifications of electors for the more numerous Houses of the Parliaments of the respective states were not uniform. This was particularly in relation to the position of women. Only South Australia and Western Australia extended the franchise to women over the age of 21. In order to ensure that those women would be entitled to vote in the Commonwealth elections, s41 precluded the Commonwealth from legislating to prevent them from voting. Section 41 however did not establish a general "right to vote". Interestingly, federal principles influenced the court in reaching this conclusion[48] and underlay the compromise represented by the provision. The so-called "right to vote" in s41 was concerned with the protection of State legislative power, more so than individual rights of women. It has been shown that the intention of the section, according to the Court, was to preserve the power of States at Federation to determine their own franchise, and thus ensure that South Australia particularly, would join the union.[49] Concern for the rights of women to vote were scant.

---

46 (1983) 152 CLR 254.

47 See the joint judgment of Brennan, Deane and Dawson JJ at 280.

48 For instance, the Court held that if a more general right was upheld it would give the States the power to destroy the Commonwealth's power to create a uniform franchise. The principles of federalism and the place of women in the constitution will be developed in another article as part of this project.

49 The South Australian delegates warned that South Australia would reject federation if South Australia lost the adult suffrage for federal elections. Mr Symon (SA) *Convention Debates*, Adelaide 1897, p132 and Mr Holder (SA) p150. See Bennett *The Making of the Commonwealth* (Cassell Australia, Melbourne 1971) p122, and more generally on the franchise, Stretton and Finnimore "Black Fellow Citizens: Aborigines and the Commonwealth Franchise" (1993) 25 *Australian Historical Studies* 521. Note discussion in Part 3 of this paper under the heading *Representation as Voters*.

The majority judgments in *Sipka* confirmed the principle underlying the majority in *Judd v McKeon*, that the power lay with Parliament to determine the extent of the franchise. There were no underlying Constitutional principles necessarily to be drawn from the Constitution in guiding Parliament.

The decision in *Sipka* once again emphasises the difficulty in discerning the Court's view of the scope or content of the principle of representative democracy at this time, save to say that it did not bode well for women and their representation.

The majority view in *Sipka* was fiercely contested by Murphy J who did seek to draw from sections 7 and 24 constitutional principles for a democratic system. These were principles that he had also relied on, as a minority, in the earlier case of *McKinlay*[50] which looked at the notion of the value of the vote. *McKinlay* also gave rise to a greater examination of representative democracy within the Constitutional system. However, some of the opinions in *McKinlay* on the principles of democracy may not necessarily have been positive for women.

An Equality Between Votes?

McKinlay involved the validity of the *Representation Act* 1905-1974 (Cth) and the *Commonwealth Electoral Act* 1918-1975 (Cth). It was essentially about the distribution of electorates, and the allocation of seats between the States. It is the distribution of electorates issue that we seek to analyse here.

The principal submission was that there was a guarantee in s24 of the Constitution, that the number of people or electors in a single member electorate should be nearly as equal as is practicable.

A majority of the Court held that s24 of the Constitution did not require such an equality of numbers, and the principles upon which this was based suggest the nature of representative democracy assumed by the court in its decision. Gibbs J held it to be clear from ss25, 30, 41 and 128 of the Constitution that people might constitutionally be denied the franchise on the grounds of race, sex, or lack of property.[51] This conclusion ignored the participatory aspect of the principle and detracted from the force of the

---

50   (1975) 135 CLR 1.
51   At 44.

argument that s24 required equality of numbers.[52] A system which did not include women in the franchise would still be representative according to this view.

A similar conclusion may flow from the opinion of Stephen J, although the opposite may also follow from a reading of his carefully nuanced approach. Stephen J dealt at length with the ramifications of s24 in light of Chapter 3 of the Constitution. Both ss7 and 24 called "for a system of representative democracy in the sense that the Houses of the legislature are to be composed of members whom the people choose".[53] Moreover, Stephen J discerned three great principles in s24 of the Constitution: representative democracy, by which he meant that the legislators were chosen by: the people; direct popular election; and the national character of the lower House. Furthermore, Stephen J held that the principle of representative democracy was predicated upon "the enfranchisement of electors, the existence of an electoral system capable of giving effect to their selection of representatives and the bestowal of legislative functions upon the representatives thus "elected".[54] However, the particular quality and character of the content of each of those ingredients was not fixed and precise.[55] Most significantly though, Stephen J was prepared to say that representative democracy is

> descriptive of a whole spectrum of political institutions, each different in countless respects yet answering to that generic description ... and in a particular instance there may be absent some quality which is regarded as so essential to representative democracy as to place that instance outside those limits altogether; but at no one point within the range of the spectrum does there exist any single requirement so essential as to be determinative of the existence of representative democracy.[56]

Whilst numerical equality was an important factor, Stephen J upheld the view that it was up to Parliament to determine the electoral system as long as it was "consistent with the existence of representative democracy as the

---

52   At 45.
53   At 56.
54   As above.
55   As above.
56   At 57.

chosen mode of government and is within the power conferred by s51(xxxvi)."[57]

Just as Gibbs J had pointed out the inadequacies of democratic principles contained in the Constitution, so too did Stephen J highlight the fact that "the Constitution in no way pretended to any perfect embodiment of some particular model of democratic principles"[58] and as such it was not accurate to determine that s24 required a practical equality of votes.

Stephen J's opinion could therefore be read in two ways. On one view his emphasis on the indeterminate content of representative democracy could be read as a prescription for labelling as "representative" any voting system, no matter whom it includes or excludes. On this view it would not be possible to argue that under-representation of women violated representative democracy. However Stephen J's view is much more finely constructed than this interpretation would suggest. His Honour was careful to state that the "quality" of any voting system may at some point lose an aspect "essential" to calling it representative.[59] He left open the question of when that occurs, and was keen to emphasise that there is no one precise moment when it does. But on this reading it can be argued that once a system of representative democracy has lost that "quality which is regarded as so essential to representative democracy"[60] it no longer conforms to the concept of representative democracy. Thus a system which under-represented women could fall "outside the [representative democracy] limits altogether".[61]

Murphy J dissented and it is in this case that some of the principles that he developed later in *Sipka*[62] were formulated. He discerned a "democratic theme of equal sharing of political power which pervades the Constitution";[63] s24 demanded it as did s30 which prohibited voters from voting more than once.

There are essentially mixed messages from the above principles, but messages, nonetheless, relevant to any assessment of how well the constitutional system represents women. Gibbs and Stephen JJ remind us that at its inception the system was not representative of women.

---

57   At 58.
58   As above.
59   At 57.
60   As above.
61   As above.
62   (1983) 152 CLR 254.
63   *A-G (Cth); Ex rel McKinlay v Cth* (1975) 135 CLR 1.

Moreover, particularly from Stephen J's description of representative democracy, there is no clear sense of what the internal principles of representative democracy actually require. However, at some point on a spectrum, certain systems fall outside the concept. The requirement of actual representation of a specific group, in Parliament, was considered by the court in a case dealing with the representation of the Territories.

The Right to Representation

Murphy J's view of democracy did receive some support in *WA v Cth*[64] when he was in the majority. The case validated Commonwealth legislation that provided for representation of the Territories in the Senate.

The concept of representation was weighed against the notion of the Senate as a States' house. Barwick CJ, Gibbs and Stephen JJ held that allowing territorial representation would distort the ability of the Senate to operate as a states' house, and in essence, held that the Australian democratic system allowed for some of the population to be excluded from the system of representative government. Three judges were, therefore, prepared to say that actual representation was not essential for representative democracy.

Even though Murphy J was in the majority, his was the only judgment that dealt substantially with the issues of democracy and representation. McTiernan, Mason and Jacobs JJ concentrated on the meaning of s122 in light of the Constitutional text.[65] Murphy J, in looking at the text, highlighted the fact that the term "representation" was significant in s122, and he went beyond the text as well. He maintained that the purpose of the Constitution and the fundamental constitutional doctrines must be kept in mind, which included the fact that "the Constitution is designed for a democratic society".[66] He examined the American system of government and the English philosopher John Stuart Mill on Representative Government, quoting from Mill's analysis:

> The only government which can fully satisfy all the exigencies of the social state is one in which the whole people participate ... In a really equal democracy every or

---

64   (1975) 134 CLR 201.
65   At 234 per McTiernan J, at 270 per Mason J, at 273 per Jacobs J.
66   At 283.

any section will be represented, not disproportionately but proportionately.[67]

The requirement for equal representation for different groups does require linkage of the elector to the electorate, in our view. And to fulfil this, one needs representation in the form of participation of particular sections within the community,[68] namely women.

The view that the Constitution encapsulates these underlying fundamental constitutional concepts was clearly a minority one in the High Court in 1975. Further, the cases discussed so far generally display a very narrow approach to representative democracy as a requirement of our Constitutional system. As a context in which to interpret the provisions, they show an overriding concern to reflect the text of the Constitution and a recognition of the non-democratic historical foundations of the system. Only occasionally does the Court indicate that some types of government may be beyond the Constitution's requirement of representative democracy.

Participation as an Essential Element of Representative Democracy.

It is in the context of freedom of political speech that the present High Court has developed principles associated with representative democracy, and it has done so in a manner that departs significantly from the views of the earlier courts which placed a strong emphasis on the Parliament's power to determine matters associated with representation.[69]

The two cases raising these issues are *Nationwide News* and *Australian Capital Television*. The first concerned the validity of s229(1)(d) of the *Industrial Relations Act* 1988 (Cth); the second, the validity of provisions in the *Broadcasting Act* 1942 (Cth). The relevant sections in each of the acts prevented certain speech. The cases established a right to free speech associated with the Australian system of representative democracy. In reaching this conclusion, some judges elaborated upon the meaning of representative democracy. These cases have been affirmed in *Theophanous v The Herald & Weekly Times Limited, Stephens v West*

---

67   At 284.
68   See p19ff.
69   Dawson J has however maintained the approach that it it is up to Parliament to determine these matters. See *ACTV v Cth* at 184.

Australian Newspapers Limited and *Cunliffe v Commonwealth of Australia.*[70]

Justice Brennan in *Nationwide* began by looking at the text of the Constitution and asserted that the text supported the principles of separation of powers, federalism, responsible government and a Parliament answerable to the people. In order to

> sustain a representative democracy embodying the principles prescribed by the Constitution, freedom of public discussion of political and economic matters is essential: it would be a parody of democracy to confer on the people a power to choose their Parliament but to deny the freedom of public discussion from which the people derive their political judgments.[71]

This was an inherent part of representative democracy and therefore was an inherent part of our constitutional system.

Deane and Toohey JJ went further and discussed the basis of the doctrine of representative democracy which they, too, agreed was a principle that underlies the Constitution: "The rational basis of that doctrine is the thesis that all powers of government ultimately belong to, and are derived from, the governed."[72]

Moreover, since the adoption of full adult suffrage, all citizens who were not under some special disability were entitled to share equally in the exercise of those ultimate powers of governmental control, in their view. This control by the people was expressed through the right to choose their representatives, and, secondly, the power to amend the Constitution through s128. This view emphasises the aspect of representative democracy which requires the electorate to be somehow linked to the elected so that the power which derives from the people is the power which government exercises. One method of achieving that linkage, according to this view, is the equal participation of citizens.

---

70   *Theophanous v The Herald & Weekly Times Limited* (1994) 68 ALJR 713; *Stephens v West Australian Newspapers Limited* (1994) 68 ALJR 765; and *Cunliffe v Cth* (1994) 68 ALJR 791.
71   *Nationwide News Pty Ltd v Wills* (1992) 177 CLR 1 at 47.
72   At 70.

Further expressions of these principles were developed in *Australian Capital Television*. Mason CJ reaffirmed that the Constitution prescribed representative democracy through the creation of Parliament, and through ss7 and 24 in prescribing for the choice by the people. He also described the theoretical basis for representative democracy:

> The very concept of representative government and representative democracy signifies government by the people through their representatives ... And in the exercise of those powers the representatives of necessity are accountable to the people for what they do and have a responsibility to take account of the views of the people on whose behalf they act.[73]

In determining essential elements of this concept of representative government, Mason CJ stated: "In truth, in a representative democracy, *public participation* in political discussion is a central element of the political process."[74]

This right to freedom of speech in our democratic system was therefore an essential part of the Constitution because public participation was an integral part of representative democracy. Again, a corollary of this view is that representation without participation may not meet the requirements of representative democracy.

Gaudron J also proclaimed that a free society governed by principles of "representative parliamentary democracy may entail freedom of movement, freedom of association and, perhaps, freedom of speech generally".[75] Each of these notions is based on the involvement or participation of the people.

These judgments reflect the Court's willingness to state that there are fundamental principles, such as representative democracy, which underlie our constitutional system. Furthermore, there is an acceptance of principles that are integral to representative democracy. Public participation, and its role in linking the elected with the electorate, are two of the principles that are developed strongly. Finally, this also reflects a Court prepared to interpret the Constitution according to present principles, rather than being confined, necessarily, to the meaning of the

---

73   At 137-138.
74   At 139.
75   At 212.

terms at the time of Federation. In this respect, the Constitution is being interpreted as a living document.[76]

These "strengthened" principles assist us in determining whether the Australian constitutional system is deficient with respect to women.

REPRESENTATIVE DEMOCRACY AND THE RELEVANCE OF GENDER

The High Court's approach to representative democracy shows that there are different conceptual levels informing constitutional interpretation. At one level, there is the text of the Constitution which contains certain rules - such as requiring members of Parliament to be directly chosen by the people. At another, there is the principle or doctrine of representative democracy which underpins the rule; and, at yet another level, there are the theories or assumptions behind the formal principle.

It is accepted that representative democracy requires some linkage of the elected and the electorate;[77] that is an ongoing requirement,[78] and that electoral systems can vary over time.[79] The crucial point in relation to under-representation of women is whether individuals or groups can nevertheless be represented in the elected assembly without physically being present themselves. Does it matter that the Australian legislature in 1995 is overwhelmingly composed of one sex at a ratio of ten to one in one house and five to one in the other? Is it necessary for women to be actually present in order to be represented?

We argue that gender is relevant to representation, and the under-representation of women in government makes the system unrepresentative. Four justifications for the view that gender is relevant to representation are identified here: the invisibility of gender; the difference between interests of men and women; the injustice of exclusion; and the nature of democracy.

---

76 This is similar to the approach of the Court in *Cheatlev R* (1993) 177 CLR 541. In that case, the Court was looking at the principle of unanimity of jury verdicts, and in the course of its joint judgment held that contemporary standards would have to be applied in determining what was a representative jury.

77 Dicey, *An Introduction to the Law of the Constitution* (MacMillon Press, London 1960, reprinted 1970) p84.

78 *Nationwide News v Cth* (1992) 177 CLR 1 at 71-72.

79 Discussion of Stephen J in *McKinlay* above. See also *Cheatle v R* (1993) 177 CLR 541 for a discussion of the nature of society changing and the effect of this on constitutional principles.

The Invisibility of Gender

This first argument stresses that gender is hidden or made invisible in current notions of a representative democracy, but it is nevertheless there, evidenced by the overwhelming numerical imbalance between men and women.

The invisibility of women in government means that no challenge is offered to the status quo of imbalance in men's representation. The imbalance appears "normal" and indeed inevitable, and maintains the necessity of natural supportive female roles.[80]

Young refers to the "paradox" of representative democracy in which men and women are formally represented, but social power renders some citizens more equal than others.[81] Thornton argues that as gender is already relevant to citizenship, albeit in a masked way, citizenship ought to become, explicitly, more "gender-conscious".[82]

The effect of this invisibility no doubt means that the agendas of governments are affected by the imbalance of representation. It is difficult, however, to determine this precisely as there is no nation that provides an example for determining the effect of equal representation. This leads into a discussion of whether men and women have different interests.

The Difference Between Interests of Men and Women

Charlesworth argues that research from a number of countries suggests a difference between men and women on political issues. As examples, she refers to women supporting peace initiatives, environmental protection, and social services more than men. She also refers to the fact that increased representation in the European Parliament in 1979 coincided with the increased concern with issues of sex equality.[83] Sawer and

---

80   Charlesworth, "Transforming the United Men's Club: Feminist Futures of the United Nations" (1994) 4 *Transnational Law and Contempary Problems* 420.
81   Iris Marion Young, "Polity and Group Difference" cited in Thornton, "Embodying the Citizen" in Thornton (ed) *Fragile Frontiers: Feminist Debates around Public and Private forthcoming* (Oxford University Press, Melbourne 1995) p259.
82   Thornton "Embodying the Citizen" in Thornton (ed) *Fragile Frontiers: Feminist Debates around Public and Private.*
83   Charlesworth, "Transforming the United Men's Club: Feminist Futures fo the United Nations" (1994) 4 *Transnational Law and Contempary Problems* 420.

Simms argue that the entry of women into the formal institutions of power in Australia has resulted in significant challenges to the content of politics. They highlight the fact that in the 1980s women politicians were airing such issues as abortion, domestic violence, sexual harassment, rape, single parenthood, women's health issues or even just the experience of suburban isolation in a manner unprecedented in Australian political life.[84] However, Rhode argues in the US context that whilst gender parity in political representation is valuable in its own right, its achievement would not guarantee a broadening of political agendas. She also refers to women supporting environmental and welfare measures more than men and greater opposition to the use of military force, but acknowledges that women have also been more conservative on some feminist issues.[85] In fact, she argues that gender is not nearly as important as education and race in predicating electoral behaviour in the US.[86] Commentators point out that issues such as sexuality, race and class influence women's views and practices as well as gender, and that each woman possesses a "multiple consciousness"[87] and thus will recognise an intersectionality[88] of interests involved.

This information raises the difficult issues associated with the "difference" debate. Briefly, difference theory, which is associated with the work of psychologist Gilligan, argues that men and women approach moral and legal dilemmas from different perspectives and therefore have "a different voice".[89] Feminist legal theorists applied Gilligan's work to argue that where law fails to recognise the different voice of women, it fails to take account of their different interests. Thus for our purposes, altering the composition of Parliament to include more women may facilitate the realisation of legislative programs more attuned to the interests of women. In a similar vein, Karst has argued that constitutional doctrines limit

---

84   Sawer & Simms, *A Woman's Place: Women and Politics in Australia* (Allen & Unwin, Sydney, 2nd ed 1993) p154.

85   The question of whether Australian women are more conservative than men is discussed in Sawer & Simms, *A Woman's Place: Women and Politics in Australia* p29.

86   Rhode, "Feminism and the State" (1994) 107 *Harvard Law Review* 1181 at 1206-1207.

87   Matsuda, "When the First Quail Calls: Multiple Consciousness as Jurisprudential Method" (1992) 14 *Womens Rights Reporter* 29.

88   Crenshaw, "Mapping the Margins: Intersectionality, Identity, Politics and Violence Against Women of Color" (1991) 43 *Stanford Law Review* 1241.

89   See Gilligan, *In A Different Voice* (Harvard University Press, Cambridge Ma 1982).

women's access to equality because they are based on a male conception of morality, rather than what he calls an "ethic of care".[90]

Other feminist scholars recognise the pitfalls of characterising women's voices as different. MacKinnon, for example, objects to Gilligan's approach because it does not acknowledge the reasons for that difference; that women's voices are different because women are in a position of subordination to men. It also fails to recognise that often women do not just speak differently to men, "A lot you don't speak."[91] Moreover, Gilligan's views contain the danger of "essentialising" women as sharing, caring and basically inferior.[92]

Whilst there are difficulties in dealing with these issues, Phillips concludes that this is no reason to completely reject the difference approach. It is *because* of the complexity and varied nature of women's interests that women themselves ought to represent their own views. Looking at these difficulties in light of the international arena, Charlesworth argues:

> How or whether women's equal participation in decision-making would affect the quality of UN decisions is not yet certain. But whatever the evidence of a distinctive woman's influence in political decision-making, it is at least clear that the realities of women's lives under the present unbalanced system do not contribute in any significant way to the shaping of UN policy.[93]

The central insight suggested by the justification remains compelling, namely that women experience the world differently to men as an undeniable matter of practical reality. Moreover, regardless of how many different voices women may have, it does not mean that men can properly represent those different voices. The personal experience of some women representatives suggests that men cannot listen to women's views.[94] If this

---

90   Karst, "Woman's Constitution" (1984) *Duke Law Journal* 447.
91   MacKinnon, "Difference and Dominance" in *Feminism Unmodified* (Harvard University Press, Cambridge 1987) p39.
92   Gilligan does state that the contrasts between male and female voices are presented to highlight a distinction between two modes of thought, and to focus a problem of interpretation, rather than to represent a generalisation about either sex. See Gilligan, *In A Different Voice* p2.
93   Charlesworth, "Transforming the United Men's Club: Feminist Futures of the United Nations" (1994) 4 *Transnational Law and Contempary Problems* 420.
94   See p33ff.

is so, how can they adequately represent and pursue them?[95] As such, the interests of women may not be adequately represented by the current, largely male, composition of Parliament. The under-representation of women skews the system of representative democracy toward one gender.

Justice

Another argument identified by Phillips is that it is unjust to exclude women from political life, just as it is unjust that they should be "typists but not directors".[96] Imagining a reversal of the gender balance emphasises the point of Phillips' rhetorical question about the British system of representative democracy: "What would men think of a system of political representation in which they were outnumbered nineteen to one?"[97]

This argument implicitly rejects the proposition that formal access to politics is sufficient to ensure equality for women. Opponents of increasing representation for groups not physically present in decision making assemblies have rejected this. They would argue that not being there *does* matter, but as these groups are not being *physically* prevented from being there, there are no obstacles to their presence which cannot be overcome by reforms aimed at achieving equality of opportunity. This argument fails to accept that there is a difference between formal equality and substantive equality.[98] As Charlesworth points out, "[i]nstitutional practices may not directly discriminate against women, but they can

---

95   We are grateful to Bridget Gilmour-Walsh for making this point so succinctly.
96   Phillips, *Engendering Democracy* p62.
97   As above, p2
98   This position is at best naive. Teson, for example, in discussing the level of representation of women in the international sphere, states that representative democracy requires the elected body to be broadly inclusive of the population, but says that liberal feminism already addresses the issue of underrepresentation with the principles of nondiscrimination and equal opportunity. "Radical feminist theory" according to Teson, would go too far by advocating other means of redress such as affirmative action. In any case, there is no "real injustice, unless feminists are suggesting that women are being prevented from voting". He poses the question: does a radical feminist solution propose appointing women "regardless of popular vote" or even "forc[ing] women who do not want to run for office to do so?" See Teson, "Feminist International Law: a Reply" (1993) 33 *Virginia Journal of International Law* 647. For a response to this in the international context see Charlesworth, "Transforming the United Men's Club: Feminist Futures fo the United Nations" (1994) 4 *Transnational Law and Contempary Problems* 420.

effectively inhibit women's participation by relying on norms reflecting male life patterns as benchmarks of eligibility or success."[99]

Democracy

Anne Phillips favours a fourth argument which concerns the revitalisation of the democratic process. She states that approximate equality between men and women when linked to "a more ambitious programme of dispersing power through a wider range of decision-making assemblies"[100] is necessary for the enhancement of the democratic process. The strongest justification is one concerned with the nature of democracy, in her view.

Some commentators argue that presence is not necessary to representation; the composition of the Parliament does not have to include particular groups in order for those groups to be represented. It is argued that taken to its extreme it would accept the proposition that only lunatics can be represented by mad people.[101] It puts too high a premium on who the representatives are, rather than what they are doing;[102] and it would lead to a "slippery slope" where parliamentary quotas are introduced for other sections of the community whether they be people with definable interests such as lesbians and gay men, and pensioners, or people with arbitrary common characteristics such as blue eyes and red hair.[103] These advocates are arguing quite explicitly that "being there", or presence, is not essential to representation.

Those arguments are rejecting the notion of linking electors to the elected. They certainly limit the concept of participatory democracy to a pure ability to vote. In addition, one must ask whether women can be categorised as a group similar to other groups? First of all, women often represent at least *half* of the community, and secondly, within the category of gender, all those other groups may also be represented.

---

99 Charlesworth, "Transforming the United Men's Club: Feminist Futures fo the United Nations" (1994) 4 *Transnational Law and Contempary Problems* 420, referring to Knop, "Re/Statements: Feminism and State Sovereignty in International Law" (1993) 3 *Transnational Law and Contemporary Problems* 293 at 304.

100 Phillips, "Democracy and Representation, Or, Why Should it Matter Who Our Representatives Are?", unpublished paper (On file with author) at 19.

101 Griffiths quoted in Phillips, as above at 3.

102 Pitkin *The Concept of Representation* quoted in Phillips, above at 4.

103 Phillips, "Democracy and Representation, Or, Why Should it Matter Who Our Representatives Are?", unpublished paper at 4.

Democratic theory is sometimes divided into three models: liberal or representative democracy; direct or participatory democracy; and civic or republican democracy. Each model includes a notion of representation, although the form it takes may alter. Thus in Anne Phillip's discussion of these models[104] she emphasises how, in a liberal democracy, the interests of the individuals who make up the citizenry are represented by representatives elected to the decision-making assembly. In a model of participatory democracy people participate in decision-making themselves. Participation occurs in local arenas such as the workplace, as well as in the political sphere. The likelihood of personal involvement through direct participation is greater according to this view, but not all people will be able to participate all of the time, and their interests will be represented by others. In this model there will normally be a closer link between the parties. A model of civic republicanism differs from both of the above, while still retaining a notion of representation. In republican democracy the people involved in public life are required to transcend localised concerns and represent a more general notion of community.

The involvement of women enhances the model of participatory democracy most. This would also accord with the recent High Court attitudes towards participation as a fundamental part of representative democracy.

Moreover, the critique of "difference", in Phillips' view, only strengthens the need for more women to represent that diversity amongst women. If interests are easily determined it matters less who represents them. When they are complex and divergent, however, there is a greater need for complexity and diversity in the representatives. To this extent, the very difficulties in defining what are in women's interests strengthen the case for more women as representatives.[105] This would enhance representative democracy for men and women, for men would also benefit from the counsel that women would afford.

In summary, representation is a significant element in democratic theory. It implies a linking between the electors and the elected in order to produce some coincidence between them.[106] Participation is one mechanism for establishing that link. The need for the elected body to be

---

104   Phillips, *Engendering Democracy* p13f.
105   Phillips, "Democracy and Representation, Or, Why Should it Matter Who Our Representatives Are?", unpublished paper at 15.
106   This is reflected in the judgments of *Nationwide* and *Australian Capital Television* as discussed above.

representative does not end once the body is elected; representation is an ongoing process. While the content of representative democracy is not set in the sense that differing electoral methods may satisfy its requirements, the system is not representative without the presence of a broad range of people and groups from the electorate. In order to be representative that range should include gender. The invisibility of the currently gendered system, the injustice of under-representing women, the difference between men's and women's interests and the need to revitalise democratic processes compel the conclusion that gender is relevant to representation. Women's representation may not be achieved by men alone, regardless of whether it will necessarily be achieved, for all women, by including more women in the representative system. Regardless of whether women speak in a different voice to men, or the same voice as each other, the gender of those present is relevant to representation, and the under-representation of one gender means that the system is not representative overall.

THE REPRESENTATION OF WOMEN IN THE AUSTRALIAN CONSTITUTIONAL SYSTEM

Representation is used in the literature in a number of different senses. First, women ought to be *represented by government* in a representative democracy. This meaning usually conveys the idea of being able to vote.[107] Second, they ought to be *represented in government*. This entails being a part of the government.[108] Third, and perhaps more controversially, if the appearance of representation is important to the existence of a representative democracy, then women ought to appear *in representations of government*. Just as the law traditionally relied on the maxim that justice should not only be done, but be seen to be done,[109] the representative nature of the constitutional system should be *seen* as well as simply assumed. In order for the Australian constitutional system to reflect the principle of representative democracy in respect of women, women should feature as those who are *represented* (as voters); as those who are *representatives* (as members of parliament); and *in representations of* the constitutional system (in visual and textual descriptions).

---

107 The reliance on ss7 and 24 as an expression of representative democracy is based upon the notion of choice by the people. See discussion above and *Australian Capital Television Pty Ltd. v Commonwealth* at 137 per Mason CJ.

108 The importance of participation in relation to representative democracy is highlighted in *Nationwide* and *Australian Capital Television*. See discussion above.

109 The oft quoted statement is of Lord Hewart CJ in *R v Sussex Justices; Ex parte McCarthy* [1924] 1 KB 256 at 259.

A range of different indicators might be used to test whether the system is representative in the sense of these three connotations. We could look at the composition of the bodies involved in the constitution-making process. For example, who drafted the Constitution? Who approved it by voting for it at referendum? We could look also at the composition of the elected assembly. Who are they and who do they claim to represent? Who voted for them? We could also look at the way in which various interests are taken into account in the debates in the legislature; in the law-making program; and in the administration of policy. How are the contributions of women viewed? And finally, how are those women represented in portrayals of the Australian constitutional system? This section explores those questions in order to demonstrate that Australian constitutionalism does not conform with the principles of representative democracy. In so doing, we adopt a combination of arguments about the relevance of gender to representation. Notions of injustice, difference and revitalisation of the democratic process inform this discussion. Similarly, we argue that as gender is already relevant to representation, albeit in a disguised manner, representation should be "gendered" explicitly to the benefit of women whose presence in the decision-making assembly has so far been minimal, despite the formal appearance of equality of opportunity for representation.

The Historical Under-Representation and Exclusion of Women From the Australian Constitutional System in Relation to Representative Democracy

Historically, women have been either grossly under-represented or totally excluded from significant aspects of the Australian constitutional system. Although the historical exclusion of women from these processes may accord with the practices of the period, it does not address the question of whether the practice accords with the notion of representative democracy, particularly when the imbalance continues into the present day. Women remain under represented, not simply as part of the story of the past but in the story of the present. This is not surprising given, as O'Donovan notes, that "[p]ast exclusions inform present practices. History is not yet abolished."[110]

---

110   O'Donovan, "Gender Blindness or Justice Engendered?" in Blackburn (ed) *Rights of Citizenship* (Mansell, London 1993) p19.

Representation in the Drafting of the Constitution

The first stage in the process of building a constitutional system based on representative democracy was the holding of a series of constitutional conventions in 1891, 1897 and 1898, at which the Constitution was drafted. Women were not merely *under represented* in this process, they were virtually not represented at all. At the 1891 Convention attended by all colonial legislatures and New Zealand, no women were present, and as none were eligible to vote in colonial elections none could contribute to the process by electing the delegates.

In 1894, South Australia had introduced universal franchise, and so South Australian women contributed to the 1897 Convention process by electing their representatives and, in the case of one particularly bold woman, even standing for office. But when Catherine Spence stood for election to the 1897 Convention as a South Australian delegate, she was the first woman to seek political office in Australia. Despite being named in the Liberal organisation's list of "10 Best Men",[111] and polling a "creditable" 7383 votes,[112] her bid was unsuccessful. Catherine Spence partly attributed her failure to comments by the South Australian Premier Charles Kingston,[113] who cast doubt over her eligibility to stand as she was a woman, an attitude in keeping with prevailing legal doctrine in which married women had (along with lunatics and children) no civil legal capacity at common law. At the 1897 Convention, Western Australia appointed its delegates, who were all men; in New South Wales and Victoria, where only men could vote and stand, only men were elected; and Queensland did not attend. No women were present in 1897, nor were they in 1898.

Unless it is accepted, as was argued at the 1897 Convention, that women can be represented at the ballot box by "their relations and male friends",[114] women were virtually excluded from this crucial constitution-making aspect of representative democracy.[115]

---

111   Haines, *Suffrage to Sufferance* (Allen and Unwin, North Sydney 1992) p60.
112   As above p62.
113   As above.
114   *Convention Debates*: Vol. 2, 15 April 1897, p637.
115   Despite their official exclusion from the process, women's groups worked hard to have their views represented in the constitution-making process by informal means. See Irving, "Who are the Founding Mothers? Women and Australian Federation" *Papers on Parliament* (Forthcoming, to be issued by the Department of the Senate, Parliament House, Canberra 1994). Numerous petitions were sent to the Conventions by women's groups. Appropriately enough, one of their major issues pursued was universal suffrage. See the *Convention Debates*: Vol

Despite the skewed nature of this process of representation, it is sometimes argued that the "founding fathers" were broadly representative of the Australian population. Craven, for example, has argued that it has become fashionable to criticise the members of the Conventions on the grounds of lack of diversity, when the Convention included a range of different interests including commercial, labour and agricultural.[116] Presumably the point of this argument is to make the claim that in view of their diversity in terms of class, political party, socio-economic background, they were representative of the Australian community. Despite the diversity, however, they all shared one significant characteristic, namely their gender. The "founding fathers" may have included a cross section of some groups in Australian society, but they did not include one major group, women.

Representation in the Endorsement of the Constitution

The next phase in the making of Australia's most basic law was the holding in each State of a referendum to seek approval for the Constitution. It is a critical moment in the development of any new nation, and in the case of Australia, the popular mandate bestowed on our Constitution by the referendum process, is often touted as Australia's unique badge of democracy. The only problem with this argument is that the electorate which endorsed the Constitution comprised only half of the population in terms of gender, and none of the indigenous inhabitants. Not only were women not represented in the Conventions which drafted the basic law, but they were virtually not represented in the electorate which endorsed it.

Little wonder, then, the anger of many women in Victoria, Tasmania and New South Wales,[117] who, having struggled since the 1860s for the right to vote, now saw the consequences of their exclusion from the franchise; they were effectively silenced in the constitution-making process. As one commented: "[i]t is manifestly unjust that this great national question of Federation should be decided by only half the adult population of New South Wales."[118]

1, 10 March 1891, p174; Vol 2, p23 March 1897,5; p24 March 1897, pp33,34; 30 March 1897, p261; 8 April 1897, p408; 15 April 1897, p637; and Oldfield, *Woman Suffrage in Australia: A Gift or a Struggle* (1992).

116   Craven, "The Founding Fathers: Constitutional Kings or Colonial Knaves?" *Papers on Parliament No 21* (1993) Issued by the Department of the Senate, Parliament House, Canberra

117   Oldfield, *Woman Suffrage in Australia: A Gift or a Struggle* p62.

118   As above.

This is a good example of how women of the time were caught in a classic cycle of discrimination. As they were not entitled to vote, they were not entitled to any say in the nature and content of the Constitution, the legal instrument which determined the very rights, such as voting, that they struggled to achieve.[119] Some of the most basic rights of representation and citizenship (for example determining what would be included in the basic law and voting for it) were denied them, because they were denied representation in the first place. The failure of the constitution-making process to conform to the principle of representative democracy boded poorly for the type of constitutional system which followed. The exclusion of women, once institutionalised in the constitution-making process, legitimated any subsequent exclusion and also provided a reason for excluding women.

Representation as voters

As women were excluded in the making or approving of the Constitution, so they were virtually excluded from voting for representatives in the new federal Parliament until 1902, when the vote was granted to all women except Aboriginal women in Queensland and Western Australia.[120]

At the State level, the franchise had been extended over a period of some 25 years. South Australia was the first colony to grant women the right to vote in 1894 after the defeat of no less than six attempts in nine years.[121] Western Australia granted women the franchise next in 1899, after three earlier attempts had been defeated.[122] Then came the Commonwealth in June 1902,[123] followed shortly thereafter by New South Wales in August 1902,[124] and Tasmania in 1903.[125] Queensland and Victoria held out against universal suffrage until 1905[126] and 1908[127] respectively, with Victoria having gone to the trouble of repealing the right it inadvertently granted to women ratepayers in 1863.[128] Many of the early attempts to

---

119   Note the discussion above on section 41 and the "right to vote".
120   Oldfield, *Woman Suffrage in Australia: A Gift or a Struggle* p64. See also generally, Sawer & Simms, *A Woman's place: Women and Politics in Australia*, above.
121   Oldfield, *Woman Suffrage in Australia: A Gift or a Struggle* p23-38.
122   As above, pp46-52.
123   As above, p64.
124   As above, p96.
125   As above, p109.
126   As above, p27.
127   As above, p156
128   As above, p132.

extend the franchise were limited to women who owned property,[129] or were married,[130] and did not always extend to Aboriginal women.[131]

At the Commonwealth level, the question of plural voting according to property holdings was the major controversial issue and little of the discussion at the Constitutional Conventions focussed specifically on female representation. At the 1891 Constitutional Convention held in Sydney,[132] one delegate, however, candidly noted that although the lower house was elected to represent the whole of the people, "it does not really do that, for it does not represent the women."[133]

Eventually the wording of cl 30 allowed the colonies to determine the qualification of electors and a proposal to exclude property qualifications was rejected. In Adelaide in 1891, and at the 1897 Convention, Holder proposed that adult suffrage be included within the Constitution. This was rejected. In a convoluted turn of logic, delegates argued that as some colonies were opposed to suffrage for women, federation would be jeopardised by agreeing to the South Australian position.[134] The matter was characterised as a conflict between "states rights" and women's rights and thus the former larger interest had to prevail. Holder then immediately proposed an amendment which guaranteed the continued right of South Australian women to vote in federal elections. It was phrased in the negative and provided that no person who held the State franchise could be restricted from voting at Commonwealth level. This amendment was eventually severed from cl 30 and became s41 of the Constitution. States continued to be able to prescribe qualifications of voters until the Commonwealth otherwise provided.[135]

Apart from ingrained prejudice about the appropriateness of women participating in a representative democracy as full citizens, Oldfield puts

---

129   See for example introduction by Caldwell of measure into SA Parliament in 1889 in Oldfield, *Woman Suffrage in Australia: A Gift or a Struggle* p30.
130   As above, p103-104.
131   See Stretton and Finnimore, "Black Fellow Citizens: Aborigines and the Commonwealth Franchise" (1993) 25 *Australian Historical Studies* 521.
132   *Convention Debates*, Sydney 1891, Vol 1, 52-3, 62, 174, 488, 614, 625, 627.
133   McIlwraith, *Convention Debates*, Sydney 1891, Vol. 1, 62.
134   *Convention Debates*, Adelaide 1897 See, for example, Wise 3:717; Howe 3:719; Fraser 3:720; Glynn 3:720; Trenwith 3:722-723. The latter three specifically claimed to support women's suffrage but thought federation was more important.
135   See the discussion above. Gibbs CJ and Stephen J drew on this historical reality in interpreting ss7 and 24 in *McKinlay*'s case, and this approach was also relied on in *Sipka* in interpreting s41 as a transitional provision.

forward a number of other reasons for the rejection of universal suffrage. The debate was stifled because of its association with the wider issue of abolition of the plural vote. For this reason the labour movement generally favoured abolition of the plural vote before the extension of the franchise to women.[136] Similarly the very fact that a property qualification was still attached to the vote indicated that the type of voting system in the fledgling democracy was not representative in any case.[137] Fear of cheap labour and that women involved in politics would not bear sufficient children to populate the sparse continent in the Asian region also influenced the debate. Finally the legal doctrine of coverture[138] assumed that, upon marriage, men and women were joined in a unity of spousehood making it unnecessary for women to vote because their relatives and friends were already representing them.

The struggle for enfranchisement illustrates a key premise of the discussion about constitutional law and women, namely that representative democracy is important for the claim of women to equality in a broad sense. The right to vote is just one of a bundle of rights which constitute full citizenship in society, a point clearly demonstrated by an examination of the issues which were linked to the suffrage debate. The debate did not solely concern a right to exercise political choice; it was intimately connected with the way in which women were, on a deeper level, subject to discrimination and inequality. For example, Oldfield surveys the issues which impinged upon the debate about granting the vote to women. They included the need to improve working conditions of women;[139] rights of women to own property;[140] automatic guardianship of children by fathers;[141] the inequality of divorce laws which still required women, but not men, to prove an aggravated adultery;[142] treatment of women prisoners;[143] legislation which provided for detention of any women suspected of engaging in prostitution;[144] and education for women.[145] Taxation of women without representation[146] and natural rights theories

---

136   Oldfield, *Woman Suffrage in Australia: A Gift or a Struggle* p174.
137   As above, p16.
138   See discussion in Graycar & Morgan, *The Hidden Gender of Law* (Federation Press, Sydney 1992) Chapter 6.
139   Oldfield, *Woman Suffrage in Australia: A Gift or a Struggle* p203.
140   As above, p204.
141   As above, p206.
142   As above.
143   As above.
144   As above, p207.
145   As above, p189.
146   As above, p187.

which demanded that every person should have the same rights[147] were also discussed. Economic, social, educational, property and family rights of women were intertwined with the issue of representation. Clearly representation was not simply about political rights but about the way women were conceived of in the new society.[148] As the Constitution is the foundation of law-making, the ability of women to vote for the law-makers was essential to the notion of representative democracy. It was a small but significant step toward women exercising their rights on an equal basis to men, although its achievement did not guarantee substantial change as indicated by the continuing prohibition on women's entry to a number of public activities including aspects of the legal profession.[149] After a long struggle,[150] a constitutional system committed to the principle of representative democracy finally granted the right to be represented to half its constituents.

Representation as Members of the Parliament

Despite the opportunity for women to stand as representatives in the Parliament, the actual history of women's election to that role is not encouraging.

Apart from South Australia, where the right to stand was introduced in conjunction with the right to vote in 1894, the right to stand for election to Parliaments of the States was generally not introduced until around the period of the First World War.[151] The right to stand for the Commonwealth Parliament was granted in 1903 along with the vote.[152]

---

147   As above.
148   See also Irving, "A Gendered Constitution? Women, Federation and Heads of Power." (1994) 24 *Western Australian Law Review* 82.
149   Thornton, "Embodying the Citizen" in Thornton (ed) *Fragile Frontiers: Feminist Debates around Public and Private* (forthcoming Oxford University Press, 1995) p6.
150   Oldfield refutes the claim by other historians that the granting of votes for women was a "gift" of the new Federation to women, by demonstrating that it was in fact the result of a 28 year long struggle by women: Oldfield, *Woman Suffrage in Australia: A Gift or a Struggle* pp14-15ff.
151   *Constitution Amendment Act* (SA) 1894; *Parliament (Qualification of Women) Act* (WA) 1920; *Women's Legal Status Act* (NSW) 1918; *Constitution Act* (Tas) 1921; *Elections Act* (Qld) 1915; *Parliamentary Elections(Women Candidates) (Vic)* 1923 cited in Thornton, above, appendix 1. See also Haines, *Sufferage to Sufferance* (1992) 73 and Sawer & Simms, *A Woman's Place: Women and Politics in Australia* Chapter 3.
152   Haines, *Sufferage to Sufferance* (Allen and Unwin, Sydney 1992) p73.

As to the actual election of women to Parliament in all States, apart from South Australia and Tasmania, women were elected fairly soon after the introduction of enabling legislation.[153] In the Commonwealth, however, no women were elected to Parliament until 1943, when Enid Lyons won the seat in the House of Representatives and Dorothy Tangney entered the Senate.[154]

The dearth of women representatives was not through any lack of willing candidates. Between 1902 and 1943, 39 women had unsuccessfully nominated for the lower house and five for the upper house.[155]

Numerous reasons, many of which still resonate today, have been put forward for these dismal statistics. Haines attributes it to greater family responsibilities of women, the fact that women generally remained outside the party system, and, that when inside, they were given unwinnable seats.[156] The idea of women representatives evoked fear on the part of male representatives: "The prospect of women occupying their hallowed parliamentary benches seemed to frighten most nineteenth-century Australian parliamentarians out of their wits."[157]

Sensationalist, and contradictory comments were made to the effect that women representatives would be at once dangerous, and feminising. "No Government would be safe against the persistent attacks of a feminine opposition";[158] "[d]o you want to bring them in here with their babies and their bottles".[159]

The persistent failure of women to win seats continued well after the election of Enid Lyons and Dorothy Tangey. In the twenty-five years between 1943 and 1969 women were successful on only five occasions,

---

153 The first woman to be elected to any Australian Parliament was Edith Cowan. In 1921 she was elected as a Nationalist to the West Australian Legislative Assembly. See Souter, *Acts of Parliament: A Narrative history of the Senate and House of Representatives of the Commonwealth of Australia* (Melbourne University Press, Carlton 1988) 358-359. In NSW in 1923, in Queensland in 1929, but in SA in 1959 and in Tasmania in 1943: Haines, *Sufferage to Sufferance* (Allen and Unwin, Sydney 1992) p123.
154 Haines, *Sufferage to Sufferance* p73.
155 As above.
156 As above, p74.
157 As above, p178.
158 *Observer* 23 July 188, quoted in Oldfield, *Woman Suffrage in Australia: A Gift or a Struggle* p179.
159 *Mercury*, 9 October 1903, quoted in Oldfield, *Woman Suffrage in Australia: A Gift or a Struggle.*

and as Haines points out, as Enid Lyons was elected three times, only three different women represented the electorate during that period.[160] At State level the figures are even worse. Of the 46 women who stood as State representatives, only seven were elected.[161]

The most disturbing data however comes from the period of the 1960s and 70s, an era in which so-called second-wave feminism had advocated successfully for a range of initiatives. In this enlightened period, women responded enthusiastically to the idea of entering the public domain as representatives of the electorate. In an eight-year period between 1969 and 1977, no less than 161 women offered themselves as candidates for election to the House of Representatives. Only 44 of these were endorsed by either of the major parties, and only one, Joan Child, was elected.[162] Equality of opportunity or not, clearly a system which produces such a run of statistics is open to question.

During the 1980s and the early 1990s, the figures have very gradually improved. At 8 November 1994, there were 136 women in Australian parliaments, out of 841 seats. This represents 16.17 %.[163] It is clear from this evidence that merely providing the opportunity for women to become representatives is not sufficient to guarantee that the constitutional system is actually "representative". Since Federation, only 50 women out of a total of 1279 parliamentarians have been elected to federal Parliament. Despite the existence of equality in the formal sense, the reality has been that the representative nature of the Parliaments of Australia has been anything but equal in relation to women. If, as noted above, one condition of representative democracy is that the Parliament be broadly representative, then this failure of Parliaments around Australia to seat women calls into question the representative nature of the Australian constitutional system.

The composition of the current Federal legislature grossly under-represents women in the Australian community.

The basic condition of representative democracy is that the composition of government reflect a broad cross-section of the community. This notion is

---

160   Haines, *Sufferage to Sufferance* p121.
161   As above, p121.
162   As above, p142.
163   The percentage of women in each Parliament on 8 November 1994 was: Commonwealth 14.35%; NSW 19.15%; Vic 12.12%; Qld 14.6%; WA 16.48%; SA 23.19%; Tas 14.82%; ACT 35%; and NT 12%: Parliamentary Research Service, Parliament of Australia.

supported by the importance of the represented being linked to the representatives and the ability of the representatives to listen to and ascertain the views of their constituents during the life of the Parliament.[164]

In common with other countries,[165] the composition of the federal parliament is not representative of the community in respect of women. "The body politic remains a predominantly fraternal organisation".[166] The current Prime Minister, Paul Keating, has labelled this gender disparity as "the great flaw in Australian democracy".[167] Figures taken from the ALRC Discussion Paper, *Equality Before the Law*,[168] indicate that representation of women in the federal legislature, and the federal executive, is grossly disproportionate to the number of women in the community.[169] In the federal parliament women comprise less that 9 per cent of members of the House of Representatives and just over 21 per cent of the Senate. Women hold less that 10 per cent of positions in a federal ministry of 32, and approximately 5 per cent in federal Cabinet. And, as noted by the ALRC "there has never been a woman Governor General or

---

164   *Australian Capital Television v Cth* (1992) 177 CLR 106 at 232-233 per Toohey J. See also the discussion above of High Court doctrine following the free speech cases.

165   The roll of the New Zealand House of Representatives lists 36 women and 1127 men: Fish, Kirby & Waring, *Petition to Members of House of Representatives of New Zealand*. In 1990 percentages in other countries ranged from between 5-6% in France and the U.K. to 10-12% in Austria, Italy and Poland, and 20-30% in Germany, the former Soviet Union and Denmark: Janova and Sinean, "Women's Participation in Political Power in Europe" (1992) 155 *Women's Studies International Forum* 117; *The World's Women: Trends and Statistics 1970-1990*, (Social Statistics and Indicators, Series K, 8, United Nations, New York 1990) p39.

166   Thornton, "Embodying the Citizen" in Thornton (ed) *Fragile Frontiers: Feminist Debates around Public and Private* (Oxford University Press, 1995) p18.

167   Kingston, "PM wants more women in Parliament" *Canberra Times* 4 December 1994. The Prime Minister's stance on this issue contrasts with his attitude toward the ability of female journalists married to Liberal party members to report Canberra politics without bias: see Kingston, "Lawrence criticizes PM's stance on women", *Canberra Times* 3 June 1994.

168   ALRC Discussion Paper No 54 at 59.

169   In this respect, the political arena is no different to other sectors of the community such as business where, contrary to popular impressions, recent survey demonstrate, women remain underrepresented. See Still, *Where To From Here? The Mangerial Woman in Transition* (Business and Professional Publishing, NSW 1993): the proportion of women in senior management fell from 2.5% in 1984 to 1.3% in 1992 as compared to a fall for men from 11.3% to 10.1%.

Prime Minister".[170] The decision by the Australian Labor Party at its 1994 annual conference to commit itself to preselecting women in 35 per cent of all winnable seats by the year 2002 is seeking to address this deficiency.[171]

The division between public and private spheres reflects and perpetuates the under-representation of women.

The gross under-representation of women in the Australian constitutional system is due partly to the division between public and private spheres. This view, common to feminist theory, is strongly argued by Pateman who claims that the abstract individual, so essential to liberal democracy, can only operate because of the gendered distinction between public and private.[172] Thus, a woman's domestic responsibilities in the private sphere impede her entry into public life. O'Donovan argues that "[w]hat goes on in the family is crucial to political life".[173]

Applying this approach to under-representation in the constitutional life of the state does not simply mean that women were impeded in entering into the public sphere. Once they had entered they still carried the double burden of their roles. The significance of a perceived distinction between public and private spheres of life continued to be a hindrance to their role as representatives. Sawer notes how the early Australian women politicians were expected to demonstrate their commitment to the private sphere, over their public responsibilities: " ... their first commitment was to traditional gender roles in the home, and ... housekeeping the state could only come later and never at the expense of the primary role."[174]

The practical consequences for women can be extreme. As Justice Elizabeth Evatt observed, women would have never agreed to s125 of the Constitution, placing the Federal capital within New South Wales, but at least one hundred miles from Sydney. Women would have recognised the impossibility of leading a normal domestic life while participating in

---

170   ALRC Discussion No. 54, above. Note that the more powerful the institution, the less likely that women will be represented on it.
171   See "Historic win for ALP women", *The Australian* 28/9/94.
172   Pateman, *The Sexual Contract.*
173   O'Donovan, "Gender Blindness or Justice Engendered?" in Blackburn (ed) *Rights of Citizenship* (Mansell Publishing, London 1993) at 15.
174   Sawer, "Housekeeping the State: Women and Parliamentary Politics in Australia" in *Trust the Women:Women in Federal Parliament* (Papers in Parliament No17, Department of the Senate, Canberra 1992) p18.

Parliament so peculiarly located that even modern-day transport has not overcome its inconvenience.[175]

The distinction also had the effect of influencing the view that women's interests differed from those of men. Sawer's study also found that early women politicians were expected to confine their discussion to women's issues affecting family, children and welfare matters.[176]

Constitutional decisions in other jurisdictions perpetuated the continuance of such a division, and thwarted women's ambitions to enter the public domain. Judge Ruth Bader Ginsburg (as she then was) notes how the U.S. Supreme Court rationalised exclusion of women from the public sphere on the basis that it was not their place.[177] So, for example, Judge Ginsburg notes that, as late as 1961, the Court could find a women's place at "the centre of home and family life" could exclude her from the obligation to sit on juries. The public/private distinction was thus constitutionalised.[178]

Simply providing equality of opportunity in the sense of removing overt barriers to women's entry to Parliament will not necessarily change the imbalance until these structural issues are also addressed. This of course includes, amongst other things, broadening the responsibilities of both parents in the domestic sphere.

The contribution of women representatives is seen as "different" and accorded less weight.

This section concerns the way in which women's interests are taken into account in the legislative process. It takes as its starting point the view that the nature of women's contribution, or "voice" differs from that of men's. This has two consequences. The first is that in order for the constitutional system to be representative, women should represent their own interests. The second, is that women's interests are given less value in parliamentary debate than those of men's because they are different from the interests of men. Just as women's "different voice" would be incorporated into the law under this view, the different voice of women

---

175   Cited in Irving, "A Gendered Constitution? Women, Federation and Heads of Power" (1994) 24 *Western Australian Law Review* 82 at 93.
176   Sawer, "Housekeeping the State: Women and Parliamentary Politics in Australia" in *Trust the Women: Women in Federal Parliament* p19.
177   Bader Ginsburg, "Remarks on Women Becoming Part of the Constitution" (1988) 6 *Law and Inequality* 17 at 19.
178   *Hoyt v Florida* 368 US 57 (1961).

would also be incorporated into the constitutional system in order to make it more representative.

The idea that in a constitutional system, women have a different interest, and therefore "voice", to men has expressed itself in the representative process. During the debate over female enfranchisement, supporters of suffrage argued that the electoral process would benefit if women were given the vote. Louisa Lawson, editor of the first women's magazine in Australia, argued that women would introduce a superior, feminine form of logic into the representative process. Women voters: "will be a power for good in every place and she will conquer error by truth and love."[179]

When women representatives first appeared in the Parliament the notion of a different voice surfaced again. According to Dame Enid Lyons, when she made her maiden speech, men wept.[180] History does not report whether it was the subject matter or style of Dame Enid's presentation which produced such an overwhelming response, but it is clear that her contribution differed from that which was usually heard.[181] There is of course an obvious point, that women's voices are different physiologically; apart from anything else they sound different. As Parliament is a forum for debate, tone and style of delivery is often important in persuasion and debating style. On the hustings too, the voice of Dame Enid was perceived as being somehow "different" from that which was ordinarily heard: "[s]he gave her own speech, talking politics in terms of 'pots and pans and children's shoes'."[182]

The view of the difference of women's contributions is still current. Introducing a proposal to encourage women from the Liberal Party to run for pre-selection, the current president of the Liberal Party federal women's committee Joan Hall was reported to have said: "Women have a different perspective on the way they view life and the way they exercise power in politics. I think Parliament will have a different sort of emphasis ... a different set of priorities."[183]

---

179   Oldfield, *Woman Suffrage in Australia: A Gift or a Struggle* pp195-196.
180   Lyons quoted in Langmore, *Prime Ministers' Wives* (McPhee Gribble, Melbourne 1992) p108.
181   According to Langmore, Dame Enid's speech was "thoughtful and substantial, compassionate and visionary": as above.
182   Langmore, *Prime Ministers' Wives* p86.
183   Lang, "Women the key to new-age Parliament" *Canberra Times* 30 August 1993.

Moreover, Sawer and Simms argue that "[w]omen in Australian political parties have often found that the price of acceptance is to agree to the sidelining or marginalising of issues concerning the status of women."[184]

Proponents of double sex representation where each sex would be represented in each electorate, argue that women who entered Parliament under the proposed system would not have to operate in the same competitive manner as men. Thus, they would not be in the mould of Margaret Thatcher, and there would be "a greater sense of co-operation, and, unencumbered by the extremes of ego that cause such posturing in the political process, the system itself would gradually change".[185]

Another variant on the idea of the difference of women's contribution is the notion put forward by some citizenship theorists that qualities associated with mothering or nurturing would enrich the ideas of representation and citizenship.[186]

There is further evidence that women may fulfil their role as representative differently to men. The Budget process is an important aspect in the way representatives exercise power on behalf of the electors. In 1993 the Australian parliamentary system was subject to change in the Budget process. Ordinarily in the Budget process, if a government needs the support of a minor party in order to have the Budget bills passed by the Upper House, the minority grouping would put a list of demands to the government. The government may be forced to make concessions. The election of two women Senators from the Greens Party has injected a new dimension into that process. Senator Christobel Chamarette and Senator Dee Margetts asked for something which had not previously been demanded: answers to questions about how the Budget would affect the people they represent.[187] The effect of this different voice may lead to different emphases in the parliamentary process and hence the constitutional system of representative democracy. Gilligan claims that women's different voice leads them to emphasise contextual relationships

---

184   Sawer & Simms, *A Woman's Place: Women and Politics in Australia* p208.
185   Macklin, "An idea whose time has come" *Canberra Times* 22 October 1993.
186   Elshtain, *Public Man, Private Woman: Women in Social and Political Thought* (Princeton University Press, Prinston 1981) cited in O'Donovan, "Gender Blindness or Justice Engendered?" in Blackburn (ed) *Rights of Citizenship* p22.
187   According to newspaper reports, the Federal Treasurer Mr John Dawkins was forced to supply a graph of the alleged effects of the Budget on taxpayers, and a complete analysis of the same. Kingston, "Greens entangle Keating" *Canberra Times* 4 September 1993.

over abstract rights.[188] The Senator's demands could be seen as an example of this approach. Instead of assessing the impact of the budget in abstract terms, they looked at the specific context of its effect. This could be seen as an illustration of the different way in which women approach moral dilemmas.

But even assuming that there is no different voice between men and women,[189] anecdotal evidence suggests that contributions by women are "heard" as different and consequently accorded less weight. Sawer's study confirms that historically male politicians either patronised or ignored the contributions of female politicians. A letter to the newspaper noted that Ministers replied to women members of Parliament with "a mixture of coyness and fatherliness that they no doubt also apply to their teenage grand-daughter's demands".[190]

If accounts of current members of Parliament are examined, this attitude still holds true. They suggest that the different nature of the "voice" of women in the Parliament leads to their views being accorded less weight than those of the male representatives. With a hindsight tinged with regret parliamentarian Kathy Sullivan reflected recently:

> It appeared that women MPs could state their views however they liked - tactfully or aggressively, sweetly or stridently, obliquely or bluntly - but if they were expressing views about women, too often a majority of the men in their parliamentary audience automatically close their ears, believing they are about to hear fringe feminist rhetoric, which was to be automatically rejected. This realisation was a painful one - considering the number of years I had spent, I thought, I had been patiently explaining modern women's aspirations.[191]

---

188   Gilligan, *In A Different Voice*, in particular Chapters One and Five.
189   Rhode is wary of this view. She states that "we cannot expect that women who internalize the norms necessary for political success and who gain vested interest in current structures will promote a transformative vision": Rhode, "Feminism and the State" (1994) 107 *Harvard Law Review* 1181 at 1206-1207.
190   *United Associations of Women News Sheet* May 1964 quoted in Sawer, "Housekeeping the State: Women and Parliamentary Politics in Australia" in *Trust the Women:Women in Federal Parliament* (Papers in Parliament No17, Department of the Senate, Canberra 1992) p20.
191   Sullivan, edited text of lecture in Main Committee Room of Parliament House September 27 1993, reprinted in *The Canberra Times* 28 September 1993.

When women speak, all some men hear is women's issues, regardless of whether they are speaking about issues relevant to both sexes. The previous federal women's minister claimed she was restrained from speaking out publicly because of the lack of credibility accorded to matters she discussed.[192] If there were equal numbers of women in Parliament, then men would be forced to reconsider their attitude to women, for half of the participants would be speaking in this different voice, and the men could not then afford to ignore them.

Women in Representations and Images of Representative Government.

The question of representation in the sense of inclusion of women and of women's interests is closely linked to another connotation of the word "representation", namely the way in which women are represented in visual and textual descriptions of aspects of the constitutional process. This part briefly introduces some thoughts about representations of women in the latter sense.

Historically, representations of women in the Australian constitutional system have been characterised by trivialisation, ambiguity, or complete absence. Women were either not there at all; there in the guise of men in drag; or there to be ridiculed. Josie Castles and Pringle conducted a study of political cartooning at Federation.[193] They noted that apart from the occasional use of women as allegories of statehood, the more common symbol of the new Australian identity was of a man dressed in woman's clothing. The authors argue that this frequent cross-dressing indicated an ambivalence, and anxiety about Australian nationhood. "A crisis in political legitimacy is signalled in the cartoon as sexual ambiguity".[194]

For our purposes there are two consequences of this analysis. First, and most obviously, the absence of female images reflected the exclusion of women from the Constitutional drafting and endorsement process. Despite vigorous informal lobbying they were hardly visible and, hence, were not portrayed in images of the nascent constitutional system. Second, if sexual ambiguity is associated with ambiguity over Statehood, then it becomes more apparent why it was necessary to keep women in

---

192   Kingston, "Feminism's new confidence" *Canberra Times* 20 October 1993.
193   Castles, J & Pringle, "Sovereignty and Sexual Identity in Political Cartoons" in Magarey, Rowley & Sheridan (eds), *Debutante Nation* (Allen & Unwin, St Leonards 1993) 136
194   As above, p142-143.

traditional roles and thereby exclude them from the processes of representative democracy. A State in transition is portrayed as a man dressed as a woman. Given the uncertainty this image conveys, it is hardly surprising that women were not encouraged to act in a way which was beyond their expected role. In a state of "semiotic restlessness", certainty about women's roles, including their traditional exclusion from representative democracy, was the least that could be counted upon. Again, women's absence confirmed traditional exclusion from representative democracy and served to lessen other anxieties Australia had about its impending status change.

Sawer and Simms note in the preface to their second edition of *A Woman's Place: Women and Politics in Australia*, that the absence of women and women's issues from discussions of Australian politics was identified in the late 1970's. In 1981, the Australasian Political Studies Association (APSA) adopted a policy that the study of women be incorporated into all politics courses. In 1991, a review commissioned by the APSA Women's Caucus concluded that "introductory textbooks in Australian government published during the last five years have contributed little to making women more visible in the analysis of Australian politics and almost nothing towards the inclusion of feminist scholarship in Australian political science."[195]

In addition to the inadequate representation of women in the constitutional system generally, women have often been represented in a trivialised manner. It is common in political debate to either belittle women politicians or, conversely, when successful, to compare them to men. Senator Bronwyn Bishop is a frequent butt of a combination of this approach.[196]

This trivialisation has a long and not so honourable history in Australian parliamentary politics. Early this century, men warned against the danger of granting women the vote because it would lead to "petticoat government".[197] In political literature and cartoons women suffragettes were depicted as less than women, as masculine; they were caricatured as unattractive, bossy, violent and ridiculous. A suffragette was "that

---

195   Cited in Sawer & Simms, *A Woman's Place: Women and Politics in Australia* xi.
196   Interesting case studies of this phenomenon would be the resignation of Ros Kelly from the Keating Cabinet in early 1994, and the "head to head" conflict between Carmen Lawrence and Bronwyn Bishop.
197   Oldfield, *Woman Suffrage in Australia: A Gift or a Struggle* p190.

creature of abhorrence to all true men and women - the masculine woman."[198] In one pamphlet of the period, entitled "The Wild Woman in Politics",[199] a large frowning woman attending a political meeting throws an egg at the man chairing the meeting, beats men with her umbrella, and tosses a man out the window in order to force her will on the meeting. She then reaches her decision not on the basis of the candidate's political views but because "he eats peas with a knife". Not only is she bossy, violent and unattractive, but she is stupid enough to decide political questions on the basis of rules of etiquette. Moreover, she is emasculating: the woman "and her family of 15" reduce "the anguished candidate" to a "limp condition."[200]

While this portrayal is not the direct responsibility of government in the same way as is under-representation in the Parliament, it is a phenomenon worth noting. The way in which people are represented may affect the way in which they act. Where women are left out or trivialised in the picture of what constitutes representative democracy, this may stifle their attempts to become more actively a part of the system. This also has importance for role-modelling, and its place in encouraging younger women to contemplate a future in politics. If there is a trivialisation of women in politics, it will not encourage other women to enter the arena.

Therefore, this section has shown, first, that historically women have been excluded from the constitution-making process of drafting and approval by referendum, and from early voting under Constitution; thus in the past women have not been adequately *represented in or by government*. Second, this is not purely an historical anomaly; the current composition of Parliament grossly under-represents women in the Australian community. Women therefore are not, to a sufficient extent, *representatives in government* in the Australian constitutional system. Moreover, the division of life into public and private spheres restricts women from *being representatives in government*. Third, the contribution of women in the Parliament has been, and continues to be, perceived as "different" to that of men's, and accordingly given less weight; *representation by women* has been marginalised. Finally, images of women in government either cast them as men or trivialise or omit them altogether. The invisibility of women in the constitutional system is confirmed in *representations of government*. In sum, the Australian

---

198   Montague Whitney "Womanhood Suffrage" quoted in Oldfield, *Woman Suffrage in Australia: A Gift or a Struggle* p192.
199   As above, p193.
200   As above.

constitutional system is not representative of women in any of the three senses of the term identified above.

BECOMING A MORE REPRESENTATIVE DEMOCRACY

This paper has documented some of the ways in which women are under-represented in the Australian constitutional system. This demonstrates a violation of the notion of representation in light of the meanings attributed to it by recent High Court doctrine and also according to the theories and assumptions that lie behind the principle of representative democracy. In the words of the Prime Minister, Paul Keating: "The ruling body of the nation should be representative of the people it serves. At present it is not."[201]

Any constitutional system which has failed in the past and continues to fail in the present, to adequately represent women cannot continue to be called "representative". Just as the notion of what is representative has altered with time from a property based to a universal franchise, so too has the content of representative democracy in relation to women. It is no longer valid (if it ever was) to label as representative a system in which one sex outweighs another at a ratio of approximately ten to one in some sectors of government, and at a ratio of infinity to nothing in others. Pressure to address the gross under-representation of women in constitutional systems around the world has led to a range of options being considered.[202]

Some aim to alter the composition of parliament and the executive directly. These include: the introduction of voluntary[203] or mandatory[204] gender quotas for the party preselection of candidates, in major political parties; double sex parliamentary representation whereby the size of each electorate would be doubled[205] and each would elect a male and a female

---

201   Kingston, "Feminism's new confidence" *Canberra Times* 20 October 1993.
202   An International Plan of Action to Correct the Present Imbalances in the Participation of Men and Women in Political Life was adopted in Paris in March 1994 by the Inter-Parliamentary Union.
203   The Liberal Party is encouraging more women to stand for preselection. Lang "Women the key to new-age Parliament" *Canberra Times* 30 August 1993. In the late 1980s the German Christian Democrat Party introduced voluntary quotas: Phillips, *Democracy and Representation* at 2.
204   The Australian Labor Party's commitment to 35% of winnable pre-selection seats to be mandatorily allocated to women women follows a trend in other countries. The British Labour Party has moved from a 50% target to be achieved within three general elections to a 1993 principle of all-women short lists for candidate selection in half the winnable seats: Phillips, as above.
205   Macklin, "An idea whose time has come" *Canberra Times* 22 October 1993.

representative; the introduction of constitutional quotas guaranteeing a certain percentage of seats to women;[206] and the inclusion in Cabinet of the Minister responsible for women's affairs.[207] A petition presented to a select committee of the New Zealand parliament calls for alteration of electoral legislation to ensure equality and parity of gender representation.[208] Other methods of group representation include the use of functional constituencies in Hong Kong representing groups such as unions and industry within the Legislative Council.[209]

Other proposals aim to alter the political and legal culture in which the under-representation has occurred. "Schooling" in parliamentary skills for women;[210] using the Upper House to "experiment" with representation for particular groups;[211] reforming parliamentary working hours;[212] and regular government reporting to international review bodies such as the CEDAW committee about percentages of women in parliamentary institutions,[213] have all been suggested.

Some suggestions are addressed to under-representation in government and government policy more generally. These include equal representation of women on all government bodies by the year 2000;[214]

---

206   The Indian constitution was amended in 1991 to allocate 30% of sets in local government to women: MacDonald, "Non-feminist female politician" *Canberra Times* 21 April 1994. In Australia see, for example, Constitutional Centenary Foundation, *Representing The People: The Role of Parliament in Australian Democracy* (Constitutional Centenary Foundation, discussion paper 1993) p9.

207   Kingston, "Cabinet to make room for women's affairs minister", *Canberra Times* 19 October 1993.

208   Written submission of Paul Hunt in support of the Petition of Jocelyn Fish, Georgina Kirby and Marilyn Waring, concerning Equality of Gender Representation in New Zealand's House of Representatives.

209   Although it is not suggested that this method necessarily leads to broader representation.

210   Phillips, "Democracy and Representation, Or, Why Should it Matter Who Our Representatives Are?", unpublished paper at 2.

211   Constitutional Centenary Foundation, *Representing the People: The Role of Parliament in Australian Democracy* p27.

212   Hewitt, edited extract of the Donald Horne address, *Canberra Times* 26 January 1994; Reported comments of convenor of Australian Governemnt's National Women's Consultative Council, "Good job ... pity about the hours" *Canberra Times*.

213   Fraser, "Women and Public Life: Articles 7 and 8 of the Women's Convention and The Importance of Non-Governmental Organizations in Creating Civil Societies" (1993) *International Women's Rights Action Watch* 9.

214   Kingston, "A Woman of Status" *Canberra Times* 23 October 1993. Federal Cabinet endorsed a stratetgy to encourage women to take positions on

mandatory representation of women in government appointments to non-government bodies such as UN committees;[215] and a requirement that departments take account of the effect on women of policy.[216] Finally, some proposals call for reform of the underlying issues which inhibit the entry of women into the constitutional system, such as inadequate education, health-care and employment.[217]

Common to all proposals is the need to make visible the gendered nature of representation in the current constitutional system, a need that has particular resonance for contemporary Australian debate about changing the Constitution, most of which has occurred without a mention of the representation of women or their interests.[218] If questions about whether Australia should become a Republic, or have a Bill of Rights, are decided without explicit consideration of women, Australia will be repeating the mistakes of the past. Adopting a neutral position clearly operates to the disadvantage of women. To avoid excluding women from the process of making, or re-making, the Constitution, it is crucial that any convention held to discuss such issues should be composed of approximately equal numbers of men and women.[219]

Unless Australian constitutional law takes seriously the challenge from women to include them and their interests in the representative process, beginning with the way in which alterations to the Constitution are debated, the constitutionality of the whole system is surely in doubt. There is a distinct possibility that over the next few years it will be said that women are adequately represented in the process by men, or even by the inclusion of one or two women. These arguments bear a striking

---

Commonwealth boards, councils and other government authorities. In 1989 the target was set at 50%. In 1994 the figures only show 25% of women in those positions. *The Age*, 8 October 1994, p3.

215   Kingston, "Feminisms' New Confidence" *Canberra Times* 20 October 1993. This recommendation followed the appointment to the United Nations world population conference committee of 10 men and no women.

216   As above.

217   Fraser, "Women and Public Life: Articles 7 and 8 of the Women's Convention and The Importance of Non-Governmental Organizations in Creating Civil Societies" (1993) *International Women's Rights Action Watch* 9 at 4ff.

218   The Constitutional Centenary Foundation has as one of its projects the issue of representation of women in the political process. See "Women's Suffrage Centenary Issue" (1994) 3 *Constitutional Centenary Foundation Newsletter*.

219   Note that one widely circulated paper calls for a broadly representative Convention (and one which includes specific representation for indigenous people), but does not mention the inclusion of women. See, Constitutional Centenary Foundation Inc, "*If We Wanted to Review the Constitution, How Would We Do It?*", 24 September 1993 at 3.

resemblance to those put at the 1897 Constitutional Convention, when it was said that women's interests could be adequately represented by their male friends and relations. It was patronising then and it is worse now.

However, there may be cause to be more optimistic in view of the recent developments in High Court doctrine. As we argued, the recent cases of the High Court state that there are fundamental principles, such as representative democracy, underlying our constitutional system. Moreover, there is an acceptance that there are principles that are integral to representative democracy. Public participation and its role in linking the elected with the electorate are two of the principles that have been developed to date.

These ideas developed by the High Court are supported by the theories and principles underlying representative democracy. There must be a link between the represented and the representatives, representation must be an ongoing process, and the meaning of representation changes over time. For the linkage to occur satisfactorily for women, and for representation to be ongoing for women, there needs to be a broad cross-section of representatives. At this time in Australian history, there needs to be an acknowledgment that women's interests are not being adequately represented at present. This has been displayed above in addressing how the present system operates for women, denying both women and men a representative democracy and the counsel that women afford.

As the Inter-Parliamentary union stated in adopting its international plan of action:

> The concept of democracy will only assume true and dynamic significance when ... politics and national legislation are decided upon jointly by men and women with equitable regard for the interests and aptitudes of both halves of the population.[220]

Or in the words of the New Zealand petition, "A society governed overwhelmingly by men is a society half-governed."[221]

For the constitutional system to reflect its underlying principle of representative democracy, women must be *representatives in government, resented by government,* and must be seen in visual and textual *representations of government.*

---

220   Quoted in *The Age* 8 October 1994 p3.
221   The petition of J Fish, G Kirby and M Waring, above.

Navigating the Newstream: Recent Critical Scholarship in International Law

Deborah Z Cass

Deborah Z Cass, 'Navigating the Newstream: Recent Critical Scholarship in International Law' (1996) 65 *Nordic Journal of International Law* 341, 341–383, doi.org/10.1163/15718109620294924 <https://heinonline.org/HOL/LandingPage?handle=hein.journals/nordic65&div=26&id=&page=>

Navigating the Newstream: Recent Critical Scholarship in International Law

DEBORAH Z. CASS*
Lecturer in Law. Australian National University, Canberra

1. Introduction

Generations of legal scholars have reinvented their fields by a ritual over-throwing of their predecessors[1] and one group within the current crop of international lawyers is no exception. These lawyers, who label themselves as Newstream,[2] are presently involved in a theory battle with those the new scholars label, somewhat negatively, as Mainstream.[3] This otherwise esoteric battle is interesting because it coincides with a changed perception about

---

* LL.B (Hons) University of Melbourne 1989, LL.M Harvard University 1995, currently S.J.D. candidate Harvard University. I would like to thank Susan Marks, David Kennedy and Gerry Simpson for their invaluable comments on earlier drafts.

[1] See e.g. the Realist school of American legal thought which was in part a project aimed at creating a new way of thinking in contradistinction to what it labeled "formalism". For a discussion of the realist critique as a response to formalism see William W. Fisher, "The Development of Modern American Legal Theory and the Judicial Interpretation of the Bill of Rights", in M. Lacey & K. Haakonssen, (Eds), *A Culture of Rights* (1991).

[2] I will use the term "Newstream" to discuss work which has been referred to variously as "New Stream" or part of a body of "New Approaches". See David Kennedy, "A New Stream of International Law Scholarship", 7 *Wis. Int L. J.* 1, (1988) [hereinafter *New Stream*] and David Kennedy & Chris Tennant, "New Approaches to International Law: A Bibliography", 35 *Harv. Int. L. J.* 417, (1994) [hereinafter *New Approaches*]. International legal scholarship which defined itself as "New Stream" first appeared around 1980: see Nigel Purvis, "Critical Legal Studies in Public International Law", 32 *Harv. Int. L. J.* 81, 89 (1991) at note 41. It has expanded considerably since then. The proportion of analyses which were so defined in 1980 was relatively small. A 1991 survey of the field noted three book length expositions and just over a dozen contributions in all: Id. At 89 and 91. Cf. In 1988 David Kennedy listed 17 scholars as pursuing "critical projects" in the field: Kennedy, *New Stream*, id., at 2. Three years later the number of analyses identified as Newstream had increased to some four hundred and fifty: Kennedy and Tennant, id., at 431–460.

[3] In this article Mainstream is intended to refer to a body of scholars who have dominated the field for the last twenty-five years. It does not indicate any homogenous category but covers a number of different theoretical approaches including realist (Schwarzenberger, Weil, Watson), classicist (Fitzmaurice), and liberal-humanitarian (Henkin, MacDougall, Falk).

the role of international law in structuring and regulating international public order. A once moribund international rule of law is assumed to have been reinvigorated by current events. The resuscitation of international law is accompanied by an optimism arising out of a perceived end to the polarized bloc politics of the late twentieth century. Actions in the Gulf and in Somalia are seen as evidence of the international community's will to collectively respond to threats to international peace and security. But that optimism is also tempered by a strange uncertainty about ordering the international plane. Besides being somewhat quelled by the experiences of Somalia and the former Yugoslavia, post Cold War confidence in international law has been replaced by a muted anxiety about its limitations. This anxiety focuses on questions which seem to have become more, rather than less, difficult to answer since the resolution of superpower politics. What is the role of the weakened nation state in the new regional arrangements of world order? How will human rights regimes overcome the chasms of cultural difference between societies? What is "culture" anyway? What is the nature of the relationship between international trade regulation and local governance? Can reconstituted units of failed federations accommodate disparate ethnic interests? It is in the service of answering these dilemmas that the new brand of legal scholarship has risen to prominence, claiming to challenge the certainties of the old. This article is about that challenge, and the attempt by the new scholars to reconceptualize the idea of what is international law.

The article is inspired by the sense that, to date, the battle between the Newstream and the Mainstream has been a rather detached, disengaged affair, and that in particular, the Mainstream has failed to respond meaningfully to Newstream critique. Instead the Newstream has been anxiously dismissed as overly theoretical or willfully obtuse.[4] Here I refine and explore some of the Newstream ideas which have invigorated the discipline and have the potential

---

[4] Despite the industry of Newstream writers, *supra* note 2, and the appearance of two lengthy survey articles (Purvis, *supra* note 2), book reviews (see e.g., Ian Scobbie, "Towards the Elimination of International Law: Some Radical Skepticism about Skeptical Radicalism", *Brit. Y.B. Int'l. L.* 339 (1990) frequent citation in scholarly journals by writers sharing similar concerns, and attention at international law conferences, (e.g., American Society of International Law Annual General Meeting 1994, panel on *Theoretical Perspectives on Sovereignty,* comments by Martti Koskenniemi and Karen Knop), to date, the new analyses have been largely ignored, or at least superficially treated, in recently revised publications of the traditional discipline. See e.g. a recently revised standard Casebook used in American law schools, Louis Henkin, Richard Pugh, Oscar Schachter, Hans Smit, *International Law Cases and Materials*, 3rd ed., (1993) which devotes two pages to "international law and the critical legal studies movement" id. at 48–49, four pages to "feminist perspectives" id. at 43–47, and occasionally refers to specific writers associated with Newstream such as Philip Allot, id. at 16. Other Mainstream scholars engage only very briefly with the critique in order to dismiss it. See e.g., Rosalyn Higgins, *Problems and Process: International Law and How We Use It,* (1994) esp. Ch. 1 "Nature and Function of International Law."

to create a productive dialogue between the bearers of the international tradition and its challengers.[5] I intend to show how this should lead to a gradual recasting of the field.

There is little doubt that a large body of compelling work has now been written, associated with the rubric of Newstream, and that its continued neglect by the Mainstream risks stultifying the field and prevents the development of a more nuanced and responsive international legal theory. The Newstream critique's major strength, its sense of a mission to create a new international law, risks being blunted by the lack of dialogue between the two approaches. Moreover, as pedagogical tools, the Newstream writings are invaluable because they offer plausible explanations of international law making, interpretation and application, at a point in time in which traditional understandings about law have been questioned by (post)modern insights into cultural fragmentation, the making of history and the role of language in law. The work also echoes a widespread interdisciplinary interest in language and its effect on the structure of ideas.

Despite these strengths Newstream scholars do not exploit the critique's potential because they often fail to make explicit evaluative choices. If they perceive law as simply a variable set of argumentative possibilities, these possibilities are not being used to effect change. There are problems internal to the critique as well, for example its often condescending and reductive tone, and its occasionally derivative and abstract theorizing.

I have thus positioned my own critique at the borderline in the hope that it will enable both sides to explore each others territory. Putting to one side the reality that at least some Mainstream and Newstream writers perceive their positions as antithetical, I will assume that any conversation between

[5] In addition to the quantitative impact of the work, it is having a substantive effect on academic and practitioners alike. An anecdotal survey of some international law teachers indicates that many use the writers discussed here in their teaching. International law texts now include references, albeit somewhat cursory, to these writings. Writers not formally identified with the approach use the various techniques identified above. See e.g., Patrick Thornberry in Christian Tomuschat, *The Modern Law of Self-Determination* 1993 (analyzing self-determination law as a "metalanguage" and proposing a reconstruction based on a new conception of the relationship between the State and its sub-groups). Practitioners in law firms, departments of state around the world, corporations, and non-government organizations are increasingly schooled in these methods of analysis. In some cases the experience of these practitioners is channeled back into the academic scholarship. See e.g., Ileana M. Porras, "The Rio Declaration: A New Basis for International Cooperation", in Phillippe Sands, *Greening International Law*, (1993) (arguing that the Rio Declaration represents a compromise between the interest in development of developing states and the interest of the West in environmental protection. Porras acted as government representative at the Rio Conference). The result of these developments has been to extend the effect of the work, so that it is beginning to reach into the public and private sectors, as well as the academy. Accordingly there is need to incorporate these materials more thoroughly into mainstream teaching and research.

theoretical positions is good for international law, because it generates a deeper understanding of what the discipline entails. My starting premise is that Mainstream scholars ought to pay greater heed to the transformative potential of some of the work of the Newstream, and the latter should acknowledge their continuing debt to the scholars who have preceded them, and continue to engage with that work. I will therefore set out in my paper what I believe to be the main arguments of Newstream work. By offering one translation of a sample of the recent scholarship I hope to demonstrate its richness and creativity; to provide a point of entry for dialogue between the perspectives; and to promote the use of Newstream work as a valuable source of information and analysis for Mainstream scholars.

2. Structure and Overview of Paper

The Newstream, positioning themselves in opposition to the Mainstream, have challenged the international law tradition at three levels. Section 3 of this paper is devoted to discussing the underlying conceptual challenge of Newstream work, Section 4 its methods, and Section 5 its strategies. In a concluding section, Section 6, I examine some recurring problems with the critique. Before commencing I will briefly sketch the three challenges: *conceptual, methodological*, and *strategic*.

Newstream writers are making a *conceptual* claim about Mainstream scholarship (Section 3) which has three parts. First, the Newstream regard Mainstream international law as having adopted a complacent approach toward questions of how to define culture and differences between cultures (Section 3.1). This is exemplified in the arid debates over self-determination and cultural relativism. By contrast Newstream writers claim that the way in which culture is defined determines the legal rule which ensues, and that the meaning of what is culture is thus primary to the doctrines which have evolved. Second, they contend that Mainstream international law represents itself as an account of history as progress in which the doctrine of sovereignty develops from an uncertain principle of naked power distribution to a more formal, regulable legal mechanism (Section 3.2). Newstream accounts suggests that the story is more complex and that sovereignty can be re-interpreted in the light of different readings of the historical development of international law, in a manner which would inevitably unsettle interpretations of important doctrines such as acquisition, or territorial integrity. Third, they argue that Mainstream scholars have maintained a fiction that law-making can be reduced to either custom (a reflexive process of locating and amalgamating the practice and belief of states), or agreement and the drafting of new treaties, and so have failed to sufficiently take into account contemporary theoretical insights relating to language and representation (Section 3.3). If law is constituted by language rather than simply objective behavior and belief, then its foundations are less certain and its reconstitution is not only possible but obligatory. In short, the Newstream argues that Mainstream literature relies upon an untenable set of ideas about culture, sovereignty, and law-making.

In addition to these substantive, conceptual claims the Newstream argues that the Mainstream has a limited approach to method. So the second level of challenge is *methodological* provoking Newstream writers to experiment with different analytical devices (Section 4). First, new approaches method often locates and dissects twinned conceptual oppositions underlying history, sovereignty and culture, thereby revealing the unstable and contingent nature of the law which they support (Section 4.1). Second, Newstream writings represent international actors as being engaged on a highly personal quest, thereby undermining the notional objectivity and formality of international rules (Section 4.2). The device of the quest also produces an evocative descriptive framework, a personal and personally revealing account of law, and a mechanism to explore the internal contradiction between international law's idealism and its ordinariness. Finally, Newstream work uses language in ways which emphasize the conceptual and methodological themes just noted (Section 4.3).

Third, there is a *strategic* level to the challenge (Section 5). Here Newstream scholars reinvigorate pre-existing reform strategies, in an attempt to shift the emphasis of lawmaking from one of reform to radical reconceptualization. This is accomplished by incorporating perspectives foreign to the discipline and hitherto absent, and by situating legal problems more fully in their political and cultural context (Section 5.1); by provocative rewritings of doctrinal history (Section 5.2); and by integrating political considerations into legal analysis (Section 5.3).

Finally in Section 6 I argue that while these Newstream challenges could be transformative tools of changing law their potential is largely unrealized. Section 6 extends my critique by highlighting previously identified recurring problems with the analyses, namely their lack of concretization, reductionism and tendency toward condescension.

3. The Newstream Conceptual Challenge to Mainstream International Law

This part of the essay will examine the way Newstream writings are redefining some foundational concepts of international law. The three themes I focus on are: culture, the relationship between history and sovereignty and the role of language in the constitution of legal doctrine.

3.1. *Culture*

The first conceptual theme that features strongly throughout this body of this work is a concern with what constitutes culture. This is presented by the Newstream writers as a challenge to what they perceive as international law's traditional complacency when describing different groups of people, or modes of social, political and economic organization.

Much of the Newstream scholarship begins from the premise that definitions of culture are central to the way in which international law has been constituted, and that the meanings used in Mainstream literature operate to include certain ideas and groups of people and exclude others. So for example, a first group of Newstream writers interested in culture contend that representations of indigenous people in Mainstream international law have tended to mimic the standard stereotypes. They have been depicted as backward, under-developed, or more latterly, noble and thereby excluded from the development of law.[6] Moreover, this portrayal is represented as an inevitable result

---

[6] See e.g., Chris Tennant "Indigenous Peoples International Institutions and the International Legal Literature from" 1945–1993, 16 *Human Rights Quarterly* 1, 7 (1994) discussing the relationship between the representation of indigenous people in international legal literature and international law's treatment of them. He argues that there is a connection between the images in the literature and international law's treatment of them. He argues that there is a connection between the images in the literature and the practices of law. Indigeneous peoples are represented in the international legal literature as either "ignoble" or noble and that both representations affect the way in which law responds to their situation. On this view, cultural (mis)representations determine law. So in the period to 1945 indigenous peoples were represented as "ignoble", located in the past, lacking and incapable of exercising political responsibility. At the same time international law emphasized strategies of technical assistance, development and assimilation, in order to bring them into the present. More recently the international legal literature has represented indigenous people as "noble", as part of a communitarian lifestyle, in harmony with the environment and detached from modernity. Accordingly current legal strategies stress "flexible concepts of self-determination and autonomy", in order to transcend the failures of modernity, Id. at 24. In both cases international processes, doctrines, and institutions are responding to representations of indigenous people and not to indigenous peoples themselves. Moreover, the different representations actually corresponded to the goals of that particular period of law. When assimilation was considered a legitimate goal of law, indigenous people were portrayed as "ignoble" and in need of civilizing; when integration lost its cachet and there was disillusionment with Western legal solutions, indigenous people were depicted as "noble" and encouraged to remain separate from Western culture. Similarly Ileana Porras, in an article on terrorism, argues that international law's definition of terrorism frequently depends upon images of Orientalism which are constructed to suit law's need to exclude this form of violence from the range of the "normal" rules: Ileana Porras, "On Terrorism: Reflections on Violence and the Outlaw", in D. Danielsen and Karen Engle Eds., *After Identity: A Reader in Law and Culture* (1995). Hence a man charged with acts of terrorism is described in the press as wearing a suit "billowing in the wind" Porras, id. 304, reminiscent of Lawrence of Arabia imagery. The depiction of terrorist actors as "other" enables their acts to be demonized as a form of violence beyond that which is "normal" and thus the ordinary rules of international law, say in relation to the laws of war, or criminal law cannot apply. The construction of cultural stereotypes determines a particular set of international rules.

of culture and so, according to the Newstream, only a concerted rewriting of Mainstream cultural depictions will lead to changes in the actual practice of law.

Not all Newstream writers confront the question of culture in the same manner. There is a marked division between those who claim that the Mainstream literature has produced a Westernized view of different cultural groups, but that this depiction can be reconstructed, and, those who argue that the foundations of international law are so saturated with partial ideas about culture, that they cannot be reconstructed.

A group representing the first viewpoint argue that international legal culture has been fashioned out of a Western set of values,[7] but ultimately they maintain that law can recognize its own subjectivity and transcend it[8] by one of two methods. International Law could become more conscious of the legal viewers' own perspective,[9] or it might apply legal rules in a manner which recognizes the particular context of the group subject to the rule.[10] In sum, according to this first group of Newstream scholars, definitions of culture, although skewed by current Mainstream work, can be reassembled in such a way so as to incorporate into law the particular practices of the exclud-

---

[7] See e.g., an exploration of the exclusionary power of Western cultural assumptions, on law in Rosemary Coombe, "The Properties of Culture and the Politics of Possessing Identity: Native Claims in the Cultural Appropriation Controversy", in D. Danielsen and K. Engle Eds., *After Identity: A Reader in Law and Culture* (1995). Coombe's focus is the development of new forms of legal protection for the cultural property of indigenous peoples. Cultural property protection is based on the European "art/culture system" which excludes an indigenous understanding of ownership and identity. Moreover, this criticism applies to both traditional copyright law, and to the emerging laws of cultural property protection which purport to protect group rights. So, for example, both the copyright protection accorded Picasso's use of an indigenous mask and newer forms of collective cultural protection legislation are based on the same Western concept of "possessive individualism": id. at 255. What is left out of both regulatory styles is the sense that both ownership and collective identity carry quite different and specific meanings for indigenous peoples. Ownership in an indigenous sense, for example, may include a bundle of ideas which cannot be simply directly translated into new Western forms of law. Hence she argues, the structure of Western law, steeped in cultural assumptions derived from its own art/culture system, precludes the creation of new forms of legal protection about indigenous art, ownership and identity.

[8] See, e.g., Frankenberg who argues that comparative lawyers are blinded by their own subjectivity: Gunter Frankenberg, "Critical Comparisons: Rethinking Comparative Law", 26 *Harv. Int. L. J.* (1985) 411. He claims that comparative lawyers fail to recognize that their own perspectives play a significant part in the way they view other cultures: id. at 441. Moreover given this subjectivity, comparative law actually reveals more about the culture from which the comparativist belongs, than about the legal system under investigation.

[9] Id. at 442.

[10] Coombe, *supra* note 7. Coombe's proposal to overcome this problem, is to "listen[. . .] to native claims in context": id. at 266. She argues that in order to develop law reflecting indigenous ways of art and culture, it will be necessary to undertake a highly specific and contextualized form of investigation into the practices of the peoples involved. Only by adopting such a localized approach will laws emerge which accommodate the concerns of indigenous peoples.

ed groups resulting in a new international law which is more contextual, comprehensive and ultimately more expressive of diverse cultures.

How effective is this form of critique? The first form argues for reconstruction. However given the underlying premise of the Newstream writers that Western social, political and economic organization dominates legal developments, it is difficult to see how law can simply transcend those limits by "listening in context."[11] The very hegemonic nature of definitions of culture will tend to work against this solution. It is unlikely, if not inconsistent, that on the one hand European culture precludes the formation of law responsive to indigenous people, and on the other to claim that if law "listens" harder, European culture can be overcome. Moreover, it is contradictory to criticize Mainstream scholars who purportedly attempt to distance themselves from their own cultural stereotyping and yet then argue that all lawyers should learn to "transcend perspective".[12] On the one hand we are entreated to "recognize we are participants of one culture and observers of another"[13] and on the other, that we can be released from the "all encompassing grip of the habit of our own truth."[14] Is it possible to recognize subjectivity and transcend it simultaneously? If one accepts the first premise, namely that as lawyers we are trapped in our own cultural vision, then it seems problematic to overcome that vision, simply by an act of will. Although there is something appealing about the possibility that knowing who we are may lead to changing what we do, it seems likely that it will take more than mere desire to achieve it.

Ultimately this first group of Newstream writers effectively exposes the role of culture in determining legal practices, but their proposals to alter it are internally contradictory. This criticism may not however be fatal in the long term. Obviously under certain conditions, and over time, concepts and ideas which are beyond law's parameters are gradually incorporated, otherwise law would remain in a form of statis. Nevertheless it would seem that in order for the argument to have real force it is first necessary for these Newstream writers to speculate as to what are those conditions and how change can occur. How can contextualized listening lead to change? In what circumstances and by what mechanisms is it likely to occur? What is the appropriate context? The claim for contextualization is, to date, too thin to support a changed practice.

[11] Id. at 266.

[12] Frankenburg, *supra* note 8 at 442. Frankenburg acknowledges that no-one can "dispose[.]" of their "cognitive history" or "baggage of assumptions", id. at 443, yet he still ultimately advocates exactly just that, the only difference being that the actor does so self-consciously.

[13] Id.

[14] Id. at 454.

While the first Newstream group advocates a redefinition of culture by either recognizing Mainstream stereotyping of cultural groups, or better contextualizing legal problem solving, or transcendence of subjectivity and other acts of will, the second group, which I now discuss, is skeptical of ever achieving these goals.[15] This second group of Newstream writers are not so sanguine about reforming the current law. For them international law does not simply rely on culture, international law *is* culture.[16] By implication, international law cannot transcend culture by recognizing group difference. It cannot undo constructed notions of culture, because the notion of culture inheres in what international law is. According to the second group of writers, the construction of culture is not only the result of human agency in creating stereotypes but results from the structures of international law, its language and its history.[17]

---

[15] The polarity within Newstream work reflects an irony which dogs much contemporary scholarship: at the same time that the critique of culture is strongest in some quarters, the embrace of difference is at its peak in others, even within the same project: See discussion of Arjun Appadurai, "Disjuncture and Difference in the Global Cultural Economy", 2 *Pub. Culture* (1990) 1.

[16] See, e.g., Annelise Riles discussion of the question of whether it is possible for law to ever overcome the categories of culture: Annelise Riles, "Note: Aspiration and Control: International Legal Rhetoric and the Essentialization of Culture", 106 *Harv. L. Rev.* 723 (1993) [hereinafter *Aspiration and Control*]. She argues that nineteenth century international law was built upon essentialized versions of European and non-European culture. Moreover, so dependent was law on these essentialized notions, that international law was collapsed into culture, even though it projected itself as separate and law-like. Culture as law came in two forms. In one case it manifested itself as a mechanism for ordering non-European peoples by requiring them to aspire to standards of European-ness, in order to be included within existing categories of law. Thus non-Europeans aspired to own territory in order to prove statehood, because a state without territory was like a man without clothes: id. at 733 quoting T. J. Lawrence, *International Problems and Hague Conferences* (1908). The other manifestation of culture as law was to order non-Europeans by controlling then in a "dizzying catalog of colonial topics", id. at 729, according to racial differences and political organization. Both manifestations relied on culture. In one law offers the possibility of assimilation, in the other it offers the threat of exclusion.

[17] See, e.g., Antony Anghie who shares Riles' skepticism about the conundrum of law and culture, yet whose focus is on the role of language and history: Antony Anghie, Constructing the Nation State: Colonialism and the Making of International Law (1994), (unpublished S.J.D. dissertation, Harvard University, on file with author). Anghie claims international legal doctrine has developed largely in response to colonialism. Many of the major developments in relation to acquisition of territory, sovereignty and personality, for example, are informed by, and infused with the imperatives of colonialism. He argues that the entire language of international law was based on a complex taxonomy which separated "uncivilized from civilized" in order to justify inclusion and exclusion in full membership of the international system: Id. at 6 041-054. European notions of culture, defining everything from political organizations, to sexual practices, were used to denote "civilized" and exclude all else. However in order to treat with those outside the model of civilization, international law had also to create ways that the "uncivilized" could become objects, (but not subjects) of the system. Anghie develops the notions of "calibrated recognition", id., at 6 068, to describe the process by

The second group argues that the very nature of international law as culture may preclude any possibility of modifying international law to make it more responsive to different cultures. Most importantly they argue that international law is inherently a European cultural form,[18] and that these forms continues to pervade thinking, even amongst those who attempt to deconstruct law.[19] In one example Mainstream international law is depicted as the cultural language of nineteenth century colonialism,[20] and so language, culture and the formation of laws are therefore inextricably connected. Moreover if this story of the genesis of major doctrines of international law is correct, then those same cultural considerations continue to inform law-making and its functioning. Hence inbuilt and structural cultural biases will not simply be overcome by contextualization, or transcendence of perspective. What distinguishes the second group of Newstream writers from the first then is their belief that the very structure of international law precluded, and continues to preclude any way of moving beyond these cultural categories.

While the two viewpoints are partially persuasive, they both leave unanswered the question of how international law can be loosened from the particular cultural moorings it has acquired over time and which are now represented in Mainstream literature. Can the different cultural settings present in the twentieth century inspire a different international legal language? Will the post-colonial culture engender a post-colonial law in the same way that colonial culture produced colonial law? And is it possible for any universal system of international law to incorporate competing cultural considerations? Some of these critical issues are taken up by other Newstream writers who adopt an explicitly feminist perspective.

Their response has been to focus on a specific issue and document the difficulties it raises in recasting a more culturally sensitive international law. This has been done in relation to clitoridectomy,[21] and the wearing of the veil[22] in order to demonstrate the important observation that feminist con-

---

which non-European groups were kept out of international law membership but sufficiently recognized, (by personality doctrine and sovereignty/property distinctions for example), so that Europeans could trade with them, make unequal treaties with them and acquire their land. "'[T]he whole edifice' of international law is constructed on a[n] initial exclusion", id., at 6 061, and disempowerment because of the conjunction of civilization and sovereignty.

[18] Riles, *Aspiration and Control, supra* note 16.

[19] See e.g. Riles' discussion of David Kennedy's and Anthony Carty's treatment of culture: Riles id. at note 81.

[20] Anghie, *supra* note 17.

[21] Karen Engle, "Female Subjects of Public International Law: Human Rights and the Exotic Other Female", 26 *New Eng. L. Rev.* 1509 (1992) [hereinafter *Female Subjects*].

[22] Lama Abu-Odeh, "Post-Colonial Feminism and the Veil: Considering the Differences", 26 *New England L. R.* 1527 (1992).

ceptions of what is (women's) culture are precarious and diffuse.[23] These studies therefore indicate that it will be even more problematic to develop an international law reflecting post-colonial culture, both where there are no clear categories of culture and where different cultural considerations, such as gender and religion, contradict and overlap.[24] While not offering any neat solutions, these Newstream writings represent an advance upon the way the debate is conducted in Mainstream literature where it tends to devolve into an irresolvable exchange about whether international law should apply universal standards or be set according to local or regional needs. The difference here is that these Newstream writers intersect and oppose gender and culture in an attempt to move the debate beyond the simple observation that when trying to construct a more inclusive international law, previously excluded cultural factors come into conflict with each other. In contrast these works attempt to

[23] Karen Engle explores and criticizes the way different feminist critiques of international human rights, identify and assimilate women's concerns: Karen Engle, "International Human Rights and Feminism: When Discourses Meet", 13 *Mich. J. of Int'l L.* 517 (1992) [hereinafter *International Human Rights*]. She categorizes feminist approaches according to how they incorporate a conception of womens' culture into human rights. A three-layered typology is produced consisting of doctrinalists, institutionalists and external critics. "Doctrinalists" work within the framework of the existing doctrine to change and improve it, id. at 522. Hence the prohibition against torture contained in various human rights instruments can be extended to a prohibition against violence in the home, through a process of reinterpretation. "Institution-alists" focus their work on the processes of law-making advocating greater participation of women ultimately affecting the production of doctrine. Those engaged in an "external critique" see international human rights law as inherently male and resistant to assimilating women's concerns into its basic framework.

[24] Drawing on the earlier typology, id., Karen Engle explores what happens when other cultural categories intersect with this range of women's cultures. Focusing on the issue of clitoridectomy, she argues that the critique which appears to be the most explicit in identifying a culture specific to women (the "external" critique) is the *least* capable of being sensitive to other non-gendered cultural contexts: Engle, *Female Subjects, supra* note 21 at 1518. The external critique fails to recognize that the issue engenders deep differences of opinion, based on ethnic culture, between women. Similarly, Lama Abu-Odeh explores the difficulties of recognizing differences between women at the same time as maintaining a skepticism toward inclusive categories of womanhood, focusing on the use of the veil by feminists in Muslim countries and Western feminism's response: Lama Abu-Odeh, *supra* note 22. She argues that it may be possible for the two seemingly opposed positions to be reconciled at the point at which the interests of the two groups intersect. This is despite contradictions between Western feminists who see the veil as a symbol of disempowerment for women, and Muslim feminists who don it as a symbol of their power to redefine its meaning. It is not the obvious point that culture and gender can clash. Instead she locates common ground upon which feminisms meet by recognizing that although the veil increases a woman's "untouchability", id., at 1530, and thus remedies a problem of sexual harassment in the street , id., at 1531, it has a "different logic" in the workplace, where it can "seriously affect the career prospects", id., at 1534, of those who wear it. Despite (significant) differences, Islamic and Western feminist attitudes to the veil, both, through different means, seek to provide opportunities for Arab women to choose their work, and lifestyle and to be free from sexual harassment. Western feminisms are portrayed as both in opposition to, and potentially in alliance with, Islamic feminisms.

problematise the issue of culture, to argue that it is no longer possible to see categories of culture, as either all the same or all different. According to this view the proposals about incorporation of difference have been superseded by a recognition that one can no longer accurately define what standard is universal or relative. Whether it be human rights standards, or indigenous art, or Coca Cola, the search for an authentically universal, or relative version of each is an idle one because, in the words of one political scientist, sameness and difference have "cannibalized" each other.[25] It is the examination of this contradiction in the Newstream writings which makes the work so provocative and worthwhile.

So far we have seen how a concern with Mainstream definitions of culture permeates much Newstream work, although it is grappled with in quite different ways. A related uncertainty within the new scholarship concerns a pronounced skepticism about ever assigning people to particular cultural groups. This problem, which pervades many of the analyses, begs the question of how to ever talk about, or generalize about a group, in order to develop legal rules. The scholarship exhibits an implicit anxiety over culture which limits and complicates the possibilities of description, of law-making, and its interpretation. One response of some Newstream writers has been to argue that, despite the instability of the concept of culture, there is something intuitively appealing about representing a group of people in terms of a particular set of common characteristics, particularly when they have defined those characteristics themselves.[26] Implicit in this argument is the view that it would be churlish and patronizing to question the self-identification of a cultural grouping such as indigenous people.

Another response has been to argue that instead of discarding cultural groupings altogether as "untenable categor[ies] of representation",[27] one needs to a reconstruct the categories of culture as they currently exist.[28] The term "perspective" is used by one writer to describe a new mode of mak-

[25] Appuradai, *supra* note 15 at 17.

[26] Maivan Clech Lam, "Making Room for Peoples at the United Nations: Thoughts Provoked by Indigenous Claims to Self-Determination", 25 *Cornell Int. L. J.* 603 (1992) arguing that indigenous peoples' participation at the Working Group on Indigenous Peoples is slowly allowing for the infiltration of indigenous concerns into international norm creation. This argument explicitly utilizes the notion of culture. Lam relies on there being in existence a recognizable, identifiable cultural category of indigeneity, just as she describes her Asian community at law school in the 1970s as an "unmistakable community" defined by "rice, fish sauce, ghost stories and anti-imperialism": id., at 604.

[27] Annelise Riles, "Disciplines and Cultures: Perspectives on International Law and the Colonial Encounter", (1994) (unpublished manuscript, on file with author) at 10 021 [hereinafter *Disciplines and Cultures*]

[28] Id.

ing and interpreting law on the basis of some method other than culture[29] and would entail accommodating the perspectives of a multiplicity of different groups, peoples and disciplinary approaches and a movement beyond its own boundaries into other fields such as anthropology. The inclusion of a wide range of perspectives would serve as a replacement for international law's singular reliance upon cultural forms, and the new perspectives would reflect against each other thus creating "a series of angles directed onto themselves"[30] giving rise to new ideas of law.[31] So having demolished culture, as defined by international law, its reconstruction might be promoted by the use of a methodology other than culture. But the danger with this version of "multi-perspectivalism" is that it must also ultimately be premised on one form of cultural, or perspectival, representation. It is not any more certain that the new perspectives would not replicate what was once referred to as culture. If the fit between law and culture is as constraining as Newstream writers have argued it is difficult to see how it can be escaped by a change in terminology.[32]

In sum Newstream work contributes to international law a sophisticated new approach to one of the basic conceptual apparatuses of the field, culture. It provides a complex rendering of definitions of culture using it to examine the inclusionary and exclusionary power of culture in doctrinal development, questions of representation of peoples, and problems of incorporating difference into law. Writers differ as to the manner in which to overcome the constraints of culture with some relying on various acts of self-will, while others argue that the nature of language, the structure of law and the problem of how to address the intersections between different categories of description make it difficult to overcome cultural definitions. On the other hand, culture may be necessary to the self-identification of peoples excluded from Mainstream processes. Ultimately no single view about culture dominates, but what emerges instead is a sometimes fraught but always provocative set

[29] Id. at 10 017.

[30] Id. at 10 035.

[31] Riles suggests that this would ultimately lead to change. "[T]he work of the discipline would be to foreground a multitude of perspectives on the perspectives that we once forced into the category of culture, and to facilitate the movement between them by representing this movement as symbolically significant": id., at 10 025.

[32] Ultimately perhaps the same criticism that was made of Frankenberg can be leveled also at Riles; how can one both be constrained by and transcend the categories of culture, or of perspective. Nevertheless Riles at least anticipates this criticism: id., at 10 033. She disassembles international law as culture in order to reassemble it, id., at 10 036, arguing in the process that the key feature to guide reconstructed perspectivalism is the increased participation of voices previously excluded from international law. In this respect, by self-consciously embracing the categories she criticizes, id., at 10 036, the analysis resembles Karen Knop's strategy, *infra*, note 129, of disassembling sovereignty and reconstructing it in a newer form taking account of the criticisms of the concept which caused it to be disassembled. While her admission lends a certain credibility to the project, it does not overcome the criticisms.

of possibilities. Culture is revealed to be both a vehicle of change and of stagnation and one the redefinition of which has much to offer to Mainstream analyses of law.

3.2. *History and Sovereignty*

The second way in which Newstream work is altering one of the conceptual bases of international law is through its redefinition of the relationship between the history of international law and the doctrine of sovereignty. Newstream scholarship maintains that Mainstream international legal history is self-servingly repetitive, excessively linear in focus, unstable, and, that it conceal interests other than the purely legal. Newstream writers therefore propose various ways in which the relationship between history and sovereignty could be reconceptualized.

A central thesis of Newstream scholarship is that international law requires rewriting because the Mainstream version constantly reiterates its own history so as to present the field as a narrative of inevitable progress and modernization.[33] And the telling of law's story corresponds to a range of other stories, conveniently buttressing each other, which are conventionally recounted about the same period of development. The organization of society from a tribal basis, to one based on communities and then on individuals; the movement from status to contract; and from religion to philosophy to law follow the same linear route. The development in law from a concern with substantive norms, to a focus on procedure; from legal rules to institutions; from naturalism to realism to pragmatism, all mirror the same Enlightenment story. By excluding stories which deviate from this format, international law is thus written to reflect the history of the Enlightenment in which law is constantly improved and refined with the progress of time.[34]

Although there is wide agreement in the new scholarship about the relationship between telling a particular history and the development of law, as with culture, Newstream writers present different versions of the Mainstream stories, and so different versions of how they could be altered. A first group

[33] See, e.g., Kennedy, *New Stream, supra* note 2 at 2.

[34] David Kennedy Lectures in International Law and Institutions, Harvard Law School, Fall 1994, [hereafter *Lectures*]. He illustrates the point by referring to a major American text which tracks a shift from a pre-modern concern with philosophy, through a classical interest in doctrine to a modern emphasis on institutions, with appropriate turning points signaled by the Peace of Westphalia in 1648, the nineteenth century rise of the nation state, and the Treaty of Versailles. See Henkin et al., *supra* note 4 at xxi–xxxi.

following the realist[35] or sociological[36] traditions, argue that international law and its history, have been constructed,[37] in such a way so that something called "law" has been made, and exists at least semi-autonomously. They are not claiming that the history which is made is fictional or fraudulent but simply that it has been made, the point being to question the Mainstream version in order to show that outcomes are chosen and not inevitable. A second group however who do not share the assumption that this process of construction has lead to the existence of a separate entity called "law". Instead (and this is discussed more fully in the next section) they contend that law may be no more than a set of argumentative practices, a form of rhetoric,[38] (although this does not necessarily make it any the less real or powerful).[39] So a concept like "the state", or "sovereignty" is actually about the relationship between something posited as law and something posited as society,[40] rather than being a thing as such.[41] If law and its history are simply structures of certain repeating practices and arguments, then these tools must be questioned and unraveled, not only revealed (as the first group advocates), in order to effect any meaningful alteration in them.

Why it is that the Newstream writers would be so keen to unsettle the conventional view of history and international law? First, they argue that an examination of sovereignty reveals that the linear, historical story is wrong, and that its acceptance has skewed our current understanding of the doctrine's meaning. Far from having progressively evolved from a nineteenth century political principle, through a positivist rule early this century[42] to a more nuanced concept today, Newstream writers argue that sovereignty has always

---

[35] "Realist" is used here to describe a conception of law a result of policy choices of judges. See, e.g., Karl Llewellyn, "A Realistic Jurisprudence: the Next Step", 30 *Col. L. Rev.* 431 (1930).

[36] "Sociological" is used here to describe a conception of law as a reflection of society. See, e.g., Roscoe Pound, "The Scope and Purpose of Sociological Jurisprudence", 24 *Harv. L. Rev.* 591 (1911).

[37] Philip Allot, "New International Law: the First Lecture of the Academic Year 20 -", in Warbrick (ed.), *Theory and International Law: An Introduction* (1991), 105 at 116: the "actual" is not "natural and inevitable."

[38] Kennedy, *New Stream, supra* note 2 at 9: "Law is a restatement of its imaginary relationship to society."

[39] One political science commentator claims "imagination has become an organized field of social practices,": Appadurai *supra* note 15 at 5.

[40] Kennedy, id., at 6.

[41] Id., at 44.

[42] The highpoint of positive sovereignty is conventionally represented by the holding that restrictions on sovereignty cannot be presumed: *SS Lotus Case* (*France* v. *Turkey*) (1927) PCIJ Ser A. No. 9.

been an unstable reference point.[43] For example, judicial decisions which have been traditionally interpreted as illustrative of the importance of sovereignty can equally be read as representing law's fealty to strict rules over morality.[44] Moreover the meaning of sovereignty has always been in a state of flux, particularly throughout the nineteenth and twentieth century when treatise writers used the term sovereignty to describe how large trading companies wielded power over colonial territories and inhabitants[45] and early judicial decisions implicitly rejected any absolute rule, developed subsequently, that restrictions on sovereignty could not be presumed.[46] Later treatise writers used the concept to discuss the status of the first universal international institution, the League of Nations, arguing for example, that sovereignty was not simply about territory and power, but the moral authority wielded by government over the rights of the inhabitants,[47] or that although the League lacked the critical attributes of sovereignty,[48] it nevertheless possessed a separate existence which was more than the sum of its member state parts.[49]

A second reason Newstream writers are critical of the Mainstream representation of history is that, somewhat paradoxically perhaps, they claim it inhibits lawyers confronting current problems, because they are always look-

---

[43] Kennedy, *Lectures*. See e.g., David Kennedy, *A New World Order: Yesterday, Today and Tomorrow* [hereafter *New World Order*], 4 Transnational Law & Contemp. Problems 329 (1994) at 350: sovereignty "means lots of things." Kennedy also argues that the critique of sovereignty itself has been a recurring one, Kennedy, *New World Order*, id., at 359, and that Newstream writers are themselves situated historically, within a "rotating critique" about sovereignty and formalism, id., at 68.

[44] *The Antelope* 23 U.S. (10 Wheaton) 66 (1825) in Deak, *International Law Cases* Vol. 1. Chief Justice John Marshall of the U.S. Supreme Court held that African slaves seized on a Portuguese ship had to be returned to their owners despite domestic abhorrence of slavery. The case is commonly understood as a landmark in the development of sovereignty, on the basis of respect for Portugal's sovereignty. Alternatively it could be seen as an example of support for the rule of law, demonstrated in the reasoning that although "public sentiment" may wish the "unnatural traffic ... to be suppressed" this would "march somewhat in advance of strict law", id., at 3.

[45] Wheaton, *Elements of International Law* (1866) 18.

[46] *Pacquette Habana* (1900) 175 US SC Rep 677.

[47] Geoffrey Butler, "Sovereignty and the League of Nations", *Brit. Y.B. Int'l L.* (1920–21), 35. His discussion questioned any singular notion of sovereignty referring to insights from the new field of psychology, French corporations theory and recognition doctrine. According to Butler "consciousness" as much as territory created sovereignty, id., at 42. The notion that a corporation could possess "personality" suggested that such concepts were artificial constructs, id., at 36. And the emergent distinction between *de facto* and *de jure* recognition implied that there could be different types of sovereignty, id., at 35.

[48] P.E. Corbett, "What is the League of Nations?" *Brit. Y.B. Int'l L.* (1924) 119. Corbett lists criteria set out by Oppenheim: the right of legation, rights of sovereignty, the right of intervention for the protection of minorities, the capacity to hold a protectorate and to declare or peace, id., at 121.

[49] Id., 148.

ing back to past developments or anticipating an inevitably reformed future, instead of focusing upon the substantive difficulties of the present.[50] The nostalgic invocation of the past[51] thus has the added effect of suspending the doctrinal development of international law in the present.

What does the adoption of such a view signify in practical terms? To take one example, if international human rights law is perceived as constantly moving toward a more progressive state, but is instead caught in limbo between a harsh past and a utopian future, proposals to regulate the present are bound to be impeded. This prognosis can be illustrated in the ambivalence in human rights law towards the well-documented problem of violence in the home, which continues to infect most societies despite widespread condemnation. While a host of factors, such as religious belief, economic structures, and assumptions about the male right to exert power, militate against its eradication, the continued belief in the inevitability of improvements also plays a role. This optimism, often unsubstantiated by facts, blunts the impetus for change in the present by encouraging women to be satisfied that some movement is occurring and so to remain patient and passive, even if in fact conditions are worsening or remaining static rather than improving in many situations.[52] Thus current realities of continuing universal abuse are hidden if international human rights law continues to passively rely upon a history in which progress is inevitable.

A third reason for the Newstream skepticism about international law history is their claim that that the Mainstream story presumes the existence of a clear demarcation between the past, in which religion, mysticism, and universalizing ideologies reigned, and the present in which society is characterized by law, rationality and the absence of ideology.[53] Newstream critiques argue that religion, although largely unacknowledged, continues to inform inter-

---

[50] The field is "constantly remembering a stable origin, foreshadowing a substantive resolution, but living in an interminable procedural present": Kennedy, *New Stream, supra* note 2 at 2. The "stable origin" of Kennedy's claim would be states choosing to join together as a community of nations in order to create an international public order; the "substantive resolution" would be the promise of a fully developed set of substantive norms; and the "interminable procedural present" is represented by the burgeoning bureaucratic structure of the United Nations, its agencies, and other international law making institutions.

[51] Id., at 12.

[52] For a recent news article substantiating the view that violence in the home continues to be a widespread problem see, e.g., "More Women Killed in Pregnancy in US as Result of Beating Than All Other Diseases" P. Bone, *The Age* 24/25 Aug. 1995. For an argument claiming that economic structural adjustment policies has a disproportionately deleterious effect on women see, e.g., Marilyn Waring, "Gender and International Law: Women and the Right to Development", 12 *Australian Y.B. of Int'l L.* (1992) 177.

[53] A major casebook on international law, Henkin et al., *supra* note 4 at xxii , differentiates the past from the present by arguing that "universalist ideologies" of earlier times have been replaced by "co-existence" in the current period, id., at xxx.

national law, because it repeats in a "secular key" religion's attitude to the sacred and profane.[54] Sovereignty with its almost deified[55] status within the hierarchy of norms could be one example of the operation of this distinction, because its "sanctity" continues to operate as a barrier to the development of principles perceived as incursions on it, such as human rights protection and humanitarian intervention.

A final reason to question the Mainstream linear view of history is that it buries inequalities which lie at the very foundation of some doctrinal developments. For example it is argued that sovereignty and its associated doctrines, acquisition of territory, territorial integrity, and self-determination, arose out of, reflected and reinforced the inequities of colonialism. Anthony Anghie examines the history of colonialism and its effect on the development of sovereignty doctrine. He argues that the whole project of sovereignty was a response to colonialism. He identifies two forces which were used in the name of the colonial project to oppress colonial peoples and form the structural basis for the development of the rules of sovereignty. The first arose as a response to the Austinian challenge to international law. Typically Austin's definition of law as rules emanating from a sovereign backed by force is viewed as inimical to the idea of international law itself. However the Austinian view of law also conflicts with the characterization of indigenous social orders as non-legal. Colonial peoples who, after all, would have satisfied the criterion of sovereignty had to be distinguished. International law answered the latter part of the Austinian challenge, according to Anghie, by refocussing the discussion over the source of authority from the sovereign to society. If society was the real source of legitimacy it was a short step toward limiting the sorts of societies which could be such sources. Hence, argues Anghie, the response of international law was to utilize colonialism's definitions of civilization in order to exclude the "uncivilized" sources from operating as a legitimate source of sovereign authority. Once excluded as uncivilized, this exclusion then formed the basis of justifications for the development of international norms relating to sovereignty. There was a circular relationship then between the rejection of Austinian definitions, colonialism, and legal doctrine. Each reinforced the other.[56]

This history has continuing ramifications for international law because it has not previously been acknowledged. Newstream advocates argue that it is

---

[54] Kennedy, *New Stream, supra* note 2 at 17.

[55] Richard Ashley, and R. B. J. Walker, "Reading Dissidence/Writing the Discipline: Crisis and the Question of Sovereignty in International Studies", 34 *Int'l Studies Q.* (1990) 367, arguing that sovereignty has variously been reconfigured as equivalent to, *inter alia*, God, nature, citizen, nation, and history.

[56] Anghie, *supra* note 17 at 47.

imperative for international law to excavate its foundational doctrines in order to determine whether they mask disadvantages which would counter international law's claim to impartiality and fundamental equality. So, for example, adopting a Newstream approach, one could examine whether there are inbuilt restrictions upon the application of principle of permanent sovereignty over natural resources and, if there are, whether these internal limits ought to be reassessed in the light of current understandings of equality and disadvantage? Another possibility of applying the Newstream historical approach would be to ask whether the GATT "special sector" exclusions for textiles and agriculture relate to their particular historical genesis and now require readjustment?

In sum Newstream methods of analyzing history and sovereignty have been combined in imaginative ways which suggest their application could have far-reaching consequences for international law. The continuing redefinition of the relationship between history and sovereignty has been used to question the linear and progressive account of history, and the sanctity of some of law's basic principles, to uncover inequalities in doctrines, and to assist in rescuing international law from its paralysis in the face of continuing violations. The potential application of these insights in fields ranging from human rights to trade is an important project for the future. When sovereignty is no longer conceived of as natural, construction can be a liberation rather than a constraint.

3.3. *Language*

The final conceptual redefinition which Newstream introduces into international law is its focus on language as a constitutive tool of law-making. While Mainstream literature on law-making emphasizes the role of custom in the form of state practice, beliefs, and values, Newstream writers borrow from ideas associated with French post-structural theory, to argue that as law is made up of language, languages generates, rather than simply describes, legal rules.

If this view of the relationship between language and law is correct then the Mainstream approach has failed to take account of an important factor in law-making. If law is a set of arguments generated by language then it is the discussion or conversation about the arguments which creates the concepts themselves, not the actual behavior of states, their consent, or their beliefs. So Newstream lawyers refer to law to as a system of "linguistic maneuvers",[57]

---

[57] Edward M. Morgan, "Internalization of Customary International Law: An Historical Perspective", 12 *Yale J. Int'l Law* 63, 65 (1987).

or as a practice of argument[58] rather than a system of rules with an *a priori* existence which is subsequently reduced into language.

The second aspect of this approach to language is that it disputes the Mainstream assumption that law is different from other forms of culture. If law is simply a linguistic phenomenon made up out of language, it has much more in common with other fields such as politics, or sociology, or even drama or of visual art, and therefore its claim to being unique is weakened. And so also, the things which make up the texts of law — its instruments, its doctrines, its institutions and processes — can be interpreted as aspects of any one of those fields. So for example, war crimes trials from Nuremberg, through Eichmann to Demjanjuk, can be seen as a form of legal drama, as "retributory theater" rather than as stages in the development of legal doctrine.[59] Or a legal forum may acquire a theatrical quality. A conference on East Timor and an academic exchange to the Royal College of Madrid become scenes in a three act drama about the disillusionment of an international human rights lawyer.[60] Or a particular doctrine, such as self-determination, can be interpreted in terms of its relationship to the artistic developments in the Modernist period.[61]

However it would be a mistake to conclude that this emphasis on law as language, or artistic narrative, reduces law to semantics or renders it any the less powerful. On the contrary the Newstream scholars depict law as a set of irreconcilable binary linguistic tendencies[62] which constitute a powerful social practice[63] with very real effects. For example it is convincingly argued that the language of state sovereignty developed in such a way as to exclude colonized peoples from the benefits of sovereignty.[64] Colonized groups, although

---

[58] Kennedy, *Lectures, supra* note 34, describing statehood doctrine as being composed of a series of "argumentative tendencies".

[59] Edward Morgan, "Retributory Theater", 3 *Am. Univ. J. Int'l L. and Pol.* 1 (1988).

[60] David Kennedy, "Autumn Weekends: An Essay on Law and Everyday Life", in A. Sarat, ed., *Law and Everyday Life* 191 (1993) [hereinafter, *Autumn Weekends*].

[61] Nathaniel Berman, "Modernism, Nationalism and the Rhetoric of Reconstruction", 4 *Yale. J. of L. and the Humanities* 351 (1992). Berman aims to show how legal innovations in the inter-war period borrowed from developments in art. He argues that the principles of self-determination and minority protection fragmented sovereignty in the inter-war period in a similar way to that in which modernism fragmented representation of the body. The appearance of a principle which undermined absolute sovereignty and invested national groups with legal significance coincided with, modernism's critique of representation and its interest in primitive expressionism.

[62] Martti Koskenniemi argues convincingly that the entire structure of legal argument is based upon certain oppositions inherent in language. He shows that law can be reduced to two sets of mutually complementary "ascending" and "descending" sets of justifications. Martti Koskenniemi, *From Apology to Utopia: The Structure of International Legal Argument* (1989) [hereinafter *Apology to Utopia*].

[63] Appadurai, *supra* note 15 at 5.

[64] Anghie, *supra* note 17.

exhibiting many of the requirements of sovereignty such as group identification, territory, political organization, and an authoritative decision maker were nevertheless not "sovereign" in the sense required by international law because they were deemed "uncivilized" according to a definition of the term which excluded non-European practices. Thus the language of law in formulating a complex spectrum of types of sovereignty determined the practice of law in a manner which made it both exclusive of non-Europeans and hierarchical toward them. Non-Europeans possessed "personality" at international law which enabled them to convey land to Europeans, and to trade with them, but nothing more. The inter-dependence between legal definitions of sovereignty and the continued subjugation of the colonized peoples is evidence of the power of language and its participation in the creation of those conditions.[65] Moreover, it is evidence of the way in which the language of colonialism and international law interacted because without the language of one the other made little sense.

It is important to acknowledge however that the focus on language is not new to international legal scholarship, although the emphasis on it is. The provisional nature of the meaning of concepts such as sovereignty has long been recognized[66] as has the normative ambiguity of legal language generally.[67] But the difference between the Newstream and earlier commentators is that although the latter were aware of the inherent ambiguity of the language of law they nevertheless believed that its true meaning could be extracted by going beyond the surface meaning to find an interpretation which best fitted the purpose of the instrument.[68] The purpose could be located in ancillary texts, for example in the travaux preparotoire (itself a thing made up of language). Where these newer commentaries differ is in their claim that even looking behind the instrument, or doctrine will not reveal the true meaning of the law, because language, with all its normative ambiguities is still the constitutive tool. There is no escape from language. According to the Newstream approach, there will always be available a linguistic justification for a particular view of law that emphasizes either the need for sovereign autonomy and or the requirements of an interdependent world community. One may in

---

[65] "Language cannot yield to empirical reality where it would lead to collapse of the system and of language itself": id., at 6 059.

[66] See discussion of the sovereign status of the League, *supra* notes 47 & 48.

[67] Myres McDougal, *Power and Policy in Quest of Law: Essays in Honor of E. V. Rostow*, (1985) 145. [hereinafter, *Power*].

[68] Id., at 154: "[w]hen the march of events inevitably lays bare ambiguities and alternatives of interpretation. . . . rationality must require that interpretation . . . which best promotes the major purposes . . . "

certain circumstances appear more persuasive than the other, but neither is inherently or objectively correct.[69]

In Section 3, I have shown that Newstream scholarship has introduced some basic redefinitions of important conceptual relationships in international law between cultural form and legal doctrine, between history and sovereignty and between language and law. In Section 4 I turn to an examination of the methods Newstream scholarship uses in making these arguments.

4. The Methodological Challenge

Mainstream writers generally draw upon a standard range of methodological tools. Upon identifying a legal problem they classify it using a common taxonomy and common history; its textual, judicial and customary sources are discussed; the intention of the drafters or state actors is identified; as are any associated norms; and the political context or realities which constrain its interpretation. The discussion usually generates two or three possible alternatives through which the prudent scholar ordinarily divines a middle course. The objection of the Newstream to this form of analysis is that it is redundant because it simply regurgitates old problems and ultimately leads to intellectual stagnation. So in order to avoid reproducing past problems, Newstream works challenge not only the basic concepts of international law by redefining them, but also its methods. The three Newstream methods which are discussed here are the use of polarities or "doubles" to construct arguments, the personal quest device, and the focus on language.

4.1. *"Doubles"*

One Newstream strategy is to locate within international law scholarship, opposing argumentative tendencies, or, as I will call them, "doubles", in order to expose the indeterminate nature of law. Martti Koskenniemi, the best known exponent of the technique, positions international legal problems on a type of metaphorical grid in which all legal arguments veer between justifications for State behavior, or advocacy of more international regulation; between being either "apologetic" in the case of the former, or "utopian" in

---

[69] Hence Koskenniemi contends that *"we cannot consistently prefer either set of arguments. Adopting a descending pattern will seem political and subjective either because it assumes the existence of a natural morality or because it creates an arbitrary distinction between States. An ascending pattern will seem political and subjective because it cannot constrain at all. . . . Both must be included in order to make law seem objective, that is, normative and concrete and, as such, something other than politics."* Martti Koskenniemi, "The Politics of International Law", 1 *Eur. J. Int'l. L.* (1990) 4 at 45 (emphasis in original) [hereinafter *Politics*].

the case of the latter.[70] So examples of the apologetic, or "ascending" justification are arguments which emphasize state autonomy, the role of consent in law-making, and concreteness in legal interpretation. Typically, utopian or "descending" arguments will emphasize justice, normativity and community. By reducing legal argument to this simple but compelling structure, Koskeniemmi convincingly demonstrates the deficiencies of the Mainstream claim that law is founded in objective, rational, or value based choices and instead shows that it is part of a mutually reinforcing system of rhetoric.[71]

As a methodology, "doubling" is not new to international law,[72] but the technique is repeated so often in Newstream methodology, that it has become a distinguishing feature or the "voice"[73] of the approach. It serves a number of functions apart from exposing fundamental linguistic oppositions inherent in international law.[74] Doubling shows how these oppositions may combine in order to produce legal change;[75] it demonstrates how legal principles are always subject to re-interpretation because they usually contain contradictory

[70] Koskenniemi, id. Even the Newstream are caught in a puzzle in which they simultaneously criticize and embrace sovereignty: Kennedy, *New World Order, supra* note 43 at 360. The mutual dependency of the opposing forces emphasizes again how law fits together as a structure; it is not just a series of rules but a "single rhetorical fabric", Kennedy, *New Stream, supra* note 2 at 38.

[71] This mutual dependency is referred to in Kennedy's work as "double movements", Kennedy, *New Stream,* id., at 17. So, for example, the structure of sources doctrine moves between consent and non-consent, between treaty and custom, between "getting in" to custom through *opinio juris* and state practice, and "getting out" via regional custom or persistent objection are defined in this way. Or, constitutional voting mechanisms at the League of Nations referred back to the politics of establishment and forward to implementation of norms, without resolution, in the same way that sources and process doctrine "produces a practice of interminable discourse.": id., at 39.

[72] Earlier international law commentators, probably drawing on the Realist school of jurisprudence, Llewellyn, *supra* note 35, observed how doctrines "travel in opposites." Also, see e.g., McDougal, *Power, supra* note 67 at 156.

[73] Kennedy uses "voice" to refer to the style or approach encapsulated by the mainstream tradition. See, e.g., the "tragic voice of post-war public law liberalism": Kennedy, *New Stream, supra* note 2 at 2.

[74] It facilitates the Newstream arguments about the constitutive nature of language and reveals the way sets of irreconcilable oppositions in law are themselves rooted in the structure of language. Following the argument usually associated with French post-structuralism, see, e.g., Christopher Norris, *Deconstruction: Theory and Practice* (1982), that language is structured into a series of binaries, law constituted by argument must also express the same oppositions.

[75] Sometimes these binarisms are characterized as combining with each other to create a particular legal regime. Nathaniel Berman, for example, argues that self-determination law during the inter-war period combined modernism's interest in primitivism with its experimentation with form, Berman *supra* note 61. Berman illustrates his thesis by comparing the work of an artist, Picasso, with that of a legal scholar, Redslob, who wrote on nationalism. Picasso's work celebrated the period's critique of representation, and its interest in cultural expression. He fractured traditional representations of women for example and he incorporated images from "primitive" art into his work. Similarly law, described by Redslob, destabilized classic forms of concepts such as sovereignty and focused on the power of a "primitive" nationalism.

impulses;[76] and it lends support to the view that lawyers ought to look beyond the discipline, in order to avoid being paralyzed by these tensions.[77] Moreover doubling exposes international law's reliance on irreconcilable ideas;[78] illustrates the claim that Mainstream work is obsessed with procedure at the expense of achieving substantive objectives;[79] and provides one important

The period's artistic emphasis on innovation with form and with technique was translated into the legal domain in new forms such as the plebiscite and minority protection regimes, id., at 375. International law of peoples, in the inter-war period, reflected a modernist alliance of two related trends, primitivism and experimentalism, id., at 369.

[76] The doubling method impels new interpretations by providing an impetus for the release of argumentative energy. For example, Lam, *supra* note 26 at 622, examines how indigenous peoples can utilize pre-existing international law doctrine such as statehood and sovereignty to further their claim for greater participatory rights. Her primary argumentative device is to characterize statehood and sovereignty as part of a "double helix" which therefore contains "multiple inheritances" for indigenous peoples to draw upon. She relies on oppositional strands of thought which have been hidden but which are released by her analysis. Similarly, Allot describes an international law class in the twenty-first century, *supra* note 37, telling his students that society can either be like a poem and focus upon human consciousness, or it can be mechanistic like a motor car, id., at 109, and it is only the "joy of law" which will save it from the latter, id., at 113. It is the energy created by this contrast which inspires Allot's argument for a new normative vision of law in the current period.

[77] Doubling encourages writers to look outside law in order to avoid the spiral created by opposites in conflict. It encourages a questioning of law's boundaries and a dissolving of the distinctions between law and other disciplines. Newstream writers draw on anthropology, Riles, *supra* notes 16 and 27; art criticism, Berman *supra* note 61; politics, Koskenniemi, *Politics, supra* note 69; and feminism, Karen Knop, "Re/Statements: Feminism and State Sovereignty in International Law", 3 *Transnational L. & Contemporary Prob.* 293 (1993) to help resolve the law's indeterminancies. Moreover precursors of the Newstream approach use similar techniques. So, for example, Berman relies on Redslob who argues that nationalism is informed by literature and politics, Berman, *supra* note 61 at 364, 365. See also Redslob's reliance on a rich background of non-legal factors to constitute a concept which has legal status, namely nationhood. Robert Redslob, "The Problem of Nationalities", *Grotius Society*, March 2, 1931, 21. Nationalism is created as a product of various influences, including, for example, a royal family, id., at 22, "the literary and artistic patrimony", and political instruments such as the Magna Carta, id., at 23. Interdisciplinarity, both of the analyses and or their historical sources characterizes the new approaches method.

[78] Ileana Porras uses the method to examine the way the Rio Declaration on the Environment contains provisions which seeks to balance seemingly incompatible goals of development and the environment, Porras, *supra* note 5. A sovereign right to exploit resources according to the State's own development policies, an injunction that environmental standards should reflect context, and that they should not distort trade, are included alongside provisions imposing state responsibility for environmental damage, the polluter pays principle, and a requirement that States reduce unsustainable patterns of production and consumption: id., citing Rio Declaration Principles 11, 16, 2, 16, 8 respectively. Despite what Porras calls this "paradox", id., at 21, she portrays the developments as basically healthy because they are an example of inclusion of developing countries interests, which forces developed countries to modify their practices as well as enabling developing countries to contribute to law making and interpretation.

[79] A function of the doubling technique is that it concretizes the Newstream arguments about the relationship between substance and process, in three ways. First, doubling emphasizes the way process avoids substance. Koskenniemi claims that classic international law developed into

organizing device for arguments.[80] In short, the use of doubles is not only characteristic of Newstream work, but facilitates the definition of many of the conceptual challenges referred to above.

4.2. *Personal Quest*

A second challenge to Mainstream method comes in the form of the personal quest device. Mainstream methods of analysis are clearly comforted by the notion that in adopting a standard methodology, as described above, one is assured that the legal conclusions which are reached are, to an extent, objective. Newstream work implicitly questions that assumption, by adopting a different set of techniques, perhaps the most controversial of which is to personalize legal issues as part of a larger quest or journey for a better international law. The quest device serves to emphasize three features: the subjective nature of law-making, the relationship between public and private, and the search for redemption within the discipline. A well known example of a writer who uses this method is David Kennedy.

Kennedy uses the quest technique to evoke the disappointment of Newstream writers with current Mainstream lawyers who, he argues, have largely inherited a pragmatic, as opposed to normative form of analysis.[81] Non-legal

proceduralism in order to avoid the problem of resolving conflict either by using fundamental values or oppressive majoritarianism, Koskenniemi, *supra* note 62 at 128, 129. Second, it lends support to the argument that process determines substance. Kennedy claims that although state responsibility presents itself as the humble servant of substantive norms, it often supplants it, David Kennedy, *International Legal Structures* (1987) 175 [hereinafter: *Legal Structures*]. For example in the *South West Africa* cases Liberia and Ethiopia were refused standing on the basis of lack of interest. In this case South Africa's breach of the mandate on the grounds of racial discrimination was never resolved, but was nevertheless indirectly determined, id., at 125. Third, doubling facilitates the new approaches view that the move to process is seen as depleting substance. Tennant cautions against the dangers of indigenous peoples vesting energy in procedural reform because it may lead to valorizing process over substance; indigenous aspirations being "captured" and "co-opted" by participation, Tennant, *supra* note 6 at 56.

[80] So for example Riles' basic thesis is to show how a Europeanized version of culture ordered colonial societies, Riles, *supra* notes 16 & 27. But to make this argument she divides the mechanisms of order into opposed, but mutually dependent forces. Colonial peoples were ordered in one of two ways. Either they were ordered because they were controllable as categories of peoples deemed to lack civilization, or they were ordered by forcing them to aspire to be civilized. In both cases her argument aims to prove how international law ordered colonial peoples, and in both cases the organizing principle of her thesis is European culture in opposition to other cultures. Similarly Tennant, *supra* note 6, organizes his argument around two opposing standards, his aim being to contrast one legal period with another. Indigenous peoples were represented as ignoble during the period of assimilation and as noble when autonomy was the preferred strategy. Doubling is an effective tool in ordering such an argument.

[81] In a thumbnail portrait of American international lawyers in the post war era, he argues that they sacrificed a doctrinal purity for institutional pragmatism and portrays them as naive

techniques, such as a literary writing style, and the frequent use of similes and metaphors characterize the work, often as stylistic devices to repeat the theme that international law has lost its idealism and its innocence, and strayed toward realism and proceduralism. So where the emphasis is on a law of human rights which is caught between an idealistic realization of its normative framework and a realistic acceptance of its limits, Kennedy describes a human rights conference in a mood which evokes a similar equivocation and disappointment, as a "smudged Xerox affair" with a "faded agenda".[82] From the terminology we know already that the conference was held in an under-resourced field of law where the aspirations of its stated norms had a slightly soiled quality, signaling a certain weariness within the field and the inevitability or likelihood of failure[83] and passive acceptance of that failure.

The personal nature of the journey is emphasized by portraying the people involved in international law-making in an informal gossipy manner,[84] or by writing in the form of a personal narrative[85] or as a kind of social anthropology of international lawyering.[86] Again the use of the personal voice allows the Newstream writer to convey a sense of disappointment and unrequited anger about the perceived failure of Mainstream international law.

---

and childlike playing with toys beyond their control. There they were, "sneaking up" on sovereignty, with their enthusiasm for administration rather than rules, but their "shiny new bureaucracies failed to produce the reform which they had prophesied.": Kennedy, *New Stream, supra* note 2 at 4.

[82] Kennedy, *Autumn Weekends, supra* note 60 at 192.

[83] Metaphor is used in the same way, to repeat in stylistic mode the harsh move toward disillusionment. So in describing the way international scholarship lost its sense of direction in the post-war era, Kennedy says that its students were "invited to choose [explanations for international law] like a debutante at a smorgasbord", Kennedy, *New Stream, supra* note 2 at 4.

[84] See David Kennedy's description of the generational development of American international lawyers from the inter-war period, through the post war phase, to the present day. Kennedy describes an international law peopled by "imperialists and humanitarians", "usually Republicans", id., at 3, in the pre war era, and "Democrats eager to rebuild in the name of democracy and decolonization", id., at 4. It is a description tinged with excitement and with pathos. The inter-war characters were lawyers of "independent intellectual vision" who "rebuilt the field after the debacle of America's absence from that quintessentially progressive institution, the League of Nations", id., at 3. They are depicted as heroic if somewhat naive in ignoring the insights of realism, or the principles of the welfare state.

[85] David Kennedy often places himself at the center of a description. International scholarship is about personal discovery. It is also as much as about how individual people behave and act as a group as it is about the texts they write or write about. Friendships and companionability are important to this international law. Ideas and rules are not self generating.

[86] The same conference is described as a "site for social relations", Kennedy, *Autumn Weekends, supra* note 60 at 202, even for "flirtation", id., at 205. Much store is placed by Kennedy on the formation at the meeting of an "affinity group" id., at 204 of like minded, slightly jaded, but savvy people.

[t]he elaborate edifice they had honored was succumbing to the erosion and fragmentation they had encouraged. Attacked from the left and right, theoretically weak, jurisprudentially behind the times, the old edifice they had so lovingly sheltered seemed hopelessly ill-equipped to the broad functions they had encouraged us to think it might perform".[87]

The voice is of the disappointed disciple who had been led to believe in international law's capacity to change the international sphere and had seen those expectations dashed[88] especially by those in the academy.[89] However it also opens the door to the Newstream to challenge its predecessors and position themselves as intellectual redeemers of the field,[90] a goal which is pursued with almost missionary zeal.[91] The reader witnesses the journey and is encouraged to identify with its success or failure.

The most distinctive feature of the quest is that it integrates the personal and public spheres, so that the twin themes of idealism and realism, of romanticism and cynicism, are repeated, eventually resolving into a sense of melancholy. So although a central theme of Kennedy's work is the tension in public international law between its potential to provide a strong, enforceable, normative framework and the actual limits of its application, he also seems engaged in a constant, perhaps therapeutic and quite public exploration of, what he calls, the "split moment"[92] between realism and idealism, best exemplified in the article about a human rights conference on the subject of East Timor.[93] This is a journey which is characterized by both romance and sexu-

---

[87] Kennedy, *New Stream, supra* note 2 at 5.

[88] The sheepish exit, id., of the ancestors seems fitting as Kennedy recounts in great detail the disaster he has inherited, berating them with their many deficiencies – theoretical, jurisprudential, political and shortsighted. What is left after this rather Oedipal outburst, is only the detritus of its former proud self, "a frail dowager, too weak to withstand sustained criticism, in need of enrichment, protection and an observant fealty," id., at 6, a group whom Spiro Agnew would justifiably label "nattering nabobs of negativism," id.

[89] In the academy all that could be offered was "an easy patois of lazy justification and arrogance for a discipline which had lost its way and kept its jobs," id. The bitterness extended to a feeling that the teachers could provide no convincing explanation for the existence of international law as law. "We were given too many reasons to believe in international law - as our teachers struggled to make good their enthusiasm after having pawned their idealism", id.

[90] Not keen to keep working in the same manner, to be a "bureaucrat, a laborer in an institutional plant that no one believed was able to respond to international racism, inequality or violence," id., the younger critics commenced on a program of reinvigoration.

[91] Their mission, their journey was to save the field of international law, to "dislodge the discipline from its stagnation in post war realism," id.

[92] Kennedy, *Autumn Weekends, supra* note 60 at 203.

[93] The conference, held in Portugal in 1991, concerns the legal ramifications of Indonesia's continuing presence in East Timor. The pervasive theme of the article is the conflict between activism and realism, but this theme is conveyed through the device of the author's reminiscence

ality, and by cynicism and mundaneness.[94] It is a journey in which the author indulges in self-aggrandizement;[95] adopts an ironic, almost flip tone;[96] and attempts to shock the reader with his purported amorality.[97]

At one level then the writing is cynical and self-indulgent, exhibiting, albeit consciously, all the worst traits of me-generation pop psychology narration: arrogance, self-centredness, too cleverness and mock mockery. However intertwined with the heavy and quite explicit cynicism of the style is a perhaps honest, serious, funny, vaguely optimistic but sad paen to the possibilities of human rights law. Its redemptive quality lies largely in its brutal self-scrutinization and revelation. [98] Moreover, the seriousness of its objectives,

upon his own participation in the conference and in the disillusionment which occurred there. His personal musings become the subject of the piece.

[94] Kennedy's disillusioning process of yearning for a transcendental idealistic normativity which characterized the beginnings of the East Timor conference and the cynicism and pragmatism of the Spanish nightclub, reads like the story of a failed romance. Cf. Allot's attachment to the "poetry" of international law over its mechanical qualities has a lyrical, but urgent edge to it, Allot *supra* note 37.

[95] East Timor falls away as an issue of concern or law, as does human rights or even self-determination. Instead we are left with an consciously indulgent personal dialogue, with a warts and all revelation of the author's misgivings, insecurities and conceits/vanities. Thus the author elevates himself as the subject of the work. He refers to himself in, what he himself labels, "messianic" terms: Kennedy, *Autumn Weekends, supra* note 60 at 197. At one point he is asked to provide an unscheduled interview for Portuguese television. He does so with what appears to be a general disdain for the process, for the subject of East Timor and for his audience. Subjected to questioning by a "charming reporter", he felt he "should admit that [he] had no idea what the U.S. position on Timor might be," id., at 199, but he nevertheless "wishes for a more forthcoming attitude from the State Department on Timor (don't they always disappoint)," id., at 200. He talked about the "number of crucial procedural hurdles" associated with the case and that "the case would need to be pursued diligently, but the importance of the norms involved could hardly be overstated. And so on," id. The explicit irony of the description, does not lessen its superior and condescending tone. Nowhere are the issues really aired, the whole process is treated as a sort of unpleasant but expected distraction satisfying only the subject's interest in media attention and his political detachment.

[96] Confessing to the reader that he was ignorant of the U.S. position in Timor, Kennedy asks "where were we on Indonesia these days anyway?" id., at 199. Small details are introduced in an irreverent tone. The author postpones his departure for the conference because he has "tickets for Natalie Cole" the preceding day, id., at 196, as if to heighten the disjunction between the hedonistic private and the altruistic public domains.

[97] Cogitating about whether to attend the conference, Kennedy confesses that he was motivated by reasons other than international law advocacy. He "had never been to Portugal" id., at 194, and "[a]t the very least, this sort of thing can sometimes be cashed in for political correctness points with students and colleagues," id., at 195. When Kennedy leaves the conference he flies home with a sympathetic colleague and they ruminate pretentiously over the event, creating a sort of primitive, high-altitude, concrete poetry during the flight, id., at 211–214.

[98] Kennedy's hyper-criticism of the nerdishness of others is easily matched by his own self-flagellation. As a participant in the conference, he fears that he is engaged (along with others) in a "great collective narcissism in the name of empathy," id., at 208. His overarching self-criticism contrasts with the collective self-righteousness that is a product of the conference itself.

one of which is to condemn the phenomenon of human rights conferencing as a sham, further undercuts the otherwise gratuitous flipness.[99] There is tragi-comedy here. Held up by a TV journalist and having no idea what the US position was on East Timor, the author "flashed rather unhelpfully on nuclear ships and New Zealand."[100] There is no question that Timor is belittled here as just another crisis. On the other hand it is the international lawyer's fate to be somewhat dilettantish, knowing a small amount about many parts of the globe and being expected to comment intelligently on them all. The speaker's shallowness becomes a reflection of the discipline's superficiality.

In short, the personal quest device allows the writer to evoke a mood of disillusionment about international law which repeats a prominent substantive theme of the work. The personal narrative style and the emphasis on the everyday behavior of people brings the discipline to life stressing the human agency involved in its creation. The ironic, sometimes aggrandizing and shocking tone of the work highlights the melancholic conclusion of the personal voyage, and the objective nature of the law-making process is further undermined. Ultimately the continual representation of law as riven by two opposing forces of idealism and realism, heightens the dramatic possibilities of the search for a resuscitated international law.[101]

4.3. Language

A final aspect of Newstream methodology is its interest in the use of language. As the last section demonstrates the Newstream style of language sometimes departs from the styles used in standard Mainstream analyses. The Newstream piece may be heavy with descriptive passages, or devices such as metaphors which are more often associated with literature than law. It may be personal and gossipy. It may contain word plays and different tones shades ranging

---

[99] When Kennedy describes himself proposing an alternative resolution to the final conference resolution it is clear that what he is expressing represents real frustration with the ineffectiveness of international law. Instead of simply calling for action which the conference participants know will not be forthcoming, he calls on the meeting to express its sheer frustration with the hopelessness of international law's prospect of real change, id., at 210. Similarly when he refers to the Dili massacre, which occurred during the Conference, he notes how this real life incident of great magnitude barely cut in to the everyday of the conference. These are not the comments of a cynic, but of someone saddened by the disjuncture between the aims of law and its application.

[100] Id. at 199.

[101] The point of this argument, and its content, is mirrored again in the writing style. Kennedy relies on a perceived contrast between what international law should aspire to and what it had become to highlight the poignancy of the quest. In relation to the despondency of international lawyers during the Vietnam War, "either they needed a new theory of law which could account for its violation or a new theory of violation which could account for America's activity. Neither was forthcoming." Kennedy, *New Stream, supra* note 2 at 5.

from irony to pretension, from mockery to gravity. Moreover, the emphasis on language features as both a conceptual theme and a methodology. The linguistic focus reiterates the theme of the quest when it refers to the goal of the Newstream as one of "disentangle[ment]",[102] or of "translation",[103] or of trying to "describe the silences"[104]. It emphasizes the conceptual theme that law is constituted by language by the use of terms which imply structure and organization, such as "taxonomies"[105] and "map"[106] and "architectures".[107] And it sometimes translates into an open discussion of its own terminology[108] again emphasizing the self-conscious and subjective nature of the Newstream scholarship.

So in various respects Newstream work diverges from the Mainstream by introducing into international law a methodology which emphasizes doubles, is quite personal and sometimes messianic in nature, and focuses on language. The introduction of these techniques increases the transformative potential of the Newstream work by challenging the form as well as content of Mainstream analyses.

5. The Strategic Challenge

To this point the paper has identified a number of conceptual redefinitions and methods introduced by the Newstream to international law. Section 5 looks at one further defining feature of Newstream, namely its strategies. These are threefold: the incorporation of multiple perspectives into the law-making process and the contextualization of legal problems in their social, political and cultural background; the rewriting of doctrinal history; and the integration of political perspectives into legal analysis. Although not new in themselves, these strategies are applied innovatively, in a manner which reflects another difference in emphasis between Mainstream and Newstream

---

[102] Koskenniemi, *Apology to Utopia, supra* note 62 at xv.

[103] Anthony Carty, *The Decay of International Law* (1986).

[104] Hilary Charlesworth, Christine Chinkin & Shelley Wright, "Feminist Approaches to International Law", 85 *Am. J. Int'l. J.* 613, at 615 (1991).

[105] Anghie, *supra* note 17 at 6 051.

[106] Tennant, *supra* note 6 at 56.

[107] See, e.g., David Kennedy, "Turning to Market Democracy: A Tale of Two Architectures", 32 *Harv. Int'l. L. J.* 373 (Spring 1991).

[108] So, for example, part of Riles' critique is to write about the appropriateness of the term "perspective" to describe her methodology, or instead to use an aural metaphor such as "polyphony", Riles, *Disciplines and Cultures, supra* note 27 at 10 033. Her conclusion is irrelevant for my point, which is to show how self-consciously the writers' interest in law's language is present also in discussion of their own work. The use of words to describe law, reflects that interest in structure.

work. Mainstream work may utilize similar techniques, but its major aim is to facilitate the drafting of new instruments or affect changes in state practice, both of which seek to reform existing rules and practices. By contrast Newstream work is self-consciously concerned with affecting radical changes in international law, largely through the use of these three strategies, which shift the conventional emphasis from remoulding legal rules to one which attempts to reconceptualize their very bases. Although this latter goal is present only in nascent form in Newstream work, its trajectory is illustrated below.

5.1. Incorporation of Multiple Perspectives and Contextualization

As discussed earlier, Newstream work seeks to redefine the conceptual bases of international law. One strategy for achieving that goal is to incorporate into international legal analysis previously excluded perspectives, whether they be cultural, gender, race, social or political in nature. This technique, of the incorporation of multiple perspectives, is reminiscent of feminist and third world critiques, many of which advocate incorporation of perspectives beyond those usually included by Mainstream analyses[109] (are assumed to be focused on the views of Western industrialized states).

In Newstream, as with feminist and third world critiques, the function of such a strategy is inclusive. By incorporating perspectives beyond those which are ordinarily included in law-making processes, international law will gradually be cured of any inherent biases favoring a Western or an implicitly male viewpoint. So, Newstream work argues, for example, that the culture of international law could be redefined to ameliorate its biases if it were to contain within it a "multilayering" of different perspectives.[110] Comparative law, too, could be transformed by focusing on previously marginalized peoples, groups, and cultural data.[111] Moreover the incorporation of multiple perspectives functions not simply as a call for a more pluralistic international law which

---

[109] For a feminist version see e.g., Charlesworth, Chinkin and Wright, *supra* note 104; for a third world critique, see e.g., Mohammed Bedjaoui, *Towards a New International Economic Order* (1979).

[110] So, for example, one of Riles' objectives is to show that "culture" as currently relied upon by international law is an "untenable category of representation", Riles, *Aspiration and Control, supra* note 16 at 21, which omits the perspectives of the non-Western, non-European viewpoint. She proposes therefore that international law adopt an entirely new method, which she calls a "multilayering" of perspectives, id., at 36. In this new strategy no single perspective would dominate, in the way European view of culture does in mainstream international law.

[111] Frankenberg also advocates a form of multi-perspectivalism, even though his basic premises are quite different from Riles', Frankenberg, *supra* note 8. He is concerned with how comparative law has conducted comparisons between cultures. He derides comparative law as being a form of "tourism," id., at 412., in which the travelers/lawyers have to date been unable to distance themselves from their own assumptions about their own legal cultures; everything

would simply enlarge the field of players, [112] but as a strategy of destablizing many of the underlying premises of the field, [113] or facilitating a rethinking of the boundaries of international legal debate. [114]

But despite the intuitive appeal of the argument (and the intellectual honesty of some proponents who apply the critique to their own work[115]), the main weakness of the strategy is that incorporation remains largely speculative in nature because few concrete doctrinal or theoretical examples have, as yet, been produced by the Newstream.[116] Presumably however the consequences of such a strategy would be similar to those found in the field of political science. There, an incorporation approach suggests that the strategy will not be easily realized. A cultural practice cannot be automatically defined as

they see is referred back to their own world view or else they delude themselves in believing they can drop their cultural baggage: "[u]niversalism and relativism tend to reproduce the dichotomy between the self and other," id., at 415. In Frankenberg's view, the answer is for comparative law to adopt a new method which would enable it to move from the "ethnocentrism" of the current approach to the "self-criticism," id., at 455., of his preferred approach. This strategy would involve adopting a "greater sensitivity to the relationship between the self and the other; recognizing that they are participant observers,", id., at 441, maintaining a skeptical attitude toward allegedly authentic interpretations and universal categories; and "focus[sing . . .] on the marginal stuff that is normally skipped for lack of relevance," id., at 443. Like Riles, Frankenberg expresses a similar optimism about the reconstructive possibilities of adopting a new strategy. However, in other important respects the analyses are quite different. First, Frankenberg claims that comparative lawyers participate in making their own culture, but are still observers in others, id., at 443. Riles implicitly rejects the idea. Her work on European colonialism emphasizes that both the categories of European and non-European culture were created according to European assumptions. Second, despite Frankenberg's skepticism about culture, there are hints in the article of a belief that with the adoption of a new strategy, comparativists will be able to ultimately discover what is authentic about cultures. So, for example, Frankenberg claims it is possible to "transcend perspective," id., at 442, as long as we recognize our participation. To Riles the idea of transcendence would be an impossibility. Ultimately Frankenberg still believes in an authentic culture, whereas Riles does not.

[112] Following Marilyn Strathern, id., at 28., Riles argues that this is not a matter of merely introducing more diversity into the field. Diversity still implies, contrary to her belief, that a cohesive whole could be produced whereas Riles rejects the reformist assumptions in ideas of cohesion.

[113] Riles portrays international law like a prism, in which the facets of the prism reflect upon each other and create a new international law based on a new series of angles or refractions of law, id., at 31.

[114] Frankenberg is optimistic that if this new strategy was adopted comparative lawyers would therefore be more tolerant of ambiguity and be able to embrace a "multiplicity of developmental possibilities and explanations", *supra* note 8, at 454. As a result, comparative law could "imagine roads not taken, to think and explore counterfactual trajectories," id.

[115] See e.g., Riles who applies the strategy to her own analysis, *Aspiration and Control, supra* note 16 at 37, acknowledging that it may lead back to the same problems it seeks to escape – perspectivalism may be a synonym for just a different form of cultural definition. To this extent, it is a courageous tactic.

[116] Cf. Frankenberg, *supra* note 8 at 448-453, who discusses the effect his approach would have on the issue of abortion.

universal or relative,[117] so that the tension between universalism and relativism cannot be resolved by a simple incorporation of interests.[118] Equally, it is impossible to identify any cultural practice as entirely authentic.[119] This challenge of the basic terms of cultural theory foregrounds further significant arguments for international law, for example, that legal categories such as territorial integrity, self-determination and sovereignty are uncertain,[120] and that we therefore may need to develop a new theory of culture which more closely approximates scientific "chaos theory",[121] than does the current paradigm. As these conclusions suggest, the incorporation of multiple perspectives by

[117] Applying a form of multi-perspectivalism to political analysis, Appadurai, *supra* note 15, finds that the simple equation of universalization of culture with Americanization no longer holds sway. An example taken from Pico Iyer's work in the Philippines has a particularly eerie quality. Iyer notes that Filipinos have embraced American 1950's pop culture in a manner that is both more faithful to a Western idea of the original than the original itself ever was, and which has no connection with the conditions in which they live. Again in Riles' terms multiperspectivalism has led to unpredictable cultural combinations. A peculiarly Filipino perspective of an American past has been grafted onto the Filipino present. Thus the "hegemony of Euro-chronology "is unstable because it has created a sense of "nostalgia without memory," id., at 3.

[118] No cultural idea can sensibly be placed in either category in a world in which "sameness and difference cannibalize each other," id., at 17, bringing to an end any confidence in finding a reasonable balance between the two.

[119] Appadurai argues that it is no longer possible to rely on an authentic version of culture. In the face of the constant dislocation between the various "scapes" (see below at n. 121) of the global economy it is not possible for small groups, families, communities, to reproduce themselves. How does the Filipino mother or father working in Saudi Arabia and going home once every few years pass on the cultural meanings of being Filipino to their family? The process is likely to be either diluted by distance or strengthened by an artificial, but understandable resolve to hold on to what it means to be Filipino in the face of the fragmentation of the cultural group. "Trans-generational stability of knowledge... can no longer be assumed," id., at 17 Appadurai has shown how a multi-perspectival strategy demonstrates the instability of combining universality and relativity, and of culture itself.

[120] In the case of territory, for example, the cannibalization of sameness and difference, id., and the instability of cultural inheritance are exacerbated by "deterritorialization", id., at 11. Mass migration, caused by war and economic dislocation, as well as use of guest-workers, separates peoples from territories. Nations and states have become "one another's projects", id., at 13. So states seek to expound their sense of nationhood, even where it is fractured by gender, class or ethnic divides, national movements search for a State, id. The effect of deterritorialization is worsened by the media industry when canny entrepreneurs cash in on nationalistic desire to create new and sometimes fictional homelands, id., at 12. Thus the mythological homeland of Khalistan, id., at 13, has become implicated in the sometimes bloody and very real struggle of Sikhs to create a homeland. The pernicious effects of cultural, media, and territorial displacement are illustrated.

[121] Appadurai argues for a new "chaos theory" to explain what has happened to the once apparently stable idea of culture, Appadurai, *supra* note 102. Cultural forms are "fundamentally fractal", and that they "possess[...] no Euclidean boundaries, structures, or regularities", id., at 20. This is because, although in the past cultural intervention occurred only through warfare or religion, id., at 1, in the present it is mediated through five "scapes" of ethnicity, media, technology, finance and ideology, id., at 7. The result is that culture is increasingly subject to both homogenization and heterogenization, id., at 5. In Riles' terms then, the new perspectives

Newstream writers, although fraught, may ultimately lead to a very different international law from one in which law reform is the major strategy for change.[122]

Closely associated with the incorporation technique is the strategy of contextualizing legal problems in their particular social, political or cultural background[123] with a view to addressing the exclusion of non-Mainstream interests from international law. This is also derivative of earlier movements. Moreover in its current form it suffers from a similar deficiency, namely a lack of guidance or detail as to how it would be applied. To be effective as a strategy, the call for context ought to include a discussion of, for example, what constitutes an appropriate context, who are the legitimate decision makers and how they should be identified, otherwise it remains subject to the criticism that analyzing problems in "context" may simply introduce anoth-

---

are being incorporated from a variety of angles, public and private, Western and non-Western, with each incorporation and re-incorporation resulting in new "angles" and perspectives upon the existing system. So for example globalization has led to the much touted McDonaldization of culture. But even when these apparently universalized forms are transplanted into a new setting they are always modified by the indigenous culture. This has the effect of creating a global system "filled with ironies and resistances," a global "hyper-real", id., at 3. In order to better understand this potent admixture, Appadurai proposes the creation of a new theory of global cultural processes which combines both a "fractal" metaphor for shape of cultures and a "polythetic account of their overlaps and resemblances", id., at 20.

[122] For a fascinating discussion of a similar debate within the discipline of anthropology see Clifford Geertz, The Culture War, New York Review of Books, November 30 1995, 4:

Anthropology is a conflicted discipline, perpetually in search of ways to escape its condition, perpetually failing to find them. Committed, since its beginnings, to a global view of human life - social, cultural, biological, and historical at once - it keeps falling into its parts, complaining about the fact, and trying desperately, and unsuccessfully, to project some sort of new unity to replace the unity it imagines itself once to have had, but now, through the faithlessness of present practitioners, to have mindlessly cast away.

[123] See e.g, Rosemary Coombe, *supra* note 7, who is concerned with the way the intellectual property system excludes indigenous peoples' understanding of concepts of ownership and property. She argues that "supposedly...universal principles" such as authorship operate in practice to exclude native claims and lead to "injustice", id., at 267. Both intellectual property law and cultural property law rely on a system of European art and culture. Native art either falls into the category of timelessness, and thus is considered an "authentic artifact;" or it is elevated into a "masterpiece," id., 257. Art labeled authentic is protected by the newer legal regimes of cultural protection which are based on an idea of "cultural nationalism." In such cases the group is conceived of having ownership in the property which coincides with its identity as a "collective individual," id., 261. Art considered to be a masterpiece is protected by traditional copyright law. But both protections, Coombe asserts, bear traces of a form of "possessive individualism" which does not take account of the way in which indigenous peoples actually construe their association with the works of art. The only way out of this dilemma is to "listen [. . .] to native claims "in context," id., 266.

er form of subjectivity into legal analysis.[124] The danger is that "context" functions for the Newstream as "sovereignty" does for the Mainstream. One empty and amorphous concept is substituted for another.

5.2. *Rewriting Doctrinal History*

Another maneuver is to excavate the past in order to facilitate new interpretations of doctrine for the present, a strategy also reminiscent of the third world critiques of the 1960s.[125] Of the strategies discussed so far, this is the most successful in the sense of demonstrating the transformative potential of Newstream work. Some examples include a reconfiguration of the doctrine of state sovereignty taking account of feminist concerns,[126] the rewriting of historical accounts of sovereignty and statehood to show how they might benefit the interests of indigenous peoples,[127] and a reinterpretation of a set of doctrines concerned with acquisition and personality to show that they reflect the history of colonialism.[128] Utilizing either earlier legal theories,[129]

[124] See e.g., Coombe who does not convincingly avoid the charge that indigenous peoples' interests cannot be objectively identified. Instead she retreats at the critical juncture into a rhetorical statement: that "[i]t is ... as politically dishonest to deny the objective identity of those making culturally nationalist claims as it is to assert an internationalism that privileges the nation-building imperialist enterprises of European countries", id., at 263, 264.

[125] See, e.g., Bedjaoui, *supra* note 109, who documented the ways in which international law had disadvantaged third world interests.

[126] Knop, *supra* note 77. Knop argues that a new approach to participation in lawmaking is emerging, which undermines the traditional view of sovereignty that law is made only by state consent. Although research is still to be done, it appears that the contributions of non-sovereign groups such as NGOs, or women, or environmental groups, at international fora are becoming significant factors in the making of custom.

[127] Lam, for example, shows how indigenous peoples can utilize pre-existing histories underlying international law doctrine: Lam *supra* note 26. Earlier I noted she does this by exploring the "double helix" of sovereignty and statehood. This enables her to reveal the "multiple inheritance" of the helix so that she can "insinuate" new concepts into the "rigidities" of the law of indigenous peoples, id., *passim*.

[128] Anghie, *supra* note 17.

[129] See Karen Knop who carefully and generously crafts an enormously diverse range of materials using and re-using earlier international legal theories: Knop, *supra* note 77. She begins the process of reconfiguration by drawing upon a variety of international law and feminist sources and using them in ways probably not intended by their authors. Drawing upon Thomas Franck's claim that a right of democratic governance is emerging, id. at 301, and Fernando Teson's view that only liberal governments are deserving of the term sovereign, id., at 302, she plots the increasing trend against absolute sovereignty. (See Thomas M. Franck, "The Emerging Right to Democratic Governance", 86 *Am. J. Int'l L.* 46 (1992), and Fernando R. Teson, "The Kantian Theory of International Law", 92 *Colum. L. Rev.* (1992)). To this ingredient Knop adds the lessons of recent practice in the Balkans, showing that recognition of statehood is becoming conditional upon respect for human rights. She also draws upon the insights of the New Haven school, id., in order to argue that actors other than states contribute to the making of law. (See Myres S. McDougal et al., *Human Rights and World Public Order*

historical inconsistencies,[130] doctrinal ambiguities,[131] or law-making in the form of cases, state practice, or draft conventions,[132] these Newstream works compel a different understanding of foundational international law concepts, such as the relationship between women, indigenous peoples, colonialism and sovereignty. What is particularly ingenious about the examples mentioned is the way they draw upon existing raw materials (without having to resort to introducing excluded perspectives or contexts) sometimes deploying those

(1980)). Finally to these sources, she adds feminist arguments about equality, participation, and the breakdown of sovereignty. Here she outlines three models: the equality model proposed by Catharine MacKinnon, id., at note 40, the difference formulation of Carol Gilligan id., at note 46; and the collective autonomy response of Denise Reaume id., at note 54. In relation to participation she refers to the work of Iris Young, id., at note 54, and Isabelle Gunning, id., at 312-315 (see also Isabelle Gunning, "Modernizing Customary International Law: The Challenge of Human Rights: The Challenge of Human Rights", 31 *Va. J. Int'l. L.* 211 (1991)). And for a feminist analysis of sovereignty, Knop draws upon the work of Jean Bethke Elsthain, id., at note 126. The arguments lead ultimately to a reconstruction of the notion of sovereignty.

[130] See, e.g., Lam, *supra* note 26, identifies four "conceptual rigidities" which have traditionally militated against the rights of indigenous peoples. The first is the reliance in Westphalian theory of the nation state as the perfected form of political organization, id., at 616. This, despite evidence to the contrary in countries such as Switzerland where a federated set of cantons allowed a degree of flexibility and autonomy to the different constituent groups. Second, she argues that the idea of nationhood itself was a invention. For example, at the time of the French Revolution in 1789, it is likely that there was little sense of French nationality, id., at 613. Lam quotes figures showing that eighty years after the Revolution French language was still not spoken in approximately one-fifth of the communes. Third, there is the mechanism by which indigenous peoples were excluded from participating independently in international affairs, namely the League of Nations practice of wardship, (invented as a foil to modernist understandings of cultural identity), id., at 615. Fourth, she labels as a "conceit" the idea that some subjugation, in the form of "saltwater" domination was worse than others, id., at 616. These are the rigidities she seeks to overcome.

[131] Anghie, *supra* note 17.

[132] Lam, supra note 26, looks for any signs in the recent history which favor indigenous peoples' independent participation in international law and finds the following. The *Western Sahara Case* and the *South West Africa Cases*, facilitated recognition of a right of self-determination, id., at 618. The break-up of the former Soviet Union and former Yugoslavia were treated with "anxiety not prohibition," id., partly as a result of sympathy for national self-expression arising from the Westphalian model. Although neither instances relate directly to indigenous peoples, Lam views these developments as historical foundations for them to exploit. Moreover in 1991 the Draft Declaration on Indigenous Peoples, formulated by an expert Working Group, for the first time, included a qualified right of indigenous self-determination, id., at 620. The Working Group also provides indigenous peoples with a forum to speak and they participate in the work of a number of UN agencies. Moreover this "interface occurs across several permeable surfaces," id., Working Group members operate on behalf of the UN and yet are also professional and independent experts. They deal with NGOs and indigenous peoples groups in a manner which has "evolved through mutual criticism, accommodation and perhaps also appreciation," id. Lam has demonstrated the continuity between the history which seemed to deny indigenous people's rights and the history of acceptance. Pre-existing histories carried with them the subversion of their own rigidities.

sources in a manner probably not intended by their authors.[133] This further demonstrates the Newstream claim above that if international law is manufactured, (in the sense of being constructed rather than fraudulent) from histories made by us, it can also "be remade by us".[134]

5.3. *Integrating Politics into International Law*

Finally the Newstream advocate an international law in which political considerations are integrated in an explicit manner, another project reminiscent of realism. The political dimension is also acknowledged by mainstream scholars. The major difference is, however, that while the Mainstream writers protest that "law is politics",[135] they rarely apply that insight to their discussion of particular doctrines. Compare, for example, David Kennedy's analysis of state responsibility,[136] with that of Louis Henkin et al.[137] Kennedy looks at the political factors motivating what he terms the shift from substance to process, whereas Henkin et al focus upon the doctrine as a set of positive legal rules.

Newstream scholars argue that international law should not and cannot be separated from politics.[138] If politics were explicitly acknowledged,[139] then doctrinal biases would be disclosed. For example a purportedly neutral legal conclusion evaluating an assertion of jurisdiction over foreign nationals might be revealed to mask political considerations of national interest. [140]

---

[133] See, e.g., Knop *supra* note 77, who relies on arguments made by Teson. Although Teson rejects the view that under-representation of women derogates from the states representativeness, Knop argues that Teson's view about sovereign legitimacy provides the "rhetorical scaffolding", id., at 302, to support a feminist re-reading of sovereign will in which the low rates of participation by women in law-making lead to questions about the legitimacy consent.

[134] Allot, *supra* note 26 at 16.

[135] Henkin et al., *supra* note 4 at 1.

[136] Kennedy, *infra* note 146.

[137] Henkin, *supra* note 4.

[138] Koskenniemi questions the separation of international law and social life: Koskenniemi, *Apology to Utopia, supra* note 62 at xiii–xvi. He argues that the only way beyond the dilemma of constantly moving between community and autonomy, between concreteness and normativity, is to abandon the idea of the objectivity of law and cease what he calls the "flight from politics", *Politics, supra* note 69 at 4–7.

[139] David Kennedy argues that international law should take more explicit account of political concerns. He says the "mantra" of the renewalists should be the "politics of private law", Kennedy, *New World Order, supra* note 43 at 374, or, in another piece that international economic law fails to answer "traditional questions about the politics of international law, David Kennedy, "The International Style in Postwar Law and Policy", 194 *Utah L. Rev.* 7 (1994) 101 [hereinafter *The International Style*].

[140] See e.g., Robert Malley, Jean Manas, Crystal Nix, "Note: Constructing the State Extraterritorially: Jurisdictional Discourse, The National Interest, and Transnational Norms", 103 *Harv. L. R.* 1273 (1990) for an analysis of the doctrine of reasonableness as it relates to questions

Or analysis of the development of a particular doctrine, such as acquisition, would show it to be hamstrung by political, rather than legal, concerns.[141]

The Newstream strategy of integrating politics into law claims to expose law's silence about politics, cast doubt upon its objectivity, and facilitates the identification of underlying biases within doctrine. And it demands that international lawyers identify the politics they pursue through international law. Once the political ramifications of doctrine are revealed, the retreat into proceduralism seems no longer possible.

In Section 5 three strategies for change arising out of new approaches scholarship have been identified. Multiplicity and contextualisation address law's exclusionary power, and rewriting doctrinal history and integrating political concerns upset its constructed and discriminatory categories. To this point the approach appears to have developed the tools for changing much that it criticizes. Why then does it sometimes fail to do so?

6. Recurring Problems and Conclusion

In this conclusion I will focus on some recurring problems with Newstream analysis. I will argue that the content of the critique can be marred by, inconclusiveness, reductiveness and equivocation, and that the style suffers from a sometimes disengaged or patronizing tone.

6.1. *Inconclusiveness, Reduction and Lack of Concretization*

Newstream critiques frequently seem to pull back from the brink of affecting real change in international dialogue. For example the consequences of alter-

---

of jurisdiction. They show that when the United States Supreme Court engages in a balancing process to assess the "reasonableness" of allowing another state to assert jurisdiction over an American national, the Court is actually concerned with how the assertion of jurisdiction will affect American national interests, id., at 1297. Thus the political question of national interest trumps a supposedly neutral legal question. They show that reasonableness doctrine masks the political consequences of power differentials between states.

[141] See e.g., Carty, *supra* note 103 at 43–60. Carty examines how political considerations have affected the development of a particular legal doctrine. He claims that despite its apparent formality, the law of acquisition is a highly politicized concept. He demonstrates this by examining how the whole edifice of the law of acquisition is based upon Roman notions of possession of land, and a capitalist conception of commodities exchange. He argues that the influence of these two political factors foreclosed the development of self-determination and permanent sovereignty over natural resources, both of which are doctrines concerned with method of use, not exchange, id., 51–60. For another discussion of the politicized nature of acquisition doctrine with particular application to Australian Aboriginal ownership of land, see also Gerry Simpson, "Mabo, International law, Terra Nullius and the Stories of Settlement: An Unresolved Jurisprudence", 19 *Melb. Uni. L. R.* (1993) 195.

native strategies of changing international law are never fully explored,[142] arguments about what is actually wrong with international law are inconclusive,[143] or fail to speculate about the conditions which might affect a change in the Mainstream perspective.[144] Moreover the Newstream calls for the integration of politics with law is not sufficiently problematised. The call is a commendable ambition but doubts remain. There is a tendency in some Newstream work for an apparently radical critique to conclude with a facile or reductive call for a move to politics, yet the political is as contested and enigmatic as the legal. While concepts such as sovereignty are being denigrated as too incoherent to underpin the legal system, a radically pluralistic politics seems an inauspicious place to find new normative consensus.

Other Newstream scholars are internally inconsistent calling, for example, for changes in Mainstream analysis while not acknowledging that the critique must apply to Newstream analysis as well[145] while others labor under a

---

[142] For example, there is something dissatisfying about being left with only the conclusion that the strategy of multi-perspectivalism will lead to a "discomforting" but "instructive void," Riles, *Discipline and Cultures, supra* note 27 at 740. It is this rather vague but vaguely engaging image which is at once the most exciting and frustrating aspect of the strategy proposed. Thus despite the intuitive appeal of the analysis, the strategy as a technique to actually change the operation and description of international law, remains largely unexplained. Riles provides no definite idea of what she means by putting new perspectives together and no concrete examples of doctrinal changes which might result. While complete specificity is not required, some hypotheses about how the strategy would apply ought to have been explored. In the absence of this the consequences of this maneuver remain somewhat speculative. What would be produced by a new melange of perspectives relating to each other in new combinations and permutations? By admitting that she does not know what exactly would be produced or how these new perspectives would relate to each other, or indeed even whether they would not replicate an idea of culture, Riles withdraws from prescribing an effective application of the strategy. This last step is crucial if the incorporation of multiple perspectives strategy is to have any effect on conventional perceptions of the international. In contrast, Appadurai, *supra* note 15, is able to demonstrate not only that cultural meanings are unstable and thus must be reinterpreted with the incorporation of new perspectives, but that this process will itself lead to new instabilities. New cultural classifications will feed off each other complicating the possibility of simply improving the current system by incorporating new perspectives. American culture suffers from this defect as much as any other, and the resulting chaos is what defines culture in the late twentieth century.

[143] See e.g., Kennedy, who analyses the common intellectual history of new approaches with earlier schools but ends only with an abrupt and sketchy call for the renewalists to differentiate their critique by examining redistributive consequences and private law, Kennedy, *New World Order, supra* note 43 at 374–375. Similarly, when discussing international economic law, it is not until close to the end of the article that he explicitly states what he believes is wrong with a regime infused with the spirit of liberal trade policy, namely, that it might fail to answer political questions about how the world trading system disadvantages developing countries, or structures the debt crisis, Kennedy, *The International Style, supra* note 140 at 101, 102.

[144] See the discussion of culture and change accompanying notes 125–127.

[145] See e.g., Frankenburg, *supra* note 8, who fails to recognize the contradiction in criticizing the Mainstream for not taking account of perspective and then entreating us to trying overcome perspective.

suffocating equivocation or unwillingness to evaluate specific legal claims.[146] The reader's expectations are constantly thwarted by these retreats as the critiques seem to peter out just as they are beginning to bite and the potentially transformative moment is lost, leaving impressive descriptive analyses lacking in effect.[147]

6.2. *Equivocation, and Condescension*

Newstream work is also dogged by recurring stylistic problems which inhibit its more widespread application. The equivocatory tone of some critics leads to a voice which seems disengaged and at odds with the general call for a more involved politics.[148] There is a tendency to patronize[149] other actors making assumptions about what will be the outcome of adopting a particular strategy. A superior condescending tone is used [150] in characterizing other interna-

[146] Kennedy, e.g., argues that state responsibility process doctrine, avoids and supplants substantive outcomes but withdraws from making a normative judgments, *Legal Structures, supra* note 79. So the International Court's reliance on standing in the *South West Africa* Cases, to preclude considering the merits of apartheid as a breach of self-determination, is an example of the oscillation within international law between substance and process. But at the conclusion of his argument, the oscillation is described as one of the "strengths": Kennedy, id., at 191, of the discipline, leaving the reader to ponder whether a strength which had appeared to lead to injustice is a good or a bad strength. Even if Kennedy is arguing that indeterminacy opens possibilities for argument, the illustrations used seem to demonstrate that oscillation is not a positive outcome.

[147] Not all Newstream writers suffers from this deficiency. Some demonstrate why, as Riles predicts, the void might be instructive, Riles, *supra* note 16 at 740. So, for example, when Abu-Odeh locates the intersection between Islamic feminism and Western feminisms' shared concerns about equality, regardless of conflicting attitudes to the veil, she signals an enrichment of Western feminism if it better understood the complex conception of veiled sexuality in Islamic culture, Abu-Odeh, *supra* note 22 at 66. When a Toronto conference summary introduces the voices of women who have traditionally not been heard in Western feminist human rights, we begin to see what benefits multi-perspectivalism might bring, Rebecca Cook, "Women's International Human Rights: The Way Forward", 15 *Human Rights Quarterly* 230 (1993) 231–261.

[148] As one proponent comments, thē method often "fails to provide answers" and that "skepticism about the material determinacy of international law seems to prevent new approaches lawyers from making normative propositions," Koskenniemi comment in Kennedy & Tennant, *supra* note 2 at 427.

[149] See, e.g., Tennant's argument, *supra* note 6, that even if participation is the goal which indigenous peoples desire, the writer assumes that it will lead to co-option. Surely if self-determination and participation have any meaning it is that the groups asserting their rights have the right to determine when and how they will utilize them. Lam is also mindful of the dangers of participation, but claims that it has led to concrete substantial goals such as realization of limited forms of self-determination: Lam *supra* note 26 at 617–618. She also notes that participation can be an end in itself.

[150] For e.g., the personal quest device of Kennedy, *Autumn Weekends, supra* note 60 at 202, while effective in some respects, also carries with it certain risks of condescension. It exposes a tendency on the part of some writers to denigrate the contributions of other participants in the

tional legal actors, and some disparage Mainstream strategies for change as ineffective without sufficient explanation. For example, it is not clear that participation has only procedural consequences,[151] or that substance is always "strong" and procedure inevitably "weak". This latter propensity to adopt a substance/procedure dichotomy in the belief that the former is strong and the latter is weak, pre-empts the reader's capacity to assess the issue. Apart from the very difficult question of whether such a content/form distinction does exist, it is a somewhat reductive way of characterizing legal practices which tells us little about the actual nature and content of the practice. Sometimes it appears to be a kind of shorthand for good and bad, rather than a useful or revealing comment upon a practice. The dangers of condescension and reductionism then, are that they trivialize, oversimplify and obscure a serious and elaborate intellectual agenda for change. These problems and others iden-

---

international sphere. For example, at a plenary where a "fashionable Latin American Woman ... in rather high pumps" id., suggests a reformatting of a conference resolution, Kennedy comments that:

> We all knew we should clearly distinguish the perambulatory recitation of norms and facts from the operational engagement with the everyday. Numbering would do the trick, indentation would help, id.

Portraying the woman's concerns as mere cosmetic artistry he reduces their importance and trivializes her contribution. The mocking tone permeates the entire recollection. By the time the final conference session arrives Kennedy muses on "enjoy[ing] the hilarity of voting as a bloc on one after another absurd amendment or proposal", id., at 209. The flippant tone of the description conveys a condescending attitude by the writer to the other participants. Personal and probably hurtful details are included. The constitution-drafting group is described as a "distinctly dull crew of Pedro's more earnest Portuguese acquaintances," id., at 199, and "the last refuge of the lawyer's lawyer, the nerd's nerd," id., at 201. The bitchy throwaway lines heighten the sense that unnecessary details are included at others' expense. The reader hovers endlessly between laughter and alienation.

[151] Tennant, *supra* note 6 at 50–55, is skeptical, or at least cautious, of the gains that would attend increased indigenous participation in lawmaking claiming that this participation valorizes process over the achievement of a substantial goal. He argues that the misrepresentation of indigenous peoples by international law (discussed above), led indigenous peoples to resist these images. That resistance has led them to argue for increased rights of participation in international law making processes. Tennant argues that although participation seems to be a worthwhile goal, it carries with it the danger that indigenous peoples will be co-opted by becoming part of the institutional process. "The danger lies in the shift from *substantive* political goals to the *procedural* goal of increased participation," id., at 50. The weaknesses in his argument are characteristic of new approaches work. First, it is not clear why increased participation, even characterized as a procedural rather than substantive goal, is not a desirable end in itself. In respect of other groups excluded from international law-making, the claim is often made that their increased participation will provide an opportunity to create norms which incorporate the concerns of those groups: Gunning, *supra* note 129. Second, there is some room for argument as to whether participation is simply procedural, and whether that label condemns it in any case.

tified throughout the discussion above have the ultimate effect of diminishing the influence of the new scholarship on the discipline generally.

This paper has sought to make explicit a debate within international law between two schools of thought labeled Mainstream and Newstream. It has argued that the Newstream critique has emerged as a significant body of criticism, with common themes, methods, and strategies aimed at redefining what it perceives as Mainstream forms of analysis. In disclosing some of the deficiencies and gaps of international law, Newstream work, is developing into a well crafted body of scholarship. It has dissected the way in which law constructs its own histories, is inherently indeterminate, masks distributive disadvantage, is decontextualised, and excludes a range of perspectives. As a first stage of any analysis, the critique has demonstrated its potential to renew and invigorate international legal doctrine. It is provocative and sometimes daring work.

Accurate and incisive dissection and description is critical to any project of transformation and if the point was to show that traditional legal analyses were demonstrably partial, exclusive and biased then this has been achieved. A critical descriptive and expositive function has been performed. But the Newstream works seem to aim to do more. They advocate change, contextualization, multiplicity, and politics. And it is this transformative potential of the critique that remains unrealized. In fact reading new approaches work can be a baffling experience, with frustrating results. The analyses lack concretization, and tend toward reductionism and condescension with the consequence that what is potentially transformative risks becoming rather unappealing.[152] Change is merely flagged as something which would eventuate if these techniques were adopted within the Mainstream. To paraphrase one of the its repeated themes, the critique itself remains suspended in an interminable present between the description of what has come before and the promise of what its implementation will bring.[153] So although Newstream work highlights previously untapped but important anxiety over what is culture; displays a fascination with the relationship between history and sovereignty; and a deep interest in the narrative structure of law; applies new methods and reinvigorates old strategies, creating opportunities for reading old material in new ways, to date it has led to an utterly altered vision of what international law *is* but not what international law *could be*.

---

[152] There is an almost poignant lack of communication between the Newstream and traditional international law. A mixture of antipathy and condescension exists between the two groups resulting in a dialogue of the deaf.

[153] David Kennedy constantly refers to an oscillation, within traditional analyses, between substance and process, Kennedy, *New Stream, supra* note 2 at 17.

Ultimately though the measure of its success may be its commitment towards enunciating another kind of international law, a commitment which is symbolized in the quest device which characterizes most of the major works.[154] Like all quests, it is characterized by a sense of sadness for what current international law has lost. Moreover what differentiates it from earlier commentators' similar journeys,[155] is the central, self-appointed, almost messianic role of the new international lawyers. Exploiting the drama of the search, the Newstream international lawyers place themselves at the center of the quest, exhibiting an almost heroic urge to save international law, and themselves, from the moral bankruptcy of indeterminate material outcomes.[156] This is the goal. But although the search and its quixotic conclusion have echoes in the modern period, the quest is all the more poignant for the postmodern realization that there can be no return either to the weak realism of the earlier phase, or to an even earlier faith in natural order. It is this melancholic view of the traditional discipline which impels the journey toward new forms of scholarship.

---

[154] For example, Allot is on a journey through "consciousness": Allot *supra* note 37 at 109; Koskenniemi tracks the trail of the disappointed jurists who "put their faith variably on logic and texts, history and power . . . ": but who lost their footholds; Koskenniemi, *Politics, supra* note 69 at 31, Kennedy deplores the "tragic voice of post-war public law liberalism": Kennedy, *New Stream, supra* note 2 at 2; and Carty is escaping international law's "decay", Carty, *supra* note 103.

[155] McDougal, *supra* note 67 at 156–157.

[156] Koskenniemi, *Apology to Utopia, supra* note 62, *passim*.

Commonwealth Regulation of Campaign Finance – Public Funding, Disclosure and Expenditure Limits

Deborah Z Cass and Sonia Burrows

Deborah Z Cass and Sonia Burrows, 'Commonwealth Regulation of Campaign Finance – Public Funding, Disclosure and Expenditure Limits' (2000) 22(4) *Sydney Law Review* 477, 477–526 <http://www.austlii.edu.au/au/journals/SydLawRw/2000/23.pdf>.

Commonwealth Regulation of Campaign Finance — Public Funding, Disclosure and Expenditure Limits

DEBORAH Z CASS* AND SONIA BURROWS†

1. Introduction[1]

A. Outline of Article

The regulation of the relationship between money and politics is a topic of perennial significance to anyone interested in the democratic process. As a subset of a discussion about public trust and public accountability it has a long pedigree in Australia.[2] State specific and comparative collections of essays on the topic have been produced[3] and both the legal and political science communities have taken an interest in it.[4] In the United States campaign finance has particular cachet because it is dealt with under the general rubric of First Amendment free speech jurisprudence.[5] Moreover interest is reignited periodically[6] when the press discovers the existence of new devices for encouraging gift-giving such as a coffee with the President, or renting a White House suite for a night.

* London School of Economics and Political Science Law Department. LLB (Melb), LLM (Harvard). We would like to thank Peta Stevenson for her research assistance with this project, and the Reshaping Australia's Institutions project at the Research School of Social Sciences, Australian National University.
† LLB (Hons) student, Australian National University.
1 The law is stated as at August 2000.
2 For example, Paul Finn, 'Public Trust and Public Accountability' (1994) 3 *GLR* 224.
3 For example, Herbert Alexander & Shiratori Rei (eds), *Comparative Political Finance Among the Democracies* (1994); Herbert E Alexander, *Financing Politics: Money Elections and Political Reform* (4th ed, 1992); Keith Ewing, *The Funding of Political Parties in Britain* (1986).
4 For example, Alexander, *Financing Politics*, above n3. In Australian political science literature, see for example, Colin Hughes, 'Australia' (1963) *The Journal of Politics* 646; Ernest Chaples, 'Developments in Australian Election Finance' in Alexander & Rei, above n3.
5 See, for example, Cass Sunstein, *Democracy and the Problem of Free Speech* (1993). The foundational US case around which discussion revolves is *Buckley v Valeo*, 424 US 1, 46 L. Ed. 2d 659, 96 S. Ct, 612 (1976) which distinguished between expenditure limits and contribution limits, finding the former were unconstitutional whereas the latter, subject to conditions, were not.
6 A recent excellent collection of views on the topic can be found in 50 *Stan LR* (1998).

Australian legal literature on campaign finance is relatively sparse[7] as, it appears, is political comment.[8] This is somewhat surprising, given that recent inquiries into government corruption in Australia in the last two decades refer to the topic as being unavoidable in any inquiries into, and attempts at, protecting the integrity of government.[9]

This article is a brief survey, from Federation to the present day, of some key aspects of campaign finance regulation related to public funding, disclosure and expenditure limits. It suggests that three features characterise the Australian regulatory approach to these issues: a steady increase in regulatory control; an increasingly complex regulatory environment which seeks to balance public and private interests; and an acceptance of the constitutional feasibility of expenditure limits. Specifically, we will argue here, first, that although the history of regulation in Australia has experienced some dormant periods, and even a period of complete de-regulation, the overall trend has been towards increasing regulatory control. Second, current regulatory techniques extend to include an emphasis upon the regulation of entities associated with political parties and candidates, rather than simply the political participants themselves. That is, at present some regulation is directed towards placing tighter controls on the conduct of traditional participants such as political parties, and some is directed toward enhancing the ability of private donors to contribute to the political process, while simultaneously controlling their behaviour. A further concern is control over public funding. The complex relationship between providing public support for elections, encouraging private participation in public political activity, regulating that activity and public controls on political party conduct is a constant theme of the current regulatory context. Third, we will argue that an historical precedent exists for the introduction of campaign expenditure limits and that precedent is unlikely to have been affected by subsequent constitutional developments in relation to free speech.

It is not the aim of this article to explore the complex theoretical premises underlying regulation, which have been examined comprehensively elsewhere.[10] Instead it is our aim to describe the history of a small, but significant selection of regulatory devices used in relation to campaign finance. Very briefly, however, it is clear that a number of principles inform the debate about campaign finance regulation. Principles of free speech; political equality; access to information; access to participation; trust in public officials; privacy; efficiency and individualism all vie for domination in the terrain of campaign finance reform.

---

7 See, for example, Keith Ewing, 'The Legal Regulation of Electoral Campaign Financing in Australia: A Preliminary Study' (1992) 22 *UWALR* 239; Finn, above n2.

8 Dr Carmen Lawrence recently stated that 'While there has been extensive debate about big money in politics in the US, there appears to be a conspiracy of silence among Australian politicians': quoted from her 17 August 2000 speech to the Sydney Institute, 'Renewing Democracy: Can Women Make a Difference'. Full transcript available online at http://www.carmenlawrence.com/says/papers/sydneyinstitute.htm.

9 See, for example, Western Australia, Commission on Government, Report No. 2 Part 2, (1995).

10 The scholarship on the topic is voluminous. For a selection of recent approaches see 'Symposium: Law and the Political Process' 50 *Stan LR* (1998) and Corrado et al (eds), *Campaign Finance Reform: A Sourcebook* (1997).

Moreover, as the vast scholarship on the topic indicates, a key problem here is striking the appropriate balance between these principles, all of which are legitimate in the abstract. So, for example, one writer referred to the Australian legislative framework as 'privileging ... political liberty over political equality'.[11]

One result of the clash of competing principles is the development of a broad range of regulatory devices. These include public funding of election campaigns, and the provision of tax credits or deductions for campaign donations. Governments may establish a regime of disclosure for donations to political participants, and/or of payments by political parties. Legislation may be aimed at achieving truth in political advertising. This article focuses on three of these devices — public funding and disclosure rules, and expenditure limits — as a means of exploring some of the ways in which the principles mentioned above operate in the legislative context.

B. Nature of the Problem Addressed by Public Funding and Disclosure Rules

The purpose of public funding and public disclosure rules is to avoid both the imputation and actuality of corruption. In general terms the underlying aim of the regulation of campaign finance is to preserve the integrity of the political process. By ensuring that the public is aware of the sums of money gifted to political parties, the public is able to judge the legitimacy of legislative proposals, and identify the avenues of influence that may affect politicians' judgments. This is the 'transparency furthers accountability' argument.

It is also said that transparency may discourage the parties from providing favours to donors for fear of reprisal from a well-informed public. Public funding of political parties reduces their need to rely on donations from external sources. Moreover, by reducing the need to rely on private donations a more level playing field for candidacy is constructed; candidates with limited private support can afford to run for political office against candidates who have access to either personal wealth or other sources of private support. This argument is concerned with equality of financial opportunity for potential political candidates.

It is clear that not all of the arguments for campaign finance regulation rely upon the supposition that interests that give money to political candidates and parties will necessarily demand their *quid pro quo* in terms of a policy outcome. For example the equality argument is not directly concerned with this possibility.

---

11 Ewing, above n7. The attempt to achieve a 'balance' of regulation assumes that the poles themselves are secure. The appearance of the principle of 'free speech' for and against regulation should immediately alert the reader to the contestable nature of any assumed opposition between these principles. One concern of this area is to recognise the way campaign finance regulation can be both rejected and justified on the basis of different conceptions of free speech; see: *Turner Broadcasting System v FCC*, 117 St. Ct. 1174 (1997).

In fact, empirical research on whether campaign donations influence policy decisions is equivocal.[12] However counter-intuitive it may seem, some commentators believe that money does not and cannot directly cause changes in policy outcomes. Professor Rolf Gerritson, appearing before the Australian Senate's Finance and Public Administration Legislation Committee in 1998, expressed this view:

> From my observations, it appears that there is no correlation between public policy outcomes and the pattern of donations; that corporations tend to donate to political parties, if you like, to reward a policy stance rather than to induce one.[13]

One of the interesting phenomena of campaign financing, and a reason why the predictability of the money/politics link is problematic, is the existence of anecdotal evidence that corporate interests give donations to more than one of the major parties, albeit in different amounts. So, for example, in the 1992 Australian election, one major Australian company, Amcor, donated $30 000 to the Australian Labor Party and $100 000 to the Coalition parties.[14] If the political contest is conceived of as occurring only between *political parties*, then this practice muddies the conclusions that may be drawn from gift-giving. It produces a kind of stalemate in which a party cannot, without criticism, claim that a donation 'bought ... decisions' from the other side of politics without tarring itself with the same brush.[15] However if the political contest is conceptualised as including interests other than political parties, such as *community groups, business and union organizations, and indeed the public at large,* then Amcor's actions, even if equal as between political parties, have bought an advantage over all these other political competitors, all of whom are legitimate actors in the political process.

Occasionally the claim is made that particular donations or monetary benefits have led to particular legislative outcomes in favour of the contributor. For example, it was claimed in the Australian Parliament in 1998 that the Liberal Party was lent $10 million by National Australia Bank for its 1996 election campaign, on the condition that, if elected, as government it would open the superannuation industry up to the banks — a legislative outcome which subsequently came about.[16]

The question of the influence of campaign contributions upon political outcomes is really unanswerable. Given the range of variables which influence

---

12 Although the Sydney Morning Herald recently quoted a Business Week/Harris Poll, surveying 400 senior executives of large public corporations in the United States and exploring their reasons for donating to political parties. They discovered that 'a worrying 41% said that at least part of their reason ... was the hope of receiving "preferential consideration on regulations or legislation benefiting our business"': Michelle Grattan, 'Money and the Politics of Schmooze', *The Sydney Morning Herald* (25 August 2000).

13 Australia, Senate, Finance and Public Administration Legislation Committee, Hansard, Electoral and Referendum Amendment Bill (No. 2) 1998, Tuesday 16 June 1988, Canberra at 21.

14 Australia, House of Representatives, *Parliamentary Debates (Hansard)*, 3 June 1998 at 4674.

15 Id at 4675–4676.

16 Bob McMullan, Australia, House of Representatives, *Parliamentary Debates (Hansard)*, 23 March 1998 at 1346.

political decision-making, it would be impossible to construct an experiment to test the hypothesis that money corrupts politics. To this extent then, the question of proof of influence is irrelevant.

However what is not irrelevant is the *perception* that the possibility that money can influence politics is enough to cause a different sort of problem for democracy, and that is the problem of a general disillusionment with the political process. It is generally accepted that increasing numbers of people are losing faith in the political process, in politicians, and ultimately in the promise that democracy can ensure a fair, equal and participatory method of governance. In a submission in 1998 to a governmental committee on electoral reform one Australian Senator described a 'crisis of public confidence concerning political parties and politicians' referring to the 'deep levels of cynicism and disillusionment within the electorate towards their elected representatives' which was reflected in opinion polling findings that less than 10 per cent of Australians believed that their politicians held high standards of ethics and honesty.[17] In relation to this form of democracy fatigue, the possibility of politics even being tainted by the influence of campaign finance is a real problem. In the words of one commentator — 'I do think the public standing of politicians is important, and I think it is being damaged by this kind of covert behaviour.'[18]

Some anecdotal evidence exists to suggest that political parties are exploiting methods that disguise the receipt of political money and its source. Devices of this sort inevitably raise questions as to the reasons for keeping sources hidden, with one answer being that it allows the protection of sources of funds in the event that the party subsequently provides them with a political benefit or advantage. One method currently widely used to disguise donation sources has been the creation of trusts and foundations through which donations are channelled. For example claims have been made in the Australian Parliament that one of the major parties received income of $7.2 million laundered through a trust.[19] This device reputedly allowed donations to the trust, which then gave the money to the political party. Since the trust was not subject to the appropriate regulatory legislation, the original sources of the contributions were not disclosed.[20]

Other techniques do not disguise donation sources, but are simply created to increase the sums of money available to compete successfully in the political market. Included amongst the new money-raising techniques of campaign financing are: the siphoning off of rents from investments;[21] the leasing out at high

---

17 Senate, Finance and Public Administration Legislation Committee, *Submissions*, Reference: Electoral and Referendum Amendment Bill (No. 2) 1998 at 38. Submission of Senator Andrew Murray (Australian Democrats).

18 Professor Rolf Gerritson, above n13.

19 It was said that the Liberal Party received $7.2 million through the Free Enterprise Foundation:
   · Australia, House of Representatives, *Parliamentary Debates (Hansard)*, 9 March 1995 at 1950.

20 Bob McMullan, Australia, House of Representatives, *Parliamentary Debates (Hansard)*, 23 March 1998 at 1346.

21 The Labor Party was reputed to have received $1.6 million from rents from John Curtin House Pty. Ltd without disclosing: Australia, House of Representatives, *Parliamentary Debates (Hansard)*, 9 March 1995 at 1950.

rates of property to government departments;[22] the giving of loans on favourable terms, which are themselves not disclosed[23] or the conversion of loans into gifts, by non-enforcement.[24] Whilst secondary to the problem of the influence of money on policy formulation, they are nevertheless important given the increasing pressure upon parties to seek illicit donations in bids to fund a successful campaign, donations which may be conditional upon political favours.

For regulators the problem is further compounded by the fact that, like tax avoidance, this area is always a case of 'catch-up politics'.[25] As soon as one loophole is closed, another will open. One recent development has been the replacement by a political party of a long-standing campaign fund-raising body with a new entity, thus avoiding the reach of the Australian Electoral Commission (AEC) and the legislative requirements of disclosure. In one case the new entity shared common trustees, postal address, and accountancy support with the pre-existing foundation, but was reluctant to provide information regarding its status to the Commission, thus thwarting the ability of the regulatory body to monitor the disclosure requirement.[26]

Whether one accepts in theory the need for campaign finance regulation or not, there are also strong practical reasons suggesting that political players ought to be more accountable. One such reason concerns the imbalance between regulation of private and public organisations apparently committed to the public interest. The argument is that organisations such as political parties, although private in nature, serve a major public interest, namely the election of representatives to represent the interests of the public in determining major political decisions, and hence

22 The claim was made in Parliament that the Labor Party had leased out at 'exorbitant rent its property to Commonwealth Departments, including the Auditor General': id at 1953.

23 See, for example, John Faulkner, Australia, Senate, *Parliamentary Debates (Hansard)*, 3 March 1998 at 200; Bob McMullan, Australia, House of Representatives, *Parliamentary Debates (Hansard)*, 23 March 1998 at 1346; John Faulkner, Australia, Senate, *Parliamentary Debates (Hansard)*, 25 June 1998 at 4174. See also Lenore Taylor, 'Liberals receive a $4.6m secret loan', *Australian Financial Review* (3 February 1998) at 3; 'Minister won't detail Greenfields Foundation $4.6 million loan to Libs', *Canberra Times* (9 March 1998) at 5.

24 See, for example, John Faulkner, Australia, Senate, *Parliamentary Debates (Hansard)*, 28 May 1998 at 3357; id at 25 June 1998 at 4174.

25 John Faulkner, Australia, Senate, *Parliamentary Debates (Hansard)*, 9 December 1999 at 11565; Lenore Taylor, '$4.6m loan to the Liberals may spark electoral law change', *Australian Financial Review* (12 May 1998) at 3.

26 The claim was made over a series of months in the Australian Parliament by members of the opposition in relation to the establishment of the Greenfields Foundation. The new foundation, Greenfields, was established with similar trustees, postal address, and accounting support as the Free Enterprise Foundation, a foundation previously identified by the Commission as an associated entity under the Act and therefore required to disclose. The Greenfields Foundation however declined to provide details to the Commission that would have enabled the Commission to ascertain whether or not it was an associated entity. The Commission lacked the necessary investigatory powers to pursue the matter. See, for example, John Faulkner, Australia, Senate, *Parliamentary Debates (Hansard)*, 3 March 1998 at 200; Bob McMullan, Australia, House of Representatives, *Parliamentary Debates (Hansard)*, 23 March 1998 at 1346; John Faulkner, Australia, Senate, *Parliamentary Debates (Hansard)*, 28 May 1998 at 3357. See also Lenore Taylor, 'Secret foundation to look at taking donations', *Australian Financial Review* (5 February 1998) at 6.

should be subject to public scrutiny and regulation, certainly no less so than are private organisations with public interests. 'Political parties are less regulated than corporations, trusts, partnerships, unions, employer organisations, welfare groups and tennis clubs.'[27] There is a disjunction between the very public role of the political party, and its very closed and private legal internal organisation. Their 'legal status is not appropriate to their actual role and their public status'.[28] Therefore, so the argument goes, the techniques of corporate regulation could be transferred to the sphere of political party regulation.[29]

Further, since 1983 political parties have been partially publicly funded and thus open accountability is required; they wield enormous power in public life; and by comparison with public listed companies and private limited companies their regulation is limited.[30]

Finally, in recent times concerns have also been raised about the use of public money to finance political advertising campaigns by incumbent governments just prior to the announcement of an election, thereby ameliorating the need to raise large sums of money and the accompanying disclosure rules. So, for example, in the lead up to the 1998 Australian election, the government was reported to have spent $A28 million in an 'election advertising blitz' prior to the official announcement of polling[31] on ads extolling the virtues of government reform, past and proposed, in areas as diverse as taxation and immunisation.

In sum, quite apart from the difficult theoretical issues concerning, for example, any contest between political equality and individualism, this section has briefly sketched the nature of the campaign finance problem and shown how regulation is said to be justified for reasons of preserving the integrity of the political process, confronting democracy fatigue, avoiding even the taint of untoward influence of money on political outcomes, and bringing public political bodies closer to regulation parity with private bodies involved in public life. The next part of the article surveys Commonwealth regulation of public funding and disclosure rules.

2. Historical Background

This part of the article will argue, first, that historical precedent exists for the current system of regulation. Campaign finance legislation in Australia had its genesis in the *Commonwealth Electoral Act* 1902 and was regularly reformed and updated over the ensuing years. The remarkable aspect of the original legislation of 1902 is that it contained most of the key elements of the current regulatory

---

27 Senate, Finance and Public Administration Legislation Committee, *Submissions*, Reference: Electoral and Referendum Amendment Bill (No. 2) 1998 at 48. Submission of Senator Andrew Murray (Australian Democrats).

28 Id at 50.

29 Id at 48, 52, citing Allan Ware, *Citizens, Parties and the State: A Reappraisal* (1987) at 91.

30 Id at 51.

31 Mike Seccombe, 'Election rumours sweep House', *The Sydney Morning Herald* (28 August, 1998).

system.[32] It contained disclosure and transparency rules; third-party regulation; it focused on the importance to campaign finance of advertising; and it contained simple regulation of the media. Historical continuity is therefore a significant characteristic of the current system.

However, the original legislation also contained one additional feature which is missing from the current system, namely, limits upon the amount of money political participants could spend in pursuit of their election.[33] This section will make an argument that in view of the long historical pedigree of expenditure limits, and the absence of any criticism of expenditure limits specifically on the basis of Australian democracy, there is a case for arguing for their reinstatement. This is not an argument about justification; the many rationales for expenditure limits are beyond the limits of this article. Instead we will suggest, simply, that the (re)introduction of expenditure limits as a form of campaign finance regulation is not a new development in Australian politics; that they were a feature of the Australian constitutional landscape for 80 years; and accordingly that arguments based on the novelty, or incompatibility of such regulation with the practice of representative democracy, need to be treated with caution.

A. The Original Legislation of 1902 — A Proposal for a System of Limited Campaign Finance

What were the key elements of the first attempt at Commonwealth campaign finance regulation?

(i) Expenditure Limits

The first attempt at regulation of campaign finance in Australia contained expenditure limits. Part XIV of the *Commonwealth Electoral Act* 1902 was headed 'Limitation of Electoral Expenses' and section 169 provided that electoral expenses be limited to £100 for candidates[34] for the House of Representatives and £250 for the Senate.

The early legislation also included some guidance as to the meaning of electoral expenses, although it is not entirely clear. Section 170 limited the range of matters which were authorised as electoral expenses to: printing, advertising, publishing, issuing and distributing of addresses by candidate and notices of meetings; general stationery expenses; hall and room hire and scrutineers.[35] Section 171 was, however, more wide ranging. It provided that the term included

---

32 *Commonwealth Electoral Act* 1918 Part XX.

33 These limits were repealed by s4 of the *Commonwealth Electoral Amendment Act* 1980.

34 It must be mentioned early on that at this point in Australia's history, political parties were not an important force — hence the emphasis upon *candidates'* expenses. The Labour Party, already strong in the colonies, particularly in NSW and Queensland (where it formed the world's first Labour Government for 7 days in 1899), became a Federal Party in 1901, but the rest of parliament consisted of various free trade and protection factions. The Farmers and Settler's Association created the Country Party in 1912, and it wasn't until 1944 that the Liberal Party was formed from a conglomerate of non-Labor members. Parties did not appear in electoral legislation until the *Commonwealth Electoral Act* 1918, a reflection of the changing reality of Australian politics.

35 *Commonwealth Electoral Act* 1902 s170.

'all expenses incurred by or on behalf or in the interests of any candidate at or in connection with any election' subject to only two exceptions, the purchase of electoral rolls, and 'the personal and reasonable living and travelling expenses of the candidate'.[36] Presumably the latter was read as subject to the former, to avoid any conflict between the two sections. In this event 'all expenses' would be authorised as long as they fell within the categories contained in section 170 and did not include electoral rolls or living/travel expenses.

It is possible that this combination of an expenditure limit and a limited definition of electoral expense may have led to a greater degree of financial equality of opportunity between candidates. With expenditure being capped there was no real advantage to greater access to resources because there was a limit upon what those resources could be spent on. Whether this translated in practice in a higher percentage of non-wealthy candidates running for office would be worth investigating.

(ii)   Disclosure and Transparency

A simple form of the disclosure requirement also featured in the early legislation. Here disclosure took the form of a requirement for the submission of expenditure returns. It was necessary for all candidates, within eight weeks of the election, to return a signed statement to the Commonwealth Electoral Officer indicating all expenses paid and all disputed and unpaid expenses.[37] Accountability and transparency were also anticipated. Receipts for electoral expenses were to be produced[38] and the returns were open for public inspection.[39]

(iii)   Third Parties — Individual and Collective Associated Entities

Independent interest groups, other organisations and individuals were all required to furnish returns if they had spent any money or incurred any expense for a political participant. The legislation was drafted broadly to require returns from '[e]very trades union registered or unregistered, organisation, association, league, or body of persons which has, or person who has, in connection with any election expended any money or incurred any expense' on behalf or in the interests of any candidate or political party.[40] Moreover the Chief Electoral Officer could require an officer of any such organisation to make an expenditure return or pay the appropriate penalty.[41]

Note that according to this aspect of the legislation third parties who spent on behalf of candidates (or political parties) were required to furnish returns, but not limited in the amount of money they spent. Also not mentioned in relation to expenditure limits or disclosure were political parties. This may have been because at the time the legislation was passed political parties were few and far between and relatively under-developed as fund-raising organisations for candidates.

---

36   Section 171.
37   Section 172(1).
38   Section 172(2).
39   *Commonwealth Electoral Act* 1905 s49, inserting s172(3) into the Principle Act.
40   *Commonwealth Electoral Act* 1911 s34, inserting s172A(1) into the Principle Act.
41   Id at inserting s172A(8) into the Principle Act.

(iv)   Election Advertising

The significance of election advertising was recognised by its specific inclusion in the list of matters that may have been the subject of expenditure by third parties. Election advertising was targeted for inclusion in third party returns.[42] A penalty of £50 attached to any failure to comply with the section, and £100 or six months imprisonment for the wilful making of untrue statements in a return

(v)   Regulation of the Media

Newspaper proprietors[43] were also required to complete a return showing the amount of paid electoral matter inserted into the newspaper and setting out space it occupied, the amount paid for it, and names of the body or persons which authorised its insertion. Failure to do so carried a penalty of £500. 'Electoral matter' was defined broadly to include advertisements and any 'other matter intended or calculated to affect the result of the election'.[44]

In addition to these modern forms of regulation a number of the more serious traditionally recognised common law electoral offences were also enacted, including bribery and undue influence,[45] although the category of illegal practices from which the latter were drawn was probably wider.

This brief description of the original legislation illustrates that there is a strong thread of historical continuity connecting early legislation with the current regulatory regime. This would indicate that the concerns of regulators have not dramatically changed over the years. The key issues of accountability and transparency are, in a sense, timeless. Early legislators, like their current counterparts, instituted a regime in which the public was able to discover the amount of money spent by political participants. They instituted a system in which those people and organisations assisting political participants in their quest for election were also subject to this requirement. Those same legislators foresaw the importance of election advertising as a crucial component of the sums of money the participants were required to spend. In recognition of the importance of the media for the dissemination of the electoral message, they imposed specific obligations on members of the media.

The only concern that the original and current legislators do not, on the face of the legislation, seem to share, is in relation to spending limits. However the existence of limits on expenditure indicates that, at the very least, there is historical precedent for their existence. Moreover these limits existed for some 80 years of this century as a central plank of the first system of campaign finance regulation introduced in Australia and survived (albeit in outdated form) for almost the entire century until they were repealed in 1980.[46] They existed in the context of a system

---

42 Id at inserting s172A(2) into the Principle Act.

43 Id at inserting s172B into the Principle Act.

44 Id at inserting s172B(2) into the Principle Act.

45 *Commonwealth Electoral Act* 1902 s173(ii).

46 *Commonwealth Electoral Amendment Act* 1980.

that was fairly described as a representative democracy.[47] Their persistence for some 80 years suggests that although their practical workability may have been questioned, this did not lead to a desire for their repeal. They were not perceived of as inconsistent with constitutional democracy, or incompatible with the aims of the campaign finance system. The reinstatement of expenditure limits would not so much involve the introduction of an entirely new principle of campaign finance, as the mere restoration of an historical precedent, compatible with Australian notions of representative democracy.

B.   Expenditure Limits and the Development of Constitutional Free Speech

The discussion so far assumes a somewhat static view of constitutional interpretation — expenditure limits were constitutional in 1902 and so they ought to be so now. Another, more evolutionary approach to constitutional interpretation,[48] might suggest a different result. According to this view, the restriction upon legislative power derived from the implied constitutional freedom of political communication, which had its genesis in Australia in 1992[49] and was reaffirmed in 1996,[50] may bar the re-introduction of expenditure limits. Adopting a similar line it has been successfully argued in the United States that any restriction upon campaign expenditure amounts to a breach of the First Amendment to the United States Constitution, which provides that Congress shall not abridge, to any extent, the right to speech.[51] However it would seem unlikely that this argument would succeed in Australia for a number of reasons.

First, as a matter of historical intent the argument would probably fail. The enactment of the electoral expense limitation in 1902, almost contemporaneously with the enactment of the Constitution, suggests that if there was any conflict between the two instruments the legislators at the time, and indeed the legal fraternity at large, did not recognise it.

Second, practice mitigates against the free speech argument. The electoral provision existed for some 80 years without challenge, again indicating either a degree of myopia of the legal fraternity, or the constitutional validity of provision.

Third, there is the specific nature of the Australian free speech right to consider. Unlike its US counterpart the Australian freedom is not a free speech right at large, but an implied right to communication in relation to political matters, specifically in connection with those matters concerned with the maintenance of the system of representative democracy.[52] So, for example, the limitation protects

---

47 Stephen J: it is 'quite apparent that representative democracy is descriptive of a whole spectrum of political institutions, each differing in countless respects yet answering to that generic description': *Attorney-General (Cth) (Ex rel McKinlay) v Commonwealth* (1975) 135 CLR 1 at 57.

48 As shown by *Sue v Hill* [1999] HCA 30, and Deane J in *McGinty v Western Australia* (1996) 186 CLR 140.

49 *Nationwide News Pty Ltd v Wills* (1992) 177 CLR 1; *Australian Capital Television Pty Ltd v Commonwealth* (1992) 177 CLR 106.

50 *Lange v Australian Broadcasting Corporation* (1997) 198 CLR 520.

51 *Buckley v Valeo* (1976) 424 US 1.

52 The Court in *Lange v Australian Broadcasting Corporation* (1997) 198 CLR 520 at 112.

the making of the direct choice by the people of their political representatives.[53] It extends to protecting the electors against a complete prohibition on the political advertising which is essential to voters' choice because it provides them with information necessary for the making of that decision.[54] However, the High Court has been unequivocal that freedom of political communication only exists to the extent necessary to protect the representative democratic system of government. It is not a freedom akin to the US form, which protects many types of speech. Hence in order to argue that expenditure limits were unconstitutional it would have to be shown that *unlimited* election expenditure was necessary for the maintenance of a system of representative democracy. This would be difficult to prove for two reasons. First, the High Court would have to first accept that election expenditure is a form of speech. Second, it would have to accept that *unlimited* election expenditure is a form of speech necessary to representative democracy.

Parallels might be drawn with other forms of conduct, such as political protest, which have been found to constitute a form of communication for the purposes of the protection. For example, in *Levy's Case*[55] at least two members[56] of the Court explicitly recognised that the communication covered by the implied freedom is not limited to traditional speech, but may include other conduct. Hence it may well be possible to argue that the spending of money constitutes a form of conduct which amounts to communication.

However this may depend on the type of conduct involved and its link to that crucial underlying feature of the Australian freedom, representative democracy. In *Levy* it was possible to show that protest is a form of conduct covered by the freedom, because political protest (even in relation to an issue such as duck shooting) is a recognised form of political communication and therefore integral to the democratic system. The expenditure of money, even by political participants, may not be quite so simple to categorise. Traditionally money is considered to be part of the field of commerce rather than politics and the spending of money is not conventionally seen as an essentially political act. However this obstacle may be overcome in view of the fact that the expenditure is being created by the political participants. This latter factor clearly provides the link to the representative democracy system that is missing in relation to other forms of expenditure, and suggests that campaign expenditure may indeed constitute communication for the purposes of the implied freedom.

Assuming that this is the case, and campaign expenditure does constitute communication for the purposes of the implied freedom, the next question would be whether this form of communication is necessarily protected by a freedom which only extends as far as the protection of representative democracy? Even if it is political speech, is it speech necessary for the maintenance of representative democracy? The Australian High Court has, on more than one occasion expressed

---

53 *Australian Capital Television Pty Ltd v Commonwealth* (1992) 177 CLR 106 (Dawson J), and confirmed in *Lange v Australian Broadcasting Corporation* (1997) 198 CLR 520.

54 *Australian Capital Television Pty Ltd v Commonwealth* (1992) 177 CLR 106.

55 *Levy v Victoria* (1997) 189 CLR 579.

56 Id at 107 (McHugh J), 157 (Kirby J).

the view that there are a wide variety of models of representative democracy, the essential features of which are not set in stone.[57] In some models of representative democracy unlimited campaign expenditure might be seen as an integral part of the communication between the representatives and the represented in order for the latter to directly choose the former. However it has also been argued that some models of representative democracy countenance restrictions on expenditure for the very reason that electoral choice cannot be made in the face of unlimited campaign expenditure because it has the potential to compromise the integrity of the political process.[58] The Supreme Court of Canada has, in principle, recognised the validity of State referendum expenditure limits as a means of ensuring electoral fairness because it was a key component of political equality under representative democracy.[59] Quoting extensively from the Lortie Commission, established to investigate Canadian electoral systems, it said:

> If the principle of fairness in the political sphere is to be preserved, it cannot be presumed that all persons have the same financial resources to communicate with the electorate. ... To ensure a right of equal participation in democratic government, laws limiting spending are needed to preserve the equality of democratic rights and ensure that one person's exercise of the freedom to spend does not hinder the communication opportunities of others. Owing to the competitive nature of elections, such spending limits are necessary to prevent the most affluent from monopolizing election discourse and consequently depriving their opponents of a reasonable opportunity to speak and be heard. Spending limits are also necessary to guarantee the right of electors to be adequately informed of all the political positions advanced by the candidates and by the various political parties.[60]

Given then that there are a variety of models of representative democracy, some of which allow for expenditure limits and some of which do not, and assuming that any legislation would not prohibit completely all expenditure, it would be difficult to argue definitively that an expenditure limit necessarily breaches the Australian implied freedom of political speech (which embodies representative democracy). The most that could be said against reinstating expenditure limits is that they are not part of the 'core' of representative democracy,[61] and therefore could not be subject to review on the basis of the implied freedom.

---

57 *Attorney-General (Cth) (Ex rel McKinlay) v Commonwealth* (1975) 135 CLR 1, *McGinty v Western Australia* (1996) 186 CLR 140.

58 A species of this argument was accepted by Brennan J in ACT TV when he upheld a prohibition on election advertising as a form of reasonable regulation: *Australian Capital Television Pty Ltd v Commonwealth* (1992) 177 CLR 106 at 159–161.

59 *Libman v Quebec*, 1997 DLR LEXIS 1511: 151 D.L.R. 4th 385. Note however that the particular legislative limits under consideration here were struck down as disproportionate to their stated objective.

60 Id at ¶47.

61 See George Williams, 'Sounding the Core of Representative Democracy: Implied Rights and Electoral Reform' (1996) 20 *MULR* 848.

Another way of addressing the issue is to argue that even if expenditure limits are seen as, prima facie, a breach of the implied freedom because they burdened freedom of communication about political matters,[62] they may yet be saved on the basis that they can be considered 'reasonably appropriate and adapted to serve a legitimate end the fulfilment of which is compatible with the maintenance of representative government.[63] It might be possible therefore, to argue that preservation of the integrity of the political process is a legitimate aim compatible with representative government, and that expenditure limits are a proportional measure to achieve that goal. In this respect the Courts' earlier invalidation of a prohibition on election advertising might lead a current Court to view expenditure limits as a less drastic measure for achieving a similar goal, and valid on that account. Again, relying on Canadian jurisprudence, an argument might be made for reasonable regulation of speech on the basis of ensuring political equality between candidates, or voters' rights to receive information in order to ensure fairness of the electoral process.[64]

Finally, recent United States First Amendment decisions suggests a limited, but notable, softening of the US Supreme Court's formerly strict approach to free speech regulation where other public values are at stake, such as increased public discussion or prevention of electoral corruption. In one case it was suggested by some members of the Court that free speech may be regulated in circumstances where that regulation increases opportunities for public discussion and informed deliberation, because these values are the underlying goals of the First Amendment.[65] One critic has commented that under this approach a cap on campaign expenditures would be valid:

> [S]o long as Congress could reasonably conclude that it would enhance equal participation in public debate, and did not burden substantially more speech than necessary to achieve it[s] goal of equal participation.[66]

More recently, in the specific field of campaign finance, the Supreme Court re-affirmed its long-standing distinction between contribution limits (which are constitutional under certain conditions) and spending limits (which are not)[67] and, in the process, reiterated the importance of allowing legislatures to limit campaign contributions for the purpose of combating real and potential corruption attributed to permitting large contributions into the electoral process.[68]

In short even given any political antipathy toward expenditure limits, constitutional doctrine does not necessarily bar their re-introduction in Australia.

---

62 Above n58.

63 Ibid.

64 Above n59 & 60.

65 *Turner Broadcasting System v FCC*, 117 S. Ct. 1174 (1997).

66 Andre R Barry, 'Balancing Away the Freedom of Speech: *Turner Broadcasting System v FCC*, 117 S. Ct. 1174 (1997)' (1998) 21 *Harvard Journal of Law and Public Policy*, 285 at 286, notes omitted.

67 In reaffirming the distinction, the Court referred back to *Buckley v Valeo* 424 US 1, and to the more recent decision of *Colorado Republican Federal Campaign Comm. v FEC*, 518 US 604.

68 *Missouri v Shrink Missouri Government PAC*, 120 S. Ct, 897 (2000).

3. Commonwealth Regulation, Deregulation, Revival and Expansion

Putting the constitutional issue to one side, the early legislation covered all the pertinent aspects of campaign finance and the next 80-odd years of regulation were relatively uneventful in a legal sense. With only a few changes to the legislation, the situation could be described as relatively dormant. In 1946 the expenditure limit was increased to £250 in the case of the House of Representatives and £500 in the case of the Senate,[69] and the categories of authorisable electoral expenses were broadened to include 'advertising and broadcasting' as well as the more traditional methods of dissemination of campaign information.[70] These were simply moves to keep up with the changing times, both inflationary and technological, and reflected a degree of satisfaction with the goals and methods of the original legislation. Similar moves were made in 1966, when the introduction of decimal currency led to the expenditure limit being revised to $1000 for the Senate, and $500 for the House of Representatives.[71]

Few other noteworthy changes were made to the Commonwealth Act in the next half-century. One of these was a prohibition on what is referred to colloquially as 'porkbarrelling'. In 1966 there was inserted into the legislation a prohibition upon candidates making gifts to clubs or associations. The penalty was, even by 1966 standards, extremely low, namely a $10 fine, although it was supplemented by 'any other penalty provided by law' and there was a three-month limitation period on bringing claims.[72] All penalties were raised in 1980 to $100 for failure to comply with the section and $200 for untrue statements.[73]

A. Virtual Deregulation — A Brief Interlude

The dormant phase came to a close in 1980 with the repeal, albeit briefly, of campaign finance regulation. All of Part XVI of the 1918 Act, except for the section requiring newspaper proprietors to furnish returns, was deleted from the statute books. In the process campaign expenditure limits and the requirement for electoral expenditure returns were removed.[74] This 'virtual deregulation'[75] came as the result of a fear that substantial non-compliance with the legislation (common amongst both candidates and organisations) could lead to national challenges,[76] following a successful challenge by the Australian Democrats to the election of a candidate to the Tasmanian Parliament under that State's laws, causing a by-election to be held.[77]

---

69 *Commonwealth Electoral Act No. 42* 1946 s4.
70 Ibid.
71 *Commonwealth Electoral Act* 1918 as amended by *Commonwealth Electoral Act* 1966.
72 Id at s150, s172A(5)–(7).
73 *Commonwealth Electoral Act No. 93* (1966) s3.
74 *Commonwealth Electoral Amendment Act* (1980) s4.
75 Denny Meadows, 'Open election funding or hide and seek?' (1988) 13(2) *Legal Services Bulletin* 13(2) 65 at 65.
76 Australia, Joint Select Committee on Electoral Reform, *First Report* (Canberra: 1983) at 28.
77 Id at 65 (Colin Hughes).

However deregulation was also accompanied by the government's stated aim to introduce a form of public disclosure of campaign expenditure, and to this end the matter was referred to an independent inquiry, which reported to the government in 1981 and was made available to the Parliament in 1983.[78]

Thus after nearly 80 years spending limits were erased from the landscape of Australian political history because a) they were often not complied with; b) the danger of electoral instability arising from an increase in successful challenges to elected candidates on their basis of non-compliance; and c) the government aimed to overhaul the entire system. The erasure of spending limits may lead some current commentators to believe that limits are new to Australian politics, when in fact they were in existence for more of the post-Federation period than they have been absent.

In any event, the release of the report by the Joint Select Committee on Electoral Reform in 1983 led to a major revamping of campaign finance. In its opening chapter the Committee commented that although electoral reform had not 'atrophied' it perhaps had 'not progressed at a rate in line with expectation'.[79] Accordingly the Committee recommended the introduction of a whole new system which included public funding and disclosure rules.[80] Although the legislation was largely well received, one commentator commented, prophetically, that there were 'more direct ways to control campaign costs', citing as an example a prohibition on paid broadcast electoral advertising.[81]

B.   The Introduction of Public Funding

The major innovation of the 1983 amendments was the introduction of a system of public funding for political candidates and parties. In its report the Joint Committee acknowledged that indirect public subsidisation of the political process already occurred.[82] Campaigns were indirectly funded as a result of compulsory voting (which saved parties a major expense in organising voter drives); access to electoral rolls; tax deductability of candidates' election expenses; and public provision of basic infrastructure needs for campaigning such as staff, telephones, offices, postage, and research. Nevertheless, a majority of the Committee concluded that public funding for electoral expenditure was warranted,[83] although they stopped short of recommending funding for ongoing administrative maintenance.[84]

The public funding system was to be based upon a number of foundational principles. Money was payable only to those with significant electoral support; it was payable according to fixed rules; the amount received would be related to

---

78 Ibid.
79 Id at 29.
80 The main provisions relating to disclosure are carefully summarised and analysed in Meadows, above n75 at 68.
81 Ibid.
82 Above n76 at 145.
83 Id at 152.
84 Id at 157.

electoral support and funds would not exceed election expenditure.[85] Participants would have to receive at least 4 per cent of the primary vote to qualify for funding which was to be calculated using a base rate linked to an indexed postage rate. It was to be paid to an accountable person in the appropriate party organisation, or where none existed, to the candidate. Only registered political parties and candidates could apply for funding; evidence of expenditure had to be provided; no advance payments were to be made; and the system was to be administered by the Australian Electoral Commission.[86]

In reaching its recommendations the Committee accepted a range of arguments the empirical basis of which is not to be found in the Report but which we have sought to test with a set of interviews with political participants, regulators and observers.[87] For example the Committee relied on the view that public funding would help avert the taint of the influence of money upon the political process. It said funding could help participants avoid donations by large and specialised interest groups,[88] and therefore it would reduce 'the necessity or temptation' to accept donations with conditions attached.[89] While it is not possible to state definitively that this view has or has not been borne out in the years subsequent to the introduction of funding, anecdotal reports would suggest that public funding has not diminished political participants' enthusiasm for seeking donations from large or specialised interest groups.[90] Nor, according to a 1991 report of the successor Committee had it led to a much greater degree of transparency generally in the system.[91] Whether public funding has reduced the temptation to accept conditional grants is impossible to test because, as we discussed above, the

---

85 Id at 156.

86 Id at 156–160.

87 Peta Stevenson, interviews with Doug Thompson, ACT Branch Secretary, Australian Labor Party (Canberra, 8 December 1998); Phil Orphin, Accountant and Party Agent, National Party (NSW Branch), (Sydney, 14 December 1998); Andrew Bartlett, Senator and Federal Campaign Director for the 1998 Federal Election, Democrats (Queensland, 15 December 1998); Mike Steketee, National Affairs Editor, *The Australian* (Sydney, 10 December 1998); Ian McKenzie, NSW Campaign Coordinator for the 1998 Federal Election, former NSW and Australian Greens Treasurer and Party Agent, Greens (Canberra, 18 December 1998); Party Official, NSW Liberal Party (Sydney, 18 December 1998); David Oldfield, Adviser, One Nation Party, (10 December 1998), Professor Rolf Gerritson, Professor of Local Government and Applied Policy, Australian Centre for Regional and Local Government Studies, University of Canberra (Canberra, 17 December 1998); Brad Edgman, Director of Funding and Disclosure, Australian Electoral Commission (Canberra, 14 December 1998).

88 Above n76 at 154. However, Mike Steketee feels that public funding has simply created new methods of hiding sources of donations: Peta Stevenson, interview with Mike Steketee, ibid.

89 Above n76 at 153.

90 For example see evidence that in the 1987 federal election the Australian Labor Party received public funding of almost $5m and donations of approximately the same amount; the Liberal Party received public funding of $4m and the same again in donations and the National Party received $1.2m in public funding and $1.7 million in donations: Australia, Joint Standing Committee on Electoral Matters, *Who Pays the Piper Calls the Tune – minimising the risks of funding political campaigns'*: Inquiry into the Conduct of the 1987 Federal Election and 1988 Referendums, Report No. 4 (Canberra: June 1989) at Table 7.1, 74.

91 In its 1989 report the Committee stated there remained an 'alarming lack of information of sources of election funding': id at 76.

influence of money on politics is only one in a range of variables that may affect public policy making.[92] Our hypothesis here is not that money does corrupt politics but that the imputation that it could is enough to warrant regulation to stop or at least stem the flow of private money into political campaigns.

The record is also probably a little harsh on another of the Committee's justifications for funding, namely to assist parties in financial difficulties.[93] Although public funding must help parties, particularly new parties, to gain sufficient financial momentum to run a campaign,[94] large parties which spend large sums of money may still experience financial difficulties under a system of public funding. Conventional wisdom has it that an impetus behind the Australian Labor Party's introduction of the *Political Broadcasts and Disclosures Bill* 1991 (which prohibited political advertising during election campaigns subject to limited exceptions) was the high level of the party's indebtedness after the 1990 election campaign due, in large part, to the high cost expended upon broadcast advertising. This financial shortcoming arose during the period of public funding, which suggests that public funding may not be the magic wand that the 1983 Committee seemed to assume that it was. It must be said, however, that most of the party representatives interviewed were fundamentally positive on the impact of public funding on the opportunities for smaller parties and those in financial difficulties. Public funding was thought to provide a degree of certainty for parties, without having to seek corporate sponsorship. One commentator suggested that parties such as the Democrats might not exist without public finding.[95] This was certainly a claim supported by the Australian Electoral Commission's Director for Funding and Disclosure[96] and also by David Oldfield from the One Nation Party who was in a position to fully understand the financial concern of smaller parties which may be unable to gain the same level of corporate sponsorship as the ALP or the Liberals.[97]

Other justifications relied upon by the Committee were the existence of similar schemes in other countries, and the equalisation of opportunities between parties. In relation to the comparative argument, it appears that a range of countries

---

92 It is further complicated by the fact that virtually all parties contend that conditional grants are unacceptable and unaccepted. Peta Stevenson, interviews with Doug Thompson, Phil Orphin & Andrew Bartlett, above n87. Senator Bartlett also stated that there are a few areas the Democrats simply refuse to accept money from, such as tobacco, uranium, and wood-chipping; Ian McKenzie & Party Official, NSW Liberal Party, above n87.

93 Above n76 at 154.

94 Interestingly enough, this is supported by the ALP and the Democrats (Peta Thompson, interviews with Doug Thompson & Andrew Bartlett, above n87) but contested by the smaller, newer parties, the Greens and One Nation (Peta Thompson, interviews with Ian MacKenzie & David Oldfield, above n87). Both of them see major problems because most new parties seeking serious representation start in the upper house, where it is very difficult to get the requisite 4 per cent support. This is compounded by the fact that public funding is not available in advance, but only *after* the election *if* you achieve the magic 4 per cent.

95 Peta Stevenson, interview with Professor Rolf Gerritson, above n87.

96 Peta Stevenson, interview with Brad Edgman, above n87.

97 David Oldfield claimed that the One Nation Party ran its campaign solely on public funding as they had no corporate donations whatsoever: above n87.

continue to maintain public funding systems. The equality argument continues to be strongly argued in the American context,[98] but no empirical studies appear to have been done to test the hypothesis that the greater the source of public funding available to support new participants into an increasingly expensive political process the more likely a wider range of people will be able to participate. However our interviews suggested that whilst public funding did assist small parties, 'it has also put money in the coffers of big parties'.[99] What does remain certain is that in countries where public funding does *not* exist the cost of entering the political contest is extremely high, is increasing every year and probably remains out of the reach of ordinary people.[100]

One final justification for the introduction of public funding seems to have been fairly weak even at the time of the Report, and that is the view that public funding would reduce reliance upon fundraising in order to allow greater concentration on policy development.[101] Again it would be hard to test this proposition but it would seem unlikely that the political fundraiser is any less of an institution in an environment of public funding and that any spare moments away from it are being spent on policy development. Moreover, policy development tends to occur separately from fundraising. The modernisation of the fund-raising process and its increasing importance to parties means that such processes are frequently handled by a specialised wing of the party,[102] and bear very little relation to those areas specialising in policy development.

The final recommendation of the Committee in relation to public funding was for further consideration to be made of the view put in evidence before it that no public funding be introduced but that free time be granted to all participants and that all political advertising be banned.[103]

However plausible were the justifications for public funding, in 1983 it was introduced as part of the *Commonwealth Electoral Legislation Amendment Act 1983*.

The provisions relevant for our purposes were contained in Part XVI of the Act entitled 'Election Funding and Financial Disclosure'. The Part was divided into six divisions dealing with: election funding; disclosure of donations; disclosure of electoral expenditure; interpretation of the legislation; agents; and other miscellaneous matters including penalties, public access to documents, and indexation of funding.

---

98 'Wealth Robs the Unwealthy of Voting Clout', *Los Angeles Times* (26 July 1994).

99 David Oldfield, above n87. Ian MacKenzie (above n87), of the NSW Greens also believes that there is such a huge gap between the Greens and the major parties that it is impossible to truly level the playing field.

100 For example, according to the US Federal Election Commission, in 1996 the cost of running for a seat in the US Senate was $US3.76 million. Quoted by the *Washington Post* (4 September 1998): <http://www.washingtonpost.com/wp-srv/politics/special/campfin/campfin.htm>.

101 Above n76 at 155.

102 Peta Stevenson, interviews with Doug Thompson, Phil Orphin & David Oldfield, above n87.

103 Above n76 at 161 (evidence of Professor Joan Rydon).

The key sections were contained in Divisions 3, 4 and 5. Division 3 established a system of partial public funding of election campaigns under which parties, candidates and groups had a general entitlement to funds. Funding was provided for candidates and groups who received over 4 per cent of the primary vote.[104] Once that threshold was reached the participants received public funding which varied according to the number of formal, first preference votes they received. House of Representatives candidates received the highest base payment, then Senate candidates elected during an election not held simultaneously with the House of Representatives election and then Senators elected during a simultaneous election.[105] Payment was made on the basis of 'total electoral expenditure', and was not to exceed this amount.[106] Hence claims had to be made in the approved form accompanied by information showing the exact total electoral expenditure of the political participant.[107] Standard reimbursable items included extra salaries and campaign novelty items, but excluded publicity for a membership drive and post election parties.[108] The agent of the registered party, candidate or group was responsible for making the claim[109] and receiving the payment.[110] Claims for payment could be made up to 20 weeks after polling day.[111]

C.   Disclosure of Donations

The Joint Committee's discussion of disclosure was noteworthy because it included some consideration, albeit short, of disclosure of *income* and of *administrative* expenditure. Although neither matter was finally incorporated into the Committee's recommendations for disclosure, their existence in the deliberations indicates the scope that remained for extending the disclosure requirements.

The Australian Labor Party put forward to the Committee the view that disclosure of all income was an 'essential corollary' to public funding because the 'long term viability of the democratic system depends on public confidence in the legitimacy and integrity of the political process and that any hint of corruption undermines public confidence'.[112]

The Liberal Party argued that disclosure of donations constituted a 'grave infringement of civil liberties', a 'violation of privacy', and that it carried the threat of 'victimisation of individuals particularly by certain trade unions'.[113] It

---

104 *Commonwealth Electoral Legislation Amendment Act* 1983 s153B.

105 There is an entitlement to a base rate of 60 cents per vote for elections to the House of Representatives; 30 cents for elections to the Senate where the polling day is the same as the House; and 45 cents for election to the Senate where the Senate election is not coincidental with the House election: s152(1)–(3).

106 Section 153C.

107 Section 153(8)(a) and (b).

108 Australian Electoral Commission, *Election Funding and Financial Disclosure Handbook* (Canberra: AGPS, 1984) at 16–17.

109 Section 153.

110 Section 153D.

111 Section 153(8)(c).

112 Above n76 at 162–163.

113 Id at 163.

proposed, therefore, that only donations above $10000 be subject to disclosure regulations.[114] Although the national, and some state, bodies of the National Party accepted the principle that undisclosed donations could potentially corrupt the political process other branches did not. The Queensland branch for example was totally opposed to disclosure of donations.

The majority of the Committee accepted the view that donations could potentially influence the political process and so public disclosure was necessary for the preservation of the integrity of the system.[115]

A number of recommendations in relation to disclosure of donations were made. Disclosure should be made of donations above $200 to a candidate or above $1000 to a party. The total amount of donations received by candidates, or parties should be disclosed. The Committee recommended a prohibition on anonymous donations with the requirement that, if received, anonymous donations should be forwarded to the Electoral Commission. They also recommended that all receipts or donations received or paid above prescribed levels by organisations or individuals (what the Report called 'front' organisations) should also be disclosed. Agents should be registered by political parties and candidates, and one of their functions would be to furnish disclosure returns. Administration and regular reporting to Parliament was to be made by the Electoral Commission. Innocent mistakes in returns were not to be penalised but severe penalties would be applied for submission of knowingly false returns.[116]

The Committee rejected any requirement for disclosure of donations to party maintenance or administrative expenditure provided they were not used for election purposes.[117] This loophole continues to the present day.

D.   Disclosure and Third Parties

In any event the disclosure provisions contained in Divisions 4 and 5 of the Act, followed the Committee's recommendations quite closely. Division 4 dealt with disclosure of donations. It established a system where all political parties, State branches of political parties, candidates, and groups running in an election were obliged to reveal details of any gifts received. In the case of political parties or State branches, they were obliged to disclose details of all gifts unless they were under $1000, or made on condition that the gift be used for a non-election purpose.[118] Candidates were to reveal all gifts over $200 and groups all gifts over $1000.[119] Independent interests were also required to reveal on the public record any expenditure over $1000 incurred for a political purpose.

---

114   Ibid.
115   Id at 164.
116   Id at 166.
117   Id at 165–168.
118   *Commonwealth Electoral Legislation Amendment Act* 1983 s153J(5).
119   Section 153J(5).

Disclosure covered a variety of matters. It stipulated that, amongst other things, the total amount of all gifts received, the number of gifts, and the 'relevant details' of each were to be listed on the return.

The legislation also targeted donors who 'split' gifts in order to avoid disclosure. If a donor gave two or more gifts during the disclosure period, with a total value of $1000 or more, then the details of each must be provided. The term 'gift' was defined in the interpretive section to mean 'any disposition of property otherwise than by will, being a disposition made without consideration or with inadequate consideration'.[120] It included the provision of a service, other than volunteer labour. It did not include public funding, or annual subscriptions.

The *Electoral Commission Handbook* also made it clear that the definition of gift included gifts-in-kind and that they should be valued at the cost to the donor or, where no cost was involved (such as office space) on the basis of income foregone.[121] Candidates' contributions to their own campaigns were not disclosable.[122]

Disposition of property was defined to cover any conveyance, transfer, assignment, settlement, delivery, payment or other alienation of property. A list of types of property caught by the definition then followed although it was not exhaustive. The list includes: shares; trusts; lease, mortgage, charge, servitude, licence, powers, partnership or interest; the release of any debt, contract or chose in action; general powers of appointment; and any transaction entered into with intent to diminish the value of property and increase the value of another person's property.[123]

Disclosure was to be made by the participants' agent through the making of a return to the Electoral Commission.[124]

The period for which disclosure was to be made varied. Political parties and state branches had to disclose all gifts received in the period from the day after polling in the last election up to polling day in the current election.[125] A first-time independent candidate had to disclose all gifts received since they announced their candidature.[126] An incumbent independent had to disclose all gifts received from the day after polling in the last election in which they stood.[127]

Despite the breadth of the legislation it contained a number of 'avoidance techniques'.[128] These included the exclusion from the disclosure requirement of membership subscriptions, importantly, loans and income derived by a party from

---

120 Section 153H.

121 Above n108 at 19.

122 Section 153H(3).

123 Section 145(1).

124 The return had to be made before 20 weeks after polling for political parties and state branches: s153J(1); 15 weeks for independent candidates and groups: s153J(2)(3) and for independent interests: s153K.

125 Section 153J(1).

126 Section 153J(2)(a).

127 Section 153J(2)(b).

128 Meadows above n75 at 68–69.

its investments or business undertakings. Large amounts of money used in campaigns could still go undetected because of the broad exception for gifts made for purposes other than a purpose related to an election.[129] Moreover a donor could give a party a large sum with the express purpose of investing it and thus avoid the disclosure provisions, even if the money derived from that investment was used for election purposes. Finally, the exclusion of party maintenance or administrative expenditure funds from disclosure in the interests of administrative simplicity, was seen as a 'loophole':[130]

> It is difficult to see how a requirement of full annual accounts from parties, who presumably must account to their members, would significantly complicate the system for the Commission or for the honest party.[131]

The same commentator also noted that the level at which the identity of small donors must be revealed was generally higher in the Australian legislation than in its US counterpart;[132] that third parties were not required to disclose campaign contributions to primary participants under the legislation's definition of electoral expenditure;[133] and that the requirement under the Act to keep records was 'far from rigorous'.[134]

The 1984 *Handbook* also excluded other items from disclosure, although it does not make clear upon what basis it made the assessment since some items could have fallen within the notion of gift, and yet were not specifically excluded by the legislation. For example, Meadows has commented that 'income derived by the party from investments or business undertakings', which the *Handbook* excluded, could constitute a gift for the purposes of the legislation.[135] The exclusion of cash raised in ad hoc collection also became somewhat problematic in the light of evidence that senior Queensland party officials received large cash donations in brown paper bags. Loans, too, might have constituted a gift, especially if they were subsequently not enforced. Offers by media to interview candidates raised the spectre of donations in the light of the known, partisan, sentiments of certain large media groups, and in view of their highly diversified and complex business interests. Media groups, who could no longer be solely identified as reporting on society because of their interconnecting interests in other commercial sectors could have been seen as making an offer resembling donation in-kind which amounted to a valuable contribution and yet avoid disclosure.

Gaps can also be found around the provision of services that are seen by the *Handbook* as examples of volunteer labour. Included here was time spent on party activity by a person who was also a director of a public company; time spend by a trade union official (except where seconded for the campaign); legal or financial

---

129 Ibid.
130 Ibid.
131 Ibid.
132 Ibid.
133 Ibid.
134 Id at 70.
135 Id at 68–69.

advice provided by a lawyer or accountant who was a party member; printing services. Effectively, if a party could find party members who are also printers, lawyers, financial advisers, trade unionists or managing directors, they could, indirectly at least, avoid the full brunt of the disclosure provisions.[136]

E.   Disclosure of Expenditure

The other method introduced to reinforce the integrity of the new public funding system was the introduction of an obligation to disclose expenditure. Although campaign election expenditure limits had been in place between 1902 and 1980, the limits had been set at the 'ridiculously low'[137] levels of $1000 for a Senate candidate and $500 for a House of Representatives candidate, and they were unenforceable. In 1980 the government established an inquiry into electoral expenditure headed by Sir Clarrie Harders, a retired senior public servant. Expenditure limits were not within its terms of reference, and instead the inquiry focused upon the introduction of a system of disclosure. The Joint Committee of 1983 reported that implementation of the Harders system of recommendations was 'not desirable', although it is not entirely clear from the 1983 Report's summary of the Harder's report what options the 1983 Committee rejected. However, the 1983 Report carries a lengthy explanation as to why disclosure of party administrative and maintenance funds on an annual basis should be rejected as this was the main recommendation on which the Committee Report differed from the Harders Report. In essence the Committee said that there was no need to require full annual accounts of party expenditure because this information was already available. A little unconvincingly the Committee states: '... most information would in non-election years relate to party maintenance functions.'[138]

The Committee even recognised that the exemption may 'be seen as a way round the disclosure provisions' but it optimistically predicted that 'public revelation of practices of this kind with its attendant opprobrium should provide sufficient deterrent'.[139]

The Committee rejected the re-introduction of expenditure limits on the basis that they were 'unenforceable' in Australia and overseas (although does not adduce any evidence for this claim) and that in any event the new scheme would render limits 'superfluous'.[140]

Expenditure disclosure was, however, to be made by political parties, candidates, interest groups and other political participants[141] in relation to costs of: television, radio and newspaper advertising (including production costs); authorised material; production and display of advertising at theatres etc; consultancies; and opinion polls.[142] Also suggested for re-introduction was a

---

136 Above n108 at 20.
137 Above n75 at 68–70.
138 Above n76 at 172.
139 Ibid.
140 Ibid.
141 Id at 174.
142 Id at 173.

requirement that media and newspaper organisations disclose advertising space or time bought by candidates, parties and other participants during a campaign, and whether it was provided at less than normal rates.[143] The Committee recommended that non-compliance with the legislation not be a ground of election invalidity on the basis that it would cause 'disruption to the political process',[144] but instead recommended a range of monetary penalties.[145]

The resulting legislation introduced compulsory disclosure of electoral expenditure by parties, state branches, independent candidates, groups, third parties, and media organisations.

The categories of expenditures which fell within the definition of this part of the Act were broadcasting, publishing, display and production of electoral advertisements;[146] election related consultant's or advertising fees; opinion polls; and other research.[147]

All participants were required to furnish a return of electoral expenditure to the Commission. Parties and state branches had 20 weeks to do so,[148] independent candidates,[149] groups,[150] and third parties[151] had only 15. Third parties were also required to do so, but only if the expenditure exceeded $200.[152]

Broadcasters and publishers also had 15 weeks within which to submit a return to the Electoral Commission setting out the particulars of each advertisement including the station or journal of publication; the authorising participant; dates; and charges.[153] They were also required to indicate whether or not the rate charged was less than normal commercial rates.[154] Publishers were only required to furnish a return if the total amount of the charge exceeds $1000.[155]

Again, returns by parties, state branches, independent candidates, and groups were to be submitted by their respective agents.

F. Penalties and Remedies

Failure to comply with any provision did not invalidate the election,[156] however failure to furnish a donation or expenditure return could have resulted in a fine of up to $5000 for a party or state branch, or $1000 in any other case. Submission of an incomplete return was also an offence resulting in a fine of up to $1000. The making of a donation or expenditure return, or a claim for public funding,

---

143 Id at 174–175.
144 Id at 176.
145 Id at 177.
146 *Commonwealth Electoral Legislation Amendment Act* 1983 ss160, 164, 164A.
147 Section 153N.
148 Section 153P(1).
149 Section 153P(2).
150 Section 153P(3).
151 Section 153P(4).
152 Section 153P(5).
153 Sections 153Q, 153R.
154 Sections 153Q(2), 153R(2).
155 Section 153R(3).
156 Id at s153Z.

containing material which the agent knew to be false or misleading by an agent of a party or a state branch, carried a fine of $10 000. The same offence by others carried a maximum $5000 fine.

G. 1983–1991 — Maintenance and Fine-tuning

Over the next eight years, between 1983 and 1991, the legislation was fine-tuned. It was renumbered in 1984, and the funding and disclosure provisions formerly contained in Part XVI became known as the Part XX provisions.[157] The definition of broadcaster was clarified so as to include the holder of any licence within the meaning of the broadcasting legislation (other than a re-transmission licence), as well as the ABC and the SBS.[158]

Three years later came further clarifications, but no dramatic change. Under the interpretive section an advertisement related to an election if it contained electoral matter, whether or not consideration was given to its publication;[159] expenditure incurred for political purposes was disclosable if it was expended during a specified period now named a 'disclosure period' (rather than election period);[160] and expenditure would be defined as incurred for political purposes when it involved publication by any means or publicly expressing views on an election issue,[161] rather than the old text which required actual 'campaigning'.[162]

H. 1991 Political Broadcasts and Political Disclosures Act — Adbans, Compliance Audits[163]

(i) Expenditure Limits, adbans, and Free time

Although the issue of expenditure limits had not been explicitly raised again since their repeal in 1980, the issue was very much in the background for the reforms of 1991. The year marked the next active stage of campaign finance reform when a prohibition on paid political advertising was introduced (along with the introduction of audits of annual disclosure returns by political parties, and of third parties' election returns). The advertising changes were brought about by a process which had commenced two years earlier, and which harked back to a recommendation of the 1983 Report to conduct an 'extended inquiry' into broadcasting and television in election campaigns so as to enable it to investigate 'indirect public funding via "free" time and standards governing political

---

157 *Commonwealth Electoral Legislation Amendment Act* 1984 s5 and Table.
158 *Broadcasting and Television (Consequential Amendments) Act* 1985 s3 Schedule. The pre-existing definition had differentiated between holders of commercial and public licences; whereas the new definition brought them all within the same umbrella of simply being licence holders under the *Broadcasting Act* 1942.
159 *Commonwealth Electoral Amendment Act* 1987 s34.
160 Section 35.
161 Ibid.
162 *Commonwealth Electoral Legislation Amendment Act* 1983 s113, amending s153K.
163 Parts of this section are based on an earlier publication by the Deborah Cass, 'Through the Looking Glass: The Right to Political Speech' in Tom Campbell & Wojciech Sadurski (eds), *Freedom of Communication* (1994).

advertising'.[164] Although this proposal was not specifically adopted, in 1989, as part of its general inquiry into the 1987 election, the Joint Committee on Electoral Reform instituted an investigation into political advertising specifically, claiming that issue had been raised by various submissions (including 'notably' the Australian Labor Party)[165] — although this was disputed in a minority report.[166] The Committee relied on an appeal to the principles of democracy to justify its investigation:

> The rising cost of television advertising time has coincided with the growing use of that medium for political advertising. This has greatly increased the reliance of parties on corporate sponsorship. The Committee is concerned that heavy reliance by parties on such sponsorship risks the distortion of our open democratic system.[167]

A majority of the Committee recommended that a system of free time be introduced for political broadcasting on television and radio during election campaigns. In a 'freewheeling' discussion they noted the pervasive influence of television in liberal democracies,[168] especially during election campaigns,[169] noting that this coincided with a dramatic increase in the costs of television advertising.

The costs of political advertising were explored briefly in Chapter 8 of the Report which noted three related problems: increased costs; scandals caused by improper fund-raising practices; and the potential for corruption. They noted the increasing gap between public funding and the amount needed to advertise during federal elections. While public funding had increased by 30 per cent in the period since its introduction in 1984, the advertising expenditure costs had risen by over 100 per cent.[170] The Committee stated that: '[t]he ability to buy television and radio advertising should not and must not play a determining part in federal elections.'[171]

Moreover the Report noted the corrupting influence money had played in overseas politics, mentioning the Recruit scandal in Japan and Watergate in the United States. Finally the Committee referred to the increasing US practices of politicians receiving substantial donations for public speaking engagements, or the charging of lobbyists to attend meals with members of Congress.[172] They concluded:

---

164   Above n76 at 181.
165   Above n90 at 19.
166   Id at 117. Dissenting Report by Mr Michael Cobb, MP, Senator James Short & Dr Michael Wooldridge, MP.
167   Id at xi.
168   Id at 24.
169   Id at 25.
170   Id at 86.
171   Ibid.
172   Id at 88.

While there is no firm evidence of corrupt practice in Australian political fundraising, the substantial increase in the cost-pressures of campaigning create the potential for such practices.[173]

They concluded that the democratic process had become increasingly dependent on who could raise the substantial funds needed to buy advertising on electronic media.[174] Although the Australian Broadcasting Corporation made some provision for free time to political parties, this was not required by legislation and was allocated on a discretionary basis,[175] and the commercial networks provided no equivalent.[176] The Committee made some rather cursory comparisons with other Western democracies, noting that some form of free advertising existed in many; that paid political advertising was permitted in only five of the 19 countries surveyed, and that Australia's system was the most 'laissez faire'.[177] In passing, the Committee referred to the fact that in West Germany political parties had adopted a 'self-imposed ceiling' on election campaign financing, and that free time was allocated equally to all parties regardless of size.[178] The majority report very briefly discussed and dismissed a range of options: increased public funding was discounted because the costs would be borne by the taxpayer and would need to be indexed to the costs of electronic media advertising;[179] tax deductibility would only favour high income earners and would involve a revenue loss to the government;[180] a ceiling on paid advertising could be subverted by political action committees (like the United States) which would be able to campaign for funds up to the stated ceiling;[181] and a complete ban on paid advertising would have a 'direct effect on freedom of speech by reducing opportunities for discussion'.[182] Moreover it would lead to benefits for the existing major parties, and a reduction in commercial broadcasting revenue.[183]

Ultimately the majority recommended the introduction of a system of free time for political advertising on the basis that it was common to many western democracies, could be introduced without any revenue loss to broadcasters, involved no additional taxpayer expense, and would relieve pressure for increased political funding.[184]

The 'free time' system was to apply to both federal and state elections and operate only in the absence of any paid political advertising, and on the basis that all political parties accepting free time disclose fully their donations incomes and

---

173 Ibid.
174 Id at 25.
175 Id at 30–33.
176 Id at 33.
177 Id at 50.
178 Id at 48–49.
179 Id at 90.
180 Id at 91.
181 Id at 91–92.
182 Id at 92.
183 Ibid.
184 Id at 93.

expenditures.[185] It was to be allocated by an independent committee, along the lines of the UK model, which would have discretionary powers[186] but be limited by a formula based upon the level of support (measured in votes received) that the party received at the previous election.[187] Foreseeing difficulties for new parties with significant support, the Committee recommended that those parties be able to apply for a percentage allocation of 5 per cent of the total amount of free time, as long as they nominated candidates for the Senate and for more than half the House of Representatives seats in any one state.[188] This threshold for free time allocation for new parties was extremely high.

(ii) Funding and Disclosure

Also contained in the report in Chapter 7 were the Committee's findings in relation to the regularly reported issues of funding and disclosure.

One issue which remained contentious was spot audits. In the previous Committee's Report, it was concluded that existing powers were sufficient and there was 'no need for spot audits'.[189] However the current Committee discussed the concern that parties might be avoiding the disclosure provisions, and there was no way for the Commission to know whether or not this was the case. The Commission likened its situation to viewing three walnut shells, only one of which was transparently labelled donation and the other two being opaque. Without the power to conduct spot audits there was no way for the Commission to determine whether the two opaque shells required investigation. In the words of the Report,

> While income from capital explains some of the extra money spent by parties the reminder must be seen as donations which may not be required to be disclosed under current legislation.[190]

The Committee concluded that as financial disclosure was an 'important adjunct to democracy', and in view of the 'alarming lack of information of sources of election funding', it was necessary to take 'brave steps' — namely to give the Commission power to conduct spot audits of political parties, and then to make public records of such.[191]

(iii) Third Parties

The other significant issue which the Committee considered was the increasing use of third parties to channel funds into the political process, either on their own behalf or on the behalf of an existing party. Here the Committee predicted correctly the increased role that third parties would play in future campaigns[192]

---

185 Id at 96.
186 Id at 99.
187 Id at 100.
188 Ibid.
189 Id at 72.
190 Id at 75.
191 Id at 76.
192 Id at 81, and see Part 4 below.

and therefore recommended that the Commission publish a full list of these bodies,[193] that they be subject to the same disclosure requirements as other political participants,[194] and that any third parties known to have a financial relationship with political parties be subject to spot audits.[195] Importantly, the Committee also recommended that third parties be required to disclose in relation to any election and not just the election bounded by the current disclosure period.[196] The reason for this was to avoid the apparently common practice of third parties of donating outside the disclosure period for the instant election and thereby avoiding the disclosure requirement.[197]

Despite the view of the committee that a ban on advertising was not warranted, when the legislation was presented in the parliament, a ban is exactly what it contained, along with some free time and disclosure provisions. The *Political Broadcasts and Political Disclosures Act* 1991 (Cth) introduced a new Part IIID into the *Broadcasting Act* 1942 (Cth). The object of the amendment was to prohibit the broadcasting, on radio or television, of political advertisements during an election period.[198] The legislation therefore purported to ban broadcasting of advertisements containing political matter[199] or prescribed material[200] and broadcasting of any matter (subject to limited exceptions discussed below) by all governments (Commonwealth,[201] state,[202] or territory[203]) and government authorities in Australia's federal system, during an election period. An election period included federal elections and referenda, and territory,[204] state,[205] and local government elections.

Broadcasting of some otherwise prohibited material was permitted under three exceptions. First, broadcasting was permitted of news or current affairs, and comment[206] or talkback,[207] as well as some advertisements for public health,[208] charities,[209] and the visually handicapped.[210] Second, a federal government statutory authority, the Australian Broadcasting Tribunal, was vested with the power to allocate free time to some participants in the political process. Ninety per

---

193 Id at 82, Recommendation 5.
194 Id at Recommendation 6.
195 Id at Recommendation 7.
196 Id at 81, Recommendation 4.
197 Id at 79, figure 7.1.
198 Explanatory Memorandum accompanying the Political Broadcasts and Political Disclosures Bill 1991 at 2.
199 *Political Broadcasts and Political Disclosures Act* 1991 s95B(6).
200 Section 95B(6).
201 Section 95B(1).
202 Section 95B(2).
203 Section 95B(3).
204 Section 95C.
205 Section 95D.
206 Section 95A(1)(a).
207 Section 95A(1)(b).
208 Section 95A(4).
209 Section 95A(3)(a),(b).
210 Section 95A(2).

cent of the free time allocation was to be divided amongst parties who were already represented in the parliament and were contesting the election, with time given in proportion to the number of first preferences obtained at the last election.[211] The remaining 10 per cent of free time was to be divided amongst two groups. Free time would be allocated to Senators who were former members of a party that had a free-time allocation.[212] The Tribunal then had discretion to allocate the remaining percentage to independent candidates and political parties.[213] The third exception to the total prohibition on advertising was that political parties already represented in the parliament might broadcast a policy launch.[214]

The insertion of Part IIID was challenged by licensees of broadcasting stations and by the State of New South Wales. The grounds of the challenge included, *inter alia,* contravention of an implied constitutional guarantee of freedom of communication in relation to the electoral process; interference with the functioning and integrity of the states; imposition of a burden or a disability amounting to discrimination against the activities of the states: contravention of the guarantee of freedom of interstate intercourse contained in section 92 of the Constitution; and contravention of section 51(31) of the Constitution concerning acquisition of property on otherwise than just terms.

In an historic decision the High Court struck down the ad-ban regime, and, in the process, identified that the Constitution contained an implied right to freedom of communication in relation to political matters derived from the concept of representative democracy.[215] A majority[216] of the court said that sections of the Constitution, including sections 7 and 24, encapsulated an essential feature of the Australian constitutional system, namely representative democracy. The judges differed as to the consequences of this finding, although all agreed that, at the very least, representative democracy required that representatives be directly chosen by the people. Direct choice included the right to communicate and receive information necessary for the making of that choice. However, whereas six of the seven judges[217] (including one from the minority, Brennan J) said that the Constitution itself must therefore protect the right to freedom of speech in relation to political matters involved in the making of that choice, one judge, Dawson J, said in a system of parliamentary supremacy individual rights were protected by the parliament, not by judges reviewing the Constitution.[218] The remaining minority judge, Brennan J, upheld the legislation as a reasonable regulation of the political process, even though it did trench upon the implied freedom.[219]

---

211 Section 95H(1)–(3).
212 Section 95L(1).
213 Section 95M(1), (2).
214 Section 95S.
215 *Australian Capital Television Pty Ltd v Commonwealth* (1992) 177 CLR 106.
216 Ibid (Mason CJ, Gaudron, McHugh, Deane & Toohey JJ; Brennan & Dawson JJ dissenting).
217 Id at 140 (Mason CJ), 149 (Brennan J), 168 (Deane & Toohey JJ), 215–216 (Gaudron J), 227 (McHugh J).
218 Id at 186 (Dawson J).
219 Id at 169 (Brennan J).

The implied freedom of communication could only be restricted where there was a compelling justification for so doing, and where the restrictive measure was proportionate to the object being addressed. The majority and one member of the minority, Brennan J, said that there was a compelling justification for the legislation, being the preservation of the integrity of the political process by limiting opportunities for corruption caused by the high cost of political advertising.[220] Nevertheless the prohibition contained in the legislation was *prima facie* an interference with the implied freedom. In the view of the majority, the measures adopted to achieve that legitimate purpose were excessive and discriminatory, and thus failed the test of proportionality. The reasons for this were varied: the Act restricted not just political advertising, but all political communication during the relevant period;[221] the provisions discriminated in favour of existing political candidates and excluded political communications by non-endorsed individuals;[222] the mode of communication being restricted (namely television especially, as the most effective mode available);[223] and the fact that other measures, such as spending limits and disclosure requirements, could have achieved the same legislative purpose.[224] The legislation did not pass the twin tests of reasonableness and proportionality, and hence contravened the implied freedom.

Other grounds argued by the plaintiffs were generally not considered in great depth by the court. In relation to interference with the functioning of the states, McHugh J said that the legislation did interfere with their functioning,[225] two judges discussed whether the scheme constituted an acquisition of property by the Commonwealth without just compensation, and all said that the rights involved were not proprietary in nature[226] and Dawson J said there was no contravention of section 92, and that the legislation did not discriminate against the states.[227]

One of the legacies of the High Court's striking down of the constitutionality of the Bill was the loss of the changes to the disclosure regime. These were taken up again the following year.

I.   *1992 Amendments — The Introduction of Annual Returns*

The *Commonwealth Electoral Amendment Act* 1992 was introduced with a major change to the disclosure regime, which had failed to survive the constitutional challenge to the broadcast ban.[228] Instead of requiring political parties and their state branches to submit election returns for donations and expenditure, they were

---

220 See, for example, id at 142, 144 (Mason CJ).

221 Id at 171–173 (Deane & Toohey JJ).

222 Id at 145 (Mason CJ), 172 (Deane & Toohey JJ), 245 (McHugh J).

223 Id at 146 (Mason CJ).

224 Id at 234–235 (McHugh J).

225 Id at 244 (McHugh J).

226 Id at 165–167 (Brennan J), 197–199 (Dawson J).

227 Id at 195 (Dawson J).

228 See *Political Broadcasts and Political Disclosures Act* 1991 s22 inserted a new Division 5A into Part XX of the Principal Act.

now required to produce an annual return disclosing all receipts, payments and debts.[229] The return had to list all transactions (payments, receipts or debts) of $1500 or more, and provide certain particulars. The amount of each transaction, plus each amount making up the sum, and its date of receipt had to be disclosed. In addition, the names and addresses of officers of the particular body involved in the transaction were also to be provided. So, for unincorporated associations disclosure extended to the name of the association, and the names and addresses of its executive committee; for trust funds and foundations, it extended to the names and addresses of the trustees and the title of the fund; and for any other cases, the name and address of the person or the organisation. This latter category would presumably include registered industrial organisations. Candidates were still required only to submit election expenditure and donation returns.

J.   1994 Recommendations and 1995 Act

One of the unfortunate legacies of the latter amendments was that they placed a new administrative burden upon political parties who were now required to list, in minute detail, every financial transaction they undertook. Partly in response to pressure from political parties, the Joint Standing Committee on Electoral Matters (JSCEM) produced an interim report in June 1994 entitled *Financial Reporting by Political Parties*, the recommendations of which it hoped would be introduced during July 1994.[230] The Committee was convinced that there was an 'urgent need to simplify the reporting requirements' and to 'alleviate the worst of the bureaucratic requirements associated with annual returns' without sacrificing the accountability goals of the legislation.[231] To this end it recommended that only total amounts of expenditure be listed by political parties in their annual returns, instead of individual transactions.[232]

Other important recommendations made in the 1994 Report included: the setting of a threshold of $500, below which individual amounts received or paid by political parties did not have to be reported (although the total of $1500 from one entity remained);[233] the abolition of the requirement of donors' returns;[234] amendment of the Act requiring disclosure of income received by a political party from a trust fund or similar account;[235] and the introduction of the same amount of public funding for Senate seats as for the House of Representatives.[236] All recommendations except the abolition of donors' returns were accepted and incorporated into legislation.

---

229 *Commonwealth Electoral Amendment Act* 1992 s12 amending sections 314AB, 314AC, 314AD, and 314AE of the Principal Act.

230 Australia, Joint Standing Committee on Electoral Reform, *Financial Reporting by Political Parties*: interim report (Canberra: AGPS, 1994) at 3.

231 Id at 2–3.

232 Id at 4.

233 Id at 5.

234 Id at 6.

235 Id at 8.

236 Id at 9.

In 1994, a Bill was introduced into the House implementing the recommendations. Four main changes were introduced. The reporting requirements were simplified so that only totals of amounts received had to be listed in the annual return, not every sum that made up the amount.[237] This removed the 'unnecessarily onerous reporting requirements for registered political parties'.[238] Moreover, parties were only required to count individual transactions of $500 or more for determining whether an individual had reached the $1500 threshold for detailed disclosure. Second, annual reporting by donors was introduced[239] so as to facilitate cross-checking[240] with political party returns which were now done on an annual basis.[241] Third, public funding was increased and equalised between the Senate and the House of Representatives.[242] The increase was justified on the basis that the costs of campaigning had increased[243] and that since disclosure had been introduced donors were more reluctant to contribute.[244] Moreover the legislative scheme for funding was altered to the effect that participants were entitled to receive funding automatically regardless of how much or whether they spent on the election campaign. This had the twin advantages, of speeding up the process for the AEC, and reducing the administrative burden to the participants.[245] Political parties were, once again, required to furnish an electoral expenditure return,[246] and the definition of electoral expenditure was amended to include direct mail.[247]

Finally, the disclosure provisions were extended to include entities associated with political parties ('associated entities' under the Act),[248] and donations to such entities were also brought within the scope of the Act.[249] For the first time, entities closely associated with registered political parties such as companies, trust funds and foundations were brought within the disclosure requirements. Additionally, associated entities were obliged to disclose capital deposits used to earn income that was subsequently passed on to parties. In introducing the Bill to the Parliament, the Minister described this as the closure of a 'loophole' which was being 'flouted' by one party which had just received $7.2 million 'laundered'

---

237 *Commonwealth Electoral Amendment Act* 1995 s3, amending s314AC(3) of the Principal Act.

238 Australia, House of Representatives, *Parliamentary Debates (Hansard)*, 9 March 1995 at 1949.

239 *Commonwealth Electoral Amendment Act* 1995, inserting new s305B into the Principal Act.

240 Explanatory Memorandum accompanying the Commonwealth Electoral Amendment Bill (No. 2) 1994 at ¶22, 6.

241 *Commonwealth Electoral Amendment Act* 1995, inserting new s314AEA into the Principal Act.

242 *Commonwealth Electoral Amendment Act* 1995, amending s294(1), (2) and (3) of the Principal Act. The actual rate of funding, adjusted for CPI, was 157.594 cents per vote: Australian Electoral Commission, *Funding and Disclosure Report Election 96* (1997) at 3.

243 Above n240 at 2.

244 Australia, House of Representatives, *Parliamentary Debate (Hansard)*, 9 March 1995 at 1950.

245 Australian Electoral Commission, above n242 at 1.

246 *Commonwealth Electoral Amendment Act* 1995, amending s308(1)(f) of the Principal Act.

247 *Commonwealth Electoral Amendment Act* 1995, amending Division 5A of Part XX (heading) of the Principal Act.

248 Id at inserting new definitions into s287(1) of the Principal Act; s19 inserting new s314AE(1) into the Principal Act; s12.

249 Id at amending subs305(1) of the Principal Act.

through a trust, which was not disclosed to the AEC.[250] The Opposition, while not opposing the Bill, did indicate that they were opposed to the 'retrospective' element of the Bill contained in the provisions relating to annual returns of trust funds. In requiring details on sources of capital that may have been contributed when there was no question of disclosure, the Bill, according to the opposition parties, was retrospective in operation.[251]

4. The Past Five Years — Associated Entities and Disclosure

A. The 1996 Federal Election

In reporting on the 1996 election the Electoral Commission made a number of recommendations for reform of the legislation. Some were largely mechanical. These included the payment of election funding in the registered name of parties or branches rather than individual party agents;[252] the increase of the threshold for disclosure of donations to candidates from $200 to $1000;[253] the increase of the threshold for disclosure of electoral expenditure by third parties from $200 to $1000;[254] and correlating the thresholds for anonymous donations with the disclosure threshold.[255]

Other matters went to the heart of the regulation of transparency. For example, one issue identified by the Commission was that since the introduction of the annual return requirement for parties, there was no longer a separate listing for donations within the receipts listing by parties. Apart from the confusion this created (with, for example, one journalist reporting maturity of an investment as a bank donation) it complicated the Commission's task of identifying donors who should be required to lodge returns.[256] Accuracy is obviously essential, and here the Commission recommended that political party annual returns be accompanied by a report from an accredited auditor.[257]

Due to the uncertainty of the definition of 'associated entity', the Commission sought broader powers of investigation and subpoena which would allow it to serve a notice upon an organisation to inspect relevant documentation to ascertain whether it fell within the definition.[258] The Commission warned of the need to amend the legislation to more tightly define what was an associated entity.[259]

---

250 Francis Walker, Australia, House of Representatives, *Parliamentary Debates (Hansard)*, 9 March 1995 at 1950.

251 Id at 1952.

252 For example, based on figures in the AEC 1996 Report an individual agent of the NSW Australian Labor Party would have received a cheque in the sum of $4 451 179.49, and the Liberal counterpart would have received a payment for $3 537 309.22: Australian Electoral Commission, *Funding and Disclosure Report Following the Federal Election held on 2 March 1996* at 3.

253 Id at 28 (Recommendation 3).

254 Ibid (Recommendation 4).

255 Ibid (Recommendation 8).

256 Id at 13.

257 Ibid.

258 Id at 17.

259 Id at 16.

In addition, the Report identified other problems without making recommendations. These included the fact that broadcaster and publisher returns disclosing electoral expenditure were rarely inspected by the public despite the considerable administrative burden they placed upon the media. However the Commission cautioned against their abolition since they may be the only source of this information.[260]

In relation to compliance audits of parties, associated entities' annual returns, and third parties' election returns, the Commission indicated that it was moving to a 'risk-based approach'[261] which would be based upon identified risk factors and levels of financial activity. They commented that in general the standard of compliance was variable, and that some significant errors and omissions had been found.[262] These were in part the result of a lack of preparation and planning for disclosure and the inadequacy of accounting systems.[263] The Commission commented that the situation could be improved by the incorporation of parties and their subjection to other financial regulation. 'Apart from enhancing the disclosure system, this would have the added advantage of protecting party finances.'[264]

Furthermore, the Commission indicated that it may be time to consider the creation of offences without the requirement of knowledge.[265]

B. Recommendations of the Joint Standing Committee on Electoral Matters' Report of the Inquiry into the Conduct of the 1996 Federal Election

One of the continuing controversies in the scheme concerns election expenditure returns. In the 1983 Act this was a requirement for all participants, and for third parties. The requirement was subsequently removed for the 1993 election[266] and then reinstated in 1995.[267]

The merry-go-round on election expenditure returns continued in the *Report of the Inquiry into the Conduct of the 1996 Federal Election* by the Joint Standing Committee on Election Matters. The Committee noted the Liberal Party view that annual and election returns contained a level of unnecessary duplication and the ALP view that annual audited accounts could replace both, and the AEC's acceptance of the abolition of the electoral return. They recommended that the electoral return be abolished and that registered parties be allowed to lodge audited accounts annually in place of annual returns, as long as the detail and format conformed with the requirements of the Commission and of the Act.[268]

---

260 Id at 11.

261 Id at 19.

262 Id at 20.

263 Ibid.

264 Ibid.

265 Ibid.

266 *Commonwealth Electoral Amendment Act 1992* (Cth) s12.

267 *Commonwealth Electoral Amendment Act 1995* (Cth) ss5 and 6.

268 Australia, Joint Standing Committee on Electoral Matters, *Report of the Inquiry into All Aspects of the Conduct of the 1996 Federal Election and Matters Related Thereto* (Canberra: AGPS, 1997) at 102 (Recommendation 60).

Other recommendations were made by the Joint Standing Committee. The Committee considered the view proposed by the Liberals that the total threshold for reporting donations be increased to from $1500 to a total of $10000, and that individual amounts received not be included unless they were over $1500. The purported point of these changes was to relieve the administrative burden of record-keeping for volunteers in local branches,[269] although in submission the AEC argued that an increase from $500 to $1500 would not achieve this. In contrast the Committee argued that donors were already able to make a donation of $1499 to each state and national branch, and that to raise the total threshold to $10000 would allow up to nine donations of just under that amount, a total about just under $90000 which could remain hidden from scrutiny.[270]

The Committee was sceptical of this view of widespread hidden money flowing in to the political system. They said that thresholds should 'more accurately reflect current financial values',[271] indicating perhaps that people can afford to donate more these days to political parties than the legislation's figures suggest. They continued, perhaps a little optimistically, that it was 'most unlikely' that donors would go to such extraordinary lengths to conceal their allegiances.[272] Even $90 000 spread over nine branches, state and federal, was 'hardly likely to engender corruption'.[273] Echoing the wisdom of Solomon, they decided to compromise and proposed to increase the total threshold to $5000, and the threshold for counting individual sums received from a person be increased from $500 to $1500.

Donor disclosure was another issue canvassed by the Committee. The Liberal Party argued for abolition of donor disclosure. This was strongly rejected by the AEC on two grounds. They pointed out that it would effectively make disclosure of donations a purely voluntary arrangement. As long as donors kept their donations in lots below $500, the threshold above which political parties were not obliged to report them, contributions could go completely undetected if there were no additional donor disclosure obligation. Moreover, as annual party returns do not distinguish between donations and other receipts, there was no way to identify which contributions to parties of $1500 were donations and which were not. The Committee recommended the maintenance of donor returns but steeply increased the threshold for disclosure from $1500 to $10000 because the current level was 'unreasonably low and must discourage many potential donors'.[274]

On tax deductibility the Committee recommended the increase of level of donation which would qualify for a deduction under taxation legislation from $100 to $1500 in order to 'encourage small to medium donations, thereby increasing the number of Australians involved in the democratic process and increasing the parties' reliance on a smaller number of large donations'.[275]

---

269 Id at 100.
270 Id at 100, 101.
271 Ibid.
272 Ibid.
273 Ibid.
274 Id at 102 (Recommendations 58 & 59).

In relation to compliance, it is interesting that the Committee rejected the submissions of the major parties to the effect that 'substantial compliance' was sufficient in view of the large number of volunteer workers involved in the collection and submission of material for the purposes of the Act. The Committee pointed out that only offences made with knowledge were subject to penalties so that there was no need for 'relaxed penalty provisions'.[276]

In relation to public funding, the Committee recommended changing the current system from a set amount for each vote to an amount based upon its share of the primary vote taken as a proportion of a total pool of public funds, which would be set by the total enrolment at the close of rolls.[277]

Finally, the Report noted the concern of the major parties with the new requirements for 'associated entities' and suggested that government 'review' their operation.[278]

C.   *Electoral and Referendum Amendment Bill 1997*

In 1997 some of the changes recommended in the Joint Standing Committee Report were adopted. The Electoral and Referendum Amendment Bill 1997 (Cth) abolished the requirement that registered political parties lodge electoral expenditure returns, and it provided that parties lodge annual returns of expenditure in the approved form or lodge audited financial statements in a form which meets the legislation's requirements and is approved by the Electoral Commission.[279]

More contentious was the question of associated entities. In the second reading debate on the Bill, Opposition member Mr Bob McMullan claimed that the government party was exploiting a loophole in the legislation by 'sidestepping the disclosure provisions'.[280] He identified a number of issues. The first was the making of donations to a foundation which then gave the money to the political party, thus avoiding the disclosure requirements of the Act because foundations were not within the disclosure provisions.[281] This loophole had been addressed by the extension of the disclosure requirements to associated entities, but problems of definition still remained. The second issue therefore was the inability of the Commission to investigate effectively whether a particular body was an associated entity for the purposes of the Act. If the body in question said that it was not, or

275   Id at 104 (Recommendation 61).

276   Id at 104.

277   Id at 105 (Recommendation 63).

278   Id at 105.

279   Explanatory Memorandum accompanying the Electoral and Referendum Amendment Bill 1997 (Cth), Item 141, 142–144.

280   Australia, House of Representatives, *Parliamentary Debates (Hansard)*, 23 March 1998 at 1346.

281   Mr McMullan referred to a situation prior to the 1995 amendments when the Free Enterprise Foundation had reportedly donated a large sum of money to the Liberal Party without disclosing the original sources of the donations: Australia, House of Representatives, *Parliamentary Debates (Hansard)*, 23 March 1998 at 1347.

simply refused to cooperate,[282] the Commission was unable to do anything more, at least until after a regular compliance audit of the party which might take up to two years after the donations were made. The third problem was the provision of loans that might be unsecured, or provided at non-commercial rates.[283]

D.   The Ongoing Issue of 'Associated Entities'

The issue of associated entities was first highlighted in 1994, when the then Labor government noted that large contributions were being made to the Liberal Party from an organisation called The Free Enterprise Foundation.[284] These contributions were not transparent because foundations such as this were not subject to the disclosure provisions. Hence when a Liberal Party disclosure was made to the Commission it stated simply that a contribution was made by the named foundation but no further details gave the original source/s of the donations.

In 1992 changes had been introduced to the Act to bring within the disclosure provisions entities which were associated with political parties.[285] However problems with the legislation remained, the main one in this respect being that the Commission lacked the investigatory powers necessary to determine whether or not an organisation fell within the definition of associated entity. The Commission could question the organisation and request information from them relating to their status, but if the organisation refused, the Commission felt it had no lawful way to pursue their investigation. In their *Funding and Disclosure Report* following the 1996 federal election, the Commission highlighted this problem saying that such a situation 'could give the appearance of disclosure only by consent and has the potential to undermine public confidence in the disclosure system'.[286] As a result the Commission recommended that they 'be empowered to serve a notice upon the officers of an organisation for the purpose of ascertaining whether that organisation has an obligation to disclose as an associated entity'.[287]

The matter was brought up repeatedly in the Parliament during the period March to July 1998.

---

282   According to Mr McMullan, the Greenfields Foundation responded to a request from the AEC as to their status as an associated entity by claiming that they did not meet the definition and therefore were not required to provide further information: Australia, House of Representatives, *Parliamentary Debates (Hansard)*, 23 March 1998 at 1348.

283   Mr McMullan speculated that when, in 1996–7, the Liberal Party reduced its debt to the National Australia Bank from $6 762 763 to $158 305 and simultaneously was lent $4 650 000 by the Greenfields Foundation that it was the beneficiary of a loan from the latter, a loan which may have been provided at less than commercial rates: ibid. The claim that any loan had been made at less than commercial rates was denied by the government spokesperson, John Fahey: Australia, House of Representatives, *Parliamentary Debates (Hansard)*, 24 March 1998 at 1424.

284   Australia, House of Representatives, *Parliamentary Debates (Hansard)*, 21 September 1994 at 1268, 1274.

285   *Commonwealth Electoral Amendment Act* 1992 (Cth).

286   Australian Electoral Commission, above n242 at 17.

287   Ibid (Recommendation 10). In the same recommendation, the AEC also suggested that such an organisation be given the right to appeal against such a notice.

For example in Senate debates about appropriation in March, the Leader of the Opposition in the Senate, Senator Faulkner, accused the Liberal Party of 'deliberately trying to breach the spirit of the Electoral Act' and of trying to 'side step .... any form of public scrutiny of what is a huge sum of money from yet unknown Liberal Party donors'.[288]

Specifically the debate raised a number of unresolved issues related to associated entities: unenforced loans; identification of associated entities; anonymous donation-making; and concessional loan arrangements. First, Senator Faulkner recounted the history of a loan of $4 million made by the Greenfields Foundation to the Liberal Party in 1996–7, implying that the loan was to repay a bank debt which the party owed to the National Australia Bank. Second, he referred to what he called 'an uncanny number of similarities'[289] between the Free Enterprise Foundation, which had been subject to the disclosure provisions, and the Greenfields Foundation, which had not. These similarities related to identification of trustees, postal address, and accounting support between the two foundations. Third, questions were raised regarding the methods of security for the funding, payment, and interest rates for the loan. Fourth, Senator Faulkner noted that although donations over $1500 must be disclosed, loans need not, although he conceded that a loan 'of itself' was 'not a problem'.[290] The real problem was in relation to the inability of the Commission to identify the Greenfields Foundation as an associated entity for the purposes of the Act, and thus the ability of the Foundation to 'collect substantial donations from sources which remain anonymous for the purposes of funding disclosure'.[291] Despite requests from the Commission, the Foundation was not under any obligation to provide information and the Commission had 'no authority .... to go behind a separation foundation on the basis of any suspicion [it] might have'.[292] Other than a regular compliance audit of the Liberal Party, which might take place every 2 years, there was no other way for the Commission to investigate.

The matter was taken up again on 10 March 1998 with a resolution by Senator Faulkner to take note of the 1996 Australian Electoral Commission Report. The Resolution drew attention to three problems: definitional uncertainty; lack of investigatory power; and the resultant undermining of public confidence in the disclosure system.[293] A month later, a further resolution was moved by Senator Faulkner noting that, in some cases, the Commission was unable to determine whether an organisation should disclose and that there was nothing to prevent an organisation from claiming it did not meet the definition. Senator Faulkner called on the appropriate Minister to amend the Act to empower the Commission to investigate whether an organisation had an obligation to disclose as an associated entity.[294]

---

288 Australia, Senate, *Parliamentary Debates (Hansard)*, 3 March 1998 at 200.
289 Ibid.
290 Ibid.
291 Ibid. See also n283 above.
292 Australian Electoral Commission, above n242 at 17.
293 Australia, Senate, *Parliamentary Debates (Hansard)*, 10 March 1998 at 735.

In debate upon the Electoral and Referendum Amendment Bill 1997 (Cth), the Opposition foreshadowed that, whilst it supported the Bill in principle, it would move a number of amendments aimed at addressing this problem. It proposed to tighten the definition of associated entity to cover entities that operated wholly *or to a significant extent* for the benefit of one of more registered political party.[295] The current definition included entities wholly or *mainly* for a party's benefit. The object of the change was, presumably, to catch organisations which may have other purposes which took them outside the ambit of the disclosure requirements, but which nevertheless operated to benefit political parties. The statement by a trustee of the Greenfields Foundation that it was a charitable foundation may have been what the amendment was addressing.

The second amendment would have altered the disclosure period so that if a loan was subsequently unenforced, converting it into a gift, the donor would nevertheless be obliged to disclose even if the gift was, as a consequence, outside the same disclosure period as the original donations.[296] Third, the Opposition foreshadowed that it would seek to amend the Act so that only financial institutions could make loans to political parties, unless certain disclosure provisions were met, detailing the terms and conditions of the loan.[297]

The matter again came to a head when two other important changes were introduced into the Parliament in 1998 in the form of changes to taxation legislation. The first of these was relatively uncontroversial and involved including within the definition of tax deductibility those deductions that were made to independent candidates, as well as those made to political party members. Bipartisan support for this measure was apparent. The second change sought to increase from $100 to $1500 the amount that was tax deductible, and to allow companies to claim donations as tax deductions. Labor members of the Committee had fought hard for the ceiling to be maintained at $1500 rather than $10000, as proposed by the Liberals. However, when the Bill came to the House of Representatives it was still objected to upon other grounds.

Labor Member, Mr Bob McMullan, criticised the Bill for two reasons. First, the increase in tax deductibility levels would costs taxpayers some $45 million over the next three years.[298] Second, and more importantly, it failed to address what Mr McMullan called the ' "Greenfields loophole" through which donations are made to the Liberal Party without any disclosure'.[299] In debate on the same Bill another Labor member, Mr Martin Ferguson, made the claim that the three largest donors to the Coalition Government were associated entities.[300]

On 25 June 1998, the Special Minister of State, Senator Minchin, moved an amendment to the Electoral and Referendum Amendment Bill 1998 (Cth) which

---

294   Australia, Senate, *Parliamentary Debates (Hansard)*, 7 April 1998 at 2183.
295   Australia, Senate, *Parliamentary Debates (Hansard)*, 28 May 1998 at 3357.
296   Ibid.
297   Ibid.
298   Australia, House of Representatives, *Parliamentary Debates (Hansard)*, 3 June 1998 at 4664.
299   Ibid.
300   Ibid.

would empower the Commission to serve a notice upon an officer of an organisation suspected of being an associated entity to produce documents to enable that assessment to be made.[301]

The foreshadowed opposition amendments were introduced into the Senate on the same day,[302] and supported by the Greens Senator on the basis that the device of making 'loans' to political parties where there is no intention to call in those loans was contrary to the intention of the legislation and was a 'potential device for hiding donations going to political parties.'[303] The Government reiterated its support for transparency and disclosure[304] but rejected the amendments because the phrase 'significant extent' was an 'unworkable' definition, and changes to the disclosure period would have a retrospective effect.[305] The opposition amendments were rejected.[306] On July 1 the amendments framed by the Government, including increasing the power of the Commission to serve notices on organisations in order to ascertain whether they were associated entities, were returned to the House of Representatives where they were agreed to[307] and the Bill finally passed as the *Electoral and Referendum Amendment Act* 1998 on the 17th of July 1998. On the 9th of February 1999, the AEC announced to the Senate Estimates Committee that it had served a 'please explain' notice upon the Greenfields Foundation on 15 January of that year.[308]

However, the issue still hadn't ended, with debate on the Taxation Laws Amendment Bill (No. 8) 1999 (Cth) focusing very much on the Greenfields issues. The area which seemed to have been causing so much controversy was the issue of tax deductibility for donations to prescribed private funds. The fear was that organisations, such as the Greenfields Foundation would be considered prescribed private funds for the purposes of the Act, thus enabling political donations via such organisations to be tax deductible as well as limiting public transparency. In view of this, the Senate moved amendments preventing certain private funds from being considered 'prescribed private funds' The amendments were returned having been rejected by the Government majority in the House of Representatives. The amendment in question restricted prescribed private funds from including any associated entities (within the meaning of the *Commonwealth Electoral Act* 1918 (Cth)) or any private fund which at any time makes, or had made, a gift, contribution or any other benefit to a political party registered under Part XI of the *Commonwealth Electoral Act* 1918 (Cth).[309] The House objected to this on the grounds that the amendment was unnecessary as the Bill was already proposing to amend the *Income Tax Assessment Act* 1997 (Cth) such that a fund could 'only be

---

301 Australia, Senate, *Parliamentary Debates (Hansard)*, 25 June 1998 at 4080.

302 Id at 4174 (Senator Faulkner).

303 Robert Brown, Australia, Senate, *Parliamentary Debates (Hansard)*, 30 June 1998 at 4463.

304 Ibid (Senator Minchin).

305 Nicholas Minchin, Australia, Senate, *Parliamentary Debates (Hansard)*, 25 June 1998 at 4178.

306 Australia, Senate, *Parliamentary Debates (Hansard)*, 30 June 1998 at 4115.

307 Australia, House of Representatives, *Parliamentary Debates (Hansard)*, 1 July 1998 at 3181.

308 Media release, 'Howard Fails on Greenfields Debt Question', Senator John Faulkner, 10 February 1999.

309 Australia, Senate, *Parliamentary Debates (Hansard)*, 13 April 2000 at 14111.

a prescribed private fund if it is established solely for the purpose of providing money to a fund or institution listed under Subdivision 30-B of that Act'. As political parties are not being listed under that Subdivsion, any fund established for the purpose of supplying money to a political party would hence not be considered a private fund. Despite this, however, Senator Kemp, the Assistant Treasurer would still not give a commitment that the Greenfields Foundation would not be considered a prescribed private fund for the purposes of the Act.[310]

However, the amendments were defeated in the Senate, following a change of heart on the part of the Democrats in order to get the Bill passed. Hence the *Taxation Laws Amendment Act (No. 2)* 2000 (Cth) was assented to on the 31st of May 2000.[311] However, the very fact that this Bill was returned to the House three times, and was passed with considerable criticism by the Democrats,[312] indicates that the issue of associated entities and political donations is far from over. This is emphasised by the recent debate over a Senate motion proposed by Senator Faulkner supporting the AEC's concerns regarding the Greenfield's Foundation[313] as expressed in the AEC's *Funding and Disclosure Report of the 1998 Federal Election.*[314]

E.   Electoral and Referendum Act (No. 1) *1999*

A further piece of legislation, the Electoral and Referendum Amendment Bill (No. 2) 1998 (Cth) , adopted a number of recommendations made in the JSCEM Report into the 1996 Election. The relevant ones for our purposes concern donations. First, it provided that political parties are only required to disclose amounts of $5000 or more, rather than the previous $1500 received from a person or organisation in a financial year.[315] Second, in calculating this sum the Bill increased from $500 to $1500 the threshold under which individual donations must be counted.[316] Third, under the proposed amendments, donors to political parties would only be required to disclose by way of a return if they donated $10000 rather than the current $1500.[317]

The Senate's Finance and Public Administration Legislation Committee considered the Bill and heard submissions concerning it in June 1998.

In relation to donors' disclosure, Senator Minchin put forward the view that the requirement was unnecessary both because it duplicated disclosure by parties, and

310   John Faulkner, Australia, Senate, *Parliamentary Debates (Hansard)*, 13 April 2000 at 14115.
311   *Taxation Laws Amendment Act (No. 2)* 2000 (Cth) No. 58, 2000.
312   Andrew Bartlett, Australia, Senate, *Parliamentary Debates (Hansard)*, 13 April 2000 at 14117.
313   John Faulkner, Australia, Senate, *Parliamentary Debates (Hansard)*, 22 June 2000 at 15504.
314   See Australian Electoral Commission, *Funding and Disclosure Report Following the Federal Election held on 3 October 1998* (Canberra: AGPS, 2000) Part 5.
315   Proposed amendment to s314AC(1). Explanatory Memorandum accompanying the Electoral and Referendum Amendment Bill (No. 2) 1998 at Item 44s & 45.
316   Id at proposed amendment to s314AC(2).
317   Id at proposed amendment to s305B(1).

on privacy grounds.[318] In relation to the aggregation figure above which amounts must be noted, there was bipartisan support for increase from $500 to $1500.[319]

The more controversial issue was the total amount that should be disclosed by political parties. A number of objections were raised before the Committee. The first was that if the threshold were increased to $5000 approximately 20–30 per cent of donations would not remain on the public record.[320] Second, it was claimed that it would exacerbate the problem of 'splitting', whereby donors spread their donations either with other members of their family or with a company with which they have an association and avoid the disclosure level altogether.[321] For example, the proposed increase would enable a donor to contribute without disclosure approximately $45000 per year, or $135000 per three-year election cycle, by contributing up to the threshold in each state and territory and national branch of a political party[322] (the practice of splitting and donating just below the disclosure threshold is quite common according to the Australian Electoral Commission).[323] The increased level would prevent the Commission from identifying where this is occurring under the $5000 limit. Third, it was felt the increase did not address the problem of large gifts being made through associated entities which creates the impression that politicians are being influenced by moneyed interests. In evidence, Professor Rolf Gerritsen stressed the reasons behind disclosure laws applying to associated entities. He posed the hypothetical case of a large media proprietor donating large amounts of money to the Greenfields Foundation which gives the money to the party which won the election, which subsequently 'donates property that belongs to Australians, that is digital television channels, to that same media proprietor'.[324] If the donation is disclosed then according to Professor Gerritsen 'the possibility does not arise of any imputation of corrupt influence of government'.[325]

The Finance and Public Administration Committee reported on the Bill in June 1998.[326] After referring to the evidence, which suggested that 20–30 per cent of donations would go undetected under the proposed amendments, and to splitting, the Committee recommended, without remark, that the Bill be agreed to without amendment.[327] The Australian Labor Party and the Democrats submitted minority reports. The ALP report supported an increase in the threshold for amounts to count towards disclosure from $500 to $1500 but opposed both the new donor threshold, and the new total over which political parties had to disclose. The ALP

---

318 Above n13 at 20.

319 Id at 21.

320 This figure is an estimate based on records kept by Professor Rolf Gerritsen between 1993 and 1998 showing 6000 reportable donors, the average of which was approximately $4000: id at 20.

321 Evidence of Mr B Edgman, Australian Electoral Commission, id at 23.

322 Id at 22.

323 Above n16 at 38.

324 Above n12 at 20.

325 Id at 21.

326 Australia, Senate, Finance and Public Administration Legislation Committee, *Consideration of Legislation Referred to the Committee — Provisions of the Electoral and Referendum Amendment Bill (No.2) 1998 (Cth)*, June 1998: <http://www.aph.gov.au/senate/committee/fapa_ctte/electoral/index.html>.

327 Id at 7.

Senators stated that these amendments were a continuation of a 15-year policy to weaken disclosure and referred to this as the Coalition parties' 'tacit approval of the Greenfields Foundation rort'.[328] The Democrats minority report also opposed these proposals.[329]

Subsequently, the *Electoral and Referendum Amendment Act (No. 1)* 1999 (Cth) was enacted after the Senate in committee produced a number of amendments which considerably altered the Bill from that which had originally entered the Senate.[330] These amendments included the acceptance of those failed amendments proposed by the Opposition to the Electoral and Referendum Amendment Bill 1998 (Cth) regarding the definition of associated entities,[331] and limiting the acceptance of loans from persons or entities other than a financial institution unless certain disclosure provisions were met, detailing the terms and conditions of the loan.[332] The more controversial issues of raising the disclosure level for political parties from $1500 per financial year to $5000, and for donors from $1500 pa to $10000, were dropped, although not entirely forgotten.

Recently, the Joint Standing Committee Electoral Matter's *Report of the Inquiry into the 1998 Federal Election and Matters Related Thereto*, revived the issue. Recommendation 44 of the report suggests that the disclosable sum received from a person or organisation during a financial year be increased from $1500 to $3000,[333] believing that 'it is illogical for the minimum disclosable sum of donations be the same as the minimum for individual amounts received'.[334] However, a dissenting minority report stated that such a move 'will only diminish the transparency of the disclosure laws and allow further donations to parties and candidates to go undisclosed'.[335] In support of this they quoted the AEC's report of the 1998 election published this year which acknowledged the continuing problem of donation splitting, and asserted that 'the only practical deterrent to donation splitting is to maintain a low disclosure threshold'.[336]

The Greenfields Foundation arose as an issue of concern in both the AEC and JSCEM Reports on the 1998 election. The Committee's report seemed to treat the issue as resolved following the passing of the *Electoral and Referendum Act (No. 1)* 1999 (Cth), but the AEC Report raised a number of continuing concerns following its investigation of the Greenfields Foundation. It made it quite clear that despite changes to the legislation 'a person, or in certain circumstance a corporation, who wished to avoid full and open disclosure could do so by a series

---

328 Id at 9.
329 Id at 10.
330 *Electoral and Referendum Act (No. 1)* 1999 (Cth).
331 Section 15 of the *Electoral and Referendum Act (No. 1)* 1999 repealed the phrase 'operates wholly or mainly for the benefit of one or more registered political parties' and inserted the phrase 'operates wholly or to a significant extent for the benefit of one or more registered political parties'.
332 *Electoral and Referendum Act (No. 1)* 1999 (Cth) s19, inserting new s306A into the principal Act.
333 Still considerably below the Liberal Party's proposed increase to $10 000.
334 Joint Standing Committee on Electoral Matters, *Report of the Inquiry into the 1998 Federal Election and Matters Related Thereto* (Canberra: AGPS, 2000) at 128.
335 Id at 158.
336 Above n313 at 14 (¶4.16).

of transactions based on the Greenfields model'.[337] It also felt that the legislative change in the definition of associated entities had merely added 'yet further imprecision'[338] to the situation[339] which it feared 'ultimately may only be able to be resolved before the courts on a case by case basis'.[340]

F.   Taxation Laws Amendment (Political Donations) Bill 1999

This Bill was first introduced to the House of Representatives on the 28th of May 1998. It proposed to widen the range of political contributions and gifts eligible for a tax deduction to include gifts and contributions made to independent members and candidates of the Commonwealth, State, Northern Territory or ACT Parliaments and Assemblies and elections, political parties registered under State or Territory legislation, and increase the maximum deduction to $1500 per year.[341] According to the Explanatory Memorandum, these amendments are designed to 'increase the number of Australians (including companies) in the democratic process and reduce a political party's reliance on a small number of large donations'.[342] It is also designed to 'provide an equivalence of treatment between contributions to political parties and gifts to independent candidates and members'.[343] These statements were supported by the Committee's report into the 1996 election.[344]

Prior to the 1998 Bill lapsing,[345] the Bill was debated in the House of Representatives where it was strongly opposed by the Labor Party on grounds relating to the transparency of political donations[346] and the cost to taxpayers (estimated at $45 million over three years)[347] – the same arguments as had been used against the same measures in the Electoral and Referendum Amendment Bill 1997. The argument was that it was not the smaller, individual donors who would be benefiting from this Bill, but the more wealthy donors and corporations.[348]

The issue of associated entities continued to rear its head. The Labor member for Melbourne, Mr Lindsay Tanner, asked the question as to whether associated

---

337 Id at 16 (¶5.6).

338 Id at 12 (¶4.7).

339 According to the AEC, '[o]rganisations continue to ask whether they fall within the definition of associated entity. Some entities submit disclosure returns accompanied by a disclaimer that it is not to be interpreted as an acceptance of their legal responsibility to do so': id at 12 (¶4.6).

340 Ibid (¶4.7).

341 Similar moves were being made at the same time with regards to the tax deductibility of donations of property valued at over $5000 to political parties in the Taxation Laws Amendment Bill (No. 8) 1999 (Cth). The original attempt to place the deduction at $1500 failed and the limit was set in the Taxation Laws Amendment Act (No. 2) 2000 at $100.

342 House of Representatives, Explanatory Memorandum accompanying the Taxation Laws Amendment (Political Donations) Bill 1999.

343 Ibid.

344 Above n268 at 104.

345 As it did when the federal election was called on 31 August 1998.

346 See, for example, Robert McMullan, Australia, House of Representatives, *Parliamentary Debates (Hansard)*, 3 June 1998 at 4664–4690.

347 Explanatory Memorandum accompanying the Taxation Laws Amendment (Political Donations) Bill 1999 (Cth).

348 Deductibility for corporations is to be included under Schedule one of the Bill.

entities, referring once again to the infamous Free Enterprise Foundation, would be treated in the same manner as political parties for the purposes of attracting political donations.[349] According to the definition in the *Commonwealth Electoral Act*, associated entities are 'controlled by one or more registered political parties; or operate wholly or mainly for the benefit of one or more political parties'.[350] The question was not answered.

Another issue brought up once again within this debate, was the persistent fear of 'heading down the American road for funding'.[351] Australian politicians fear the Australian political system becoming like the United States, in terms of financial requirements for candidates and politicians. Moreover there is a belief that 'the people who own the country ought to run it'.[352] Such an argument has been brought up regularly over the years, within both Parliament and the political media, with frequent reference to the astronomical costs of running for the Senate, and the exclusivity of the political race in the United States.

Debate on the taxation Bill was adjourned in the Senate on the 30th of August 1999[353] and was to be taken up again in the following session of parliament. It will be interesting to see the impact upon the debate of the successful Opposition amendments to the *Electoral and Referendum Act (No. 1)* 1999 (Cth) and *Taxation Laws Amendment Act (No. 2)* 2000 (Cth) and it is probable that debate on the provisions regarding tax deductibility of donations it will continue to be heated.

5. Conclusion — A Full Circle?

Campaign finance regulation in Australia has undergone considerable re-vamping since the original 1902 legislation. Apart from spending limits, the key principles of regulation — equality, transparency, and accountability — have remained essentially the same, and even the methods have not so much changed as merely adapted to suit changing times. As noted above, the problem for regulators is that this area is always a case of 'catch-up politics'.[354] As soon as one loophole is closed, another will open. Equally, as previously noted, what is important in this area is the *perception* that money can influence politics. Findings such as those in the 1998 opinion poll, showing that less than 10 per cent of Australians believed that their politicians held high standards of ethics and honesty[355] are, perhaps, the greatest impetus to politicians whose very livelihood depends (theoretically) upon popular support and a certain level of belief in their credibility. Naturally, this concern is combined with a determined effort to see that 'the other side' has as

---

349 Australia, House of Representatives, *Parliamentary Debates (Hansard)*, 26 August 1999 at 9182.

350 *Commonwealth Electoral Act* 1918 s287(1), although this was subsequently amended by s15 of the *Electoral and Referendum Act (No. 1)* 1999 (Cth).

351 Australia, House of Representatives, *Parliamentary Debates (Hansard)*, 26 August 1999 at 9193–9194, 9202, 9247.

352 Id at 9183, Mr Andren (Calare), quoting US 'founding father' John Jay.

353 Two weeks prior to the passing of the *Electoral and Referendum Act (No.1)* 1999 (Cth).

354 Laurie Ferguson, Australia, House of Representatives, *Parliamentary Debates (Hansard)*, 3 June 1998 at 4676.

355 Above n17.

little an advantage as possible, particularly in an area such as campaign finance that can have such an impact upon a party's future. However, it is that very impact which seems to be the focus of the next wave of regulations regarding campaign finance. The use of public funding appears to be coming increasingly under the spotlight following the last federal election with increased calls for it to be subject to tighter regulation.

The presence of the One Nation party in the 1998 federal election also had a controversial effect for reasons other than their policies on immigration and indigenous peoples. According to members of the current JSCEM, following the election, One Nation made a number of public comments indicating that the party viewed the election as a 'money gathering exercise through public funding'.[356] The obvious concern this raises is that political parties are not utilising public funding for appropriate purposes.[357] At the JSCEM inquiry into the 1998 Election Mr Gary Gray, National Secretary of the Australian Labor Party, made the point that:

> Whereas political parties certainly gain freedom from the way in which current disbursement of public funding takes place, I believe that we should be prepared to take some limitations on that freedom in order to prevent profiteering out of federal elections .... Therefore our first recommendation is to consider a change to the act whereby we move back to a system of reimbursement for outlays made by political parties.[358]

This issue was raised in both the Joint Standing Committee on Electoral Matters' *Report of the Inquiry into the 1998 Federal Election and Matters Related Thereto*,[359] and the Australian Electoral Commission's *Funding and Disclosure Report of the 1998 Federal Election*.[360] Both concluded that 'the reimbursement scheme is not a guarantee that profits could not be made on election funding'.[361]

A more radical call in terms of public funding has been made by the Independent member for Calare, Mr Peter Andren, on a number of occasions. To some extent his solution, which involves the introduction of a cap on public funding, brings this article full circle. While not identical to the 1902 Act, which limited electoral expenses but did not envisage public funding, the Andren proposal is similar in that both approaches seek to restrict amounts spent in election campaigns. In a speech to Parliament against the Electoral and Referendum Amendment Bill (No. 2) 1998, Mr Andren stated:

> The moral of the story is that millions in donations to political parties are a good investment considering the billions that can be ultimately saved through government favour .... The amount of money taxpayers fork out through public funding of elections should be enough on its own without our political parties

---

356 Joint Standing Committee on Electoral Matters, Official Committee Hansard, *Conduct of the 1998 Federal Election and Matters Related Thereto*, Canberra, Thursday 1 April 1999 at EM20.

357 See, for example, W Brown, 'Party funding and other touchy political issues', *Courier Mail* (5 February 1999) at 17.

358 Ibid.

359 Above n334 at 125.

360 Above n314 at 4 (¶2.7).

361 Above n334 at 126.

having to resort to taking secret donations on top of that. I estimate a cap of $50 000 per candidate would be absolutely adequate for any campaign at federal level in this country.[362]

This may be a considerable increase from the original legislative provisions limiting expenses to £100 for candidates for the House of Representatives and £250 for the Senate[363] but it is not a radically new idea. Similarly a desire to contain the cost of election campaigns, whether publicly funded or not, appeared in the JSCEM's *Report of the Inquiry into the 1998 Federal Election and Matters Related Thereto* where a number of submissions argued that restrictions should be placed upon the amount which could be spent on election campaigns in order to reduce the amount of public spending.[364] Others called for the elimination of public funding to political parties for election campaigns altogether.[365] Dr Carmen Lawrence, in turn, has suggested a ban on donations from corporations and other large organisations and a cap of $1500 on individuals.[366] In light of the release of figures showing a $31 103 228.82 bill for taxpayers following the 1998 election,[367] and combined with the proposed $45 million bill if the Taxation Laws Amendment (Political Donations) Bill 1999 passes unamended, there are likely to be further questions raised about the efficacy of public funding in combination with the benefits handed out to further encourage individuals and corporations to donate to political parties.[368]

In short we have argued, first, that bar brief periods of inactivity, the overall trend has been one of increased regulation and an increasingly complex regulatory environment. Issues under regulation include: control on the conduct of political parties and private donors in terms of transparency and disclosure requirements; enhancement of the ability of private donors to contribute to the political process by way of tax incentives; use of public funding by political parties to maximize their financial position; capping public funding; contribution limits for individuals and for corporations. Underlying all these matters is the tension between increasing private participation in the public political activity of elections whilst at the same time funding elections from the public purse. Tighter regulation of public funding is likely to be a key question in the future, as is the relationship between public funding and private contribution. In respect of the latter in the past five years, legislation has extended to include regulation of entities associated with political parties and candidates, rather than the political participants themselves. But while the involvement of groups beyond the traditional political participants has been encouraged on the whole, the conflict between 'popular participation'

---

362 Australia, House of Representatives, *Parliamentary Debates (Hansard)*, 2 December 1998 at 1178.

363 *Commonwealth Electoral Act* 1902 s169.

364 Above n314 at 123 and Submissions ppS214 (GW Spence) and S632-S633 (E Lockett).

365 Id at 123 and submissions ppS592 (H&M Whitton), S667 (M Goldstiver) and S1844 (A Tuck).

366 Dr Carmen Lawrence, quoted in Michelle Grattan, 'Money and the Politics of Schmooze', *The Sydney Morning Herald* (25 August, 2000).

367 Media Release, '1998 Federal Election Funding Payments Announced', Australian Electoral Commission, 29 October 1998.

368 Moreover, Recommendation 6 of the AEC's *Funding and Disclosure Report of the 1998 Federal Election* has made it clear that the issue of 'associated entities' is not over yet.

through monetary contribution and the fear of financial influence will no doubt be brought out again in the Senate discussions of the Taxation Laws Amendment (Political Donations) Bill 1999, and in debates following the release of the JSCEM and AEC reports into the 1998 elections. Indeed, Dr Carmen Lawrence, in an address to the Sydney Institute in August 2000 expressly addressed this issue[369] noting that whilst public funding on elections was supposed to reduce the parties' alliance on private, corporate and union donations, 'all that has happened is a blowout in both public (doubled since 1993) and private funding as parties engage in an increasingly expensive bidding war at elections'.[370]

Second, we have suggested that, spending limits aside, despite the increased reach of the Australian regulatory system the same themes and concerns permeate the current framework as its historical predecessors. Far from being recent innovations, the requirements of the current system regarding disclosure and transparency, third party regulation, contribution limits and an emphasis on media regulation were all present in the early system. Moreover, although spending limits are not a part of the current regulatory framework, they were an accepted element of the Australian political and legal landscape for over 80 years before their abolition in 1980.

Third, and finally, we have argued that in view of the historical precedent for campaign expenditure limits, and their compatibility with representative democracy as interpreted in the Australian constitutional context, the development of an implied right to freedom of political communication would be unlikely to operate as a barrier to the re-introduction of expenditure limits. This is most important in the context of the discussion of public financing taking place following the last federal election. The recommendations of the JSCEM inquiry into the 1998 federal election will no doubt spark increased debate into the use of public monies, and almost certainly re-introduce this issue into the political and legislative arena.

---

369 A complete transcript of the August 17 2000 speech on 'Renewing Democracy: Can Women Make a Difference' is available online at <http://www.carmenlawrence.com/says/papers/sydneyinstitute.htm>.

370 Dr Carmen Lawrence, quoted in Grattan, above n366.

Contributors

Antony Anghie
National University of Singapore, University of Utah

Professor Antony Anghie is Professor of Law at the National University of Singapore and the University of Utah. His research interests include the history and theory of international law, Third World approaches to international law, international economic law and globalisation, and human rights. He is currently the Secretary-General of the Asian Society of International Law.

Dan Cass
University of Sydney Business School

Dan Cass has worked in the fields of science, environment and energy for almost three decades. He is currently Energy Lead at the Australia Institute and a research affiliate at the University of Sydney Business School. Dan has an Honours degree (first class) in history and philosophy of science from the University of Melbourne and is undertaking graduate studies in energy law. He has been a science curator at Museum Victoria, a communications specialist for international environmental non-government organisations, a political adviser, and a consultant to companies on climate and energy policy. He is regularly seen in the media explaining the benefits of the clean energy transition. He is Secretary of the Deborah Cass Prize for Writing.

Hilary Charlesworth
Melbourne Law School, The Australian National University

Professor Hilary Charlesworth is a Melbourne Laureate Professor at Melbourne Law School and a Distinguished Professor at The Australian National University (ANU).

Catherine Hawkins
Office for Women
Department of the Prime Minister and Cabinet

Catherine Hawkins is the First Assistant Secretary for the Office for Women in the Department of the Prime Minister and Cabinet. Catherine joined the Office for Women in May 2019 after her time at Home Affairs, where she led work on strategic briefings for the incoming government. Catherine has extensive experience in public policy, including over 20 years with the Attorney-General's Department. She has policy experience in transnational crime, anti-corruption, human rights, court reform, copyright and access to justice. She has also led aid-funded overseas assistance work, and extradition and mutual assistance casework. Catherine has an arts/law degree from University of Sydney and a Masters in Public Policy from Princeton University. Catherine brings a lifelong commitment to gender equality and the work of the Office for Women.

Rosanne Kennedy
The Australian National University

Dr Rosanne Kennedy is Associate Professor of Literature and Gender, Sexuality and Culture at ANU. Her research interests include cultural memory studies; testimony and trauma; law, literature and human rights; feminist theory and cultural studies; and environmental humanities. One strand of her research focuses on Australian materials and case, drawn from literature, film, memoir, human rights reports and legal cases, which she brings into transnational dialogues on cultures of memory, law and human rights, with the aim of identifying the distinctive iterations of an Australian memory culture as it interacts with Australia's deep Indigenous history and global currents. Another strand focuses on the transnational movement and circulation of aesthetic and legal texts engaging with memory and human rights.

Jenny Morgan
School of Law
University of Melbourne

Jenny Morgan is a Professor in Melbourne Law School, University of Melbourne, where she has worked since 1988. Jenny served as Dean of Melbourne Law School from July 2017 until February 2018, and was Deputy Dean from 2003 to 2007, and has served on numerous committees in the university. Jenny has been a member of the Social Security Appeals Tribunal, a Commissioner with the Australian Law Reform Commission on their Equality Before the Law inquiry, and a Hearing Commissioner with the Human Rights and Equal Opportunity Commission. She was a founding Director of the Victorian Sentencing Advisory Council and a consultant to the Victorian Law Reform Commission on their Homicide Law Reform reference. She is currently a member of the Victorian Police Registration and Services Board. She has been on the management committee of various community organisations, including Women's Legal, CASA House and Women's Domestic Violence Crisis Service. She worked for many years with VicHealth on their violence against women agenda. Jenny's research interests are in the areas of violence against women, homicide, feminist legal theory, reproductive rights and law reform. Jenny is perhaps most well-known for her book, with Reg Graycar, *The Hidden Gender of Law*, published by Federation Press in 1990, with a second edition in 2002. Much of her more recent work has focused on media representations of violence against women.

Kerry Rittich
University of Toronto

Kerry Rittich is a Professor in the Faculty of Law and the Women and Gender Studies Institute at the University of Toronto. She writes in the areas of labour law, global governance, law and development, and gender and critical theory. She has previously been a fellow at the European University Institute, the Mackenzie King Visiting Professor of Canadian Studies at Harvard University, Visiting Professor at the Watson Institute for International Studies at Brown University Sciences Po Law School, and Professor and Academic Director of the Center for Transnational Legal Studies, London.

Kim Rubenstein
Faculty of Business, Government and Law
University of Canberra

Kim Rubenstein is a Professor in the Faculty of Business, Government, and Law and Co-Director of the 50/50 by 2030 Foundation at the University of Canberra. A graduate of the University of Melbourne and Harvard University, she is Australia's leading expert on citizenship, both around its formal legal status and in law's intersection with broader normative notions of citizenship as membership and participation. This has led to her scholarship around gender and public law, which includes her legal work and her oral history work around women lawyers' contributions in the public sphere. She was the Director of the Centre for International and Public Law at ANU from 2006 to 2015 and the Inaugural Convener of the ANU Gender Institute from 2011 to 2012 and now holds an appointment as Honorary Professor in Law at ANU. She is a Fellow of the Australian Academy of Law and the Academy of the Social Sciences in Australia.

Gerry Simpson

Department of Law
London School of Economics and Political Science

Professor Gerry Simpson was appointed to a Chair in Public International Law at the London School of Economics (LSE) in January 2016. He previously taught at the University of Melbourne (2007–2015), ANU (1995–1998) and LSE (2000–2007), and was an Open Society Fellow between 2003 and 2008 (based in Tbilisi, Georgia). He is the author of *Great Powers and Outlaw States* (Cambridge, 2004), which was winner of the American Society of International Law's Prize in 2005 and translated into several languages, and *Law, War and Crime: War Crimes Trials and the Reinvention of International Law* (Polity, 2007). He has coedited (with Kevin Jon Heller) *The Hidden Histories of War Crimes Trials* (Oxford, 2014); (with Raimond Gaita) *Who's Afraid of International Law?* (Monash, 2017) and (with Matt Craven and Sundhya Pahuja) *International Law and the Cold War* (Cambridge, 2019). Gerry's current research projects include an Australian Research Council–funded project on Cold War international law with Matt Craven (SOAS University of London) and Sundhya Pahuja (Melbourne) (www.coldwarinternationallaw.org/), and counter-history of International Criminal Justice. He is currently completing a book called *The Sentimental Life of International Law*, about international law's interior life, and co-writing a study of the Cold War (*Lawful Interregnum*, forthcoming, Cambridge, 2021). Gerry is a Fellow of the British Academy.

Margaret A Young
School of Law
University of Melbourne

Margaret Young was the inaugural Research Fellow in Public International Law at Pembroke College and the Lauterpacht Centre for International Law, University of Cambridge, before joining the Melbourne Law School. She has held grants from the Australian Research Council to research international adjudication (with Professor Hilary Charlesworth) and climate change mitigation (with Professor Lee Godden, Professor Kirsty Gover and Dr Maureen Tehan). Professor Young's work has been recognised by several international awards including the Certificate of Merit in a Specialized Area of International Law by the American Society of International Law (2019), the University of Melbourne Woodward Medal in Humanities and Social Sciences (2016) and the International Union for Conservation of Nature Academy of Environmental Law Junior Scholar Prize (2012).

www.ingramcontent.com/pod-product-compliance
Lightning Source LLC
Chambersburg PA
CBHW042319210326
41599CB00048B/7151